# The Modern Caribbean

Edited by

Franklin W. Knight

and Colin A. Palmer

# The Modern
# CARIBBEAN

The University of North Carolina Press · Chapel Hill and London

©1989 The University of North Carolina Press
All rights reserved
Manufactured in the United States of America
Library of Congress Cataloging-in-Publication Data

The Modern Caribbean / edited by Franklin W. Knight and Colin A.
Palmer.

   p.  cm.

   Bibliography: p.

   Includes index.

   ISBN 0-8078-1825-9 (alk. paper). ISBN 0-8078-4240-0 (pbk.)

   1. Caribbean Area. I. Knight, Franklin W. II. Palmer, Colin A.,
1942– .

F2156.M63   1989                    88-25022

972.9—dc19                           CIP

93  92  91  90  89     5  4  3  2  1

Design by April Leidig-Higgins

# Contents

# Preface

The *Modern Caribbean* is a collection of original, analytical, interdisciplinary essays suitable for both the general public and college-level courses. Written by twelve of the foremost Caribbean scholars representing five academic disciplines, this book covers a number of issues relevant to an understanding of the Caribbean islands and the mainland enclaves of Belize, Guyana, French Guiana, and Suriname during the past two hundred years.

Together the authors provide a broad, comprehensive analysis as they consider the comparisons and contrasts, the uniformities and contradictions, the convergences and divergencies that have plagued the difficult attempts at social construction, adaptation, and reconstruction in this exciting and important region of the tropical Atlantic World.

The essays cover the history, politics, economics, and culture of the region, and provide intellectually stimulating reading not only for regional specialists but also for the general public. The references and citations have been deliberately kept to a minimum, but the bibliography appended provides a guide for further reading as well as the source material for the individual chapters.

In the overview essay, Franklin Knight and Colin Palmer outline some of the salient features of the region, indicating characteristics that are common or peculiar to all or some territories. David Geggus describes the trajectory of the Haitian Revolution—the beginning of the period of state formation in the Caribbean—and its impact on Atlantic, American, and imperial history as well as its relationship to the demise of the system of slavery in the New World. Francisco Scarano explores the disintegration of the Caribbean slave systems and the rise of free peasantries during the nineteenth century, noting the problems of labor adjustment endured by the plantation structures as they tried to find a satisfactory substitute in contracted or indentured Africans, Asians, and East Indians. In her essay Bridget Brereton discusses the relationship between material culture, including forms of dance and popular entertainment, and the various segments of society in the British and French West Indies. She shows how race, color, and economic status continually affected community relations.

The chapters by Colin Palmer and Herman Bennett represent evaluations of social and political discord and the continuing search for identity in Jamaica and Trinidad, respectively. Palmer bases his observations of the deep-seated ambivalence of Jamaicans toward race and color on extensive reading of the island's major newspaper, *The Daily Gleaner*. Bennett explains why the government of Eric Williams and the People's National Movement confronted the first significant nonelectoral challenge to the established authority in any of the major English-speaking territories. Blanca Silvestrini reviews the evolution of the special relationship between Puerto Rico and the United States, stressing the enduring contrasts permeating all facets of that relationship; and Franklin Knight points out that the success of the Cuban Revolution greatly boosted regional self-consciousness and self-confidence.

Teresita Martínez Vergne's treatment of nationalism in the Spanish Caribbean reveals that a common Hispanic tradition did not result in a common pattern of national development for Cuba, Puerto Rico, and the Dominican Republic. Bonham Richardson ranges across the region to illustrate that migration has long historical and cultural roots, producing problems that defy easy solution. Jay Mandle and Anthony Maingot examine the economic and political prospects and problems on a regional scope, while Roberto Márquez demonstrates his remarkable versatility in exploring the main currents of Caribbean literature along with the principal national and international influences that have nurtured its creativity.

# Acknowledgments

**W**e would like to express our appreciation to a number of individuals and institutions for their support while this manuscript was being prepared. We found all our contributing authors to be models of cooperation, patience, and understanding, and their competence and collegiality made our editorial task both delightful and easy. Mary Butler and Bridget Brereton took precious time from their very busy schedules to read the entire manuscript and offer invaluable suggestions and corrections. The two anonymous readers for the University of North Carolina Press provided extensive, constructive comments which we seriously considered, and most of which we—both authors and editors—tried to accommodate in some way. Nevertheless, the final responsibility for this book rests with the authors and editors.

The efficient and indefatigable Linda Stephenson at the University of North Carolina at Chapel Hill and Maggie Blades, Karen Carroll, and Linda Morgan at the National Humanities Center in North Carolina all provided superb typing services under seemingly impossible deadlines. Jean Houston, Alan Tuttle, and Rebecca Vargha at the Center Library performed miracles locating and securing our bibliographical requests; and Charles Flowers prepared the bibliography. We remain grateful not only for their valuable service but also for their continuing friendship, which on several occasions we had reason to believe had been placed in jeopardy by our exasperating requests.

During the academic year 1986–87, Franklin Knight was supported at the National Humanities Center by grants from the Johns Hopkins University, the Ford Foundation, and RJR Nabisco. He is especially grateful to those institutions for their financial assistance.

The research for Chapter 6 by Herman Bennett was supported by a Younger Scholar's Grant from the National Endowment for the Humanities.

The final version of Chapter 7 by Blanca Silvestrini was prepared during the author's tenure as a Fellow at the Center for Advanced Study in the Behavioral Sciences. The financial support provided by a National Endowment for the Humanities Fellowship and the Andrew W. Mellon Foundation is gratefully acknowledged.

Finally we thank Lewis Bateman and David Perry of the University of North Carolina Press for their unfailing encouragement and support through the years as we brought this project to fruition. Their humor, courtesy, and perfect balance between firmness and latitude made them exemplary representatives and partners in an association that was both friendly and helpful.

# The Modern Caribbean

Franklin W. Knight and Colin A. Palmer

# The Caribbean

A Regional Overview

The modern Caribbean states represent a unique and challenging experience in the history of mankind. Situated on the sparsely populated periphery of an irregularly populated continent in 1492, the region rapidly became the dramatic proscenium of the European invasion and domination of the Americas. This transformation of the Americas was a highly complex process, aptly described by D. W. Meinig as the "radical reshaping of America."[1] Beginning with the impact of the Spanish and Portuguese—and followed more than a century later by the neighboring Europeans—the indigenous societies of the Americas experienced a complete metamorphosis. The European intrusion abruptly interrupted the original pattern of their historical development. It severely altered their physical environment. It diversified their diet, complicated their epidemiological systems, produced new biological strains, and linked them inextricably to the wider world beyond the Atlantic Ocean. There they have remained. The European expansion into the Americas not only changed the history of the indigenous population; it also changed the rhythms of their daily lives forever.

Since that fateful event in 1492, the Caribbean region has oscillated between the center and the periphery of international affairs. Sometimes the victim of "benign neglect," other times the venue for the flexing of the American military muscle to subdue legitimate local aspirations or score points in an extraregional geopolitical rivalry between the superpowers, the international interest in the Caribbean intensifies and wanes with predictable regularity. The local people cope with the changes as best they can.

Its historical trajectory permanently impressed by the twin experiences of colonialism and slavery, the Caribbean has produced an unusual collection of societies with a population mélange that is different from any other region in the world. There, Europeans, native Americans, Africans, and Asians came together to create a new society, a new economy, and a new culture. It is an eclectic blend of all its components. This new Caribbean society constantly changes in response to the challenges of nature and the intervention of man. In the beginning it was a revolutionary society, and to a certain extent it remains revolutionary. It is, in many respects, a society of striking contrasts.

During the sixteenth century the region was of greatest value to the Spanish Empire, whose dominance was contested in the seventeenth century when the English, Dutch, and French entered the area. By the eighteenth century it produced the most important colonies of empires anywhere, as the exploitation of land and people generated enormous individual and national wealth from the production and sale of sugar, coffee, cotton, tobacco, and a host of spices. By the nineteenth century the Caribbean was really only economically significant to the Spanish and the North Americans—to the Spanish because Cuba contributed to its national treasury, and to the North Americans because Manifest Destiny (and the Monroe Doctrine) had created visions of their unavoidable hemispheric hegemony. In the twentieth century, the Americans have tried to accommodate themselves to the tantalizing implications of this destiny. But hegemony has not been easy. After more than a century of military invasion and political and economic intervention, the United States still finds the Caribbean a major problem area. The long-standing pattern of direct North American intervention in the Hispanic Caribbean—most recently demonstrated by the attempted invasion of Cuba at Playa Giron, or the Bay of Pigs, in 1961 and the invasion of the Dominican Republic in 1965—extended to the English-speaking Caribbean when the United States conspired to suspend the constitution of British Guiana in 1953 and put pressure on the British to delay the grant of independence in the early 1960s. In 1983 a U.S. military invasion toppled the victors of the short but bloody civil war in Grenada. Despite their widespread regional appeal and general popularity, these interventions in the British Caribbean are symptomatic of continuing U.S. problems with the expansion of nationalism in the region, especially among the anglophone Antilles or Commonwealth Caribbean states.

The proliferation of ministates among the former British colonies makes the implementation of a coherent North American policy in the region more difficult. But the process of increasing mini-nationalism is as yet incomplete, with the political status of Puerto Rico unresolved, the situation in the Dutch West Indies undergoing review, and islands like Montserrat, Anguilla, and the British Virgin Islands remaining colonies. Moreover, the relatively small size, limited population base, diversity of race, color, and ethnicity, and precarious domestic economies of many of the territories appear to be prescriptions for enduring political instability and social conflict.

## Definition

The Caribbean has been defined in any number of ways, depending on the purposes to be served. The most conventional definition—followed in this volume—includes the islands from the Bahamas to Trinidad, and the continental enclaves of Belize, Guyana, Suriname, and French Guiana. Though not the only useful definition, it does include all those territories with a closely related history, whose patterns of evolution have followed a remarkably parallel trajectory in the modern period.[2]

Altogether the region possesses nearly 30 million inhabitants, slightly more than the seven Central American states. The population growth rates vary considerably. Between the late 1970s and the mid-1980s, Montserrat, Guadeloupe, and Martinique were losing population at the rate of about 0.5 percent per year. Barbados, Cuba, Dominica, Guyana, Suriname, and the Netherlands Antilles were growing at less than 1.0 percent per year; while the other states were growing at rates varying between 1.5 percent and 2.8 percent per year. The Cayman Islands, with a small population, were increasing at the phenomenal rate of 4.7 percent per year. Yet, the population profile of the region is equally important. For most of the states, over half of the population is less than eighteen years of age, placing inordinate strains on the national economies since this group requires services well in excess of its contribution to the gross domestic product.

Politically, the region is fragmented into independent states, associated states, and colonial dependencies. Antigua, the Bahamas, Barbados, Belize, Cuba, Dominica, the Dominican Republic, Grenada, Guyana, Haiti, Jamaica, Saint Lucia, Saint Kitts-Nevis, Saint Vincent and the Grenadines, Suriname, and Trinidad and Tobago are independent states. Together these states represent about 90 percent of the population and an equal proportion of the landed area. French Guiana, Guadeloupe, and Martinique are considered as integral Overseas Departments of France and are so administered. Each Department elects three deputies to the French National Assembly, two senators to the Senate, and one councillor to the Economic and Social Council. In addition, each Department has a prefect appointed by Paris, and an elected General and Regional Council. The Netherlands Antilles comprising Saba, Saint Martin (shared with the French), Saint Eustatius, Curaçao, Bonaire, and Aruba are self-governing territories associated with Holland, although discussing their eventual independence. Puerto Rico is associated with the United States. The British Virgin Islands, the Cayman Islands, Montserrat, and the Turks and Caicos islands remain colonies of the United Kingdom.

There is, of course, no political coordination within these different entities. History and culture coincided to create insular divisions, even as they were producing the broad context against which the particular evolution of each society would take place. Thus, part of the centrifugal legacy of colonialism remains permanently expressed in the island of Hispaniola, divided between the French-speaking state of Haiti on the western end and the Spanish-speaking state of the Dominican Republic on the east. Similarly, the miniscule island of Saint Martin (or Sint Maarten) is divided between French and Dutch administrations.

Other than the three Departments of France, the only group that approximates a form of unity and cooperation appears to be the Commonwealth Caribbean, which consists of the English-speaking territories. These are mainly the Commonwealth of the Bahamas (about seven hundred islands based around Nassau and the New Providence Islands), the Turks and Caicos islands (Grand Turk, Salt Cay, South Caicos, Middle Caicos, North Caicos, East Caicos, Five Cays, Pine Cay, and Providenciales)—referred to as the "Northern Islands" in this volume—Jamaica, the Cayman Islands (Grand Cayman, Little Cayman, and Cayman Brac), the Leeward Islands (the British Virgin Islands of Tortola, Beef Island, Virgin Gorda, Anegada, Jost van Dyke, and a number of uninhabited islands, as well as Saint Kitts-Nevis, Antigua, Barbuda, Anguilla, and Montserrat), the Windward Islands (comprising Dominica, Saint Lucia, Saint Vincent and the Grenadines, Barbados, and Grenada), Trinidad and Tobago, and the continental enclaves of Belize (formerly British Honduras) and Guyana (formerly British Guiana).[3] Although the British Empire employed varying combinations for its Windward and Leeward island administrations, the island of Martinique divided the two zones for nautical purposes.

## Natural Resources

The natural resources of the Caribbean are extremely limited. Cuba has nickel and iron ore deposits. Jamaica, the Dominican Republic, and Guyana have extensive deposits of bauxite, some of which is mined and processed locally into alumina, and sold mainly to the United States. In addition, Jamaica has large quantities of gypsum. Trinidad has petroleum, pitch, and natural gas. The

Dominican Republic produces small amounts of gold, and Guyana has gold and emeralds. Small, noncommercially viable deposits of manganese, lead, copper, and zinc are found throughout most of the islands. But most of the territories possess nothing more valuable than beautiful beaches, marvelously variegated seas, and a pleasant climate conducive to the promotion of international tourism.

Agriculture constitutes a declining role in economic activity. In 1985 farming accounted for less than 25 percent of the gross domestic product in Guyana, less than 10 percent on Jamaica, Barbados, and Puerto Rico, and less than 3 percent in the Bahamas and Trinidad. The sugar industry, once the mainstay of the Caribbean economies, has fallen on hard times. In Cuba, the Dominican Republic, Barbados, Guyana, and Jamaica agricultural workers form the major sector of the employed labor force. In 1980 agriculture employed about 30 percent of the labor force in Jamaica, 25 percent in Guyana, 23 percent in the Dominican Republic, 11 percent in Trinidad and Tobago, 9 percent in Barbados, and 2 percent in the Bahamas. But the contribution that sugar makes to the gross national product has been steadily declining, except in Cuba where sugar accounts for more than 80 percent of export earnings. Barbados and, to a certain extent, Guyana have kept their sugar industries going against great odds. But they have steadily reduced the dependence on sugar exports and diversified their economies. For example, in 1946 Barbados had fifty-two sugar factories producing nearly 100,000 tons of sugar and employing more than 25,000 persons during crop time. By 1980, the number of factories had declined to eight, although production had increased, and the number employed was slightly less than 9,000; the proportion of the gross domestic product contributed by sugar and sugar products declined about 37 percent to slightly above 10 percent. In Martinique and Guadeloupe the sugar industry is being scaled back mainly to supply local needs and the important rum industry.

Industrialization varies from territory to territory. Since the 1950s, manufacturing, mining, and the processing of foods and other commodities have been used to bolster employment and increase the local economies. While these sectors have been important contributors to the gross domestic product of the individual states, in no case does this contribution exceed 20 percent of the total. Moreover, industrialization has provided neither sufficient jobs nor sufficient wealth for the states to offset the decline in agricultural production and labor absorption.

Except for Cuba, which conducts most of its trade with the Socialist bloc countries, the Caribbean states trade mostly with the United States. From the regional perspective, the United States accounts for between 20 percent and 50 percent of all non-Cuban imports and exports.

## The Colonial Period

The start of the sugar plantation society—based on slave labor—in the mid-seventeenth century created an important watershed in Caribbean history. Introduced by the Dutch after their expulsion from Brazil in 1640, the sugar plantation system arrived at an opportune time for the fledgling non-Spanish colonists and their precarious economies. The English yeoman farming economy, based mainly on the cultivation of cotton and tobacco, was facing a severe crisis. While the Spanish had proved incapable of dislodging the new settlements, and would be forced to recognize them eventually, there were other problems. English Caribbean tobacco could compete neither in quality nor in quantity with that produced in the mid-Atlantic colonies. Until then tobacco had been the basic staple and its demise threatened the economic viability of the islands. As a result, the colonies were steadily losing population to the mainland. Economic salvation came from the introduction of sugar and slavery, and from what has been called the Caribbean "sugar revolutions." The sugar revolutions were the series of interrelated changes that transformed the agriculture, demography, society, and culture of the Caribbean, as well as its politics and economy.

In terms of agriculture, the islands were converted from zones of small farmers producing cash crops of tobacco and cotton with the help of a few servants and slaves—often indistinguishable—to sizable plantations requiring large expanses of land and enormous capital outlays to create the sugarcane fields and factories. Sugar, which had become increasingly popular on the European market throughout the seventeenth century, provided an efficacious balance between bulk and value—a relationship of great importance in the days of relatively small sailing ships and long sea voyages. Thus the conversion to sugar severely altered the landholding pattern of the islands.

### The Sugar Revolutions and Slavery

The sugar revolution was both cause and consequence of the demographic revolution. Sugar production required a greater labor force than that available through the importation of European servants and irregularly supplied African slaves. Between 1518 and 1870 the transatlantic slave trade supplied the highest proportion of the Caribbean population, creating the present legacy of the strong African component. The eighteenth century represented the apogee of the slave system, although the sugar plantation remained a fixture of Caribbean economies until the twentieth century. About 60 percent of all the Africans who arrived as slaves in the New World came between 1700 and 1810. This was the century when Saint Domingue, Jamaica, Barbados, and the Leeward Islands peaked as sugar producers. By 1790 the volume of slave imports had declined to about 40,000 per year, despite the strong market demand in Cuba, Puerto Rico, and Brazil. Antislavery societies had sprung up in England and France, using the secular, rationalist arguments of the Enlightenment to challenge the moral and legal basis for slavery. At the same time, the economic foundations of the slave system were being eroded both by the changes in capital and market and the increasing resistance of the slaves to slavery. Denmark abolished its slave trade in 1803. The British, the major carriers of slaves, abolished their trade in 1807 and energetically set about discouraging other states from continuing. The abolition of the slave trade, coming in the wake of the disintegration of the slave society in French Saint Domingue about 1804, was a blow from which the wider slave system in the Caribbean could not recover.

When the slave trade ended in the nineteenth century, the Caribbean had taken approximately 47 percent of the 10 million or so African slaves brought to the Americas. The white populations, although they maintained their superordinate social positions, had become a numerical minority in almost all the islands. In the early nineteenth century less than 5 percent of the total population of Jamaica, British Guiana, Grenada, Nevis, Saint Vincent, and Tobago were white. Less than 10 percent of the populations of Anguilla, British Honduras, Montserrat, Saint Kitts, Saint Lucia, and the Virgin Islands were white. Anguilla, the Bahamas, Barbados, Cuba, Curaçao, the Dominican Republic, Guadeloupe, Martinique, Puerto Rico, Saint Eustatius, Saint Martin, and Trinidad each had more than 10 percent of the total white population. By contrast, slaves comprised less than 20 percent of the population in only the Dominican Republic and Puerto Rico.

The social consequences of this demographic revolution were significant. Rather than a relatively homogenous ethnic group divided into categories based on economic criteria, the Caribbean society represented a complex form of overlapping divisions of class and caste. The three basic divisions were free whites, free nonwhites, and slaves. The legacies of this division still remain.

The Post-emancipation Societies

The second great watershed in Caribbean history came with the abolition of slavery. In Haiti, this occurred as a result of the great slave revolt of 1791–1804. The Haitians abolished slavery in the Dominican Republic when they conquered it in 1822. For the British Caribbean, this came with the passage of the Abolition Act of 1833 and the premature collapse of the apprenticeship system in 1838. Antigua abolished slavery without an apprenticeship system in 1834. France abolished slavery in Cayenne, Guadeloupe, and Martinique in 1848. The Netherlands abolished slavery in 1863, while Spain abolished slavery in Puerto Rico in 1873 and in Cuba in 1886.

All the Caribbean societies had difficulty adjusting to a majority of new citizens who could not be denied the civil rights already grudgingly extended to the few. The extension of those civil rights, then as now, was neither easily nor gracefully achieved. It was also a difficult time for the political systems, which had existed for centuries as the narrow instruments of the small, white, landed elite, largely absentee, who were now threatened by the removal of their special trade preferences. But most of all it was a difficult time for the economy. Sugar prices were falling, and Caribbean producers faced severe competition not only from other British Empire producers such as India, South Africa, and Australia and nonempire cane sugar producers such as Cuba and Brazil, but also from beet sugar producers in Europe and the United States. Falling prices coincided with rising labor costs, complicated by the urgent need to regard the ex-slaves as wage laborers able and willing to bargain for their pay.

To mitigate the labor difficulties, the region resorted to the importation of nominally free laborers from Mexico, India, China, and Africa under contracts of indenture. Apart from the condition that they had a legally defined term of service and were guaranteed a set wage, these Asian indentured laborers were treated similar to the African slaves they partially replaced in the fields and factories. Between 1838 and 1917 nearly half a million East Indians came to work on the British West Indian sugar plantations, the majority going to the new sugar producers with fertile lands. British Guiana imported 238,000; Trinidad, 145,000; Jamaica, 21,500; Grenada, 2,570; Saint Vincent, 1,820; and Saint Lucia, 1,550. Between 1853 and 1879 British Guiana imported more than 14,000 Chinese workers, with a scattering to some of the other colonies. Asians also went to work on sugar plantations in Martinique, Guadeloupe, and Surinam. Between 1841 and 1867 some 32,000 indentured Africans arrived in the British West Indies, with the greatest number going to Jamaica and British

Guiana. Cuba imported more than 100,000 Chinese between 1847 and 1873 in order to facilitate the transition from slavery to free labor.

Indentured labor did not resolve the problems of the plantations and the local governments in the Caribbean during the nineteenth century. But it enabled the sugar plantations to weather the difficulties of the transition from slave labor. The new immigrants further pluralized the culture, the ethnicity, the economy, and the societies. The East Indians introduced rice and boosted the local production of cacao and ground provisions (tubers, fruits, and vegetables). While some East Indians eventually converted to Christianity and even intermarried with other ethnic groups, the majority remained faithful to their original Hindu and Muslim beliefs, adding temples and mosques to the religious architecture of the territories. The Chinese moved into local commerce, and by the beginning of the twentieth century the corner Chinese grocery store and Chinese restaurants and laundromats became commonplace. The Africans gave a fillip to popular African-based religions such as Santería in Cuba, and Shango, Myal, and Kumina in Jamaica, Trinidad, and British Guiana.

The general emancipation of the slaves provided the catalyst for the rise of an energetic, dynamic peasantry throughout the Caribbean. A large proportion of the ex-slaves settled in free villages, often forming cooperatives to buy bankrupt or abandoned sugar estates where they could. When they lacked the capital they simply squatted on vacant lands and continued to cultivate many of the food crops that the planters and the colonial government had imported during the days of slavery. The villages, while largely independent, provided a potential labor pool that could be attracted to the plantations. The free villagers produced new crops such as coconuts, rice, bananas, arrowroot, honey, and beeswax as well as the familiar plantation crops of sugarcane, tobacco, coffee, cacao, citrus limes, and ground provisions.

## Education

Although the Spanish brought with them a system of higher education and established the University of Havana in 1728, general popular education was not available in the Caribbean before the nineteenth century. Only in the twentieth century has elementary education been made compulsory in most territories.

After 1870 a mini-revolution occurred in public education throughout the region. This coincided with the establishment of free compulsory public elementary education in England and in individual states of the United States. A system of free public primary education and limited secondary education became generally available in every territory, and an organized system of teacher training and examinations was established.

But the main thrust of public education in the nineteenth and early twentieth century came from the various competing Christian denominations. The Roman Catholic church, the Church of England, the Baptists, the Moravians, the Wesleyans, the Presbyterians, and the Jesuits all operated elementary and secondary schools. Education became important throughout the Caribbean as a lever for social and economic mobility.

## The Modern Period

### The Development of Political Systems

The political systems of the region developed in the twentieth century under different auspices. Cuba, Haiti, the Dominican Republic, and Puerto Rico all had strong political and economic influences from the United States, which intervened militarily in the first three states to "safeguard life and property" when it felt local government had broken down. The British Caribbean colonies had a different experience which helps to explain the retention of British institutions as well as the affinity for more openly democratic political systems after independence.

The colonial experience produced two groups in the British West Indies. The first identified closely with the British system—especially with the Fabian Society of radical thinkers within the newly formed British Labour party—and sought political reforms through the conventional parliamentary channels. The most ardent representatives of this group were individuals in the local legislatures such as Sandy Cox and J. A. G. Smith in Jamaica, T. Albert Marryshow in Grenada, D. M. Hutson in British Guiana, or Andrew A. Cipriani in Trinidad. Although they did not depend on the masses for political support (since the masses did not yet have the vote), they knew how to incorporate the masses into political action, and joined the municipal and parish councils in urging a reduction in the privileges of the old planter classes and more local representation in local affairs. They also advocated legal recognition of the fledgling trade union movement in the Caribbean.

The second group was a mixture of populists, independent intellectuals, and those inspired by a semimillenial spiritual return to Africa. From this group came writers such as John Jacob Thomas, the articulate sociolinguist and formidable literary opponent of James Anthony Froude; Claude McKay; H. S. Williams, founder of the Pan-African Association in London in 1897; George Padmore, the gray eminence of Kwame Nkrumah of Ghana; Richard B. Moore; W. A. Domingo; and Marcus Mosiah Garvey, founder of the United Negro Improvement Association in Jamaica (1914) and in Harlem (1916). Thomas, Williams, and Padmore came from Trinidad; McKay, Domingo, and Garvey from Jamaica; and Moore from Barbados.

In addition to these men, there were a number of individuals from all the colonies who had served abroad in World War I in the West India regiments. Some of them were of African birth, and after the war were given land and pensions in several territories where they formed the nucleus of an early Pan-Caribbean movement. Their war experiences left them critical of the British government and British society, and they tended to agitate for political reforms to bring self-government to the Caribbean colonies.

It was the political agitation of these groups that laid the groundwork for the generation of politicians who later dismantled colonialism in the British Caribbean: Norman Manley and Alexander Bustamante in Jamaica; Robert Bradshaw in Saint Kitts; Vere Bird, Sr., in Antigua; Eric Matthew Gairy in Grenada; Grantley Adams in Barbados; Uriah Butler, Albert Gomes, and Eric Williams in Trinidad.

The political agitation that periodically enveloped the British Caribbean had roots in the dismal economic situation. The colonial government had placed its faith in sugar and the large plantation, and sugar was not doing well economically. Increased productivity in Jamaica, Barbados, Trinidad, and British Guiana could not mask the difficulties of price and marketing. Unemployment was rife. Many of the smaller islands abandoned sugar production altogether. Wages on sugar estates were one-quarter to one-half of those paid on Cuban sugar estates during the same period. Not surprisingly, large numbers of English West Indians emigrated for economic reasons to Venezuela, Panama, Costa Rica, Nicaragua, Guatemala, Cuba, Mexico, and the United States. When these economic opportunities ended with the Great Depression, the returning migrants and the frustrated laborers erupted in violent discontent throughout the region between 1935 and 1937. Yet it should also be remembered that the 1930s were a generally disruptive decade, with the Cubans overthrowing the dictatorship of Gerardo Machado and the Puerto Ricans beginning a new round of political violence.

## Labor Organizations

Political experience came most immediately and directly from the difficult growth of the labor movement throughout the Caribbean. The tendency toward trade unionization derived in part from the plethora of mutual aid and benevolent societies among the Afro-Caribbean population that had existed from the period of slavery. By the mid-nineteenth century, Cuban printers and tobacco workers were already striking for the right to form unions. In 1908 Marcus Garvey's printers' union in Jamaica lost a strike which contributed to his decision to leave the island. As the sugar industry expanded and the wage structure began to fluctuate in response to the international market, workers increasingly found the need to organize for better wages and working conditions. Without the vote and a representative voice in the corridors of power, the lower classes formed organizations for their mutual social and economic assistance. To obtain political leverage the working and employed classes had only two recourses: the general strike and the riot. Both were used effectively regionwide in winning the legal right to organize.

Between 1880 and 1920 the Caribbean witnessed a proliferation of labor organizations, despite the marked coolness of the authorities to them. A number of these alliances represented middle-class workers such as teachers, banana growers, coconut growers, cocoa farmers, cane farmers, rice farmers, lime growers, and arrowroot growers. Sometimes, as in the case of the Reformist Association in British Guiana and the Ratepayers Association in Trinidad, they had overtly middle-class political aspirations: a widening of the political franchise to allow more of their members access to political office. But more and more workers were forming their own associations of fledgling unions and agitating for better wages and working conditions. And, as in the cases of the 1905 riots in British Guiana and the Water Riots in Trinidad, the two sets of organizations worked in concert—though the martyrs to the cause were from the working and unemployed classes. One reason why the middle class and the working class could work in concert was their common determination that political reform of the unjust and anachronistic colonial administrative system could best achieve their divergent goals.

To the middle classes and the workers—and, to a certain extent, to the masses of urban unemployed—social and economic justice would be possible only if they themselves controlled the political machinery, and there were only two ways to gain access to the political machinery—through persuasion or by force.

Legal recognition for trade unions did not come easily. The oldest continuously organized union in the Caribbean is probably the Free Federation of Labor, organized in Puerto Rico in 1899. The largest union in Puerto Rico is currently the Puerto Rico Federation of Labor, organized in 1952. In Cuba in the 1920s, a number of new unions were formed in direct response to the deteriorating working conditions occasioned by the collapse of sugar prices. Both the Havana Labor Federation (organized in 1920) and the Communist-dominated Cuban National Labor Confederation (organized in 1925) were suppressed under the dictatorship of Gerardo Machado. But with the overthrow of Machado, new labor organizations sprang up in the 1930s and unified under the Confederation of Cuban Workers in 1939. In the French Antilles, official recognition came with the establishment of the Confédération Générale du Travail in Martinique in 1936 and the Union Départmentale de la Confédération Française des Travailleurs Chrétiens in Guadeloupe in 1937. Also about that time the oil workers in the Dutch Antilles organized trade unions under Catholic auspices.

During the same period, labor unionization was winning slow recognition in the British Caribbean. There the fledgling unions won the support of the British Labour party, especially its Fabian wing. But the Fabians did more. They actively sought to guide these fledgling political associations along a path of "responsible reform," thereby hoping to avert revolutionary changes or the communist domination that was manifest among some Cuban unions in the 1920s and strong in other parts of the British Empire, especially India. The results of Fabian tutelage and reformist policies appeared to fail when workers engaged in spontaneous demonstrations throughout the Caribbean, beginning in Saint Kitts in 1935 and culminating in Jamaica and Guiana in 1938. A hastily dispatched Royal Commission, dominated by Fabians and chaired by Lord Moyne, toured the region and reported on the dismal conditions with strong recommendations for significant political reform. The Moyne Commission noted the increased politicization of workers in the region, deriving from the war experiences of West Indian soldiers; the spread of elementary education; and the influence of industrial labor unrest in the United States. But after the riots the union of the middle classes and the workers was formalized. The British government extended the franchise to all adults over age twenty-one and set about building the apparatus for modified self-government with greater local participation.

In this way Jamaica came to hold the first general elections under universal adult suffrage in 1944, and the other territories followed soon afterward. The alliance of professionals and labor leaders easily captured the state apparatus from the old combination of planters and bureaucrats. Thus, in most colonies a close bond developed between the political parties and the workers' unions. In Jamaica, the Jamaican Labour party drew its basic support from the Bustamante Industrial Trade Union. Its rival, the People's National party, was at first affiliated with the Trade Union Council but, after the purge of a number of avowed Marxists in 1951, created the National Workers' Union—the popular base that would later catapult Michael Manley to political eminence. In Barbados, the Barbados Labour party depended in the early days on the mass base of the members of the Barbados Workers' Union. Likewise, labor unions formed the catalyst for the successful political parties of George Price in British Honduras, Vere Bird in Antigua, Robert Bradshaw in Saint Kitts, Eric Gairy in Grenada, and Cheddi Jagan in British Guiana. The notable exception was Eric Williams in Trinidad. His People's National Movement, established in 1956, succeeded despite a constant struggle against a sharply divided collection of strong unions.

After World War II, and until the late 1960s, a sort of honeymoon existed between the political parties and the labor unions. Expanding domestic economies allowed a substantial concession of benefits to workers, whose real wages increased significantly as unionization flourished. This trend reversed itself when the local economies began to decline.

## The West Indies Federation, 1957–1962

As part of its decision to push modified self-government the British authorities encouraged the experiment in confederation. The idea had floated about the Colonial Office since the late nineteenth century, but was brought to new life with a regional conference held at Montego Bay, Jamaica, in 1947. The British were interested in administrative efficiency and centralization. The West Indians talked about political independence. A compromise was worked out. The West Indian Meteorological Services and the University of the West Indies as a College of London University were set up, and plans were made for the creation of a political federation that would unite the various territories and eventually culminate in the political independence of the region. These new regional organizations joined others already in existence such as the Caribbean Union of Teachers, established in 1935; the Associated Chambers of Commerce, organized in 1917; and the Caribbean Labour Congress, inaugurated in 1945.

The West Indies Federation began inauspiciously with the leading politicians in Jamaica (Norman Manley, then premier, and Alexander Bustamante, leader of the opposition) and Trinidad (Eric Williams) refusing to contest the Federal elections personally. This uneasy federation of ten territories (excluding British

Guiana and British Honduras) lasted from 1957 to 1961, when Jamaica opted to leave. Doomed from the start by lukewarm popular support, the federation quickly foundered on the uncompromising insular interests, especially of its principal participants, Trinidad and Jamaica. The former would not accept unrestricted freedom of movement; the latter would not accept a binding Customs Union. But personalities and domestic politics overshadowed the decision to hold a referendum in Jamaica in 1961 to decide the issue of continued participation. On September 19, 1961, 54 percent of the Jamaican electorate voted to end its participation. It was the lowest popular vote in any Jamaican election, but the government accepted the decision and initiated the plans to request complete independence for the state. Attempts by Trinidad and Barbados to salvage the federation after the withdrawal of Jamaica failed. Beginning in 1962, Jamaica and Trinidad began the parade of anglophone Caribbean political independence. Barbados and Guyana gained their independence in 1966; the Bahamas in 1973; Grenada in 1974; Dominica in 1978; Saint Lucia, and Saint Vincent and the Grenadines in 1979; Belize, and Antigua and Barbuda in 1981; and Saint Kitts-Nevis in 1983. Montserrat, the British Virgin Islands, the Cayman Islands, and the Turks and Caicos islands remain English Crown colonies with limited internal self-government whereas Anguilla, having broken away unilaterally from Saint Kitts-Nevis in 1967, became an associated state of Great Britain in 1976.

The non-English-speaking Caribbean had already achieved measures of political independence: Haiti, unilaterally in 1804; the Dominican Republic, first in 1844 and finally in 1864; and Cuba, in 1902. The French Antilles gained departmental status in 1946, and Puerto Rico inaugurated the Associated Free State or Commonwealth in 1952.

## Nationalism

Since World War II nationalism has intensified throughout the Caribbean. Political independence has strengthened this nationalist sentiment. The Cuban Revolution of 1959 was a strong catalyst. In the Bahamas, Jamaica, Barbados, and Guyana, a strong two-party political system has developed and the performance of third parties has been dismal in elections.

Trinidad has a multiparty system, which, between 1956 and 1986, was dominated by the People's National Movement, first under the leadership of Eric Williams (1956–81) and then George Chambers (1981–86). Both in Trinidad and Guyana, ethnicity constitutes a part of the political equation of Afro-Caribbeans and Hindu and Muslim East Indians.

In the smaller islands, a number of factors have coincided to make dual-party, democratic politics a difficult achievement. In some cases the populations are simply too small to provide the critical mass of diversity and anonymity. Familiar and kin relations make secret balloting and privacy elusive goals. History did not provide the large numbers of associations and cooperative organizations that formed part and parcel of life in Jamaica, Barbados, Trinidad, or Guyana. As a result, political stability and coherence of the type found in the larger units have been elusive. Between 1979 and 1983 the government of Grenada was taken over by a group of young populists led by Maurice Bishop and Unison Whiteman. The People's Revolutionary Government, as it called itself, tried to create a new type of politics in the English Caribbean, a government based on the Tanzanian model. It ruled without elections and established very cordial relations with Cuba. The experiment ended abruptly in confusion and the military occupation of the country by U.S. troops in October 1983. After that, the United States supervised elections which returned parliamentary government—and higher rates of unemployment than prevailed under the Bishop government.

## Social and Cultural Characteristics

The Caribbean is a diverse region. Whites, mestizos, and mulattoes form significant components of Cuba, Puerto Rico, and the Dominican Republic. East Indians comprise the ethnic majorities in Suriname, Trinidad, and Guyana. Most of the remaining Caribbean states have predominantly African-derived populations. Race, class, and color, while they do not constitute the mutually reinforcing cleavages found elsewhere, remain important considerations in the various societies. No regional political or social organization, however, exists exclusively based on race, class, or color. Overt forms of racial segregation and discrimination do not exist, and crude political appeals to race and color have so far been largely unsuccessful.

Despite the common official language, common institutions, and common historical experience, each island and state has its distinct set of characteristics. Sranan is commonly spoken in Suriname along with Dutch and English. The local inflection of the English spoken in Jamaica varies significantly from that of Barbados, or Trinidad, or Guyana. Similar variations can be found in the spoken Spanish of Cuba, Puerto Rico, or the Dominican Republic—just as variations exist between British English and American English. Papiamento accompanies Dutch in Aruba, Curaçao, and Bonaire. Literacy rates vary from percentages in the high seventies in Jamaica and Saint Lucia, to the very high nineties in Trinidad, Cuba, Barbados, and the Bahamas.

All of this suggests the heterogeneity of Caribbean populations. In a region with continuous biological mixture over centuries, any ethnic ideal clashes with the observed reality of everyday life. Nevertheless, ideals exist, often based on European models, which vary from the expressed rhetoric of the political majority which tries to emphasize the African cultural heritage. Yet politics and culture do not offer an easy solution to the delicate personal and familial problems of the plural society. And at all levels of Caribbean societies tensions operate between the centrifugal tendencies of state policies and ideals and the centripetal forces of beliefs, family, and kin. These tensions are exacerbated by the fragile political structures and even more fragile economic foundations on which a viable, cohesive nationalism must be forged among the Caribbean peoples.

Politics and economics comprise a vicious circle in the Caribbean, jeopardizing the endurance of personalities, policies, and the very essence of nationalism. The resolution of the region's economic problems requires some bold, unpleasant, and difficult political decisions, sometimes with potential hazards for those who either articulate or execute these ideas. For the simple reality is that every Caribbean political leader has to contend not only with a domestic constituency, but also with public opinion and the politicians in the United States. Local policies that do not coincide with the perceived interests of the United States can have serious political and economic consequences.

One major problem regionally is the scarcity of reserves in hard currency, making the states' balance of payments deficits extremely burdensome. Given the discrepancy between the value of exported agricultural products and the value of imported industrial products, the terms of trade are unlikely to swing in favor of the Caribbean. Tourism is the largest hard currency earner in many states, yet it is a highly unreliable source, dependent on the condition of the economies of North America and Europe and the whims of the traveling public.

Local attempts to increase the production of food and other agricultural crops have often been hampered by weather and crop diseases. In 1980 sugar production plummeted in Cuba as a result of sugarcane rust, and the island lost almost its entire tobacco crop from blight. Hurricanes and heavy rains severely impeded production in Jamaica, Haiti, Dominica, Grenada, Guadeloupe, the Dominican Republic, and Guyana in the early 1980s, while a series of floods followed by droughts decreased production in Jamaica, Martinique, and Trinidad in the mid-1980s. Lower local food production increases the need to purchase abroad, driving up the prices and escalating domestic discontent.

Not surprisingly, violence has become endemic throughout the region. This stems, in part, from the accumulated frustrations of the dispossessed in societies where the system has proved itself incapable of delivering on the promise of better conditions of life for all citizens. With the exception of Cuba, none of the Caribbean societies has made serious, creative, and sustained efforts to correct the structural problems that retard their economic development. The failure to develop essentially self-reliant economies with indigenous capital has led to an unhealthy dependence on external sources. As Jay Mandle argues in Chapter 11 of this volume, foreign capital exacerbated the structural weakness of the economies with the result that the Caribbean has "experienced growth but not development." Economic growth did not generate large-scale employment and create better opportunities for the poor. Increasingly, their dissatisfaction with the system has taken and will continue to take a violent form.

It must be recognized, on the other hand, that some of the violence is also associated with the narcotics trade, particularly that related to the production of marijuana for export and the transshipment of cocaine and heroin for the U.S. market. There is, in short, a high degree of criminal violence directed at persons and property, as well as politically inspired violence often aimed at destroying the existing polities. The most serious cases of overt political violence have occurred in Haiti, Jamaica, Puerto Rico, Guadeloupe, Trinidad, Guyana, Grenada, and Suriname.

The challenges that contemporary Caribbean societies confront, as many of the chapters in this volume indicate, are at once clear and daunting. They must find ways to effect profound systemic changes that will lead to an improvement in the material conditions of life for all citizens. This is certain to test the ingenuity of the leaders inasmuch as their efforts will be impeded by the scarcity of technical expertise and natural resources, the severe population pressures in some societies, and the readiness of the United States to use its power to oppose and stymie changes that it dislikes. The racial tensions that exist in some countries are additional complicating factors. Similarly, the apparent failure of substantial numbers of the individuals of African descent to espouse and embrace a healthy pride in themselves and their heritage continues. The maintenance of open political systems in the face of these problems poses unique challenges and places an awesome burden on average citizens as well as their leaders.

# Notes

1. Meinig, *Atlantic America*.

2. Until President Ronald Reagan initiated his overtly political "Caribbean Basin Initiative" in 1981, this was the standard definition of the Caribbean. What is now considered the Caribbean basin was usually referred to as circum-Caribbean, or greater Caribbean, or Meso-America.

3. The location of these islands conforms to the standard practice and follows the definition employed in *Caribbean Databook*. Dominica here, and in every other source consulted, has been geographically a part of the Windward Islands chain. See also Chernick, *Commonwealth Caribbean*, pp. 3–4.

## 2

David Geggus

# The Haitian Revolution

R acial equality, the abolition of slavery, decolonization, and nation-hood first came to the Caribbean with the Haitian Revolution. Between 1791 and 1803 the opulent French colony of Saint Domingue was transformed by the largest and most successful of all slave revolts. After twelve years of desolating warfare, Haiti emerged in 1804 as the first modern independent state in the Americas after the United States. For slaves and slave owners throughout the New World, the Haitian Revolution was an inspiration and a warning. The most productive colony of the day had been destroyed, its economy ruined, its ruling class eliminated. Few revolutions in world history have had such profound consequences.

## Saint Domingue in the 1780s

In the period between the American and French revolutions, Saint Domingue produced close to one-half of all the sugar and coffee consumed in Europe and the Americas, as well as substantial amounts of cotton, indigo, and ground provisions. Though scarcely larger than Maryland, and little more than twice the size of Jamaica, it had long been the wealthiest colony in the Caribbean and was hailed by publicists as the "Pearl of the Antilles" or the "Eden of the Western World." Moreover, it was still expanding. In the long-settled coastal plains, the number of sugar plantations grew only slowly but the mountainous interior was the scene of bustling pioneer activity, where new coffee estates were being cut out of the mountain forests to meet rising demand in Europe and North America.

By 1789 Saint Domingue had about 8,000 plantations producing crops for export. They generated some two-fifths of France's foreign trade, a proportion rarely equaled in any colonial empire. Saint Domingue's importance to France was not just economic, but fiscal (in customs revenue) and strategic, too, since the colonial trade provided both seamen for the national navy in wartime and foreign exchange to purchase vital naval stores from northern Europe (hemp, mast trees, saltpeter). In the Môle Saint Nicolas, the colony also contained the most secure naval base in the West Indies.

Although colonial statistics are not very reliable, Saint Domingue's population on the eve of the French Revolution consisted of approximately 500,000 slaves, 40,000 whites (including transient seamen), and over 30,000 free coloreds, who constituted a sort of middle class. In broad outline, Saint Domingue society thus conformed to the three-tier structure common to all sugar colonies. However, there were some significant differences.

The tiny white community was united by racial solidarity but also divided to an unusual degree along class lines. The resulting tensions pitted sugar and coffee planters against each other as well as against merchants and lawyers, and separated all of these from the turbulent *petits blancs*, or poor whites, an amorphous group that included plantation managers, artisans, clerks, shopkeepers, seamen, and peddlers. Such tensions reflected the wealth and diversity of Saint Domingue's economy. Also, because France was a much more populous country than Great Britain or Spain, and possessed fewer colonies, Saint Domingue inevitably attracted uncommonly large numbers of indigent young men seeking employment. The richest planters, on the other hand, were able to reside in Europe living off their revenues. This was typical of West Indian sugar colonies. At the same time, however, the extent of less profitable secondary economic enterprises such as coffee, indigo, and cotton meant that Saint Domingue also possessed a sizable resident planter class, like the southern United States or Cuba. Residence in the colony, its competitive position in the world market, and its ability to produce much of its own food were factors that encouraged some planters to envisage its eventual independence.

Saint Domingue's free colored sector was exceptional both for its size and its wealth. Elsewhere in the Caribbean free coloreds were generally a very small minority and they rarely rose above the position of prosperous artisan. In Saint Domingue, however, the *gens de couleur* outnumbered the whites in two of the colony's three provinces, and they included in their number rich and cultivated planters who had been educated in France. In Saint Domingue anyone with a black ancestor, no matter how remote, was subject to the humiliating restrictions of the legal system of separation typical of all slave colonies in the eighteenth century. Free coloreds were banned from public office and the professions, and forbidden to wear fine clothing, ride in carriages, or sit with whites in church or when eating. They were not only unequal before the law but also suffered extralegal harassment, especially from poor whites with whom they competed for jobs.

The gens de couleur thus covered an extremely broad social range, from recently freed black slaves to rich landowners and tradesmen who were almost indistinguishable in appearance or culture from their white counterparts. They constituted merely a legal category (those neither slave nor white) rather than a class. Probably a majority of the men were artisans or smallholders. The women were usually petty traders or white men's mistresses. As most were of mixed racial descent, the term "mulatto" was often applied to the entire free colored community. Many had both whites and slaves for relatives. Their position within Saint Domingue society was therefore highly ambiguous. Though held in subjection by the whites, they were often slave owners themselves or acted as slave catchers in the rural police force.

Despite the spread of liberal ideas in Europe, the laws governing the free coloreds in France, as well as Saint Domingue, grew increasingly severe in the late eighteenth century—a paradox of the French Enlightenment. At the same time, the free coloreds grew rapidly in number, and in wealth as they profited from the coffee boom. By the 1780s they not only dominated the rural police force but in addition formed the backbone of the colonial militia.

Saint Domingue's slave population was easily the largest in the Caribbean. It was nearly twice the size of Jamaica's, its closest rival. The imbalance between slave and free, black and white, was not unusually extreme, but for most of the 1780s the number of slaves grew at a faster rate than probably anywhere else. During the period 1785–90 over 30,000 manacled Africans were imported each year. Despite the influx of white immigrants and the growing community of free coloreds, Saint Domingue was actually becoming increasingly African. Young men around twenty years old comprised a significant proportion of the black population.

The slave community was not at all homogeneous, being even more segmented than the white and free colored groups. Split up into small units, tied six days a week to plantation labor, the slaves constituted a random agglomeration of individuals from diverse cultures, speaking different languages and at different stages of assimilation into colonial society. On a typical sugar estate of two hundred slaves there would be Africans from twenty or more different linguistic groups. Mountain plantations were much smaller and even more isolated. Everywhere in Saint Domingue, however, Bantu slaves known as "Congoes" constituted the largest of the African groups, and formed a third of the population in the plains and well over half in the mountains.

On the lowland sugar plantations about half the adults were Creoles—that is, individuals born locally and raised in slavery; they made up perhaps one-third of the total slave population. Accustomed to producing their own food and marketing the surplus, they tended to be better off than the Africans. Fluent in the local creole tongue, superficially Christianized, and united by at least limited family ties, they constituted the slave upper class. From their ranks were chosen the domestics, artisans, and slave drivers who formed the slave elite. Elite slaves would have some familiarity with French, the language of the master class, and a few could read and write.

Little is known about how these groups interrelated. Plantation labor, social interaction, and the common experience of slavery inevitably imposed some sort of solidarity, which was symbolized in songs of call and response, networks of fictive kin, and a strong sense of locality. Moreover, slaves from different estates could meet at weekly markets, at Saturday night dances, and in more secret assemblies associated with the Voodoo cult. Voodoo apparently served to integrate different religious traditions—West African, Bantu, and Christian—and doubtless helped release anomic tensions. Nevertheless, the diversity of the slave community must be accounted one reason why, in a comparative context, Saint Domingue's slaves seem to have been remarkably unrebellious. It is true that in the twenty years before the American Revolution poisoning scares swept the colony, but these had as much to do with white paranoia as with real resistance; in the 1780s little was said about poison. Compared to the British or Dutch colonies, organized, violent resistance in Saint Domingue was relatively slight.

This paradox underlying the greatest of all slave revolts has received little scholarly attention. The planters themselves tended to attribute the absence of slave revolts to Saint Domingue's military-style government, which precluded the democratic dissensions of the self-governing British colonies, and which placed far more stress on militia training. Certainly the slaves seem to have been no better treated than in any other sugar colony. Perhaps most importantly, the colony's size and low population density meant that slave discontent was most easily channeled into running away to the mountains and forests. Other slaves fled over the frontier into the even more sparsely populated Spanish colony of Santo Domingo, as well as to towns such as Port-au-Prince and Cap Français. While some runaways formed armed bands which attacked travelers or isolated plantations, they were never very numerous and the 1780s saw a definite downturn in such activities. Although this is a controversial area, it seems clear that desertions were usually short-term and offered little threat to the system. Moreover, in 1777 an extradition treaty was signed with Santo Domingo. As new settlements spread into the remaining frontier regions, and as the colony's forests were felled, it was becoming increasingly hard to be a successful maroon. It may be, therefore, that by the 1780s slave dissidents were coming to see revolt as a more viable alternative.

## The Influence of the American Revolution

Vulnerability to slave rebellion and foreign invasion made all West Indian colonies especially dependent on their mother countries for military and naval protection. Nevertheless, the desire for self-government had a long history in Saint Domingue, and among a minority of radical planters it was notably strengthened after the North American colonists won their independence from England. Apart from its ideological impact, the American Revolution gave Saint Domingue a tempting taste of free trade. When France intervened in the conflict, it opened the colony's ports to Yankee traders, who supplied its needs more cheaply than could French merchants. These commercial contacts were sustained after the war through a new system of-free ports, but the trade was heavily taxed and subject to frustrating prohibitions. Moreover, smuggling was severely curtailed by new measures reminiscent of British action in North America twenty years before. Such conflicts of interest encouraged planters to think of themselves as "Americans" rather than Frenchmen.

The War of Independence, perhaps, had its greatest impact on the free colored community. A special regiment of free coloreds was raised and sent to Georgia to fight alongside the rebel colonists. It included André Rigaud, Jean-Baptiste Chavannes, J. B. Villatte, Henry Christophe, Jean-Pierre Lambert, and Louis-Jacques Beauvais; its muster roll reads like a roll call of future revolutionaries. These men returned to Saint Domingue with military experience and a new sense of their own importance. Leading mulattoes secretly drew up a report attacking the caste system and in 1784 sent a representative to France. The government, however, for fear of offending the whites or exciting the slaves, dared not yield an inch.

The abolition of slavery in Massachusetts and other northern states must have been discussed in Saint Domingue by American seamen and local whites, but it is not known how this affected the slaves. By the end of the 1780s news was anyway arriving from France itself of a French antislavery society, the Amis des Noirs. At the same time, government reforms aimed at limiting abuses on the plantations outraged the planter class. Hitherto, whites had presented a solid front on the question of slavery. Now cracks were starting to appear in what had been a monolithic white power structure.

## The Impact of the French Revolution, 1789–1792

Historians do not agree on just how close Saint Domingue came to having a revolution in the 1780s. Whether the whites' desires for autonomy, the free coloreds' for equality, or the slaves' for liberty would of themselves have led to violent conflict must remain a matter for speculation. No one doubts, however, that the French Revolution of 1789 precipitated the colony's destruction. If Saint Domingue was a dormant volcano, as contemporaries liked to say, it needed only the shock waves of the political earthquake in Paris to provoke its eruption.

The ideological impact of the French Revolution is not easy to distinguish from its political impact. The ideals of liberty, equality, and fraternity proclaimed by the revolutionaries in Paris were peculiarly dangerous for Caribbean societies, which represented their complete negation. But at the same time, the overthrow of the Old Regime in France also directly undermined the traditional sources of authority in the French West Indies—governor, intendant, law courts, garrison, militia, police. The French Revolution thus enflamed social and political aspirations, while weakening the institutions that held them in check.

The influence of the French Revolution was felt first at the peak of the social pyramid and thereafter worked its way inexorably downward. Although colonists were not invited when the States-General was summoned in 1788 to recommend sweeping changes in French government, wealthy planters in both Paris and Saint Domingue met in secret committees to elect deputies and ensure their representation. Their activities in fact merged with movements already under way to protest against recent government reforms in the colonies. It was the fall of the Bastille, however, and the creation of a National Assembly in the summer of 1789 that overturned the Old Regime in Saint Domingue as well as France. While mobs of poor whites adopted the tricolor cockade and celebrated riotously the news from Paris, planters, merchants, and lawyers became politicians and elected assemblies in each of the colony's three provinces. In many parishes and towns, elected committees and municipalities emerged alongside or replaced local military commanders. The militia was converted into a National Guard dominated by the plantocracy. The intendant, former strongman of the administration, was driven out of the colony, and the governor, uncertain of support from France, was forced to accept what he could not prevent.

From April to August 1790, a Colonial Assembly met in the town of Saint Marc. Though illegal, it declared itself sovereign and boldly drew up a constitution severely restricting French control even over matters of trade. Its most radical deputies openly discussed the idea of independence. The extremism of these *Patriotes* brought about a backlash, which temporarily united the Assembly of the North with the governor and military. In 1789 the elegant northern capital of Cap Français had been in the forefront of the revolution. Thereafter its big merchants and establishment lawyers became a moderating influence, and sprawling and shabby Port-au-Prince took over as the center of colonial radicalism. Lower-class whites came to exercise increasing control over its politics, notably after its garrison mutinied in March 1791 and caused the governor to flee to Le Cap.

Colonial politics was an affair of factions and demagogues. Without previous political experience, Saint Domingue's whites threw up local leaders of ephemeral fame who maintained the Creole's reputation for turbulence and impulsive egotism. Divided by regional, class, and political loyalties, colonists disagreed as to what degree of autonomy Saint Domingue should seek, how much militancy they should employ, what classes of whites should vote and serve together in the militia, and whether the colony should be represented in the National Assembly or cooperate directly with the king's ministers. The great majority agreed, nonetheless, on two things—that no one should tamper with the institution of slavery, and that the system of white supremacy should be rigorously maintained. Increasingly, however, the revolution in France came to be seen as a threat to both these pillars of colonial society.

In 1789 the society of the Amis des Noirs gained new prominence as the revolution provided a platform for its leading members (Mirabeau, Brissot, Condorcet). It campaigned only for the abolition of the slave trade and for equal rights for free coloreds, and disclaimed any desire to interfere with slavery. However, to the colonial mind which saw racial discrimination as an essential bulwark of slavery, such action endangered white lives in the West Indies. Encouraged by the Amis des Noirs, free coloreds in Paris demanded that the National Assembly live up to its Declaration of the Rights of Man. Were they not men, too? At the same time, the autumn of 1789, free colored property owners in Saint Domingue also gathered to demand equal rights with whites. Some also seem to have called for the freeing of mixed-race slaves, and those in Paris spoke of an eventual, though distant, abolition of slavery. In general, however, the free coloreds acted like the slave owners they were and were careful not to have their cause confused with that of the black masses.

In a few parts of the colony, the early days of the French Revolution saw free coloreds and whites attending meetings together and sitting on the same committees, but this was rare. The mulattoes' request to adopt the tricolor cockade created great unease among whites. Before long they and their few white allies became the victims of intimidatory acts of violence, including murder. Fears for the stability of the slave regime reinforced deep-seated prejudice, so that by 1790 it was clear that the colonists were determined to maintain the status quo and keep the free coloreds out of politics. The Assembly of the West even demanded from them a humiliating oath of obedience. Faced by mounting persecution, some now fortified their plantations, but a small armed gathering in the spring in the Artibonite plain was easily dispersed. The free colored militia joined the governor's forces which suppressed the Colonial Assembly, but the administration proved no more willing than the colonists to grant concessions.

Meanwhile, however, the mulattoes were acquiring leaders from among wealthy nonwhites now returning from France, men who had been accustomed to equal treatment. These included Villatte, J. B. Lapointe, and Pierre Pinchinat, but it was the light-skinned Vincent Ogé (an unsuccessful small merchant) who decided to force the whites' hand. He had been a prominent spokesman of the free colored activists in Paris, where he had tried and failed to gain the cooperation of the absentee colonists. One of his brothers apparently was killed in the skirmish in the Artibonite. In October, Ogé secretly returned to his home in the mountains of the North Province. With Jean-Baptiste Chavannes he rapidly raised an army of over three hundred free coloreds and demanded that the governor put an end to racial discrimination. Despite the urging of Chavannes, Ogé refused to recruit any slaves. Free coloreds were not numerous in the North; and though they initially created great panic among the whites, Ogé's men were soon routed. Mass arrests and a lengthy trial followed. Twenty rebels were executed, Ogé and Chavannes suffering the excruciating punishment of being broken on the wheel. In the West and South, free coloreds had also taken up arms but there they were peaceably persuaded to disperse by royalist officers. Military men were often more sympathetic to the mulattoes' cause, if only because they saw them as a counterweight to the colonial radicals. In the North, all free coloreds were disarmed except a few fugitives from Ogé's band who remained in hiding in the forests.

Up until now the National Assembly in Paris had maintained an ambiguous silence on the color question. France's Revolutionary politicians were extremely embarrassed by events in the Caribbean and the issues that they raised. Colonial self-government, racial equality, and freedom for the slaves all posed serious threats to France's prosperity. The news of the barbarous execution of Ogé and Chavannes, however, shocked the National Assembly into making a compromise gesture. On May 15, 1791, free coloreds born legitimately of free parents were declared equal in rights to whites. Although the measure concerned a very small proportion of free coloreds, news of the Assembly's vote created a violent backlash in Saint Domingue. Whites, now meeting to elect a second colonial assembly, seemed determined to resist the decree with force. A few talked of secession. When the governor announced he would not promulgate the decree, the patience of the free coloreds was exhausted. In August, those of the West and South began to gather in armed bands in the parishes where they were strongest. At the same time, news arrived from France that King Louis XVI had revealed his hostility to the revolution by attempting to flee from Paris.

It was in this rather complicated political situation, with civil war brewing between whites and free coloreds, with tensions rising between conservatives and radicals, with rumors circulating of secession and counterrevolution and a new assembly gathering in Cap Français, that the slaves took everyone by surprise. At the end of August 1791, an enormous revolt erupted in the plain around Le Cap. Beating drums, chanting, and yelling, slaves armed with machetes marched from plantation to plantation, killing, looting, and burning the cane fields. From the night it began, the uprising was the largest and bloodiest yet seen in an American slave society. Spreading swiftly across the plain and into the surrounding mountains, the revolt snowballed to overwhelming proportions. Whites fled pell-mell from the plain, and military sorties from Cap Français proved ineffective against the rebels' guerrilla tactics. By the end of September, over a thousand plantations had been burned and hundreds of whites killed. The number of slaves slaughtered in indiscriminate reprisals was apparently much greater, but this merely served to swell the ranks of the insurgents. Nevertheless, a cordon of military camps managed to confine the revolt to the central section of the North Province.

Most slave conspiracies in the Americas were betrayed before reaching fruition, and most rebellions were quashed within a few days. The circumstances surrounding the August uprising are therefore of great interest. The divided and distracted state of the whites and the alienation of the free coloreds probably explain much of the rebels' success, both in gathering support and in overcoming opposition. Their aims, however, are less clear. Many slaves appear to have believed they were fighting to gain a freedom already granted them by the king of France but which the colonists were withholding. They in fact rebelled, not in the name of the Rights of Man, but as defenders of church and king. How far this was a deliberate ploy (perhaps designed to win aid from their conservative Spanish neighbors), is hard to say, but the influence of French Revolutionary ideology on the revolt would seem slight. Since 1789 slaves had called the tricolor cockade the symbol of the whites' emancipation, but in revolt they adopted the white cockade of the royalists. Rumors of a royal emancipation decree had circulated in Saint Domingue in the autumn of 1789, along with news of an insurrection in Martinique, which was itself prompted by similar rumors that may have had their roots in late ancien régime reforms. The Saint Domingue uprising was one of the first of a new type of slave revolt, soon to become typical, in which the insurgents claimed to be already officially emancipated. Apparently beginning with the Martinique rebellion of August 1789, this development probably owed more to the antislavery movement than to French Revolutionary ideals.

Contemporary interrogations of captives revealed that the slave revolt was organized by elite slaves from some two hundred sugar estates. Later sources connect their meetings with the voodoo cult. The colonists, however, refused to believe that the slaves acted alone. Royalist counterrevolutionaries, the Amis des Noirs, secessionist planters, the remnants of Ogé's band, and the free coloreds in general were all accused by one group or another in the devastating aftermath of the rebellion. However, if any outside elements were involved, they soon found that the slaves were determined to decide their own fate. Their early leaders, Jean-François and Biassou, imposed an iron discipline on the disparate bands that they formed into armies. Yet, when they attempted, fearing famine and defeat, to negotiate in December a sell-out peace with the planters, their followers forced them back onto the offensive.

Free coloreds from the parishes of Ogé and Chavannes certainly did join the slave rebels when the northern mountains were overrun, but in this they had little option. Elsewhere in the North, free coloreds fought against the slaves until they learned that the May 15 decree had been withdrawn. This was a fatal move by the wavering National Assembly. Although civil war between whites and free coloreds had broken out in the western and southern provinces, the whites had been swiftly compelled to accept the mulattoes' demands in these regions where the free coloreds predominated and showed exceptional military skill. Now, however, fighting began all over again. The towns of Port-au-Prince and Jacmel were burned and, as in the North, fearful atrocities were committed by all sides, making future reconciliation the more difficult. In parts of the West, white and colored planters combined to fight urban white radicals. In the South, they divided along color rather than class lines, while in the North free coloreds joined the slave rebels. All sides began to arm slaves to fight for them, and plantation discipline slackened. Slave revolts broke out intermittently in the West and South, but the rebels were usually bought off with limited concessions, so that in general the slave regime remained intact though shaken.

Beginning in December 1791, troop reinforcements started to arrive in small numbers from strife-torn France. The soldiers died rapidly, however, from tropical diseases, and, needed everywhere in the colony, they had little impact on an enemy that avoided pitched battles. Not until France finally granted full citizenship to all free persons in April 1792 did the situation begin to stabilize. Prejudice and resentment remained strong; but in most areas outside the main towns, white and mulatto property owners now grudgingly came to terms and turned their attention to the slaves. However, the civil commissioners who arrived in September to enforce the decree rapidly alienated most sections of the white population. Léger-Félicité Sonthonax and Etienne Polverel were dynamic and zealous radicals who scorned colonial opinion and who immediately adopted the cause of the Republic on learning that the French monarchy had been overthrown. After deporting the governor, they dissolved the Colonial Assembly, all municipalities, and political clubs. Royalist officers, autonomist planters, and racist small whites were imprisoned and deported in large numbers, and free coloreds were promoted to public office in their stead.

Separated from the race war, the slave rebellion assumed more manageable proportions. The 6,000 troops and National Guards who came out with the civil commissioners were left inactive for months, but the northern plain was nonetheless easily retaken in November 1792. When a full offensive was eventually mounted in January 1793, Jean-François and Biassou were driven from one after another of their mountain camps, and thousands of slaves surrendered. By this time, however, the new French Republic was being propelled by its leaders into a world war that would leave Europe and Saint Domingue irrevocably changed.

## War and the Rise of Toussaint Louverture, 1793–1798

By refuting the ideology of white supremacy and destroying the governmental structure that imposed it, the French Revolution thus brought the free coloreds to power in most parts of Saint Domingue in alliance with the Republican officials from France. This transfer of power to the free coloreds also gained impetus from the outbreak of war with England and Spain in the spring of 1793. The colonists looked to foreign invasion to free them from the civil commissioners, who in turn grew intolerant of any white in a position of power. Port-au-Prince was bombarded into submission by Sonthonax and its jails were filled with recalcitrant colonists. The southern coast was already a free colored stronghold, but, following a massacre of whites in Les Cayes in July, it became effectively autonomous under the mulatto goldsmith André Rigaud. In the plain of Arcahaye the ruthless J. B. Lapointe established himself as a local dictator, while in the plain of Cul-de-Sac behind Port-au-Prince, Pinchinat, Lambert, and Beauvais became the dominant influences. At Cap Français, Villatte would achieve a similar local dominance after the burning of the town in June and the flight of some 10,000 whites to North America.

With the white colonists eclipsed and the slave revolt close to suppression, the spring of 1793 represents the high point of mulatto control in Saint Domingue. The rest of the colony's history, indeed that of independent Haiti, may be viewed as a struggle between the emergent power of the black masses and the predominantly brown-skinned middle class. Whether the slave revolt in the North could actually have been suppressed, and whether slavery on the plantations of the South and West would have continued as before, of course no one can say. However, the onset of war quite clearly transformed the situation not only of the veteran fighters in the northern mountains but also of all the blacks in Saint Domingue.

As soon as war was declared, both the Republican French and the Spaniards, preparing to invade from Santo Domingo, began competing to win over the black rebels. They offered them employment as mercenaries and personal freedom for themselves. Both in Europe and Saint Domingue, the fortunes of the new Republic were at their lowest ebb. Half of the soldiers sent to the colony in 1792 were already dead, and no more could be expected from a France racked by civil war and itself facing invasion. The civil commissioners' rhetoric about Republican virtues therefore had little impact on Jean-François, Biassou, and the other black chiefs. They preferred to take guns, uniforms, and bribes from the Spaniards and continued to attack Frenchmen and free coloreds in the name of the king. Increasingly, Sonthonax and Polverel were compelled to turn to the masses in general to shore up Republican rule. First they liberalized the plantation regime, then freed and formed into legions slaves who had fought in the civil wars. To forestall a counterrevolution by the new governor, they offered rebel bands the sack of Cap Français; and when an English invasion was imminent, they abolished slavery completely on August 29, 1793.

The decree of General Emancipation was felt in the colony like an electric shock. It was greeted with hostility by mulatto and white planters and with some skepticism by the blacks; Sonthonax had acted unilaterally and might yet be overruled by the French government. Sonthonax's intention was to convert the slaves into profit-sharing serfs, who were to be tied to their estates and subject to compulsory but remunerated labor. Almost nothing is known about how this system of forced labor functioned, either in 1793 or later years, but among the decree's initial effects were a disruption of plantation discipline and an increasing assertiveness on the part of the blacks. The hitherto powerless began to fully appreciate their latent power.

British and Spanish troops, sent from the surrounding colonies and welcomed by the planters, were to preserve slavery in most of the West and part of the South, but in some of the districts they occupied their arrival itself provoked uprisings and the burning of the plantations. Even without such militant action a social revolution was quietly proceeding, for where planters abandoned the countryside, work in the fields ceased and the blacks adopted a peasant life-style centered on their provision grounds. Moreover, to supplement their scanty forces the British, like the Spanish, were to recruit thousands of blacks as soldiers, further weakening the plantation regime. Above all, to repel the invaders, the Republican forces were also, during five years of warfare, to arm thousands of former slaves who until then had not left their plantations. As to the psychological effects of participating in a war of liberation, one can only guess, but in military terms the results were obvious. The civil commissioners in the North and West, André Rigaud in the South, the Spanish, and eventually the British all came to rely on armies predominantly made up of blacks.

One may argue, therefore, that though the Spanish and British occupations were intended to save the slave regime and the plantation economy, they had precisely the opposite effect. The outbreak of the European war greatly extended the effects of the slave revolt, breaking down the mental and physical shackles of slavery and plantation habit, and enabling the ex-slaves to develop the military skills with which to defend their freedom. At the same time, it made the former free coloreds increasingly dependent on the martial ability of the blacks. More than this, foreign intervention completely divided the *anciens libres* (as the free coloreds were now called) and isolated the large communities of the West from their cousins in the North and South. Slave emancipation was a fatal dilemma for the members of this classically unstable class. The Republic had guaranteed their civil rights but then took away their property and offended their prejudices. Many, therefore, opted to support the Spanish and British, though of these a large number soon changed their minds. Rigaud and

Villatte remained committed to the Republic, but friction between them and Sonthonax and the French general Laveaux mounted as the latter looked more and more to the blacks for support.

While this gradual shift in the internal balance of power lay in the logic of the political situation, it also came to acquire enormous impetus from the meteoric career of a single black general, Toussaint Bréda, who in August 1793 adopted the name Louverture. A few months before, he had joined the Spaniards independently of Jean-François and Biassou, under whose command he had served. During the next ten years, he was to emerge as a military commander, diplomat, and political leader of consummate ability. He would achieve international renown and be acknowledged in some quarters as one of the great men of his day. Of the previous fifty years of his life little can be said with certainty.

Like the majority of slave leaders who achieved prominence, Toussaint was a Creole who had belonged to the slave elite. He had been a coachman and in charge of the livestock on the Bréda estate just outside of Cap Français, whose manager appears to have favored him. At some point he had become a devout Christian. Though his command of French would always remain fairly basic, he had learned to read, and late in life (between 1779 and 1791) to write his name. Despite his degree of acculturation, Toussaint did not lose touch with his African roots. He is said to have spoken fluently the language of his "Arada" father—apparently the son of a chief—and to have enjoyed speaking it with other slaves of his father's ethnic group. He seems also to have become skilled in the medicinal use of plants and herbs. Such slaves who lived at the interface between white and black society needed to know the ways of both worlds. To maintain their standing in both communities, they had to be shrewd observers of human nature and skilled performers of a number of roles. It is not so surprising, then, if among Toussaint's dominant characteristics in later life were his ability to manipulate and his virtuoso use of deception. The plantation house was in this respect a good school.

This is perhaps one reason why it has only recently been discovered that Toussaint was no longer a slave at the time of the French Revolution. He had actually been freed around the age of thirty. While he appears to have maintained a close connection with the Bréda estate and its manager, he also owned and rented at different times both slaves and small properties. He thus belonged to the class of free colored slaveholders, into whose lower ranks he and his children married. One gets a picture, then, of a man of diverse experience, who was at home in various social milieus: among the white colonists, who thought well of him; among creole slaves and free blacks; and among *bossales* newly arrived from Africa.

Two versions exist of Toussaint's behavior during the August 1791 insurrection, both shakily supported by contemporary documentation. Most historians suppose that Toussaint had nothing to do with the uprising and at first protected the Bréda plantation, until after a few months he threw in his lot with the rebels. Others suggest that Toussaint himself secretly organized the rebellion. They claim he acted as an intermediary for counterrevolutionary whites, using his contacts among leaders of the slave community but remaining shrewdly in the background. Similar puzzles exist with regard to many other events in his life. It is certain, however, that within three months of the August uprising he had achieved prominence among the rebel blacks and was apparently one of Biassou's advisers. He interceded successfully for the lives of white prisoners, and, as one of the free colored negotiators used by the slave leaders, he transmitted their offer to the whites to help suppress the rebellion in return for the freedom of a few score leaders. Despite the amnesty France offered to free coloreds in rebellion, Toussaint stayed with the slave rebels through the dark days of 1792. His relations with Jean-François, who called himself the "Grand Admiral," and with Biassou, self-styled "Generalissimo," seem to have been stormy, but he remained one of their leading subordinates commanding a small force of his own with the rank of field marshal.

After he joined the Spaniards around June 1793, Toussaint's star rose rapidly. In the great jumble of mountains of the North Province, he immediately won a series of startling military victories against the French and free coloreds. These early campaigns reveal at once a leader of acute intelligence, who was adept at ambush and at totally confusing his opponents. They also reveal a man both ruthless and humane, capable of making barbarous threats but of sparing even those who had double-crossed him. This policy reaped rewards. White and mulatto property owners surrendered to him, knowing his reputation for mercy. As arms and ammunition fell into his hands, so his tiny army grew. Lances and machetes were exchanged for muskets. Free colored and even French soldiers joined its ranks and helped train its levies. If the essence of things creole is creative adaptation, this was a truly creole army. In nine months, it grew from a few hundred to several thousand men.

Meanwhile, the Spanish troops stayed cautiously on the Santo Domingo frontier, paralyzed by a series of epidemics. The forces of Jean-François and Biassou, for their part, gave up campaigning for quarreling among themselves and for living it up outrageously at the expense of the king of Spain. The

Spaniards soon realized that they had bitten off far more than they could chew. Such successes as they had, they owed almost entirely to Toussaint. The handsome Jean-François they found vain and fickle, and the impetuous Biassou, gross and overbearing. But in Toussaint, Spanish officers recognized a military commander of ability and a man of honor and personal dignity. They were also much impressed by his piety and the hours he spent in church. Nonetheless, however much the Spanish might respect piety, honor, and military ability, they found themselves stuck with Jean-François and Biassou and compelled to recognize them as principal commanders.

This raises the difficult question of Toussaint's volte-face, his sudden desertion of the Spaniards in the spring of 1794 and his rallying to the French Republic. According to one interpretation, it was frustrated ambition and increasing friction with Biassou that led Toussaint to leave the Spanish and seek promotion under the French. Others attribute the changeover to a desire to win freedom for all the blacks in Saint Domingue. Specifically, they link his change of direction to the decree of February 4, 1794, by which the French government ratified Sonthonax's actions and abolished slavery in all France's colonies. However, though it would seem logical that these two great events were connected, the decree was not in fact known in the colony until long after Toussaint began negotiating with the French general Laveaux, and not for at least a month after he had turned on his Spanish allies.

Even so, Toussaint's volte-face was not a simply self-interested affair. His concern for the liberty of the blacks was genuine. Although in 1791–92 he was prominent among the chiefs who offered to force their followers back into slavery on the plantations, this was at moments when defeat seemed certain. Unlike Jean-François and Biassou, Toussaint never rounded up plantation blacks for sale to the Spaniards, and at least by mid-1793 he had become associated with the idea of General Emancipation. There is some evidence that his delay in joining the Spaniards was specifically due to his attempts to get the French to declare slavery abolished. His refusal to join the French thereafter was probably attributable to the Republic's precarious position. Anyway, having joined the Spanish, Toussaint played a double game, fighting to preserve the plantation regime but at the same time speaking to the blacks of liberty and equality. This doubtless helps explain why his army grew so rapidly. It was also at this time that he adopted the name Louverture ("the opening") with its cryptic connotation of a new beginning.

Matters came to a head early in 1794. After Spanish troops had arrived from Cuba and Venezuela, hundreds of French refugees began returning to the occupied districts. Only now, after almost a year of inaction, could the Spanish seriously contemplate restoring slavery on the plantations and launching an attack on Cap Français. Resistance came from various quarters—from plantation blacks who had not taken up arms but who refused to be coerced back into the fields, from free coloreds disenchanted with their treatment by the Spanish, and from some of the black mercenary troops as well. It was behind this movement that Toussaint decided to fling his weight as of the beginning of May 1794. For several months, nevertheless, he kept up his astonishing double game while he assessed the political situation. Though he told the French general Laveaux he was fighting hard for the Republic, he remained largely on the defensive, assuring the Spaniards that such hostilities as occurred should be blamed on his disobedient subordinates. At the same time, he tried to allay the suspicions of Jean-François and he also promised his allegiance to the British forces who were threatening him from the south. In the meantime, news trickled through from Europe of Republican victories and of the abolition of slavery, while in Saint Domingue the spring rains brought fevers that decimated the Spanish and British troops. Cunningly choosing his moment, Toussaint then fell on each of his opponents in turn with devastating effect.

Whether motivated by idealism or ambition, Toussaint's volte-face was therefore tortuous, cautious, and protracted, and it was not a single-handed initiative. It was nonetheless the turning point of the Haitian Revolution. Now associated with the ideology of the French Revolution, black militancy became unequivocally directed toward the complete overthrow of slavery for perhaps the first time in the Americas. The balance of power tipped against the alliance of slave owners and foreign invaders, and French rule in Saint Domingue would be saved for another decade; but having gained a leader of genius, the movement for black self-liberation henceforth held center stage.

The next four years were a period of almost constant warfare. For much of this time, Toussaint's ragged soldiers, "as naked as earthworms" as he graphically described them, were perpetually short of food, clothing, and ammunition. They died by the hundred in their attacks on the well-entrenched positions of the British and Spanish, but in the process was forged a formidable army. The development should not be taken for granted. Unlike the free coloreds, who had a reputation as horsemen and sharpshooters, few slaves can have had much experience of firearms or artillery, even if they had been warriors in Africa. Since 1791 they had shown themselves skillful in their use of surprise and in exploiting terrain, capable of great endurance, and difficult to pin down. To these qualities Toussaint added the ability to maneuver in large numbers, heightened esprit de corps, and a tactical brilliance few could equal. He gathered around him an experienced officer corps, which was mainly black and ex-slave but included many mulattoes and a few whites as well. Already prominent by the end of 1794 were the youthful Moise, whom Toussaint called his nephew, and the vigorous and stern Jean-Jacques Dessalines.

By then, the Spaniards and their black auxiliaries were almost a spent force in Saint Domingue. They had lost half of their conquests and even their own frontier towns of San Raphael and San Michel on the grassy central savanna, stormed by Toussaint in October. They held the strategic northeastern seaport of Fort Dauphin, but the massacre there of 800 French colonists by Jean-François's soldiers, smarting from defeat, had ended all hopes of reviving the plantation regime. Instead, Spanish and black officers cooperated in stripping the sugar estates and sending their slaves and equipment to Cuba. Defeated in Europe and the Caribbean, Spain withdrew from the war in July 1795 and became an ally of the French Republic the following year. Santo Domingo, Spain's oldest colony, had become untenable and was surrendered to France, which for the time was too weak to occupy it. Jean-François and Biassou with 800 of their followers went into pensioned exile in different parts of the Spanish Empire. In the mountains of the northeast, however, many of their soldiers fought on in the name of the king until 1797.

Toussaint's forces occupied a cordon of some thirty camps stretching from the central mountains of the North Province along the fringe of the Artibonite plain to the port of Gonaives. He thus controlled access from the North to the West. Most of the northern littoral, however, was in the hands of Villatte and other semi-independent mulatto leaders. Laveaux, now governor, was confined with his few surviving white troops to the northwestern port of Port-de-Paix. The broad flood plain of the Artibonite became something of a no-man's-land, but the whole of the West Province to the south of it eventually fell to the British and their planter allies, although independent bands of blacks continued to harry them from various mountain strongholds. The British also held the naval base of the Môle Saint Nicolas and, at the tip of the southern peninsula, the prosperous coffee-growing region of the Grand Anse. The rest of the southern peninsula was a mulatto fief ruled from Les Cayes by André Rigaud. Launching successive attacks against the Grand Anse and Port-au-Prince, Rigaud, like Toussaint, built up an army mainly consisting of ex-slaves. By 1798 he commanded some 10,000 soldiers and Toussaint around 20,000.

Up to 1796, the British government had hoped to conquer Saint Domingue and add it to its tropical empire. Thereafter, it became resigned to failure but dared not withdraw for fear the black revolution would be exported to its own colonies. During their first two years in Saint Domingue (the only time they had any prospect of success), the British forces averaged barely 2,000 men.

Though they were massively reinforced in 1796, British commanders continued with a mainly defensive strategy that condemned most of their troops to die in the seaports of epidemic diseases. Throughout these years of war, yellow fever flourished in the Caribbean, fueled by the huge influx of nonimmune European troops and their concentration in the region's ports. During the five-year occupation of Saint Domingue, the British lost 15,000 of the 25,000 soldiers they sent there. The British also gravely blundered early on by alienating the free coloreds, many of whom deserted them. Even so, the most valuable part of the occupied zone was the plain of Arcahaye, where the local commander, the ancien libre Lapointe, kept the plantations in full production. By 1798 the costs of occupation were found to be prohibitive; and under mounting pressure from Toussaint and Rigaud, the British staged a gradual evacuation. Only then for some 60,000 to 70,000 blacks did slavery come to an end.

During these years Toussaint's position within the Republican zone grew steadily more dominant. Early in 1796, Villatte and the anciens libres of the North Province attempted to overthrow Governor Laveaux in an apparent bid for independence, which seems to have been secretly supported by André Rigaud in the South. According to some sources, Toussaint knew of the planned coup and with supreme cunning actually encouraged its instigators. But once it had broken out, he intervened in force and crushed it. The French government was left in no doubt on whom it depended for keeping Saint Domingue in French hands. Toussaint, the ex-slave, was proclaimed deputy-governor.

For the time being, however, the Republican position remained precarious. Not only were the British now pouring troops into the colony, but also dissension was rife in the Republican zone. Having fled to France in 1794, Sonthonax returned to Saint Domingue in May 1796 with four other civil commissioners and 900 white soldiers. Their attempts to centralize control of both the war effort and the economy of the Republican parishes quickly made enemies. As Laveaux had found, mulatto leaders who had become accustomed to complete local autonomy resented attempts to take over abandoned property they themselves were exploiting. Efforts to raise the productivity of the surviving plantations also spread fears among the ex-slaves (now called "cultivators") of a restoration of slavery. This was especially true of the northwestern peninsula, where the plantations had suffered relatively little, and whose coffee was sold to American traders for food and munitions, as in the mulatto South. From the failure of Villatte's coup to the end of 1796, the Northwest witnessed a succession of uprisings by black cultivators, in which were killed the few remaining white colonists in the region. Local mulattoes were probably behind at least some of these revolts. They show, nevertheless, that even in these districts least affected by the slave revolution a complete break with the past had by now occurred in the minds of the rural blacks. This did not mean, however, that such blacks were willing to defend their freedom by leaving their homes and becoming soldiers in Toussaint's army. Sonthonax had distributed guns to plantation workers; but when in a moment of crisis he tried to conscript all young males for military service, the extent of rebellion increased. At the same time, the mulatto South broke away from French rule, when the tactless commissioners sent to Les Cayes were expelled by André Rigaud and more whites were massacred.

The Republic was to weather these crises but only at the cost of seeing more and more power pass into the hands of Toussaint Louverture. It was his homespun diplomacy that finally pacified the blacks of the Northwest. The African General Pierre Michel, hero of the northeastern campaigns and a favorite of Sonthonax, was then arrested. Earlier rivals of Toussaint had already disappeared. With the aristocratic Governor Laveaux, Toussaint had formed a remarkably close friendship, referring to him in his correspondence as "Papa," though the two men were about the same age. Even so, by the autumn of 1796 Toussaint was intimating that Laveaux could best serve Saint Domingue if he were in Paris, where angry planters were demanding the restoration of West Indian slavery; Laveaux was promptly elected a deputy for Saint Domingue and returned home to France. Next it was the turn of Commissioner Sonthonax. In the summer of 1797, Toussaint suddenly accused him of plotting to make Saint Domingue independent. Though still popular with the blacks, he also was forced to depart.

Smitten with life in the West Indies and threatened by political reaction in Paris, Sonthonax may indeed have wished to see Saint Domingue sever ties with France. Nevertheless, Toussaint's accusation suggests a neat sense of irony. While continuing to play the role of a loyal servant of the French Republic, he eliminated one by one all his rivals within the colony. The French government was becoming alarmed and in 1798 dispatched a new representative, General Hédouville. In six months, he, too, was deftly outmaneuvered, though with all due courtesy, and driven out of Saint Domingue by a supposedly spontaneous uprising. Whether or not Toussaint was aiming for independence, or even supreme power, at this time, historians will probably never agree. However, the growth of Toussaint's power was inexorable.

# The Ascendancy of Toussaint Louverture, 1798–1802

Toussaint's expulsion of Sonthonax facilitated a rapprochement with Rigaud, which enabled the two men to cooperate in driving out the British. Thereafter, only Rigaud himself stood between Toussaint and complete domination of Saint Domingue. Rigaud now controlled all the southern peninsula; Toussaint, all the North and West. Once their common enemy had been eliminated, relations between them rapidly deteriorated. Even today, the conflict between Toussaint and Rigaud is regarded by Haitians as one of the most sensitive topics in their history. It has become known as the War of Knives. Although it was in essence a regional power struggle, it tended to divide the light-skinned anciens libres from the new class of black military officers, though most of the troops on both sides were black ex-slaves. Many of Toussaint's light-skinned officers, though they had been with him for years, sided with Rigaud; and when Toussaint invaded the South, they staged rebellions against him. The fighting was desperate, and Toussaint's reprisals were brutal, although prudently delegated to subordinates. The details are disputed, but the black general Dessalines has been accused of waging something like a war of genocide against the southern mulattoes. Toussaint later reproved him: "I ordered you to prune the tree not to uproot it." Rigaud and most of the leaders fled to France.

By the middle of 1800, Toussaint ruled supreme in Saint Domingue and of necessity was recognized as its governor. A small, wiry man, very black, with mobile, penetrating eyes, he greatly impressed most who met him, even those who thought him ugly. He had lost in battle his upper set of front teeth and his ears were deformed by wearing heavy gold earrings, but his presence was commanding and suggested enormous self-control. Whether socializing with white planters or pacifying angry plantation workers, his manner was reserved but dignified. In private, the whites might mock his rusticity (his headscarf, his limited French) or his "pretensions" (his huge watch chains, his moralizing piety), but in his presence no one laughed. Though Toussaint maintained the external pomp of previous colonial governors and he acquired much landed property, his private life was frugal. Wary of being poisoned, he ate little, and he slept only a few hours each night, invariably working late with his secretaries. His prodigious activity astonished people, as did the air of mystery he deliberately cultivated. Still an excellent horseman, he often rode over one hundred miles a day, making frequent changes of direction so that no one could be sure where he would appear next.

With the war ended in the south, Toussaint could now set about rebuilding the colony and restoring its shattered economy. Although fiercely committed to the liberty of the blacks, he believed it essential that the plantation regime be revived in order to restore Saint Domingue's prosperity. With no export economy, there would be no revenue to maintain his army of 20,000 to 40,000 men. And without the army, the gains of the revolution would be at the mercy of France's unstable politics. Toussaint therefore continued with the schemes of Commissioner Sonthonax, whereby the ex-slaves were compelled to work on the plantations in return for a share of the produce. It was a difficult policy to implement, for increasingly the blacks preferred to establish smallholdings of their own and had little desire to work for wages. This was especially true of the sugar estates, which depended on regimented gang labor and where the working day was long and arduous. Already accustomed to marketing their own food crops, most blacks preferred to concentrate on extending their family provision grounds, cheerfully letting the fields of cane and coffee choke with weeds. Toussaint, however, refused to break up the great estates. He used the army to impose the regime of forced labor and sanctioned the use of corporal punishment; he even supported the reintroduction of the slave trade to make up the loss of manpower. As most estates had been abandoned by their owners, they were leased out usually to army officers and other privileged figures in the new regime. In addition, Toussaint also encouraged the return from exile of the white planters to take charge of their properties and to work toward the creation of a new Saint Domingue.

The return of the planters, of course, raised grave suspicions among the plantation blacks and also among some of Toussaint's officers. They also resented the white advisers he appointed, and the pleasure he evidently took in inviting planters and merchants to his social gatherings. A naturally taciturn man, he seemed to be becoming increasingly remote. These tensions were given violent expression when the very popular General Moise staged a revolt in the northern plain, which caused the deaths of several of the returned planters. When Toussaint had him executed, many thought his policies were going awry. It is usually argued that Toussaint thought the technical expertise of the whites and their social polish were necessary to the rebuilding of the colony, and that he therefore was committed to a multiracial Saint Domingue. Recent work, however, has stressed that, although Toussaint encouraged the whites to return, he rarely gave them back their estates. These tended to remain in the hands of his army officers who constituted a new, black, landholding class. The return of the planters served to camouflage this development, and also to provide hostages.

It is by no means clear how successful Toussaint was in reviving the plantation economy. Export figures for the twelve months following the war against

Rigaud (1800–1801) show coffee production at two-thirds the 1789 level, raw sugar down by four-fifths, and semirefined sugar, the most valuable item, almost nonexistent. On the other hand, it is likely that trade figures were deliberately understated to allow the amassing of secret funds and the stockpiling of munitions. The administrative confusion and the autonomy of local army commanders, of which white officials complained, probably fulfilled the same function. According to his critics, Toussaint kept his generals' loyalty by allowing them to amass personal fortunes. Their troops went unpaid but the soldiers in turn were allowed to exercise a petty tyranny over the cultivators, whose provision grounds were subject to army requisitions. Only on the generals' plantations, however, were the labor laws effectively applied. Other commentators painted a more enthusiastic picture of the regime, insisting that a new spirit was abroad in the colony. Race prejudice was diminishing fast. Towns were being rebuilt. Justice was administered impartially. Even some schools were established (though this was a French initiative). All one can say with certainty is that the new regime was given very little time to prove itself.

Late in 1799, France, like Saint Domingue, also acquired a military strongman for a ruler. Napoleon Bonaparte and Toussaint Louverture had much in common. Both were seen as defenders of basic revolutionary gains of the previous decade, particularly of new land settlements. Both were autocrats who extinguished all political liberty in their respective countries. Both were destroyed by their own ambition. In July 1801, shortly before Napoleon proclaimed himself consul for life, Toussaint promulgated a constitution for Saint Domingue which flagrantly concentrated all power in his hands and which made him governor for life with the right to choose his successor. Drawn up by planters with a secessionist background, the document came within a hairbreadth of a declaration of independence. Toussaint had anticipated by 160 years the concept of associated statehood. Napoleon was infuriated. However, the first consul had already determined that French rule should be restored in what had been France's most valuable possession.

There was, nevertheless, nothing inevitable about the epic clash between Toussaint and Napoleon. Although he was constantly under pressure from vengeful planters, merchants, and colonial officials, Bonaparte had resisted for well over a year their clamor for a military expedition. His original policy was to leave Toussaint in control of Saint Domingue and to use the colony as a springboard for expanding French power in the Americas. Black troops would be sent to conquer the slave colonies of France's rivals. As part of the plan, Louisiana was purchased from Spain. However, by the spring of 1801 it was apparent that, under its black governor, Saint Domingue would be of little use to France; it was de facto already an independent state. Though France was at war with Great Britain, and unofficially with the United States, too (the Quasi-War of 1798–1800), Toussaint had made a secret commercial treaty and non-aggression pact with both these powers. This involved expelling French privateers from the colony. His purpose was to preserve the trade on which Saint Domingue, and his army, depended. The United States supplied vital foodstuffs, livestock, and munitions; the British navy controlled the sea-lanes and would otherwise have blockaded Saint Domingue. This is why, when the French and mulattoes tried to foment a slave rebellion in Jamaica, and sent agents there from Saint Domingue, Toussaint betrayed the plot to the Jamaican administration. Whatever his interest in black liberation, he needed to keep on good terms with his neighbors so as to preserve his autonomy.

In spite of Toussaint's independent foreign policy and his ambiguous behavior toward the planters, Napoleon's intention remained down to March 1801 to work with the black leader, not against him. However, the last straw for Napoleon came when Toussaint suddenly annexed without reference to France the adjoining colony of Santo Domingo, which was then French territory. The ex-slave thereby became master of the entire island of Hispaniola. It was the high point of his career. Suspicious of French intentions, Toussaint aimed to deny a potential invasion force use of Santo Domingo's harbors. But it was precisely this event that persuaded Napoleon that an invasion was necessary. Toussaint's new constitution merely enraged him further. Nevertheless, the fatal decision to attempt to restore slavery in Saint Domingue was not taken for another year, long after the invasion force had landed. Although usually presented as an act of vicious megalomania, the Napoleonic invasion of Saint Domingue was more like a last-ditch attempt to keep the plantation regime in French hands.

Toussaint had grossly miscalculated. If he was willing to antagonize Napoleon to this degree, some say, he should have gone all out and declared complete independence, rallying the black masses behind him. Instead, he kept up the fiction of loyalty to France, sending envoys to Napoleon to explain each act of defiance. He continued to assure local whites of his goodwill and to admonish the blacks on the necessity of hard work. The ambivalence of his double game was to critically weaken black resistance to the coming invasion. Toussaint's failure to declare independence was doubtless due to a number of factors. Caution, the need for white administrative personnel, and the fear of alienating the slaveholding Americans and British were probably the most important. By stopping short of de jure independence, Toussaint evidently thought that Napoleon would negotiate rather than fight. Perhaps he overrated the military lessons he had taught the Spanish and British. Or perhaps he believed that the British navy would prevent a French fleet from crossing the Atlantic.

The British, however, would support the black governor's rule only so long as it weakened France's war effort, and the Anglo-French war was now drawing to a temporary close. The British government feared both Toussaint and Napoleon, but regarded the latter as the lesser of two evils. To see the two embroiled in internecine conflict would be a perfect compromise solution to a threatening situation. In October 1801, as soon as peace preliminaries were signed, the British gave their assent to an invasion of Saint Domingue.

## The War of Independence, 1802–1803

Napoleon's brother-in-law, General Leclerc, landed in Saint Domingue at the beginning of February 1802 with some 10,000 soldiers. By sending out a large force in the healthy winter months and deploying it rapidly, Napoleon avoided the worst mistakes of the British and Spanish. His troops were also far superior to those previously sent there, and their numbers were doubled within two months. Leclerc's orders were nevertheless to seize the colony by ruse, winning over where possible the black generals. Only later, once he had allayed their suspicions, was he to disarm their soldiers and then deport all the black officers. The plantations would be returned to their owners. Slavery would be restored in Santo Domingo, where it had never been officially abolished, but in Saint Domingue the forced labor regime would be retained. Leclerc both said and thought he was reestablishing French rule but not slavery.

Uncertain of French intentions, the blacks failed to offer any concerted resistance and Leclerc quickly occupied all the colony's ports. Cap Français, under the eye of Toussaint, was burned by its commander, Henry Christophe, as was Saint Marc by Dessalines, but several of the generals surrendered without a fight. They were now planters themselves and had property to protect. Toussaint, Christophe, and Dessalines, however, took to the mountains, fighting heroic rearguard actions and destroying all that they left behind. Battle casualties were heavy and from the beginning the war was marked by frightful atrocities on both sides. Fearing the return of slavery, the rural population rallied to the black army and produced guerrilla leaders of their own. However, as successive generals surrendered, their troops were turned against those who still held out. Through the month of April Toussaint kept up a vigorous guerrilla campaign with great persistence but dwindling resources.

He surrendered early in May and retired to private life on one of his planta-tions. Christophe, Dessalines, and the other generals were maintained in their posts and used by the French to mop up remaining guerrilla resistance.

It may be that all three leaders were biding their time. Leclerc's army was already severely weakened and the blacks well knew that during the summer it would be decimated by disease. Nevertheless, when within a month Toussaint was accused of plotting rebellion, it was Dessalines and Christophe who helped denounce him. The old leader was kidnapped, hastily deported, and died in a French dungeon in April 1803. Despite this devious maneuvering by the military chiefs, small bands of insurgents fought on in the mountains in the tradition of the maroons. As Toussaint declared on leaving the colony: the French had felled only the trunk of the tree of liberty; it had strong roots and would grow again.

The situation changed dramatically in July 1802, when it was learned (by the blacks and Leclerc almost simultaneously) that the French government had decided to restore slavery in all France's colonies. Attempts to disarm the rural population now met with massive resistance, just when hundreds of French soldiers each week were dying of yellow fever. The campaign of terror launched by Leclerc proved counterproductive. As thousands of black prisoners, men and women, went stoically to their deaths, a new sense of unity was forged based on racial solidarity. By the autumn, the French were fighting the entire nonwhite population of Saint Domingue. Even the free coloreds who had fled the South in 1800 and returned in Leclerc's army now combined with their former opponents. Led by Rigaud's protégé, Alexandre Pétion, they accepted the overall leadership of Jean-Jacques Dessalines, who finally deserted the French in late September. As Toussaint's inspector of agriculture, the conqueror of the mulatto South, and then Leclerc's chief collaborator, Dessalines had been responsible for the deaths of very many blacks and anciens libres. However, he was the ideal person to lead the struggle to expel the French, and not only because he was the senior general. A menial slave under the old regime, he had none of the liking for white society which Toussaint, and the former domestic Christophe, shared with the mulattoes. He spoke only Créole, the language of the cultivators. And he was possessed of demonic energy, his battle cry being, "Burn houses, cut off heads!"

After Leclerc himself died of yellow fever, the repugnant General Rocham-beau openly waged a war of genocide against the black population, but to no avail. No one can say how far Napoleon would have gone in this hopeless venture, but once war was resumed with Great Britain in May 1803 he had to admit defeat. Until then he had sent 44,000 troops to Saint Domingue. Thereafter the British navy prevented any reinforcements from crossing the Atlantic. Napoleon's western design was at an end. Louisiana was sold to the United States. With British ships blockading the coast of Saint Domingue, and Dessalines's forces besieging the coastal towns, the remains of the French army evacuated the colony in November. Since 1791, some 70,000 European soldiers and seamen had died in the attempt to maintain slavery. Of the few thousand whites who optimistically stayed behind, most died in a series of massacres in the following months.

## International Repercussions

On January 1, 1804, Dessalines declared Saint Domingue independent and gave it the aboriginal Amerindian name of "Haiti." "I have given the French cannibals blood for blood," he proclaimed. "I have avenged America."[1] During the war of independence some of the blacks referred to themselves as "Incas" (perhaps an echo of the Peruvian uprising of 1780), and some European writers also fancifully depicted the ex-slaves as avenging the Arawaks exterminated in the sixteenth century. Archaeological finds probably made for a general awareness among the blacks of these fellow victims of colonialism, whose patrimony they were now inheriting. While anchoring the new state to the American past, the country's new name meant above all a symbolic break with Europe. All whites were henceforth forbidden to own land in Haiti.

Having destroyed the wealthiest planter class in the New World and defeated the armies of France, Spain, and England, the former slaves and free coloreds now went about making laws for themselves and erecting a state apparatus. In a world dominated by Europeans and where slavery and the slave trade were expanding, the new state was a symbol of black freedom and a demonstration of black accomplishments. For both abolitionists and the proslavery lobby, Haiti was a great experiment, a crucial test case for ideas about race, slavery, and the future of the Caribbean. In Haiti itself, publicists and statesmen spoke out against racism, colonialism, and enslavement. Nevertheless, all the early Haitian statesmen took pains to disclaim any intention of intervening in neighboring colonies. Like Toussaint, they wished to do nothing that might provoke a maritime blockade or an invasion by the slaveholding powers. The exception to this policy was the annexation of Santo Domingo, which Dessalines attempted in 1805 and was finally accomplished in 1822. As in the 1790s, rumors about the activity of Haitian "agents" continued to circulate, and these are given credence by some historians, but official involvement in any of the slave conspiracies or rebellions of the post-1804 period has yet to be proven. The only clear case we have of subversive proselytizing is by agents of the French Republic during the 1790s, most particularly by Victor Hugues, who from Guadeloupe helped foment rebellions among the French-speaking free coloreds of Grenada and Saint Vincent. Haiti nonetheless did make a major contribution to the abolition of slavery (and to decolonization) in the New World. This was in 1815, when Alexandre Pétion gave vital assistance to Simon Bolívar that enabled him to relaunch his campaign for South American independence. Pétion demanded as payment that the planter aristocrat declare slavery in his homeland abolished, which he did on his return to South America.

From 1792 onward laws were passed all around the Caribbean and in North America restricting immigration from strife-torn Saint Domingue. Even when the likelihood of direct interference was not considered strong, slave owners feared the revolution's inflammatory example. Within a month of the August 1791 revolt, slaves in Jamaica were singing songs about the uprising, and before long whites in the West Indies and North America were complaining uneasily of a new "insolence" on the part of their slaves. Several plots and insurrections were partly inspired by events in Saint Domingue and the Emancipation Decree of 1794. Most notable of these were the conspiracies organized by free coloreds in Bahia (1798), Havana (1812), and Charleston (1822). However, many factors were at work in the slave rebellions of the period, and to suppose that mere inspiration from abroad was critical in provoking resistance would be to underestimate the difficulties confronting dissidents in this age of strong colonial garrisons.

France did not abandon its claims to its former colony until 1825, when the Haitian government agreed to pay a large indemnity to the expelled colonists. The debt the country thereby incurred was among the factors retarding its growth in the nineteenth century, and the concessions then given to French merchants further shifted the export economy into foreign hands. Britain and the United States had early established trade relations with the new state (later interrupted by Jefferson as a favor to Napoleon), but full diplomatic recognition was withheld by these countries until they had abolished slavery and no longer deemed Haiti a threat.

## The Legacy of Revolution

Created from a unique experience of slavery, war, and revolution, Haiti was to be like no other state. The fledgling black republic began life with its towns and plantations in ruins and under constant threat of another French invasion. Its population had been decimated; it was severely lacking in technical skills and almost totally without experience in administration or government.

Despite the attempts to maintain production on the plantations, the ex-slaves had for a decade been building new lives for themselves as either soldiers or peasant cultivators. Fear of invasion and institutional self-interest were to burden Haiti with an exceptionally large army for the rest of the century. The earliest governments, particularly that of Henry Christophe (1806–20), continued the struggle to revive the sugar plantations with forced labor. However, the masses' desire for land and hatred of estate work, and the falling world price of sugar, forced the attempt to be finally abandoned by 1830. Haiti became essentially a country of peasant smallholders who grew food crops and a little coffee, either on land distributed by the government or on which they squatted. The postwar population was presumably young and mainly female, and therefore grew rapidly. The relative abundance of land meant that the peasants probably lived reasonably well in the nineteenth century. The Voodoo religion, though persecuted by all the early leaders as subversive to authority, became entrenched in the countryside.

Government revenues came primarily from taxing coffee exports. As in colonial times and during the revolution, the government remained military and authoritarian in character, though constitutional forms were to vary widely and regimes change rapidly. After declaring himself emperor, Dessalines was assassinated in 1806 and for the next fourteen years Haiti was divided between a mulatto republic in the South and West and a northern state, ruled by Henry Christophe, which became a monarchy in 1811. Dessalines had made great efforts to preserve the fragile wartime alliance between blacks and anciens libres but tensions continued to run deep, even after the reunification of the country in 1820. Haitian politics developed as a struggle between the uneducated black officer corps which controlled the army, and the brown-skinned professional and business class which made up most of the country's elite.

This conflict was mirrored more broadly in the elaboration of two competing ideologies, one "black," the other "mulatto." In Haitian society the color line was not at all absolute, but these two opposing camps, fronted by the Liberal and National parties, tended to be divided by phenotype as well as by culture, religion, and attitudes toward national development and toward the country's revolutionary past.

## Note

1. Archives Nationales Paris, Cols., CC9B/23, proclamation of 28 avril 1804.

## 3

Francisco A. Scarano

# Labor and Society
# in the Nineteenth Century

n 1790, the Caribbean region was at the peak of its development as mercantilist Europe's foremost colonial sphere. As demand for tropical staples increased steadily during the eighteenth century, local production of sugar, coffee, tobacco, indigo, and other crops climbed at a steady pace. Indeed, never before had the Caribbean plantation trade been so voluminous or so significant a branch of commerce within the European colonial system. Moreover, other signs of prosperity abounded in the region's peculiar mercantile life. Primarily under British and French auspices, the volume of the transatlantic slave trade had reached its zenith in the latter decades of the eighteenth century. As a result, the total slave population of the islands and the neighboring continental areas (the Guianas, Surinam, and Belize) was at its highest point since the genesis of the slave trade to the Americas in the sixteenth century. Slaves constituted four-fifths of the region's population, and the institution of slavery was the predominant, and as yet seemingly indestructible, form of labor exaction in all but the Spanish colonies of Cuba, Santo Domingo (the Dominican Republic of later years), Puerto Rico, and Trinidad. And in most of these, the economic and demographic significance of slaves was by the 1790s increasing at a steady pace.

One hundred years later, the social and economic panorama of the Caribbean had been profoundly transformed. The slave trade, which dwindled in the 1840s and ceased altogether in the mid-1860s, was by the 1890s a fading memory. More significantly, slavery had been declared illegal across the entire region, the last of the slaves having been emancipated in Cuba in 1886. The plantation economy was at a crossroads. In the wake of pronounced shifts in European-dominated world trade, which prompted the emergence of tropical commodity producers in disparate corners of the world, the Caribbean had by the 1890s lost much of its former preeminence in international commerce.

Commodity production in all its forms was sharply depressed. The sugar industry, for centuries the cornerstone of the regional economy, had entered into a period of stagnation and reorientation as a result of European beet sugar supplies and a decline in the planters' effective control over labor arrangements. As the twentieth century approached, only cocoa, bananas, and coffee, which thrived in a few of the islands, appeared to have an economic future in the Caribbean—and even that future would not seem quite so bright a couple of decades hence. Not surprisingly, the political and economic importance of the colonies (with the exception of Cuba and Puerto Rico) had by 1890 reached a historic low.

Our purpose in this chapter is to review the outstanding features of the transformation of Caribbean labor systems in the nineteenth century. The foremost themes implied in that evolution were the extinction of slavery, the rise of peasantries in some areas and their weakening in others, and the development of rural and urban working classes that, by the end of the nineteenth century, were beginning to mature organizationally and politically, albeit within the framework of the planters' continued social and political hegemony. In addition to these overarching developments, the history of Caribbean labor systems in this period encompasses a second crucial set of themes: the struggle between planters and workers over the control and use of basic resources—primarily the land, but also credit and labor. As this contest unfolded, ancillary social processes emerged: for example, the recruitment of contract laborers, particularly from India and China; the workers' participation in the anticolonial struggles that took place in the Spanish-speaking islands; the growth of a middle class composed mainly of people of African descent, and the attendant conflicts between that class and other social groups; and finally, the initial steps toward the creation of workers' institutions for the advancement and protection of their collective interests.

## The Ordeal of Free Labor in the Caribbean

Seen from the vantage point of nearly five centuries of history, the parallels observed between the many societies of the Caribbean during the nineteenth-century transition to free labor appear rooted in the region's underlying historical unity, a unity forged from its involvement in a common pattern of relationships with the European-centered world economy. Beginning in the 1500s, the Caribbean occupied a unique position in Europe's fledgling mercantile system as the foremost producer of tropical staples (principally sugar, but also tobacco, cotton, ginger, indigo, and others), and, along with Brazil, as the largest consumer of the African labor needed to produce such coveted commodities. Under the aegis of commercial capitalism, Europeans converted the islands and some of the outlying coastal areas into their primary sphere of tropical colonial exploitation. Although the timing and intensity of processes associated with this assigned role varied from one territory to the next, and from one imperial zone to another, each of the principal geographic units of the Caribbean, regardless of European affiliation, experienced one or more relatively prolonged cycles of export agriculture and trade. Conversely, the region supplied Europe with a majority of its tropical imports, at least until the second half of the nineteenth century. The multiple legacy of such a specialized assignment in the international division of labor clearly helped shape the response of Caribbean actors to the novel demands and constraints of free labor in the increasingly competitive international economic environment of the nineteenth century. Local initiatives and reactions to the conditions encountered after emancipation were, in short, firmly grounded in the peculiar dynamics of earlier history.

Between the sixteenth and nineteenth centuries Europeans imported into the Caribbean several million African slaves, forcibly subjecting them to one of the harshest and most demanding labor regimens ever conceived. Settlers from all of the European powers that carved out for themselves a share of the archipelago exploited the labor of these bondsmen, some clearly with greater success and on a larger scale than others. The slaves, particularly those who labored in the sugar industry, typically worked on *plantations*, a distinctive type of large-scale agricultural enterprise organized with the support and financial backing of their monarchies and of metropolitan merchants and other capitalists. Almost from the beginning Europeans had defined their Caribbean possessions as places that were meant to satisfy the home demand for tropical staples; slave plantations staffed with dozens and sometimes hundreds of Africans and their creole descendants became the institutional means by which such a colonial project came into fruition. Plantation slavery consisted, then, of a set of economic institutions geared toward the extraction of a maximum amount of labor from the largest possible number of involuntary migrants from Africa. Profitable production was its principal aim, and the efficient organization of labor its principal intermediate objective. Inasmuch as the slave plantation system succeeded in doing both for so long and under such diverse structural and ideological conditions, it was, as Sidney W. Mintz aptly characterizes New World slavery as a whole, "one of the most notable inventions in human history."[1]

By the early decades of the nineteenth century, all of the islands and outlying territories of the region where appropriate ecological conditions existed had experienced sustained cycles of slave plantation development. Some, like the Spanish possessions of Cuba and Puerto Rico, had only begun to tread that course in the latter years of the eighteenth century and were still in an ascending phase of the cycle; others, particularly in the British and French colonial orbits, were beginning to wind down after reaching eighteenth-century peaks of economic activity and slave importations. Planter indebtedness, outmoded processing technologies, rapacious field techniques leading to soil exhaustion, and the gradually increasing costs of purchasing and sustaining the slave labor force were some of the factors that accounted for the progressive decay of some of the long-standing producers of the British and French Caribbean.

The rise of abolitionism in Great Britain also threatened the slaveholding order. Between the 1780s and the first decade of the 1800s, British abolitionists began to act on their convictions in the political arena. In this effort, directed first against the slave trade, three more or less definable groups took the lead: the evangelical religious community (the Quakers and Methodists, especially), the working classes, and the imperialists and free traders. This broad-based antislavery movement soon spread throughout the British body politic. In 1807 the movement won a decisive first victory when Parliament forbade the involvement of British nationals in all phases of the slave trade, thus putting an abrupt end to a formerly important branch of the nation's commerce. In a dramatic reversal, Great Britain, the prime carrier of African slaves across the Atlantic in the 1700s, turned its back on the business for moral and political reasons and launched a crusade to compel other European slaving powers to follow its example.

By the early 1800s, then, the prospect that slavery might soon be extinguished by metropolitan decree became a sobering certainty of colonial life, not only in the British colonies but throughout the slaveholding societies of the Caribbean. At this juncture, as the dominant classes began to prepare for the eventual liberation of their bondsmen, they raised what would become the central issue of nineteenth-century Caribbean social discourse: how to maintain profitable plantation production in the absence of slavery's harsh restraints on the labor force. In the absence of legal means to coerce the laborers to work at the accustomed levels of effort and with the accustomed regularity of work attendance, the planters' dilemma would turn on how to secure an adequate labor supply at a cost that they deemed affordable within the parameters imposed by deteriorating market conditions. Therein lay emancipation's challenge to the slave owners—the crux of the "social question," as the Cubans and

Puerto Ricans euphemistically called it. For the slaves, on the other hand, emancipation portended the satisfying prospect of taking control of their lives and improving their conditions of life and labor. While perhaps they did not harbor any illusions as to the degree of self-determination that legal freedom would bring under the continued aegis of the planter class, the slaves undoubtedly believed that they could aim for greater autonomy and a more dignified existence.

The demise of slavery was a protracted, complex process that lasted nearly a century and exhibited significant differences of disposition and outcome across the region. That process began in 1791 in French Saint Domingue, where a slave rebellion sparked a revolutionary upheaval unlike any other in New World history. The slaves of Saint Domingue were the first to experience freedom on a massive scale, a freedom fashioned of their own volition and given meaning by their own deeds. Years later, in the wake of a Haitian invasion of neighboring Spanish territory, slavery became extinct in Santo Domingo as well (1822). In both cases, emancipation was accompanied by the destruction of the plantation system and the emigration of the planter classes. Attempts to revive the Haitian plantation system after independence in 1804 met with failure, after which the state began a redistribution of land that paved the way for the development and articulation of a strong freeholding peasantry throughout the remainder of the nineteenth century. In the Dominican case, emancipation and the flight of large landowners gave an already established peasantry a significant boost. After independence from Haiti in 1844, several decades would pass before the Dominican Republic embarked on a state-directed effort to promote the immigration of persons with capital intent on founding new sugar estates. By the end of our period (1890), then, both Hispaniolan societies still contained predominant peasant populations, although a renaissance of the sugar industry was in its incipient stages in the Dominican Republic.

The Haitian experience raised throughout the Caribbean the unsettling specter of emancipation by the slaves' forceful initiative, but it did not establish a historical precedent. Violent commotion on the scale of Haiti was avoided elsewhere, and the norm became abolition by imperial mandate rather than by insurrectionary conflagration. The first slave-owning class to meet the challenges of emancipation in this fashion comprised the masters of the British West Indies, where final abolition arrived in 1838 after a four-year transitional period of "apprenticeship." They were followed by the French and Danish West Indians in 1848, the Dutch in 1863, the Puerto Ricans in 1873–76, and the Cubans in 1880–86. In the latter two cases, as in the British West Indies, slavery officially came to an end in two steps: the adoption of partial abolition followed by a period of *patronato*, a transitional regimen akin to the British apprenticeship during which the freedmen were compelled to remain under their masters' "tutelage" for several years.

Among those countries where slavery ended as a result of imperial action, at least two general patterns of abolition are discernible. The first was typified by the British, Dutch, Danish, and French colonies (excluding, of course, Saint Domingue). As a rule, these societies featured large slave majorities predominantly employed on plantations, with relatively small minorities of "free coloreds" (blacks and mulattoes) and whites. With the exception of British Guiana and Trinidad, plantation production had a longer history of continuous exploitation there than elsewhere in the Caribbean, dating in some cases to the middle of the seventeenth century.

The second pattern held true in Cuba and Puerto Rico, whose demographic composition and social structures contrasted sharply with those of the first group by virtue of the islands' late development as slave plantation colonies. In Cuba, free people comprised at least half of the population; in Puerto Rico, they were the overwhelming majority. Moreover, there was a very large free colored group, mostly composed of peasants and other rural dwellers with a long tradition of autonomy and self-sufficiency. The abolition of the slave trade (between 1850 and 1865) and slavery (between 1876 and 1886) occurred comparatively late, and mechanisms to effect a smoother transition to free labor were adopted in anticipation of the loss of slave labor—in other words, concurrent with, rather than after, abolition. Finally, the Cuban case is exceptional because at one juncture the abolitionist thrust became associated with, and was eventually accelerated by, a bloody and prolonged struggle for independence.

In both sets of colonies the process of abolition was fraught with tension and uncertainties. But the onset of emancipation was particularly troubling to the ruling classes in the countries of the first group (e.g., the British and French West Indies). The plantations had long relied almost exclusively on the labor of slaves, and comprehensive measures to prepare for the economic shock of abolition had not been launched in anticipation of the slaves' deliverance. At the time of final emancipation in these colonies, the planters' assessment of its potential consequences was understandably bleak. Convinced that the aim of the abolitionist campaign had been to undermine their economic interests, they believed that once the slaves were freed it would be impossible to garner sufficient labor to meet their needs. In spite of the masters' pessimism, however, the abolitionist movement neither intended to destroy the plantation system nor attempted to alter the basic relations of property and power in the colonies. Abolitionists were generally satisfied with a constitutional victory over the slave owners that would inaugurate "freedom" in the legal sense of the term, even if "freedom" in a philosophical sense did not materialize. As the humanitarian campaign typically lost momentum after emancipation, the planters gradually came to realize that they could define the new rules under which labor would be appropriated without undue metropolitan interference. The principal obstacles they would face were the ex-slaves' own conception of freedom and their determination to strive for its realization.

As they tried to anticipate the freedmen's reaction, planters in the first group of colonies devised two immediate objectives. The first was to keep the laborers working on the estates to guarantee a reliable supply of labor; the second, to maximize labor's efficiency, maintain its reliability, and, if possible, reduce its cost. The priority assigned to each of these objectives varied according to certain structural conditions. The first obviously posed a more serious problem in places like Trinidad, British Guiana, and Jamaica, where a plentiful supply of unoccupied or relatively inexpensive land was still available at the time of emancipation. Given those conditions, the future of the plantations seemed to depend on avoiding a massive flight of freedmen from the estates or their environs; that is, on preventing them from becoming independent freeholders and peasants. On the smaller islands where land was scarce and therefore expensive, the freeholding alternative did not exist. Hence, the most pressing concern was to maximize labor's efficiency and reliability and to reduce its cost. The French and Danish West Indies, the British Leewards, and Barbados all conformed to the latter situation.

While planter objectives in the post-emancipation era centered around the supply, reliability, and cost of labor, it must be borne in mind that, in the long run, in order for the strategies designed around those goals to be truly fruitful, they had to be part of a more comprehensive economic project. In the second half of the nineteenth century, the economic survival of individual sugar producers and even of entire national industries hinged on the initiatives taken on several technical and economic fronts. Producers of cane sugar all over the world were forced to come to grips with an increasingly competitive environment that made technological modernization—the adoption of highly complex and costly processing machinery which brought about a gigantic increase in the scale of operations—imperative, and that required a significant reduction of unit costs to remain profitable.[2] Augmenting the labor supply and imposing a rigorous labor discipline could, in the short run, transfer some of the costs attendant on the modernization effort to the workers, but these endeavors alone could not provide the solution. In fact, some of the more repressive strategies of labor control could backfire on the planters and leave them vulnerable, as occurred in Jamaica when the freedmen withdrew from the plantations in obvious disenchantment with conditions created by estate owners in the immediate aftermath of emancipation.

The success of pre- or post-emancipation efforts to render the labor force more controllable, more disciplined, or cheaper must therefore be assessed in terms of the long-range survival and economic vigor of the plantation system in a given area. Some countries or groups of countries, like the British Leeward Islands, Danish Saint Croix, or even Puerto Rico, were relatively successful in molding a post-emancipation labor force that satisfied the imperatives of abundance, discipline, and low cost. Yet they ultimately failed to sustain the sugar economy on a viable economic footing. Starved for capital or for productive soils, their modernization effort faltered and their industries lost their ability to compete with the better endowed and/or better capitalized producers. To planters on these islands, the "labor problem," which once seemed decisive, was ultimately of secondary significance.

However, the sugar interests did not always recognize the complexity of a predicament that included a host of other issues besides the supply and control of labor: technological modernization, improved agricultural practices, liberalization of tariff restrictions in the consuming nations, the cost and availability of credit, and many others. As soon as the supply of additional slaves from Africa dwindled or ended altogether, the planters began to focus intensely on the labor question, articulating possible strategies that could be adopted to hinder the workers' freedom of movement. As we have noted, the actual implementation of such strategies differed in timing between the two groups of colonies previously identified; whereas planters in the British, French, Danish, and Dutch Caribbean typically framed their solutions to the "labor shortage" after the slaves were legally freed, hacendados in the Spanish Caribbean, abetted by colonial authorities, embraced a variety of mechanisms *during slavery* to make the eventual transition to free labor swifter and less abrupt.

But in spite of this difference, which may be attributed to Cuba's and Puerto Rico's delay in ending slave importations and abolishing slavery, the strategies adopted for the appropriation of nonslave labor were comparable across the region. They also had much in common with policies adopted in other New World plantation systems, particularly in the sugar-producing regions of some Latin American nations like Peru and Argentina. Such labor strategies took many different forms and occurred in variable combinations, depending on a country's individual needs and financial capabilities, market conditions at any particular moment, the degree of imperial acquiescence and support, and the homogeneity and solidarity of the planter classes.[3]

One of the most common procedures was to restrict or deny the laborers access to the land wherever it was available and inexpensive. A planter-controlled colonial legislature or a colonial governor might impose a minimum acreage requirement or price on land transactions, forbid purchases by groups of more than a stipulated number of buyers—to forestall the practice, which was customary in the British colonies especially, of collective land acquisitions by freedmen on the basis of pooled resources—or impede third parties (like missionary churches) from acting on behalf of laborers who wished to become freeholders but lacked the means to procure land in the first place. Alternatively, authorities might persecute squatters on public or private lands or even establish a minimum acreage requirement for anyone engaged in farming in order to forestall the growth of a smallholding class or even eradicate an existing one. The latter requirement was usually accompanied by a stipulation that all those who did not meet the minimum landholding must work for wages or be subject to stiff penalties. Such measures were included, for instance, in a coercive legal formula (the *Reglamento de Jornaleros*) that was enforced in Puerto Rico between 1849 and 1873, which also required day laborers (*jornaleros*) to move from the rural areas to the fringes of towns, and to carry a workbook on which the employer kept track of the laborer's work attendance and discipline. As the Puerto Rican experience indicated, however, such attempts to convert established smallholders into wage earners by the enforcement of a minimum landholding rule carried a high price tag and achieved dubious results. The smooth operation of such compulsory labor systems was predicated on intensive (and therefore expensive) police vigilance, the exercise of which could not guarantee, in any event, the attainment of an invariably elusive goal.[4]

Another expedient strategy of labor exaction and control, typically favored in colonies with low population densities, was the sheer augmentation of the number of workers by "mechanical" means, that is, by the volume importation of (coolie) workers, who were obligated by contract to perform plantation labor during a specified period. The main sources of such immigrants were India and China, although at certain times the planters experimented with other distant suppliers, even in Africa itself. We will discuss indentured immigration in greater depth below, but for now it is sufficient to note that the traffic in coolies was second only to the transatlantic slave trade in the number of "fresh" laborers that it brought to the Caribbean during the nineteenth century. So significant were the indentured populations in several host countries (i.e.,

Surinam, British Guiana, Trinidad, and, to a lesser extent, Cuba), that their presence caused meaningful and lasting changes in the ethnic and linguistic character of these societies. Moreover, as the hundreds of thousands of Asian coolies entered social environments where a gulf of sizable proportions already separated the Afro-creole majorities from the ruling white elite, indentured immigration exacerbated cultural divisions and gave rise to ethnic animosities that have persisted to this day.

In addition to restricting the laborers' access to the land and sponsoring coolie immigration, the planting interests used their financial leverage to enforce labor's permanence and discipline. One widely used practice of this kind was the promotion of worker indebtedness as a tool for curbing labor force mobility. In a relevant discussion concerning Latin America as a whole, Arnold Bauer has rightly cautioned that what contemporaries and many historians have called "debt peonage" may have encompassed a wide range of employer-worker relations, including, he says, those in which the debtor was not actually a "peon" in a state of virtual slavery but rather a shrewd participant in a financial transaction.[5] But whether or not one employs the term "debt peonage" to describe particular instances of worker indebtedness in the nineteenth-century Caribbean, it is clear that landowners there construed the cash advance or its equivalent as an effective means of restricting the workers' economic and spatial mobility. In advancing the workers money or goods, planters took advantage of their superior liquidity and access to credit in an economic environment that left workers, even those with access to some land, increasingly in need of hard currency to pay for marketed goods and services and to satisfy their tax obligations. The phenomenon of indebtedness was so widespread that it occurred, for instance, in situations of apparent labor abundance, as in Puerto Rico's coffee highlands in the late 1800s, where not only wage workers but also small landowners habitually fell into debt with coffee hacendados and merchants, as well as in cases of manifest labor "scarcity," such as in British Guiana during peak periods of demand for East Indian coolies.

By modern capitalist standards, many Caribbean countries of the latter nineteenth century had, in the economists' term, rather poorly "irrigated" economies, where money circulation was deficient and hard currency was continually scarce. In order for indebtedness to function effectively as an instrument of labor control under such conditions, certain other institutional practices had to be fashioned. Among the more prevalent were the use of plantation stores (*tiendas de raya* in the Spanish-speaking islands) and the disbursement of wages in coupons (*vales*) or tokens redeemable solely at the estate shop or in designated local stores. Plantation stores, coupons, and tokens became especially popular in Cuba and Puerto Rico, where monetary instability and deficient currency circulation were endemic during the last century of Spanish rule. At the estate store laborers typically received their "wages" on account, and, as their consumption outstripped the sum of accrued wages, they inevitably ran up relatively large debts with the landowners or merchants. It was not unusual for workers to owe their employer several months' wages, in a hopeless cycle of obligations that left little room for mobility or escape. On the other hand, tokens afforded laborers slightly more maneuverability, since they were usually honored by networks of merchants and storekeepers within a certain perimeter.

If planters believed that they lacked the liquidity to pay wages on a continual basis, they might also be inclined to promote certain forms of sharecropping with the workers. Such labor arrangements characteristically emerged in islands where the plantations, although controlling most of the arable land, were financially strapped. For Nevis, to take one example, Richard Frucht has shown that after emancipation the planters, who were heavily indebted to metropolitan creditors, allowed some freedmen to use estate lands for the cultivation of crops selected by the planter (usually sugarcane) in exchange for a portion of the proceeds, paid in kind. Planters provided the seed, crop supervision, and other necessities except for the simple tools used in cultivation, which the workers were asked to supply. Thus the estate owners avoided having to pay cash wages and were poised to receive two additional benefits: (1) by allotting to the croppers portions of their holdings previously fallow, the owners could extend the cultivated area within their domains; and (2) they were better able to harness the labor of entire households, since the sharecropping arrangement undermined the laborers' opposition to the estates' employment of other household members, particularly women and children. Alternatively, for a share of the produce a landowner might allow tenants to determine which crop to plant, provided that they supplied the seeds, tools, and other necessary inputs. In either case, the sharecropping agreement gave rise to a novel social type that Frucht regards as being neither "peasant" nor "proletarian," but having characteristics commonly associated with both.[6]

By now it should be clear that the transition to free labor in the Caribbean was both complex and multidimensional. To be sure, the state of the world sugar markets imposed uniform constraints, which translated into the application of similar technologies, management techniques, and philosophies of labor control in the plantation sector. But sugar was not the dominant crop everywhere; in fact, one of the more significant regional developments of the nineteenth century was the move toward economic diversification, whether by adding new crops to the export sector or by expanding the acreage devoted to traditional food crops. Moreover, even where sugar was predominant, differences in factor endowment (in the relative availability of land, labor, and capital), in ecological conditions, and in the specific economic, social, political, and cultural legacies of slavery exerted a highly variable influence on the nature of labor arrangements after emancipation. A more detailed look at the British West Indies and the Spanish possessions of Cuba and Puerto Rico will help to illustrate this variation.

## The British West Indies

At the turn of the nineteenth century, England ruled over a group of colonies which, taken as a whole, had achieved the highest level of slave plantation development in the Caribbean region. Although effective colonization by British subjects had begun more than a century after the first Spanish settlements were established in the Greater Antilles in the late fifteenth and early sixteenth centuries, it took the British settlers only a few decades after initial colonization to discover the potential for great profit in the sugar business operated with African slaves. Around the middle of the seventeenth century, the fertile island of Barbados had been the first to take up sugar on a grand scale. Other islands in the Leeward group soon followed, and Jamaica, taken from the Spanish in 1655, was not far behind. By the middle decades of the eighteenth century, just as Great Britain's navy was beginning to gain a decisive superiority in Atlantic waters, its Caribbean possessions had matured into the largest, the most efficient, and arguably the most profitable colonial mercantilist enterprise in the world.

At their peak of development in the eighteenth century, the British sugar islands were the centerpiece of a broad-based and highly complex mercantile network, which historians for many generations have referred to as the triangular trade. This system of trading relationships linked three distant continents, involved hundreds of thousands of workers on land and at sea, and was responsible for the generation of profits substantial enough to be counted among the more significant individual sources of capital accumulation in England on the eve of the first Industrial Revolution.

If the triangular trade attracted investments from British merchants and other citizens of considerable means, it was because slave labor—relatively inexpensive and superexploited slave labor—was the cornerstone of this multifaceted branch of overseas commerce. And since before the nineteenth century the slave populations, in the British Caribbean as elsewhere, were peculiarly incapable of replenishing themselves through natural reproduction, the sugar islands always depended for their economic sustenance on the importation of fresh laborers from Africa. The African slave trade was therefore a sine qua non of Caribbean sugar production; the latter could not maintain adequate levels of production, and much less expand, without the former.

As sugar production reached its eighteenth-century peak in the British Caribbean, then, so did the British "branch" of the African slave trade. In the 1700s British subjects and British bottoms were responsible for the importation into the Americas of a staggering number of African slaves, the largest ever transported by a single slaving nation in any comparable period. According to one reliable estimate, in the period 1701–1810 the British colonies purchased about 1.75 million slaves, 80 percent of whom were introduced in the labor-thirsty sugar islands of the Caribbean. The activity of British slavers had gradually intensified as the century wore on and had reached its zenith in the 1780s. As a result, more than half of the total for the 110-year period had been transported from Africa in the 50 years between 1761 and 1810.

With the passage of the 1807 bill outlawing the slave trade, British abolitionists hoped that the extinction of colonial slavery would follow naturally and swiftly. To their dismay, reality took a different course. For one, the number of slaves in the British West Indies did not decline rapidly. The British West Indian slave population had numbered approximately 775,000 in 1807; in 1834, on the eve of abolition, 665,000 people remained enslaved. Significantly, the pattern of decline was not uniform across the different geographical and historical conditions that prevailed in the Caribbean possessions of Great Britain. In some of the colonies, like Demerara-Essequibo and Trinidad, where sugar production began comparatively late and where the slave population was unstable (with high proportions of African-born and male slaves) due to the effects of recent African importations, the decline was fairly pronounced throughout the period. Jamaica, the most populated and economically diverse of the British West Indies, occupied a kind of middle ground; there, the slave population diminished slowly until about 1820, after which date the decline became slightly more pronounced but yet the curve did not slant downward as sharply as in the late-developing sugar colonies. But the older, more established plantation colonies, with populations that were more stable as they were further removed from the disfiguring effects of the Middle Passage, did not see their slave stocks decrease inordinately. In one, Barbados, the slave population even managed to grow slightly between the abolition of the slave trade and emancipation on account of an unusual surplus of births over deaths during the period.

But if the institution of slavery itself persisted in the British West Indies after the cessation of the African slave trade, it was because the plantation economy proved to be more adaptable to the new demographic and economic conditions than had been envisaged. Two decades after the abolitionists' parliamentary victory of 1807, the West Indian planters were certainly hampered in their ability to make a profit. Still, slavery had not collapsed, and the slave owners were not yet willing to give up on their property altogether. When Parliament approved the emancipation bill in 1833 to become effective the following year, it did so over the angry protests of colonial planters and slaveholders, although the law called for a transitional period of apprenticeship and for compensation to the slaveholders for the loss of their capital.

The British West Indian planters' adaptation to the demographic and economic conditions of a closed slave trade after 1807 illustrates the tenacity of slavery in the Caribbean's nineteenth-century plantation economy. The point that needs to be emphasized here is that, after the abolition of the slave trade, changes in the population's composition reduced the attractiveness of slave labor without entirely undermining its viability. The planters' inability to replenish their aging stocks varied the composition of the slave labor force in ways that, in the planters' oft-stated view, were harmful to the profitability of plantation enterprise. As the age-sex structure of the slave population became more stable, for instance, the costs of maintaining less productive slaves— children and the aged—increased. Moreover, since the percentage of both female and creole slaves grew, time-honored prescriptions for the allocation of work roles had to be revised; more women and "weaker" Creoles had to be sent out to the fields to perform gang work, from which many of these classes of slaves had formerly been exempted. The employment of creole male slaves in low-status occupations seems to have had especially undesirable consequences, for it violated the expectation of higher status to which some of such slaves had become accustomed.

In the decades before emancipation, then, the masters awoke to the realization that their slaveholdings constituted a less flexible work force than before. When the slave trade had been active, planters had made selective purchases from slavers to maintain "ideal" plantation stocks—for example, a preponderantly male population in the most productive ages. Now that the choice no longer existed, the age-sex structure of the servile population tended to become more balanced (with a higher proportion of women, children, and older people) and hence less suited to the strenuous tasks of cane agriculture and sugar making. Besides, the proprietors suddenly had to cope with a new rebelliousness among slaves (especially the creole slaves) that could have potentially catastrophic results, as the Jamaican rebellion of 1831–32 (the Baptist War) frightfully demonstrated. But the crucial point need not be missed, which is that because the actual volume of slave labor available to the plantations did not diminish drastically, and because productivity per slave was not adversely affected by the demographic shifts, it is difficult to maintain that slavery had ceased to be a viable labor institution in the British Caribbean at the time of emancipation. That in the early 1830s the plantation system was in failing health is beyond question. Yet, recent research has underscored the argument that the malady was grounded more firmly in other economic factors—for example, the falling prices of sugar, the overall loss of the sugar industry's competitiveness, and, in the older sugar colonies, the planter's reluctance to adopt more rational methods of cultivation and manufacture—than in a failure of the institution of slavery to satisfy the labor needs of the estates.

When Parliament approved legislation to abolish slavery in the colonies in 1833, concerns for the masters' property rights were paramount in Great Britain. Because most Britons, even those in the antislavery camp, believed that the freedmen would not readily work for wages without coercion, the Colonial Office devised a plan to assign the freedmen to the tutelage of their former masters for a period of six years (later reduced to four). In addition, the project called for compensation in the amount of 20 million pounds to be paid to West Indian slaveholders. The formula that became part of the emancipation statute of 1833 left to each island legislature the drafting of specific rules to implement the principles sketched in the law. While the Colonial Office oversaw such legislation as it was sent to London for approval, the office usually avoided contradicting the white colonials' wishes, on whom imperial officials relied to bring about an uneventful transition to free labor. Therefore, planter-dominated legislatures in the West Indies were virtually free to adopt whatever means they considered necessary to bring about the new system of free labor. In so doing, some of them tried to coerce the ex-slaves to work on the plantations under circumstances not altogether different from those of slavery.

Although apprenticeship was adopted almost universally in the British West Indies, there were significant differences in the way that the system was implemented in the various colonies, as well as in the meaning and importance of that experience for the establishment of labor systems under freedom.[7] As a general rule, however, the transitional regimen was harsher and led to greater bitterness between the parties in those colonies (principally Jamaica, Trinidad, and Demerara-Essequibo) where uncultivated and unclaimed lands were plentiful, and where the planters feared, for good reason, that freedmen would flee the plantations and settle lands outside of the restrictive perimeter of the estates. And generally it did not arouse as much controversy in those islands with relatively closed resources, where the planters were confident of their exercise of strict control over their labor force after all legal coercion had been abolished. Even so, some of the islands in the latter group experienced considerable turbulence during the era of apprenticeship; in Saint Kitts and Montserrat, for example, military force was needed to maintain order after the workers resisted the planters' stratagems.

Events in Jamaica help to illustrate the severity and failure of apprenticeship wherever the planters were guided by the fear of forfeiting their supply of controllable and disciplined labor at the end of the transitional term. After August 1834, upward of 300,000 Jamaican ex-slaves became apprentices, subject to a series of burdensome rules, drawn up by the planter-controlled legislature, that dictated their relationship with their former masters. The apprentices were supposed to work no more than a five-day week (40 hours maximum) and were to be paid a stipulated wage, but often such restraints on their employment and the specified compensation went unheeded. A grievance system was instituted but the planters resisted its enforcement and made it often ineffectual. Other planter abuses, including evictions from the estates and the reappearance of corporal punishment and whippings (expressly forbidden by law), soon vitiated the system and disillusioned the apprentices with their new condition. The workers for whom emancipation had held out the promise of freedom vehemently protested the planters' attempts to impose labor obligations and a work discipline that were tantamount to, if not actually harsher than, the demands formerly placed on them as slaves, while at the same time the former masters withheld some of the petty prerogatives accorded the laborers under the former regimen. The apprentices' protests were echoed on the other side of the Atlantic by the abolitionists, who pressed Parliament for the extinction of the transitional experiment in forced labor. The protests were successful, and in 1838 Parliament abolished the apprenticeship system in the British West Indies.

The extinction of apprenticeship in 1838 was undoubtedly a watershed in British Caribbean history, for it marked the true passing of the institution of slavery. Although the planters remained firmly in control of colonial politics and continued to monopolize available resources, freedmen now faced the critical issue of fashioning for themselves an array of economic, social, and cultural institutions—or, more precisely, completing or reforming those that they had begun building under slavery—that would infuse real meaning into their newly gained liberty. As they attempted to build those institutions, their most pressing concerns revolved around the norms, rules, and conditions under which they would be willing to provide plantation labor. As Walter Rodney insightfully describes it, for most British West Indian freedmen the burning issue after 1838 would turn on the question "whether the ex-slaves, the freed slaves, could create a new way of life in which labor enters a relationship with capital under conditions that are at least partially determined by labor, whether labor could free itself from some of the absolute controls of slavery."[8] The alternatives ranged from staying on the plantation "niggeryards," which the freedmen naturally loathed, working for wages that the planters could conceivably stabilize at very low levels, to abandoning the plantation areas altogether—especially in the larger colonies with relatively open resources—and establishing themselves as yeoman farmers or peasants. In this continuum of possibilities, the middle ground comprised some type of peasant adaptation that entailed part-time employment on the plantations to supplement the income derived from the sale of produce in local markets.

Given this continuum of possibilities, how did the freedmen react and why did they choose a particular course of action over another? The answers to these questions are necessarily complex, for conditions in the British West Indies after 1838 varied considerably from colony to colony and even across time within each geographic unit. The planters' strategies for the control of labor followed several distinct, sometimes even contradictory, paths; the freedmen's responses to such challenges were likewise varied. The prevailing disparity of power between capital and labor clearly meant that the laborers were at an initial disadvantage, and thus were placed in a reflexive position, in their dealings with the planters and their instruments of control. Almost everywhere the planters quickly adopted laws and regulations that were intended to severely restrict the workingmen's choices; among such coercive devices were vagrancy laws, compulsory contracting between the parties, and wage/rent systems that used estate housing and provision grounds as a means to depress wages and impose work discipline.

Yet because the freedmen were far from powerless in the face of the planters' assault, their initiatives decisively influenced the final outcome of labor systems after slavery. The nature of those initiatives hinged on several factors, including, of course, the freedmen's own analysis of the power equation and their choice among alternative courses of action. But invariably it also depended on forces that were beyond the control of local actors, such as the price of sugar and the relative competitiveness of a given colony's industry. This dialectic between planter strategies, freedmen's choices, and the British colonial market followed, once again, two general directions that correspond to the contrast in resource availability outlined above. Where the freedmen's range of alternatives was relatively broad, one kind of social dynamics prevailed, and another where the freedmen's choices were strictly limited by the planters' monopoly of resources and power.

In attempting to make sense of the transition from slavery to free labor, historians of the Caribbean have long believed that wherever land was plentiful the freedmen practiced their "natural inclination" to flee the plantations in order to escape planter control altogether. No sooner were they liberated from slavery's chains, than they fled the estates en masse to become independent freeholders, provided that land prices made it feasible to do so. This interpretation is consistent with the opinions and protestations of a "labor shortage" voiced by contemporary planters. Moreover, it is supported by evidence which shows, in the case of the larger colonies, that many—in some cases, most— freedmen had abandoned the plantations and settled in peasant villages a generation or two after the end of slavery. In this conception, the formation of peasantries in the British Caribbean after 1838 followed logically from circumstances that prevailed during slavery. For not only did the peasant accommodations constitute an outgrowth of the freed slaves' resentment toward the harsh, often brutal, conditions of labor in sugar plantations, but also it was a historical product of the "proto-peasant" practice of cultivating provision grounds for subsistence and sale in local markets during the era of slavery. Once freed, the slaves chose a course of action that was consonant with their past: they flocked to the land and turned their backs on estate wage labor as a way of asserting their independence.

However, scholars have more recently questioned whether the freedmen's flight from the plantations occurred as suddenly and as mechanically as the foregoing discussion supposes. While reaffirming the basic point that where land was abundant (i.e., in Jamaica, Trinidad, and Demerara-Essequibo) *the principal long-term outcome* was indeed the establishment of a strong peasantry with relative autonomy from the estates, some scholars, notably Douglas Hall and the late Walter Rodney, have contended that the freed slaves' *initial reaction* was to remain on the estates and, from their newly strengthened bargaining position, to transact with the planters for higher pay and better working conditions—in other words, for a higher standard of living. If freedmen indeed left the plantations in large numbers, it was only to achieve better control of their own and their families' labor by undermining the planters' ability to dictate labor conditions simply on account of their command over estate provision grounds and housing. The exodus from the plantations, argues Rodney, initially "did not occur in order to run away from plantation labor, but to strengthen the bargaining position of labor in dealing with planter capital by putting the laborer in a position where one would be unafraid of the threat that one might be kicked out of the house."[9] To bolster this point, Rodney alludes among other things to the freedmen's formation of independent jobbing gangs that moved from one estate to another in search of the highest wage rates. A carryover from the days of slavery, when some planters would organize such gangs and hire them out to other employers, the jobbing gangs organized by creole African workers were, in Rodney's view, an eminently *proletarian* reaction to the contractual conditions of employment that full emancipation inaugurated.

Equally significant for the interpretation of the freed slaves' response to capital was a series of strikes that occurred in the British West Indies within a decade of the elimination of apprenticeship. Strikes by freedmen were fairly widespread in the early years of the free labor system, even in those colonies where land scarcity virtually precluded the establishment of a freeholding peasantry. "Strikes," affirms Woodville K. Marshall on evidence gathered primarily in Barbados and the Windward Islands, "sometimes lasting as long as two or three weeks, occurred in most islands; many ex-slaves refused to surrender their provision grounds and some resisted violently; and nearly all of them objected to the wage rates."[10] In these territories, though, the most common outcome was some type of proletarian accommodation, which Marshall calls "a fragile industrial peace" created on "the basis of a few concessions—small wage increases, a shorter working week for women and guarantees of rights to growing crops [on estate grounds] in the event of eviction."[11] In British Guiana, however, the outcome was substantially different. There the workers organized fairly widespread labor stoppages in 1842, barely four years after full emancipation, and again in 1848. But while the first of these appears to have fulfilled at least some of the strikers' objectives, the second, which erupted after the arrival in British Guiana of nearly 6,000 contract workers from the Portuguese island of Madeira, was much less successful because the contract workers weakened the freedmen's leverage vis-à-vis the planters. As the number of people living in the Guyanese free villages (newly organized communities of freeholders) or in the so-called "creek-and-river movement" increased substantially after each strike, it appears that the workers' perception of their failure to wrest satisfactory concessions from capital played a crucial role in the decision of many to become freeholders.[12]

Clearly, then, the establishment of labor systems after slavery was not predicated on simple formulas. Neither the planters' continued exercise of nearly unrestricted control over their work force nor the flight of laborers from the sugar estates and the establishment of a freeholding peasantry were necessary by-products of the termination of slavery under different conditions of resource availability. In both open and closed resource situations many freedmen believed at first that they could fashion a satisfactory existence within the framework of the plantations, but only if the planters relinquished several key elements of their former hegemony, such as their ability to command the labor of entire families and to use estate provision grounds as a mechanism for maximizing labor output and depressing wages. Where the independent freeholding alternative was sharply restricted because land was in short supply and expensive, the characteristic outcome was a negotiated agreement between planters and laborers which usually included concessions of specific rights over estate provision grounds and stipulated wage rates. In other cases, like that of Barbados, in addition to a resident labor force there arose a relatively small independent peasantry. But while this group managed to move away from the estates, it continued to furnish these with more or less steady labor and in some cases even agreed to grow sugarcane for sale to the estates at a fixed price, under a contractual arrangment that resembled the *colono* system found at a later stage in the development of several other Caribbean sugar economies.

The most dramatic consequences undoubtedly occurred in Jamaica, Guiana, and Trinidad, where a widespread thrust toward freeholding had by the 1850s thoroughly altered the colonial social structure. In Jamaica, for example, where in 1838 more than 300,000 apprentices had gained their freedom, a majority of them having lived on the estates, an American observer sympathetic to the freedmen estimated in 1861 that there remained only 40,000 laborers who sold their labor on a "transient" basis to the plantations; and, of these, only half were working at any given time.[13] Many contemporaries blamed the accelerated decline of Jamaica's export economy after 1838 on this massive withdrawal of the freedmen from estate labor. In reality, however, economic decline and the founding of free villages reinforced each other. Sugar estates had begun to experience serious difficulties before emancipation. But later, as the freedmen set out, with the help of Baptist, Methodist, and other missionaries, to found communities independent of the plantations, the consequent disruption in the labor supply led to further economic difficulty for, and repression by, the planters. Once caught in this downward spiral, many Jamaican proprietors had no alternative but to cease operations; consequently, the number of plantations on the island fell drastically between 1833 and 1847 and continued to decline well into the second half of the century. The existence of a large number of ruinate plantations in turn depressed land prices and gave further impetus to the freeholding movement.

The numerous free villages that sprouted in the larger British Caribbean colonies in the 1840s and 1850s had understandably diverse origins, economic objectives, and social composition. In some cases freedmen purchased entire sugar estates and set out to either operate them as before (only now on a quasi-corporate basis) or to subdivide their lands into individual provision grounds. The first of these options was usually the least fruitful, for the freedmen ordinarily lacked the capital and market skills that were necessary to operate sugar estates successfully at a time of sharply depressed prices. The second alternative—to carve out free villages from the remains of sugar estates—was far more viable and common. By mid-century, in some parts of Jamaica, Trinidad, and Guyana that formerly harbored expansive sugar fields, the familiar landscape had been transformed. An observer, writing of the environs of Morant Bay in Jamaica at an early date (1840), described the picture as follows:

> The progress of the rural population in establishing themselves as small freeholders has been rapid and unceasing. Within a few miles of Morant Bay, three extensive villages have been established on sugar plantations that have been thrown out of cultivation for many years. These freeholds vary in extent, from one to ten acres, and the cottages, amounting to upwards of 300, are neat and comfortable and surrounded by gardens and provision grounds. Independent of these villages there are many other small freeholds scattered over the district.[14]

To be sure, British West Indian villagers of the post-emancipation period were not all—perhaps not even largely—independent peasants occupying one- to ten-acre plots of land to which they held legal title. The Morant Bay scenario may have been atypical of social evolution elsewhere in Jamaica and throughout the larger British West Indies. In the second half of the century, villagers in Jamaica, Trinidad, and Guyana were more likely to be tenant farmers cultivating small provision grounds than freeholders along the model described above. Some villagers did not have access to land at all, or, having gained it, they had lost it; in either case they turned for their subsistence to occasional estate work, domestic employment, huckstering, and a host of other activities. Thus village society was far from universally "peasant." Within the village economy, moreover, there was a general tendency toward concentration of land in fewer hands, just as in a more particular way the Jamaican free village movement seems to have lost much of its early momentum and sense of purpose in the decades after emancipation. By the end of our period, peasant dispossession and the emergence of a class of wealthier farmers were deeply entrenched tendencies of village life. So, too, was the development of an educated middle class of teachers, store clerks, minor civil servants, and the like, whose socially mobile members could trace their roots to the creole African villages or the coolie ships of yesteryear.

But in the wake of emancipation, scenes like Morant Bay's deeply disturbed planters everywhere. In desperation, they used their influence in colonial legislatures to prevent the further spread of villages and the consequent hemorrhage of plantation labor. Beginning in the 1850s, for example, British Guiana enacted a series of laws that drove land prices upward and discouraged freedmen from making group purchases of ruinate plantations or forbade squatting on Crown lands, practices that were fairly common until that time. As Alan Adamson has shown, partly because of this planter reaction the freeholding movement began to lose momentum in the early 1850s. By then, however, almost 50,000 people had sought sanctuary in the colony's free villages.[15]

But among the planters' decisions, the most consequential was not the attempt to hinder the growth of freeholding. A more extreme resolution was to replace many of the estranged laborers with indentured and other migrant workers from distant lands. The indentured workers chiefly came from India, which supplied at least two-thirds of the total, but fairly large contingents also arrived at various times from Madeira, China, and even Africa. A parallel labor migration occurred within the British Caribbean, as noncontract migrant workers moved, frequently on a temporary basis, to the labor-thirsty colonies from closed resource islands like Barbados and Antigua.

Projects to replace a declining slave population with "East Indian" (i.e., Indian) immigrants had been drawn up by some planters and colonial officials at the time of the abolition of the slave trade in 1807, but the idea did not prosper until after the end of apprenticeship in 1838. That year, an experiment with East Indian contract laborers began in British Guiana when 396 of them arrived in the colony, "the first trickle of a stream that was not to dry up until 1917 [in British Guiana]."[16] The experiment did not mark an auspicious beginning for the new system of labor recruitment. The workers, many of whom were ignorant of where their long voyage had taken them (some believed they could walk back to their homeland!), toiled for wages that the former slaves would have found intolerably low and suffered a succession of abuses and brutal treatment; in the end, a large number of them died before the survivors were able to return home several years later.

The failure of this early episode did not deter the planters, who continued to press for immigration projects both at home and in the metropole. In 1843, after considerable debate in Great Britain on the merits of coolie immigration as a solution to the West Indian "labor shortage," the Colonial Office adopted a policy favorable to state-controlled immigration. The policy, reaffirmed by the imperial government several years later, opened the floodgates of contract immigration. Between the early 1840s and the extinction of the practice in 1917, several hundred thousand Asian and other coolies were brought to the British Caribbean expressly to labor on sugar plantations. The bulk of them went to Trinidad and British Guiana, with lesser numbers reaching Jamaica and the Leeward and Windward islands. British Guiana alone received approximately 200,000 East Indian immigrants over the course of six decades, in addition to several thousand Chinese, Madeirans, and Africans. The peak of this traffic in contract laborers occurred between the 1860s and 1880s (both inclusive); in a typical year during these decades, about 5,000 East Indians were shipped to Great Britain's Caribbean possessions.

In contrast to the creole Africans, coolies were clearly a more controllable and cheaper labor force. Contracted for a fixed number of years (five was the norm) and customarily housed in estate barracks, the immigrants supplied regular labor at stable rates. Coolies were also not as likely as the villagers to put up effective, organized resistance to the planting interests by resisting them "at the point of production [on the estates] or in the wider social arena."[17] But the indentured East Indians were not passive either. Like other Caribbean workers in this period, they alternated between accommodation and resistance in their relations with employers. According to Rodney, "seasoned" immigrants were more likely to employ resistance tactics, which explains why proprietors often preferred "fresh coolies." Reindentured workers, those who signed new contracts after the original agreements had expired, were better informed, more independent (many set up residence outside the plantations), and, having acquired job skills during their first indenture, usually had greater leverage in the contest over wages and work rules and conditions. Significantly, Guyanese East Indians were involved in frequent strikes and other work-related disturbances during the 1870s, 1880s, and 1890s, by which time the immigrant community had matured and most of its members who still were plantation laborers had become reindentured.[18]

By the 1890s the pattern of labor recruitment by means of the indenture system was firmly set, and in the broader scenario of British West Indian life the processes of disintegration and reconstruction were all but consummated. Slightly more than a half century after the end of apprenticeship and final slave emancipation, a superficial glance at the societies in question might reveal an all-too-familar panorama, a landscape of striking continuities from the slavery period. The economic and social predominance of commercial agriculture had not diminished; rather, it had been enlarged in some ways and in some places by the consolidation of numerous plantations under absentee corporate owner- ship and by the increase in productive scale brought about by the central factory system in the sugar industry. On the other hand, the colonies' political and economic subordination to Great Britain had not lessened, and in some colonies (e.g., Jamaica) it had actually been accentuated with the inauguration of Crown Colony government, a form of colonial administration that rigidly curtailed the prior autonomy of the insular legislature. And finally, the working majorities continued to struggle for their subsistence within the narrow con- fines of capitalist productive relations and planter hegemony.

But if continuities with the slavery period were apparent, the changes that had transpired in the half century before 1890 were certainly no less striking and significant. The abolition of property rights in man had afforded the creole Africans an opportunity to exert greater control over their lives, particularly with regard to labor and kin—an opportunity they had eagerly seized. In the larger colonies, two entirely new social groupings had emerged: a village society that was relatively autonomous from the estates and an ethnically diverse rural proletariat. The two groups overlapped, and they eventually came to identify common grievances and forge joint endeavors of resistance and political action. Furthermore, as the century came to a close, a motley array of upwardly mobile groups—the new "middle sectors" of colonial society—had begun to take shape, the joint product of the free colored sector of slavery times and of the internal differentiation of village and urban society. In time, these educated middle sectors would also find common ground with the villagers and the estate workers, although such alliances in the end proved to be institutionally fragile and short-lived.

## Cuba and Puerto Rico

As previously noted, an important distinction obtained between the British West Indies and their Spanish counterparts of Cuba and Puerto Rico during the transition to free labor. This contrast was to a large extent a function of the timing of their development as slave plantation societies and of the sequence of events leading to emancipation. Whereas the British possessions turned to sugar monoculture as early as the seventeenth century and imported several million slaves in the 1600s and 1700s, Cuba and Puerto Rico did not begin their plantation careers in earnest until the later 1700s (Cuba) and early 1800s (Puerto Rico). Thus when plantation slavery and large-scale sugar manufacture made their debut in these islands after a hiatus of two centuries, slaves were a small minority in a population that featured a numerically large class of peasant freeholders and squatters. There existed, in short, a long tradition of independent farming that relied little on the labor of black slaves.

With the opening of European and American markets for Spanish Caribbean sugar, especially after the Haitian Revolution brought about the collapse of that country's industry, and in the wake of the enactment by Spain of commercial and immigration reforms that prompted the founding of new plantations and removed barriers on the slave trade, the stage was set for the nineteenth-century boom of the plantation system in the Spanish islands. When in 1817, giving in to British abolitionist pressure, Spain signed an agreement with Great Britain to terminate the slave trade to its colonies (the treaty became effective in 1820), Cuba's sugar industry was already within reach of the premier position among the world's cane producers. Stimulated by an influx of immigrant capital, Puerto Rico was also poised at the time to develop into one of the Caribbean's largest producing nations. But if the burgeoning slave trade were to cease as a result of the Anglo-Spanish agreement, might not the promising Spanish colonial experiment with commercial agriculture be rendered still-born?

Although this possibility worried the planters, merchants, and officials of Cuba and Puerto Rico, events soon allayed their fears. For three decades after 1820 the two islands witnessed a period of voluminous and unprecedented slave importations. A massive traffic in Africans developed to satisfy the labor needs of Spanish Caribbean sugar plantations, a trade which was, strictly speaking, clandestine, although it was carried out openly and with the conniv-ance of both local and metropolitan authorities. On two further occasions, in 1835 and 1845, Great Britain and Spain agreed on stronger provisions to persecute violators of the ban on slave trading; but while the latter treaties made it more difficult and expensive for slavers to perform their activities, they did not immediately put an end to the irrepressible Cuban commerce. While the heinous traffic from Africa to destinations in Brazil (the other large slave importer of the nineteenth century) came to a halt around mid-century, slaves continued to be smuggled into Cuba from 1850 to 1865 in even greater numbers than before. On the other hand, higher prices, more effective British vigilance, and more attentive compliance by Spanish authorities discouraged further importations by the Puerto Ricans after about 1850.

In Cuba and to a lesser extent in Puerto Rico, the development of a slave-driven sugar industry effected profound changes in population composition and social structure. Such changes were more sharply drawn in the larger of the two islands, where sugar occupied a position of greater relative economic importance. Cuba provides in fact the most dramatic nineteenth-century example of the manner in which sugar and slavery could affect a society, even one with a long-standing, articulated peasantry and in an age when prospects for the long-range survival of *any* slave system were, at best, minimal.

In his judicious study of the volume of the transatlantic slave trade, Philip Curtin estimates that approximately 550,000 slaves were introduced in Cuba between 1811 and 1865.[19] As this figure exceeded population gains by European immigration and natural reproduction, one can readily grasp how the slave trade modified the island's demographic composition. While in 1774 the slaves, 44,000 in number, comprised only 26 percent of the island population, by 1846 there were 324,000 slaves out of a population of some 900,000; in the latter year, those in bondage constituted 36 percent of the island's total population and probably more than half of its active labor force. Significantly, moreover, in 1846 slaves and free coloreds (150,000 people or close to 17 percent of the population)—the population of African descent—together accounted for more than half of the Cuban population for the first time since the middle of the sixteenth century. These figures underscore Franklin Knight's claim that by the middle of the nineteenth century Cuba had been transformed into a slave society.[20]

To be sure, Cuban slave society differed in several respects from the prototype of the pre-emancipation sugar islands of the British and French Caribbean. The population profile provides one of the most illuminating contrasts. Even at the height of slave importations in the 1840s, six of every ten Cubans were free, and more than four in ten were classified in censuses as "white." At no time were such high proportions of nonslaves and whites found in the classic sugar colonies, and assuredly not at the peak of African importations. Moreover, three additional characteristics distinguished Cuban demography from the Caribbean model of slave society. First, the island continued to be an attractive destination for European migrants; just as slavers called into Cuban ports with large numbers of *bozales* (native African slaves), many other vessels arrived with European (predominantly Spanish) settlers. Second, beginning in the second half of the eighteenth century, the free population, particularly its white segment, experienced rapid natural growth (due to a surplus of births over deaths), a demographic behavior that set it apart from the Caribbean norm during slavery times. And third, Cuba was proportionally more urbanized than any other country in the Caribbean, with all that this implies for occupational and social differentiation and for the development of craft and service industries, whether associated with, or independent of, the plantation sector. By the mid-nineteenth century, the bustling port city of Havana alone, with close to 200,000 inhabitants, surpassed the *combined* population of all other capitals in the Caribbean region.

In spite of the continuing Cuban involvement in the slave trade after 1845, that year may be regarded as a turning point in the evolution of rural labor in both Spanish Caribbean islands. After the second Anglo-Spanish treaty, the writing on slavery's future was on the wall, and Spanish West Indian planters began to search for alternative labor sources to replace a declining and aging servile population. As in the non-Hispanic colonies, the alternatives contemplated by hacendados and colonial authorities ranged from the enactment of laws to persecute "vagrancy" to the wholesale importation of coolies.

In Puerto Rico, as we saw, the colonial government, in consultation with the landed interests, chose the first alternative. The sugar industry of that island had developed strongly since about 1820, and until 1845 numerous fresh slaves from Africa formed the basis of its prosperity. However, Puerto Rico's economy was more diversified than Cuba's, its peasant sector was proportionally greater, and consequently the percentage of slaves in the total population never exceeded 14 percent. After 1845 Puerto Rican hacendados, who on the whole were financially weaker than Cuban planters, were hard pressed to run the risks, and pay the attendant higher prices, of new importations from Africa. It was at this juncture that coercive labor practices which allowed planters to tap into the large peasant labor pool became an attractive option. The ensuing Reglamento de Jornaleros (in force between 1849 and 1873) was designed to effect a swifter transition to free labor in the export sector by undermining peasant resistance to hacienda work. The law set minimum landholding requirements, forbade the common practice of squatting, required day laborers to congregate on the fringes of towns, and compelled them to carry a workbook (*libreta*) with the employer's notations on work attendance, discipline, and the like. In 1864, in an attempt to ensure stricter compliance, the state organized a rural police force (the Guardia Rural) to persecute violators.

Although from the Puerto Rican planters' point of view the libreta system was plagued with difficulties, it made available to them an inexpensive mass of labor power which otherwise they might not have commanded at the low wage rates they were willing to pay. Jornaleros were not the controllable work force that slaveholders had become accustomed to; irregular work attendance was a pervasive problem, as was the workers' refusal to perform the most demanding tasks of sugar manufacture (e.g., the boiling house procedures). Yet, as the date of Puerto Rican emancipation neared, jornaleros supplied roughly one-half of the labor needs of sugar plantations (albeit the larger and more efficient estates still relied more heavily on slaves). Meanwhile, in the burgeoning coffee industry of the island's interior, nonslave labor had been the standard for quite some time.

This is not to suggest that there were no disruptions in the labor supply when Spain decreed emancipation for Puerto Rico in 1873 and when it abolished the disappointing apprenticeship regimen three years later. As in the British West Indies more than thirty years later, some freedmen (libertos) abandoned the estates while others used their enhanced leverage—or employed strike tactics—to extract significant concessions from the owners. Nevertheless, one cannot avoid the conclusion that the coercive labor laws of the preceding quarter century succeeded at least partially in mitigating the economic shock of emancipation and cushioning the impact of the novel labor prescriptions on the Puerto Rican hacienda system.

In Cuba, on the other hand, the transition to free labor required potentially costlier means of substituting increasingly scarcer and aging slaves. Just as in the 1840s the dominant interests in Puerto Rico were reaching an agreement of sorts on the most expedient means to replace slave workers, the planting interests in Cuba were developing a consensus on the utility of Chinese coolies to achieve a similar purpose, if on a much larger scale. Such contract workers began to arrive in Cuba in 1847 and continued to be introduced until the 1870s. Unlike the traffic of East Indians to the British West Indies, of course, the Cuban business of importing Chinese contract workers flourished while the African slave trade was still active. But in ways that were quite similar to the British experience, the Cuban coolie trade subjected an alien population to the rigors of slavery in all but the legal sense. Given such oppressive conditions, it is not surprising that historians have regarded the use of coolie labor as an efficient mechanism of labor exaction during the transition to free labor. The Chinese entered into a relationship with the sugar planters that differed little from slavery in terms of the maneuverability and mobility allowed the workers; clearly, this was advantageous to the slaveholders and injurious to the workers.

Yet one should not lose sight of the fact that, in spite of indentured labor's adaptability to planter needs, Chinese immigrants supplemented but did not replace the slaves. Displaying a combination of pragmatic flexibility and opposition to radical change, Cuban planters adapted to the progressive decomposition of the slave system by employing coolies and some salaried Creoles while struggling to retain control over their slaves as long as possible. In this endeavor the Cuban slaveholders seem to have had greater success than their counterparts in other slave societies, to judge from the evidence that in the 1870s bondsmen still supplied the bulk of estate labor. Significantly, although some scholars believe that the thrust to mechanize sugar manufacture gave birth to a fateful contradiction between slavery and industrial progress, recent research indicates that reliance on slaves was in fact higher in districts with larger and technologically more advanced sugar works. Industrialization therefore may not have doomed Cuban slavery after all.

Even though slaveholders tried to cling to their chattel as long as possible, at the turn of the 1870s that goal proved, for many owners at least, increasingly difficult to achieve. During those years internal and external forces eroded the demographic and political foundations of slavery in Cuban society. As Rebecca Scott has shown in her study of Cuban emancipation, the disengagement of slavery began when, in a gradual and geographically uneven fashion, increasing numbers of slaves obtained their freedom either by metropolitan prescription—that is, by the force of partial abolitionist measures emanating from Spain—or by the slaves' shrewd manipulation of cleavages in the masters' monopoly of power, fissures created by the abolitionist movement itself and by an anticolonial insurrection at home.[21]

Two interrelated events functioned as catalysts of the liberation process: the enactment of the Moret Law (1870), a Spanish statute that called for the freeing of slaves over age sixty and those born after September 17, 1868; and the Ten Years' War (1868–78), an anticolonial struggle confined primarily to the eastern provinces. The Moret Law was significant not only because it helped to reduce the total number of slaves from 363,000 in 1867 to 199,000 ten years later (even though the total number of able workers did not decline by the same proportion), but also because it clearly indicated that between master and slave there existed a higher authority capable of being the arbitrator of, and eventually of dissolving, that relationship. Scott argues convincingly that the law's provisions "led to institutional and attitudinal changes that—to a limited extent—disrupted the social order of slavery."[22] Once abolitionism had exposed the master-slave bond as a matter over which the state had ultimate control, the slaves cleverly and assertively pursued their freedom through the various legal channels open to them.

The Ten Years' War had similar, if more dramatic, consequences. The insurrection began in eastern Cuba, where the plantation system was not as developed as in the central and western provinces and where slaves comprised, by island-wide standards, a small minority. One of the first seditious acts of Carlos Manuel de Céspedes, the rebellion's chief figure, was to liberate his own slaves and call for the indemnified abolition throughout Cuba. But as the Cuban historian Raúl Cepero Bonilla recognized many years ago, the members of the rebel leadership did not intend in the beginning to abolish slavery or upset the social order. Their call for emancipation was more symbolic than real, since their expressed policy was to free the slaves within the territorial limits of the insurrection *after* the rebellion had succeeded. Thus, when in February 1869 the rebel directorate declared all Cubans free, it called for a transitional regimen by which libertos were to remain in their former masters' service and be paid a stipulated wage. The experiment with an apprenticeship system in the midst of war was a bold and dangerous step. As in revolutionary Saint Domingue eight decades before, events in eastern Cuba in the 1870s would prove once again that slavery could not survive when social stability was subverted by the force of arms.

As the conflict dragged on and victory eluded the rebels, it became increasingly difficult to conduct the military effort without following through with the promise of freedom. The insurrection, already staffed by a motley army of creole blacks, mulattoes, and whites, needed the additional manpower. Many freedmen joined the ranks of the insurgent forces never to return to their former condition; they thus fulfilled the maxim that once armed, a slave would no longer remain a slave. In addition, the proclamation of nominal abolition prompted the freedmen of eastern Cuba to openly challenge the masters. Many took advantage of the chaos to flee and to establish small communities of runaways, shielded by the region's mountainous terrain. It is true that among those who remained under the masters' tutelage, some did not experience meaningful changes in their socioeconomic standing and living conditions. But others took to heart their new status as freedmen to wrest concessions and claim broader rights without breaking free entirely from slavery. The overall result was that, when in 1878 the rebels and Spanish authorities signed a truce to end the stalemated hostilities, the slave system of the eastern provinces of Puerto Príncipe and Santiago de Cuba had been shattered. The combined slave population of the two provinces, which had numbered 62,000 in 1867, had declined to a mere 15,000 ten years later.

For a variety of reasons, then, more than half of the approximately 400,000 bondsmen enumerated in the Cuban and Puerto Rican censuses of 1867 had ceased to be slaves ten years later. Most of those who remained enslaved, however, were tied to one of the most modern and efficient plantation systems in the world: the sugar industry of western and central Cuba. In light of that industry's economic vigor, it is not surprising to find that slavery's erosion had not affected the central and western planters as much as it had the eastern proprietors. As the year 1880 approached, the institutional resilience of slavery was evident in the age structure of the servile population of the larger, more mechanized Cuban *ingenios*. Scott's data for selected plantations indicate that slaves in the 14–40 age groups still composed a remarkably high portion of the slave stocks—considerably more than half of all slaves in the average plantation, and as high as 80 percent or more in certain units.[23] When the remaining slaves did not furnish all the needed labor, hacendados resorted, as we have said, to Chinese coolies, rented slaves, or wage workers. Flexibility and adaptation were the key; in the most advanced sector of the industry, planters who adapted typically confronted the abolitionist decree of 1880 with a core of (still) relatively young and productive slaves coupled with an additional group of contract, rented, or free laborers.

Against this backdrop of labor usage on the more important sugar ingenios, one is better able to understand the ambiguity of the Spanish abolitionist decree of 1880. Although claiming to emancipate the bondsmen, the law maintained the basic legal relationship between masters and slaves, now called *patronos* and *patrocinados*. The Cuban patronato, like the British apprenticeship that preceded it by almost half a century, included safeguards for the humane treatment of apprentices, decreed the payment of wages, and protected the integrity of the worker's family. In this regard it "resembled a liberal slave code," as Scott has noted.[24] But the patronato differed from a benign slave code in several key respects. The law specified a time limit for the patrocinados' service (all would be free by 1888 according to the law), created local and regional grievance boards, broadened the right to self-purchase (recognized by Spanish slave codes for many centuries), and commonly punished the patronos' infractions by granting apprentices their freedom. Such prescriptions opened up greater opportunities for the freedmen's libertarian actions, fissures in the slaveholders' monopoly of power which patrocinados used to their advantage. In the end, the law allowed numerous apprentices to purchase or otherwise secure their exemption from the patronato, and thus to achieve unconditional emancipation. After 1880, increasing numbers of patrocinados gained full legal freedom; by 1883 only about half of the nearly 200,000 slaves enumerated in 1877 remained in the transitional regimen, and by 1885 a mere 53,000 endured the patronato's controls. Finally in 1886, two years before it was supposed to, Spain put an end to the patronato in Cuba.

## Conclusion

The emancipation of Cuba's slaves in 1886 marked the end of slavery in the Caribbean. Nearly a century had passed since the seditious slaves of Saint Domingue initiated the systematic destruction of that most pervasive of regional institutions, and more than half a century since the first emancipation by imperial decree had taken effect in the British West Indies. Along the course of those one hundred years the Caribbean region had witnessed a diversity of abolitionist experiences and outcomes. As we have said, there was a close correspondence between the aims and aspirations of the principal actors everywhere: the large landowners and employers of labor wished to maintain the plantation system on a profitable basis and to retain their own internal dominion; imperial officialdom yearned to keep the existing power imbalance between metropole and colony; and the workers desired to exert greater control over labor, family, and leisure, and to avail themselves of—or retain, as the case may be—a share of land for their subsistence. To a large extent these parallel expectations were rooted in a common set of historical relations with the European world system and in the uniform constraints present in the nineteenth-century world sugar markets. But rigid rules of social change could not apply in a region where the forces that conditioned the behavior of slaveholders and slaves, planters and laborers, existed in such diverse combinations and played themselves out at different historical moments. As the foregoing discussion of the British and Spanish West Indies has shown, the social history of each country or group of countries was unique in many basic respects.

As the nineteenth century came to a close, certain features of contemporary labor relations in the Caribbean began to appear in sharper focus. For one, in most economic sectors there was a movement toward capitalist relations of production. More and more working people were either unable to acquire or incapable of retaining access to the land, so that the sale of their labor power became their principal, if not the sole, means of subsistence. This trend manifested itself everywhere, even in those countries where emancipation had engendered a fairly strong freeholding class. Second, as workers increasingly came to rely on the labor market for their sustenance, many of them fell into either permanent or seasonal unemployment. This was particularly true of workers in the sugar industry, where the adoption of the central mill system accentuated the seasonal nature of employment, as many more workers were needed during the harvest than in the off-season. Third, where unemployment developed into a critical problem (e.g., the British Leewards, Barbados, Puerto Rico, and the Danish West Indies), workers began to emigrate on a seasonal or permanent basis. Before 1900, most Caribbean workers who emigrated chose destinations within the region; Barbadians went to Trinidad, for example, and Puerto Ricans went to the Dominican Republic and Cuba. After the turn of the century, of course, the perimeter of labor emigration would expand to include destinations outside of the Caribbean.

Finally, proletarianization bred class consciousness and fostered the creation by workers of institutions for the defense of their collective interests. In many of the countries of the region by the 1890s workers had launched mutual aid societies, cultural and social clubs, and newspapers devoted to disseminating information on the plight of laboring men and women. Infused, in many cases, with anarcho-syndicalist and socialist ideas, these associations coalesced at a later stage into labor unions and workingmen's federations that put up effective resistance to capital and accomplished legislative reforms that addressed worker concerns. The organized working class henceforth became a powerful player in the political life of Caribbean nations, much as organized capital had been since the epoch of slavery.

## Notes

1. Sidney Mintz, "Slavery and the Afro-American World," in Mintz, *Caribbean Transformations*, p. 62.
2. Rice, "Enlightenment, Evangelism, and Economics," p. 123.
3. For a stimulating collection of essays on strategies of labor control in nineteenth-century Latin America, see Duncan and Rutledge, *Land and Labour.*
4. On the Puerto Rican Reglamento, see Picó, *Libertad y servidumbre*, and Bergad, *Coffee.*
5. Bauer, "Rural Workers in Spanish America."
6. Frucht, "A Caribbean Social Type."
7. The sole exception to the application of apprenticeship was Antigua, where the planters decided to bypass the transition and allowed the ex-slaves to have their freedom outright. This decision did not arise out of sheer magnanimity, but rather from the realization that the freedmen's opportunities for procuring an independent existence were nil.
8. Rodney, "Plantation Society," p. 646.
9. Ibid., p. 654. See also Hall, "Flight from the Estates Reconsidered," and Fraser, "The Fictive Peasantry."
10. Woodville K. Marshall, "Commentary," p. 247.
11. Ibid.
12. In British Guyana, the creek-and-river movement involved settlement of unoccu-

pied lands along the banks of the Demerara River by individual freedmen. For a description, see Adamson, *Sugar without Slaves*, pp. 36–37.

13. Sewell, *Ordeal of Free Labor*, cited in Bolland, "Systems of Domination after Slavery," p. 599.

14. Stipendiary Magistrate Ewart, cited in Paget, "The Free Village System," p. 12.

15. Adamson, *Sugar without Slaves*, p. 37.

16. Ibid., p. 42.

17. Rodney, *A History*, p. 160.

18. Ibid.

19. Curtin, *The Atlantic Slave Trade*, p. 234.

20. Knight, *Slave Society in Cuba*.

21. Rebecca J. Scott, *Slave Emancipation in Cuba*.

22. Ibid., p. 68.

23. Ibid., p. 96.

24. Ibid., pp. 128–29.

## 4

Bridget Brereton

# Society and Culture in the Caribbean

## The British and French West Indies, 1870–1980

n the decades of the 1830s and 1840s, metropolitan initiatives and internal social and economic pressures converged to effect the abolition of formal slavery in the British and French Caribbean colonies. This important change in the legal and institutional framework of West Indian society has traditionally been seen as the great break in Caribbean history, as the watershed dividing "slave society" from "free society." Thus, 1838 for the British and 1848 for the French colonies are the conventional starting points for any discussion of the "modern" (i.e., post-slavery) period.

Yet how important was formal emancipation for the people of the British and French Caribbean, where legal freedom was not the result of revolutionary initiatives nor of nationalist wars against colonialism? It is almost a truism that emancipation did not transform the nature of Caribbean societies, nor the fundamental patterns of race relations, nor the way power was held and exercised, nor even the values and attitudes that had most prestige. Because the plantation was still the most important unit in most of the islands, a rigid class/race stratification continued to exist, reinforced after 1838–48 by new divisions of race, religion, and language. Not all the Caribbean laboring people were able to free themselves from the need to work for the plantations at low wages and under serflike conditions; indeed, in some territories the majority of the ex-slaves and their descendants found themselves locked into this situation at least up to the 1940s. The grossly unequal distribution of economic resources, of wealth and poverty, was not fundamentally altered in the century that followed emancipation.

While the fundamental socioeconomic structures established during slavery remained largely intact in the hundred-odd years following legal freedom, it seems clear that emancipation opened up the possibility of change. It provided the legal conditions for social development, for the emergence of new social formations and groups. For many ex-slaves, it did make possible social and economic independence of the plantation. Emancipation allowed for popular cultures, secular and religious, to develop and sometimes to flourish, though not without difficulties. Some of the people were able to take part in political life as jurors, voters, and even as legislators. In sum, emancipation broke the stranglehold that slavery had held over the society and its institutions, and it set free new forces and new energies.

In the immediate post-emancipation decades, the Caribbean colonies were the focus of considerable metropolitan attention as the theater for the working out of a "great experiment," the attempt to transform masses of African and creole slaves into law-abiding, thrifty, hardworking, Christianized wage laborers; an attempt which, perhaps, met with more success than is often acknowledged. In these decades, the different socioeconomic groups struggled to adapt to the new legal arrangements, helped or hindered by the metropolitan visitors: Christian missionaries, abolitionists and Republicans, governors and officials, journalists and propagandists. But, by the 1870s, much of the drama seemed to have played itself out. The turbulent years of adjustment to freedom, often painful, seemed over; the great experiment had succeeded, or it had failed dismally, according to the ideology or class interests of the observer. Metropolitan interest waned perceptibly, and the Caribbean colonies gradually became forgotten backwaters, familiar but uninteresting corners of the expanding British and French colonial empires, their apparent somnolence only disturbed by a riot here or a natural disaster there.

To some extent, the decades between the 1870s and the 1930s–40s can be seen as "quiet times" for the British and French colonies, although outbursts of violent protest certainly occurred from time to time, especially just after World War I. But fundamental social and economic structures continued to dominate, and change was slow. It seemed, in fact, as if metropolitan efforts to create a sort of stability in the post-slavery Caribbean had met with some success. Yet much was happening beneath the placid surface. Many immigrant groups entered the Caribbean from Africa, Europe, Asia, and the Middle East, bringing completely new racial, cultural, and religious elements and fundamentally changing the colonies' demographic structures. Within "creole society" proper, the society made up of the former slaves, the former slave owners, and their descendants, the most striking change was probably the growth in the middle strata. By the 1930s many members of the various immigrant communities had also entered these middle strata. Race relations became more complex, involving quite "new" elements; class stratification moved slowly away from the crudely simple system of slave society and of the immediate post-emancipation era.

If social change had been relatively slow between the 1870s and the 1930s, the Caribbean colonies entered into a new era during the decades of the 1930s–40s, when the pace of socioeconomic development clearly accelerated. The depression of the 1930s, the labor protests between 1934 and 1938, the impact of World War II, and the efforts of nationalist movements led to important political, economic, and social transformations. Out of the regional labor protests emerged trade unions and political parties, and a new labor/political elite, which took the British colonies into postwar decolonization and eventual independence. In the French colonies, political and labor organizations were slower to develop, and the constitutional change of 1946 which made them *départments* of France was largely the result of metropolitan initiatives.

Economic developments after the war, with the partial industrialization of some colonies, the growth of mining (bauxite, oil), the new importance of tourism, and the massive expansion of the tertiary and services sector, had predictably crucial social repercussions. At the same time, and as part of the same processes, agriculture declined nearly everywhere; Caribbean peasantries came under heavy pressures as subsistence farming on small plots became increasingly less viable, or less attractive to the young; landlessness increased and large sectors of the former peasant strata were proletarianized. Tourism and light manufacturing, and emigration to the metropoles, absorbed some—but, inevitably, only some—of these people. Moreover, after about 1940 the population of the Caribbean colonies increased rapidly as death rates fell while birthrates continued at high levels well into the 1960s, and uncontrolled urbanization on a large scale was experienced as masses of peasants and rural laborers sought to escape the poverty of the countryside by drifting into the towns, especially the capital cities. Postwar urbanization continues to be a fundamental aspect of Caribbean social change.

Upheavals and painful adjustment in the immediate post-emancipation decades; relatively "quiet times" of slow social formation and economic stagnation between the 1870s and the 1930s; political transformations and accelerated social and economic change after World War II: here we have in summary a chronological framework of Caribbean social development since the mid-nineteenth century. We can now try to analyze the social structure of the Caribbean colonies, their patterns of race relations, as well as the material and nonmaterial culture of their people.

## Afro-Caribbean and Euro-Caribbean Relations

One of the most important legacies of slavery was the three-tier social structure. Society in the British and French Caribbean was divided—at the time of formal emancipation—into three major tiers or sectors, in descending order of power and status: the white upper class, the colored middle stratum, and the black masses who had just been freed. Few questioned the position of the white upper class as the dominant group, backed by economic hegemony, social prestige, and often effective political power (though this was less true of the French colonies after the establishment of the Third Republic in 1870). The middle group was generally separated from the black masses by phenotype; and because its members had acquired some formal education, possessed in greater or lesser degree a command of the English or French language and of metropolitan culture, held white-collar jobs, or, as in the case of small planters and middling merchants or shopkeepers, owned some land or small businesses, they were somewhat better off economically than the masses. In the nineteenth century most people in the middle stratum were of mixed African-European ancestry, but as time went on increasing numbers of blacks, as well as persons of Asian, Middle Eastern, or Portuguese origins, entered this group. At the bottom of the three-tier structure, the creole masses were mainly of African descent, the descendants of the slaves. They were largely excluded from political life, though in the French colonies formal rights of citizenship, including voting rights, were given to black men between 1848 and 1851, and again after 1870. Usually poor and badly educated, if indeed they had any formal education at all, their life-styles and cultural/religious practices were despised by most members of the upper and middle groups.

This three-tier class-racial structure remained the basic framework of Caribbean society right up to the 1930s–40s and indeed, some may argue, to the present day. But, within the system, change and diversity were both present.

Notably, a fourth tier or sector was added after the mid-nineteenth century to the social structure of some colonies: the immigrants from Asia, especially from India. In Trinidad and Guyana (and in Suriname), so many Indians settled that they came to form a large and separate sector of the population, separated from the other three groups by culture, religion, and race, and (well into the twentieth century) legal restrictions. And by their relatively late arrival, they entered the society at a time when the basic three-tier system had already been firmly established. Although Indians became a significant minority in Martinique, Guadeloupe, Jamaica, Saint Vincent, Grenada, and Saint Lucia, it is probably only in Trinidad and in Guyana that we should see them as forming a fourth distinct tier in the social structure. Neither the Chinese nor the Syrian/Lebanese communities were ever large enough to form a significant separate tier in any territory. As time went on the more successful Chinese and Syrian/Lebanese tended to move up toward, and even into, the top tier.

There were considerable variations, too, in the position of the whites in the different Caribbean societies. Most whites belonged to the upper class/tier— whether Creoles or Europeans—and the men were mainly landowners and planters, businessmen, professionals, and officials. But some colonies had a very small white population, too small in fact to form a separate class/tier. In Belize, for instance, the white population dwindled rapidly after emancipation until by 1881 only 375 white persons lived there—one percent of the total population—and 271 of these were adult men. Obviously there were very few settled white families, as opposed to European men doing a job in the colony for a few years. Guyana and the British Windward Islands also had a relatively small white community, and these territories lacked a deeply rooted white "aristocracy" such as Trinidad had in its French Creoles and Martinique in its grands békés. By contrast, Barbados and the Bahamas had much larger white communities, long established in these islands and secure in their control over them.

Moreover, a few colonies had small but distinct communities of "poor whites," notably Barbados, the Bahamas, and the Saintes (a group of small islands dependent administratively on Guadeloupe). These people, though more or less all of pure English or French ancestry (for they made a great point of never marrying outside their own little groups), were extremely poor and despised by everyone including the blacks. In Barbados they were called "Redlegs," probably because of their bare, sunburnt legs, and in the Saintes and Saint Barthélemy similar isolated and endogamous communities existed, racially "pure" since the seventeenth century, like their counterparts in Barbados.

In addition to these long-established poor white groups, the Portuguese immigrants who came to the Caribbean after the 1830s were not considered to be part of the white upper class/tier, though they were Europeans. Because they arrived as penniless laborers from simple peasant backgrounds in Madeira, spoke little or no English, and possessed a distinctively Portuguese culture, their ethnicity alone could not win for them upper-class status. They were marked off as a separate group on their own, and some censuses of the period had a category "Portuguese" which was separate from "Europeans." But by the late nineteenth century some of them had been absorbed into the first or second tiers as a result of successful trading activities, and this movement would accelerate in the postwar period as wealthy and educated Portuguese families in colonies like Trinidad and Guyana continued to enter the upper tier.

Finally, we may note that some very tiny islands hardly had any class/racial stratification system at all, for their small populations were nearly all people of African descent and roughly similar in economic position, life-style, culture, and status. Carriacou, an island dependency of Grenada, when studied by M. G. Smith in the 1950s possessed no Chinese or Indian immigrants, no white planters or businessmen (the only white residents were normally the Anglican and Catholic priests, the doctor, and the magistrate), no middle class, and virtually no mixed-race people. It was a simple society of creole blacks living a peasant and seafaring life and following similar Afro-Christian cultural patterns. In other words, Carriacou was culturally and socially homogenous, with no clearly defined class or status system. This was also broadly true of the Saint Vincent Grenadines, Anguilla, some of the tiny French islands like Desirade, and most of the British Virgin Islands group.

Within the basic three-tier structure that came down from slave society, the most important changes after the mid-nineteenth century were the gradual increase in the size of the middle stratum and the improvement in social status experienced by the more prosperous and better educated members of this stratum.

There is no doubt that there was considerable movement up into the middle group by people from the creole masses. Often the children of ex-slaves or creole laborers were able to climb up to middle-class status through teaching in the elementary schools: a secondary education was not necessary for this and so it was a favored channel of social mobility for young people from poor but "respectable," church-oriented families. Or the climb might be accomplished through successful economic activities, usually either independent farming or one of the skilled trades. Such "self-made" men and women, often uneducated, acquired cash and land through hard work and sacrifice, and money and land enabled them to move into a social position different from and above that of the mass of laborers and poor peasants. Frequently, their children, along with the children of elementary schoolteachers, were able to win a place in a secondary school (grammar school in the British colonies, lycée in the French), and with a secondary education they might be able to enter middle-class occupations that brought with them a rise in social status. They would also acquire with their schooling a command of "good" English or French and some familiarity with European literary culture, both essential requirements for successful upward mobility. In the French Antilles, the rural petty bourgeoisie had some access to local political offices after 1870, when many blacks were elected to the Conseils Municipaux; this was less possible for their counterparts in the British colonies. People in the middle stratum typically worked in white-collar jobs as teachers, clerks, shop assistants, druggists, journalists, printers, nurses, and minor civil servants. Though many lived in the towns, especially in the capital cities, there was also an important rural middle class of primary school head-teachers, postmasters/mistresses, village dispensers, and planta-tion staff, men and women of great local influence who were the natural social and religious leaders of their small communities.

At the higher levels of the middle stratum were the senior civil servants, professionals, and businessmen, both colored and black, but more typically of mixed racial origins. Their numbers increased after the post-emancipation period and their socioeconomic position in general improved. Indeed, some of them, usually light-complexioned, were able to climb into the top class/tier because of economic success and/or professional or educational standing.

In the French Antilles, for instance, the coloreds were the chief beneficiaries both of the decline of the sugar industry and of the establishment of the Third Republic in 1870. With no institutional barriers to their mobility, they en-trenched themselves after 1870, and in Martinique especially became a virtual oligarchy with a strong grip on the colony's political life. Their chief strategy for upward mobility was to monopolize administrative, political, and teaching posts in the colonies, except for the few top positions reserved for metro-politans, and to exploit the relative availability of secondary schools (the government lycées established after 1880) and university education in France. The eruption of Mount Pelée in 1902 and the destruction of Saint Pierre, Martinique's chief commercial center, accelerated the rise of the coloreds by killing many of the Antillean whites who had held important professional and administrative posts. Though the békés retained their hold on economic activi-ties, especially the exploitation of the land, the coloreds in both Martinique and Guadeloupe (along with many rising black families) were strongly en-trenched politically and socially by the time département status was granted in 1946.

Much the same sort of thing (though on a smaller scale) took place in the British Windward Islands in the late nineteenth and the first half of the twentieth centuries. Here the white population, small even before 1838, de-clined further and the coloreds were able to move into elite positions with relative ease.

But most members of the middle stratum, at least until the 1950s or 1960s, were not at all well-off economically. Primary school teachers, clerks, assistants in city stores, and junior civil servants were all badly paid, but had to "keep up appearances" in a way that the laborer did not. Yet even the most financially insecure middle-class man, as a rule, felt himself to be superior to the masses, taking pride in his "clean" and "dignified" job, symbolized in dress (collar and tie, stockings, expensive shoes), language, and behavior, marking him off from the "ordinary" people. Race was also significant, for members of the middle stratum (who ranged in complexion from very fair to "pure" black) tended to be obsessed with skin color and "good" (European-type) features and hair. They emphasized the values of "respectability," which meant subscribing more or less to middle-class British/French norms of family organization, sexual behavior, and life-styles; more positively, they stressed the importance of educational advancement for their children.

It is clear that many members of the West Indian middle class adopted uncritically the European prejudices, viewing the black working classes with open contempt, or at best an indifference born of ignorance. Too preoccupied with their own successful mobility within the system, these people showed little concern for the masses. By the early twentieth century, however, a small but significant group of middle-class persons, with allies from the masses, was beginning to agitate for social and political change. After the 1930s, as nationalist movements developed, much of their leadership came from precisely the middle stratum.

Class stratification systems in the Caribbean after slavery, it is well known, were hopelessly enmeshed with racial divisions, and the simple three-tier structure corresponded (with some discrepancies) to white/brown/black. Racism pervaded West Indian society in the nineteenth and twentieth centuries, and skin color was a crucial determinant of the West Indian's life-chances at least until the postwar era, though it would be foolish to imply it was the only determinant. (It was not always the most important determinant either: in the French Antilles, the rich black man automatically became an honorary *mulâtre*.) Nevertheless, racism, as well as sensitivity to color or shade, were strong everywhere and the pattern of race relations developed on the basis of an officially sanctioned belief that people of African (and Indian) descent were inferior, intellectually and morally, to people of European origin. Needless to say, that belief survived long after the destruction of the slave system that did so much to entrench it.

Of course, some West Indian white communities were more overtly racist than others, and discrimination against blacks was practiced more strictly in some colonies than in others. Barbados and the Bahamas, two English colonies with large creole white populations, were especially noted for open racial discrimination which persisted well into the 1950s–60s, despite the absence of any official system of segregation. As late as 1945, a Bahamian governor noted that the local whites bitterly opposed the nomination of a colored man to the Executive Council because they and their wives might have to meet him at social events at Government House. A little later, the English writer Patrick Leigh Fermor found out that there was virtually no public place in Barbados (restaurant, club, hotel, or whatever) where he could meet and talk with the island's black chief minister, a situation that Grantley Adams (according to Leigh Fermor) accepted with resignation. In the middle 1950s, in fact, Adams felt impelled to threaten the passage of antidiscrimination laws when Barbados's chance of becoming the capital of the Federation of The West Indies was harmed by the belief, reflected in the report of the Federal Capital Site Commission, that open racial discrimination existed in the island.[1]

In Jamaica, the white community remained to a significant degree socially aloof from the colored middle stratum and the masses until the postwar years. W. P. Livingstone, writing at the turn of the twentieth century, noted that Europeans coming to Jamaica soon learned "that colour and race are the most powerful influences regulating the destiny of the colony" and soon came to share the prevailing racism. Livingstone's observations led him to conclude that most white Jamaicans regarded their black laborer "like a mule," abusing him whenever he made a mistake and treating him just as so much brute force; and that in the home, most white housewives dealt with their domestics in similar fashion, substituting "the lash of the tongue" for the whip. Neither the planter nor his wife tried to deal with their workers as valuable and sensible employees, Livingstone noted, because the white Jamaican did not see black men and women as fully human, let alone as equals.[2] At least up to the 1940s, these attitudes remained typical of most Jamaican whites, and of many middle-class coloreds and blacks too.

For race prejudice came as easily as breathing to most whites living in the West Indies: it was part of their deepest feelings, learned early in childhood if they were Creoles, or quickly picked up if they were settlers from abroad. The whites felt themselves to be a group set apart from, and far above, the rest of the population. Even in small islands where the resident white community was tiny, the whites remained isolated from the people in whose midst they lived and on whose labor they depended. This kind of attitude was especially typical of the white Creoles: for them, it was even more essential than for the Europeans to preserve their racial "purity" because of their long history of association with the blacks as slave owners and employers.

In Trinidad, for instance, the powerful "French Creoles," descended from

French, Spanish, Italian, and even German and Irish settlers who had come to the island generations ago, felt this need with special strength. They could only marry within the group and, above all, they could never marry a person suspected of having "colored blood." In one of his novels, first published in 1934, Evelyn Waugh describes a fictional French creole girl, going home to Trinidad from school in Paris to get married. She explains to someone on board the ship: "There are so few young men I can marry. They must be Catholic and of an island family . . . there are two or three other rich families and I shall marry into one of them." The poor girl was limited to seven possible candidates, and one of them was ruled out because although very rich "he isn't really a Trinidadian. His grandfather came from Dominica and they say he has coloured blood."[3] Apart from the crucial question of marriage, French Creoles did not mix with nonwhite Trinidadians on an equal basis. They would not be invited to private gatherings in French creole homes, and even more public contacts in political and official life, in business and the professions, or in church activities, were limited. In Trinidad, as elsewhere in the Caribbean, the whites organized exclusive social clubs (recreational, sporting, or business-oriented), and conducted much of their social life within them.

Much the same situation was to be found in the French Antilles. In Martinique especially, the békés formed a powerful, closely knit endogamous elite, maintaining until very recent times rigid castelike barriers against nonwhites in all private social relations. Guérin described the Martinique elite, in the 1950s, as "an exclusive caste made up of a dozen or so families including at the very outside a thousand individuals who see eye to eye, help each other financially, take care to preserve the plantations undivided, marry within their circle."[4] Although only a very small nucleus enjoyed real wealth and power, the békés' sense of community ensured that no Martiniquan white fell into real difficulty. Endogamy was almost absolute, interrelationships were correspondingly dense, and any white Creole who fell on hard times was more or less guaranteed a job or a loan so that caste prestige was not endangered. Up to the 1970s, the Martinique békés preserved their social distance both from the colored middle class and from the metropolitan civil servants who had flocked into the island since 1946. In Guadeloupe the white elite was always smaller and less entrenched than in Martinique, yet it too fought to preserve its privileges and its sense of superiority. A perceptive French writer noted of the Guadeloupe white Creoles in 1890 that "a white family will not go where it will be exposed to meeting a family of mulattoes or negroes." They took refuge from the decline of the sugar industry and their political eclipse under the Third Republic in racial solidarity, declining to mix with colored society and keeping up pretenses despite real poverty: "half-savages, full of bitterness and scorn for the men and things of the present epoch, very proud and almost arrogant in their poverty, always ready to mount on their high horses when one waves the burning questions of politics and colour before them."[5]

Of course, the social exclusiveness of the whites in the British and French Caribbean, striking though it undoubtedly is, was never absolute. No formal system of apartheid existed, and intimate relationships between whites, coloreds, and blacks, including sexual ones, continued to be formed. There was interaction at many levels, and it is clear that white Creoles were deeply influenced, in their life-styles, their ways of thought, their material culture, and even their use of language, by the Caribbean creole society and cultural complex of which they were an integral part.

## The Newer Immigrants

The pattern of race relations inherited from Caribbean slavery essentially involved relationships between black, brown, and white people, the components of the original "creole society." But after formal emancipation, people from many different parts of the world were brought into the region to supply labor for the sugar plantations. Their arrival and settlement—above all, that of the immigrants from India—further complicated the pattern of race relations and the structure of society.

Constituting by far the largest group of new arrivals, the Indians entered the Caribbean as indentured laborers between 1838 and 1917. Because of their large numbers, because they brought religions, languages, and cultural forms quite different from any found in the region, they greatly complicated as well as enriched these societies. They were neither black nor white, they were not Christians, they had their own ancient culture; there were too many of them to be simply ignored or pushed to the margins of Caribbean society.

Two other groups of immigrants from Asia were too small to pose a serious challenge to the established pattern of social and racial relations: these were the Chinese and the Syrian/Lebanese. Chinese laborers were imported, like the Indians, to work on the plantations; they brought their own language and culture. Some soon adopted Christianity and mixed freely with the Creoles; others held on to traditional cultural patterns well into the mid-twentieth century. Like the Portuguese, the Chinese tended to enter small shopkeeping, and soon the "Chinee shopman" was as typical a figure in the country towns and villages all over the West Indies as his "Potugee" fellow. The latest arrivals were the Syrian/Lebanese, who began to come to the Caribbean around 1890. Most were Maronite or Catholic Christians, though a minority were Moslems, and they spoke Arabic. Although few in numbers, they settled in nearly every West Indian colony and quickly carved a secure niche as a closed ethnic group involved almost exclusively in retailing cloth, clothes, and household goods. Starting as humble peddlers, many Syrian/Lebanese families prospered and set up thriving stores, becoming in the postwar period an important element in the economic elite of several colonies, owning conspicuous businesses in cities such as Port of Spain, Kingston, and Fort-de-France.

Most of the post-emancipation immigrants were imported to provide labor for the sugar estates after many ex-slaves had "deserted" them. But an important additional reason for bringing in Indian, Chinese, and Portuguese laborers was to further divide the society: the planters and whites in general, as well as government officials, believed that these workers would be a check on the creole population. They hoped that the resulting divisions of race, religion, language, and culture would prevent the people from ever effectively uniting against white control. For instance, the manager of an estate in Berbice, Guyana, believed in 1848 that the safety of the whites depended on the "want of union" among the laborers, arguing that the Indians, Chinese, and Portuguese would always "stand by the whites." Things had not changed fifty years later; in 1897 a Guyanese planter said of the Indians and the Creoles: "they are totally different people; they do not inter-mix. That is, of course, one of our great safeties in the colony when there has been any rioting. If the Negroes were troublesome every Coolie on the estate would stand by one. If the Coolies attacked me, I could with confidence trust my Negro friends for keeping me from injury."[6]

Indeed, relations between black Creoles and Indians in Guyana and Trinidad (where Indians had come to form about one-third of the total population by the time immigration ended in 1917) were often difficult. Not that they were always bad. For instance, in both colonies, black Creoles took part in the Moslem Hosé festival, helping to build and carry the *tadjahs* (elaborate temple-like structures) and beating the drums. On the estates, resident workers of both races labored together and tolerated each other's ways, even though a tendency developed for Creoles and Indians to do different, specialized tasks: Creoles worked in the factory and cut canes, Indians did the routine cultivation jobs. But there were sources of friction on the plantations, and later in the villages where Indians settled after about 1870, which caused tensions between the races.

Black drivers (headmen) of Indian gangs on sugar estates were often harsh and unfair, and creole policemen also tended to bully Indians and abuse their authority by stopping Indian workers and demanding to see their "papers" without adequate reason. In both colonies there were sporadic outbursts of violence between the races on the plantations, though such events were not common. Off the estates, Indians came into contact with black creole villagers. Tensions might arise when Indians began to compete for jobs previously held only by black villagers, or when they bought land that had been owned by Creoles, or when the colonial governments (after 1869 in Trinidad and after 1880 in Guyana) set up special settlement schemes for ex-indentured Indians.

Still, conflict between the two races was not common between the 1840s and the 1950s, and creole-Indian relations in Trinidad and Guyana were generally peaceful, if not exactly friendly. Each group had a low opinion of the other, based on misunderstanding, ignorance of each other's culture, and the tendency to adopt European prejudices about each race. The planters, as we have seen, did what they could to discourage cooperation between the races. After the 1870s, Creoles in Trinidad and Guyana increasingly took the better-paid, skilled jobs on the estates, or moved into cocoa (Trinidad), or worked as artisans, clerks, teachers, and urban laborers, or took jobs in gold and diamond mining (Guyana) and in the oil industry (Trinidad), while most rural Indians remained field laborers or peasants, still essentially Oriental in religion and culture and well behind the other races in educational attainment. Each tended to despise the other, but each also tolerated the other's presence, and the de facto residential segregation which was the result of occupational divergencies reinforced this uneasy, yet essentially peaceful, coexistence.

In the postwar period black-Indian relations deteriorated in both colonies, but notably in Guyana. There were, probably, two main reasons for this important but complex development. First, by the 1950s significant numbers of Indians had acquired a secondary education and even university and professional training, and they began to seek and obtain administrative or professional positions, positions that had traditionally been considered the special preserve of colored and black Creoles. When the vast majority of Indians remained safely isolated in the rural villages or on the plantations as laborers and as poor farmers, they presented no great threat to the creole middle stratum; but that situation had clearly changed by 1950. Second, with the grant of adult suffrage and the advent of mass electoral politics, it was almost inevitable that political parties would develop which were based on ethnic constituencies, and that their leaders would exploit racial tensions. In Trinidad, creole-Indian relations were especially tense in the period between 1956 and 1962, the last stages of formal decolonization; in Guyana, tragic communal violence culminating in 1961–62 took many lives and left a legacy of bitterness and mistrust that clouded Guyana's political and social future after independence in 1966.

## Economy and Society

The material culture of most West Indians in the post-slavery era was dominated by poverty, underdevelopment, and a grossly skewed distribution of economic resources. The colonies' wealth was concentrated in the hands of a very small group in the society, nearly all belonging to the white upper tier/class which controlled most of the resources, along with foreign (British, French, later American) capitalists. This group continued to own most of the good farming land, especially in the larger colonies; it controlled the larger business enterprises and the financial institutions; and its members dominated the professions and the top ranks of the administration.

In Martinique, for instance, 3 percent of the total number of landowners in 1935 (208 persons) owned 61 percent of the cultivable soil, and 5 percent of the total (365 persons) owned 75 percent of the soil. By contrast, 72 percent of the owners (4,696 persons) held 7 percent of the farming land. By the 1950s just five large corporations effectively controlled Martinique's agricultural production. Indeed, the whole of Martinique's economy was in the hands of a few béké families who "maintain a grip on every penny of the sugar industry's profits, control the banks, the export-import trade in its virtual entirety, and run the island's administrative circus."[7] In 1960 one estimate concluded that the békés held 66.4 percent of the invested capital in the island, with 11 percent held by metropolitans; in Guadeloupe, 62 percent was held by metropolitan interests and 23 percent by Martiniquans.[8] Such a picture, in varying degrees, would also be accurate for most of the other islands, except, perhaps, for the smaller, impoverished territories where there was little investment or production of any kind, like French Guiana.

Most West Indians, after the post-emancipation decades, continued to work for the plantations as wage laborers, whether as full-time resident workers or as casual, irregular laborers during harvest times and at other busy seasons, supplementing their meager earnings from their own cultivations. In Trinidad and Guyana most full-time, resident workers on the sugar estates after 1870 were Indians. Elsewhere planters continued to rely on creole laborers, sometimes supplemented by Indians as in Guadeloupe, Martinique, and Jamaica. In the French Antilles, resident plantation workers were the *gens casés*, housed on the estates, to be distinguished from the *cultivateurs*, independent peasants who gave casual labor to the plantations. Wages were everywhere very low, and lower still for women and children, who formed a crucial component of the estate labor force. As late as 1937–38, official surveys found that women in such British colonies as Saint Kitts, Grenada, Saint Lucia, and Jamaica were receiving between ten pence and one shilling a day for field work (weeding and hoeing), between one-half and one-third the average wage earned by men. These were more or less the same wages as women received one hundred years earlier in the immediate post-emancipation period.

But if most people were forced to seek some kind of a living as plantation laborers, some were engaged in other occupations. A significant number had succeeded in becoming independent peasant farmers during the nineteenth century. This was especially the case in Jamaica, in the British Windward Islands like Tobago, Dominica, and Grenada, and in Guadeloupe, but peasants were to be found in most places. In Trinidad, for instance, peasants produced cocoa, especially after 1870, and both Creoles and Indians grew canes as small farmers after the 1880s. Tobago, by 1900, was almost exclusively a peasant island, and so was Dominica, where the great majority of the population earned no wages in the 1930s, depending solely on their subsistence production. In the French islands, a peasantry developed slowly after 1848, especially in Guadeloupe. Here the local government granted small plots between 1898 and 1922; plantation lands also passed into the hands of peasant smallholders during the sugar depression of the 1880s and 1890s, and again after 1946 when many medium-sized plantations could not afford the new minimum wages imposed after the island became a département. By about 1950 Guadeloupe had some 16,000 smallholders owning two and one-half acres or less.

Although the peasants enjoyed some independence, and may have eaten better than the plantation laborers and town workers, most were very poor. Only a small minority of peasants owning, say, between ten and fifty acres could be described as prosperous, making enough from the land to feed their families well, to support children in school, and to take an active part in local religious and social affairs. The great majority farmed less than ten acres, many depending on tiny plots of under one acre, the soil often exhausted after generations of use. For these people, independent farming provided only a bare existence, if that: many were forced to seek jobs to add to their small income from the land, or to drift into the towns. The small plot of "family land"— "microscopic cabbage patches" in Guérin's phrase—which was all that most West Indian peasants could farm certainly provided a sense of security and made outright starvation unlikely, but it could not provide anything like a decent living for a rapidly growing rural population. Nor did the various land settlement schemes carried out by many colonial governments, especially after 1918, bring substantial improvement to the situation of large numbers of smallholders, except in a few places.

The West Indian people found many other ways to make a living. Some were seamen and fishermen, especially in the smaller islands like Carriacou, Anguilla, and the Bahamas chain (where "wrecking" and sponge fishing were the major industries between the 1830s and the 1930s). Others found a living in the forests as woodcutters, in places like Dominica with its thickly wooded interior, in Guyana, and in Belize where the export of mahogany and logwood was always the chief economic activity. Domestic service employed large and growing numbers everywhere, especially women. Thousands of women were full- or part-time seamstresses and washerwomen; Lafcadio Hearn has left a romantic portrait of the Martiniquan *blanchisseuse*—whom he considered to be probably the hardest worker in the entire population—around 1890.[9] And the towns provided jobs for a few as stevedores, porters and messengers, shop assistants, and, after the war, factory workers in the new light manufacturing industries.

West Indian laborers typically received low wages for their work; but their situation was made worse by the irregular, seasonal employment of so many: underemployment was the norm for most. Work on the estates had always been seasonal except for the small core of resident laborers. Loggers, goldminers, wreckers and sponge fishermen in the Bahamas, stevedores, porters and coalers on the docks—all faced intermittent employment and long periods of no work and no wages. The problem of low wages was made far worse by irregular earnings.

To escape low wages and seasonal employment, as well as impoverished existence on small peasant plots, thousands left the country and went to the towns. The general depression in the Caribbean sugar industry between 1880 and 1914 had an adverse impact on rural living conditions in many territories, accelerating the movement to the towns. By the 1930s this urban drift had created serious social problems, for the towns had few jobs to offer the new arrivals, and health and housing conditions soon deteriorated as people crowded into the slums. Kingston, Fort-de-France, Port of Spain, and the rest expanded rapidly with uncontrolled, haphazard settlements springing up; Fort-de-France, for instance, tripled its population between 1901 and 1946, and between 1954 and 1966 alone its population grew from 67,000 to 115,000 inhabitants.

Another way of escaping poverty and unemployment was emigration. Many thousands of West Indians took the decision to leave their colony, perhaps to leave the Caribbean, especially between the 1880s and the 1920s, and again after World War II. Indeed, emigration became a way of life for the people; in some smaller islands like Saint Kitts, Nevis, or Carriacou, the majority of adult males expected to work abroad for some years. They went wherever work was available: Trinidad and Guyana, especially in the nineteenth century; Bermuda; the Dominican Republic and Cuba; Panama and Central America; the United States. Thousands of Bahamians escaped dire poverty by migrating to Florida. Jamaicans and Barbadians went to Panama, Costa Rica, and Cuba in large numbers between the 1880s and 1920s. After World War II, migration to the metropoles became important as thousands went to Britain and (in much smaller numbers) France. The earnings of men and women who had emigrated were sent back to family members as remittances, and this money became an extremely important source of income for poor West Indians, especially between about 1880 and 1924, the great age of emigration, and again after 1945.

For most West Indians, poverty was an inescapable fact of life. An impressive array of missionaries and clergymen, officials and commissioners, journalists and writers testified to the appalling material destitution endured by the masses of the people. Impoverishment was especially severe in very small islands with precarious resource endowments, like Saint Kitts, Anguilla, or the Bahamas "Out-Islands." In these places actual hunger and outright starvation were experienced at times; in "normal" circumstances people hovered at the edge of subsistence. Generally speaking, conditions were usually better in the larger colonies, yet even here thousands lived in great poverty. In Guyana the creole laboring population was showing signs of increasing distress by about 1880, prompting the government to investigate the extent of poverty in the coastal villages and the need for relief. In Trinidad the condition of the Indian sugar workers living in the central and southern parts of the island was especially desperate by the 1930s. Their wages were both low and irregular, their diet was inadequate, and they suffered from a host of diseases caused mainly by poor food and bad sanitation. The Jamaican rural masses experienced grinding poverty, with particularly "hard times" in the 1860s and again in the 1930s. In the French Antilles, metropolitan observers as late as the 1950s spoke of the islands as "a panorama of disgrace and misery"; a member of the French legislature, in 1954, told the National Assembly that he defied anyone "to travel a mile through either Guadeloupe or Martinique without being appalled by what he can find out with his own two eyes."[10]

Survival in these conditions was a daily struggle. Some emigrated, some stayed but received money from relatives abroad; many had "family land" to fall back on, even if it could provide only the barest of needs; people did odd jobs or engaged in petty trading—what the Jamaicans call "scuffling" and the Trinidadians "hustling." It is important to note, moreover, that the people had a strong tradition of self-help and mutual aid. Poor as they were, they helped relatives and friends, they took in destitute children and elderly people, with a real spirit of generosity and sacrifice. W. M. MacMillan noted in his survey of the British colonies in the 1930s the "African generosity" of the people in sharing the last crumb with very poor relatives and friends.[11]

The consequences of poverty were squalid living conditions, ill health, and misery. Housing for the masses of the people was appalling: most lived huddled together in primitive huts (the *case-nègres* of the French Antilles), or in tiny rooms in plantation barracks, or in shacks or barrack-range rooms in the urban slums. Overcrowding often reached unbelievable levels, and sanitation and ventilation might be almost nonexistent. Conditions were perhaps equally bad in the hut of the impoverished peasant farmer and in the barrack range on the estates, though the peasant probably had a degree more security and privacy. On many plantations, the old slave barracks—the "nigger yard" in the vivid Guyanese phrase—were simply fixed up for the indentured Indians, or new ranges were built for them—"bound" or "Coolie" yard. By the 1930s most larger plantations had phased out barrack housing for their married workers, providing instead crude wooden or earth huts, an improvement in terms of privacy if nothing else. Yet the Royal Commission, which investigated social conditions in the British colonies in 1938–39, was appalled at the housing conditions of the poor; "conditions are such," it noted, "that any human habitation of buildings now occupied by large families must seem impossible to a newcomer from Europe." The poorer West Indian child, the commission went on, "may know only a small unlighted hovel with wooden shutters tightly closed by night in order to shut out evil spirits or thieving neighbors. Privacy of any sort is impossible when a family of ten or twelve have to sleep in one small room, some on the floor, some under the bed, some in it, and all in a stifling and foul atmosphere."[12]

Of course, these conditions affected the family life and health of the people who endured them. Because of poverty, unbalanced diet, bad water supplies, and appalling housing, the West Indian masses were chronically ill. Epidemics of cholera, smallpox, and typhoid swept the region from time to time. Endemic diseases like malaria were only brought under partial control in the 1920s and 1930s. Hookworm infestation, caused by bad sanitation, was chronic nearly everywhere up to the 1940s, debilitating its victims. Venereal diseases were rampant, and so was yaws, an infectious skin disease: in the small island of Saint Lucia, over 1,000 cases of yaws were treated in 1935 alone. Tuberculosis, a classic disease of poverty, was the single most important cause of adult deaths in Jamaica in the 1930s. After the 1920s–30s, adult death rates began to fall steadily as the major killer diseases were brought under control, and infant mortality rates also declined in most places after about 1945; but preventable, nonfatal conditions and diseases which brought debility and suffering to the victims were still very widespread. Even minor problems like a cut or a bad tooth might become serious because medical care and medicines were unavailable or too expensive for ordinary people.

The plight of infants and children was grave; infant and child mortality was extremely high everywhere until after the 1930s. This, of course, was due to poor maternal and child nutrition, as well as bad water supplies and sanitation. Working mothers often had to stop breast-feeding after the first few weeks (if their milk had not already failed because of poor diet), and milk was expensive. Infants received gruel or "pap" which was low in nutritional value and often the source of gastric infections. In addition to malnutrition, babies and children were especially vulnerable to a host of infections and diseases. In Grenada, around 1890, nearly one-half of all the babies born to poor mothers died before their first birthday. Of all babies born alive in Jamaica in 1896–97, 17.5 percent died before their first birthday and 26.8 percent before their fifth. In rural Martinique as late as 1952, infant mortality was calculated at 23 percent, long after adult death rates had entered a period of steady decline in the colonial Caribbean generally.

Moreover, medical care was not available to most ordinary people before the 1960s. In Guyana, nearly half of all the deaths recorded in 1871 took place without any medical care at all for the dying person. In Jamaica, the sick poor rarely got to a doctor; by 1898 there was only one doctor per 19,400 Jamaicans, and 75 percent of all deaths in 1896–97 took place without any medical intervention. As late as the 1950s, Le Monde reported that only about a quarter of Martiniquan patients needing hospital treatment received it because of a shortage of beds. Indeed, most West Indian peasants and rural laborers up to this period probably looked to the local healer, village midwife, or Obeah-man/woman (quimboiseur in the French Antilles) rather than to the formally trained doctor for medical and psychological aid in times of illness.

## Religious Practices and General Culture

Religious faith and practice were important aspects of the lives of West Indians in the nineteenth and twentieth centuries. Most were deeply religious and their whole way of life and thought was profoundly influenced by their faith. By the mid-nineteenth century, most of the people were already Christians or at least under Christian influence as the various churches and missionary bodies extended their work in the region; the Christian presence was by then very deep and permanent, in both its Roman Catholic (the French Antilles, Trinidad, Saint Lucia, Grenada, Dominica) and its Protestant (Jamaica, Guyana, Barbados) manifestations.

At the same time, African religious influences remained strong. African beliefs in the spirit world, the idea of a person having several souls or spirits with different functions, concepts of death and the afterlife, and many other African religious rites and practices continued to shape the way West Indians looked at the world. Although some blacks, especially those who personally remembered Africa or who had been influenced by African-born relatives, managed to practice their religion almost unchanged, it was more usual for them to merge African and Christian beliefs and rituals: syncretic Afro-Christian religions and sects emerged and flourished in the century after about 1860. The religious scene was further complicated by the arrival of large numbers of Hindus and Moslems from India. Though the majority of Indians kept their faiths, some accepted Christianity, and here too some syncretism between Hinduism and Christianity, sometimes with African religious elements added, began to emerge.

The well-established Christian churches, whose ministers were mainly Europeans and who looked to Europe for leadership and guidance, enjoyed the most prestige among all the social groups in the Caribbean just after emancipation. Over the next hundred years there was, to some extent, a shift in membership among black West Indians from the established churches to the various fundamentalist Protestant churches or sects introduced into the region mostly by American evangelists, such as the Church of God, the Church of the Nazarene, the Seventh Day Adventists, and the different Pentecostal churches. Still, in 1938 as in 1980, nearly every West Indian of African descent could claim formal membership in a Christian church or sect.

Yet belief in spirits was almost universal among the masses, and much of the African spirit world was still alive in their minds. The Obeahman/woman—the magical specialist who could control spirits to harm someone, or, if he or she chose, to cure and heal and ward off ill-intentioned spirits—was a powerful figure in the rural communities of the Caribbean well into the postwar period. Lafcadio Hearn thought that in the Martinique of the 1880s the quimboiseur "wields more authority than the priest, exercises more terror than the magistrate, commands more confidence than the physician,"[13] though all his clients were, of course, Mass-attending members of the Roman Catholic church. The quimboiseur and the French priest coexisted, and the former was probably more important to people's daily lives. At death, Catholic rites and creolized African practices marked the passage to the afterlife.

Powerful Afro-Christian faiths emerged after the mid-nineteenth century, combining Christian and African beliefs, rites, and deities/saints. The dominant form of Jamaican popular religion after the 1860s was Revivalism, a movement that linked several Revivalist sects, all featuring practices like visions and trances, spirit possession, prophesy, speaking in tongues, and healing by touch, by water, or by other means. Revivalism satisfied the people because it combined their deepest African beliefs with Christianity, as well as giving them a chance for leadership, for it was usual that a Revivalist congregation would be dominated by a strong leader or prophet, man or woman, like Alexander Bedward who led a Jamaica-wide Revivalist movement between the 1890s and the 1920s. Many other territories developed similar sects and prophets, who were usually faith healers as well as religious leaders, using special rites often involving water and traditional herbal remedies to cure and comfort the sick. The ordinary West Indian might well prefer to go to a balm-yard (as the healer's place was known in Jamaica) rather than to a doctor or clinic, not only because the healer cost less, but also because he or she could offer advice and comfort for emotional problems as well as cures for physical ills.

The West Indian people sought relief from the harshness of their material existence in the world of religion, and in traditional festivals and popular celebrations. Most of the territories had some kind of traditional Christmas celebration which was often held right through to New Year's Day. In Jamaica the main Christmas festival was called Jonkonnu and it featured costumed troupes, street processions, miming, dancing, and musical bands. The festival combined West African characters with traditional English mumming figures. Jonkonnu was also held (with variations) in Nassau (Bahamas) and in Belize City. Many other colonies had Christmas festivals involving costumed or masked figures, processions, and street music, sometimes with troupes performing elaborate skits in public or in people's houses.

While these traditional Christmas celebrations seem to be chiefly found in the Protestant islands (Jamaica, the Bahamas, Belize, Saint Kitts, Tortola, Antigua), the pre-Lenten Carnival was definitely associated with Catholicism. It was in Trinidad (British since 1797 but strongly Catholic) and in Martinique that Carnival was most fully developed. It combined, of course, Catholic and southern European influences with African traditions. With emancipation, in both islands the black masses were now free to take part in the white folks' Carnival as they chose, and gradually it was transformed into a much more rowdy, lively, popular celebration, centered on the streets of Port of Spain, Saint Pierre (before 1902), and Fort-de-France. There were traditional costumes, characters, and "bands" (groups of costumed masqueraders), ritualized dancing and stick fighting between the champions of rival bands, street processions, and the singing of topical songs on people or events (which developed, around the turn of the nineteenth century, into the modern calypso). Although the Trinidad Carnival came increasingly under official control after the 1880s, with many of its more risqué costumes suppressed on grounds of obscenity and its band fights largely put down, it never lost its liveliness or its anarchic folk spirit, out of which both the calypso and later, the steel band, would emerge.

Other popular festivals were held on the first of August in the British colonies to mark Emancipation Day and often also to celebrate Cropover (the sugar harvest), and on All Souls' or All Saints' Day in all the Catholic territories, French and British. At all these festivals, dance was important; indeed, it was crucial to the culture of the people. Traditional African dances survived in many places, like the Que-Que dance performed in Berbice (Guyana) up to the 1950s by people who considered themselves to be of Ibo origin. It involved drumming, songs (which referred to the Ibo Nation), and dancing in a circle. People of the Cromanti (Ashanti) and Congo nations held their own dances with different dance steps and drum beats. Similar Nation Dances were held, for example, in Grenada and Carriacou. In the French islands and the French-influenced British colonies (Trinidad, Saint Lucia, Grenada, Dominica), the main traditional dances were the Calenda, the Bamboula, and the Belair; the latter word was also used for the calypsolike song that was sung in *Créole* as part of the Belair dance, also known as *biguine*. These traditional dances and songs reflected a French Creole-African cultural complex that linked Martinique and Guadeloupe (and Haiti) to Trinidad, Saint Lucia, Grenada, and Dominica.

Of course, more modern forms of recreation were also important to the people. Horse racing was a great popular passion in all the larger colonies, attended by people of all classes and races and involving a great deal of gambling, cheating, drinking, and fighting. Indeed, gambling was an important aspect of folk life everywhere. Chinese number games were popular, like *whé-whé* in Trinidad and *peaka pow* in Jamaica, both illegal. The Creoles of the British colonies were mad on cricket, one of England's most successful cultural transplants to its colonies. Every open space would become a cricket pitch, an oil tin would serve for wickets and a palm-leaf rib for a bat. At the higher social level cricket in each colony tended to be dominated by upper-class organizations, mainly if not exclusively white until the 1950s, but it had a genuinely popular following everywhere.

From the early 1900s, the modern mass media penetrated the region: the cinema, radio, cheap newspapers, and, finally, television after 1960. They were all vehicles for transmitting Euro-American values and ideas and for spreading the gospel of modernization, consumerism, and middle-class Western life-styles.

The formal education systems established in all the colonies in the nineteenth century were also, of course, extremely influential in shaping social development and cultural change. After emancipation, local and metropolitan governments moved slowly to establish systems of public primary education, which involved in some cases church schools in receipt of state grants, or a combination of state-aided church schools with government-controlled secular schools. Of course, most upper-class West Indians (and many metropolitan officials too) were at best lukewarm about spreading education among the children of the masses whose only role in life was to be field laborers. A retired Trinidad inspector of schools commented in 1898, "How often have sugar planters and others said to me, 'what do you want to educate little niggers for? Put hoes in their hands and send them to the cane pieces.'" It was the mentality of the prominent Guyana planter and politician who is said to have muttered, when he heard about a newly qualified black lawyer, "another good shovelman spoilt."[14]

With these attitudes among the upper classes and many officials as well, it is easy to understand why funds for primary education were always very limited and at times were cut altogether. Elementary schools, especially in the countryside, were often badly housed and very poorly equipped; teachers were miserably paid and inadequately trained (often they were untrained). Though most West Indian children did attend a primary school, irregularly, for a few years by the 1930s, both enrollment and attendance levels were quite low. In 1937, while 88 percent of the children aged six to fourteen were enrolled in school in Barbados, the proportion was under 70 percent in Belize, 51.5 percent in Grenada, and only 46.5 percent in Saint Vincent. And average daily attendance rates were always far below enrollment: in 1937, average attendance as a percentage of those enrolled could be as low as 57 percent (Saint Lucia) or as high as 74 percent (Barbados). On the whole, the French did better in their colonies; the assimilation policy tended to dictate a higher level of expenditure on education, and greater efforts were made by the French to reproduce in the Antilles the full range of curricula and amenities found in metropolitan schools. By the 1960s Martinique and Guadeloupe probably enjoyed, overall, a stronger public education system than the British colonies. In 1966, 96 percent of the children aged seven to fourteen attended a school in the French islands as compared to 60 percent in Jamaica in 1960; 31 percent in the age group ten to nineteen attended some secondary institution as compared to only 5 percent in Jamaica.

Until after the war, secondary education was largely the preserve of upper- and middle-class children in the British colonies; only a tiny handful of children who passed through the primary schools ever got to one of the secondary institutions. Most of their pupils were white or colored, with a few blacks and (in Trinidad and Guyana) a sprinkling of Indians by the 1930s. They offered a highly elitist form of education, based on the English upper-class public or grammar school—just as the French lycée, established in the Antilles after 1880, followed the identical curriculum and used the identical textbooks as the metropolitan model. Because so few children from peasant and working-class families could gain entry to the secondary schools before the 1950s or 1960s, they served to deepen and sharpen class distinctions.

Yet with all its deficiencies the system of formal education established in the Caribbean colonies was a major social force. By the 1950s most West Indians were more or less literate in English and French, and that in itself was a major achievement. Education had also played a key role in shaping the growing middle class: the school was one of the most important social institutions allowing for upward mobility. The schools spread European values and culture among all sectors of society. They spread knowledge of French in Martinique and Guadeloupe where *Créole* was the popular language. In British colonies where English was only a minority language such as Trinidad or Saint Lucia in the nineteenth century, the schools were probably the most important means for the gradual advance of English at the expense of the French *Créole* spoken by the masses. Where there were large numbers of Indians as in Trinidad and Guyana, the schools helped Indian children to adjust to their new societies and adopt some Western ways as well as the English language. Clearly, the schools were modernizing, westernizing agencies which spread European culture and values among the people.

In this they were especially successful in the French Antilles. The schools transmitted French language, literature, and culture; they offered a strictly metropolitan education, and any effort to modify it to meet "special colonial needs" was indignantly rejected by the middle class and those who aspired to that status. In short, they created an elite of good Frenchmen and women who, in comparison with the elites of the British colonies, had a far deeper attachment to France and French culture and a far greater alienation from their own societies. It is true, of course, that the provision of substantial material benefits by the metropole, especially after 1946, contributed to the French Antilleans' sense of identity with France. Yet, all in all, the Antilles seemed to represent France's greatest success at "assimilation" and the *mission civilatrice*. What assimilation did was to offer human and civil rights to French West Indians, but at the price of denying their cultural rights: it necessarily meant the suppression of West Indian culture and encouraged cultural alienation among the upper and middle strata to a far greater degree than British colonialism produced in the British West Indies.

Yet the decades since the 1940s have been marked, in the French Antilles as well as in the English-speaking territories, by a search for an original and authentic Caribbean culture. The elites were largely preoccupied with demonstrating their command of European culture and their intellectual "equality" with their metropolitan counterparts, but after the war a minority split away and made contact with the people, drawing inspiration from popular cultural and religious forms and trying to express in literature and art their aspirations and their anger. This movement, which had first begun in the islands with political independence (Haiti, Cuba), slowly spread to the colonial Caribbean, first to the British islands, finally to the French colonies, where, we have seen, the attachment to French culture was especially deep. It was characterized by an interest in popular languages (*Créole*, English Creoles), in Afro-Christian religion, in folk forms of dance and music, and in the daily lives of the masses. By the 1960s and 1970s this movement toward cultural authenticity was in full bloom. It was the counterpart of the contemporary search for effective national sovereignty, self-propelled economic development, and substantial social justice; and even if it was less compelling politically, it was just as important for the long-term prospects of the Caribbean people.

## Notes

1. Fermor, *The Traveller's Tree*, pp. 147–49.
2. Livingstone, *Black Jamaica*, pp. 165–68.
3. Waugh, *A Handful of Dust*, pp. 163, 166.

4. Guérin, *The West Indies*, p. 38.

5. A. Corré, *Nos Créoles* (Evreux, 1890); quoted in Renard, "A Social History," pp. 428–29.

6. Quoted in Moore, "East Indians and Negroes in British Guiana," chap. 7.

7. Guérin, *The West Indies*, pp. 37–38.

8. Brian Weinstein, "The French West Indies," p. 257.

9. Hearn, *Two Years*, pp. 243–47.

10. Quoted in Guérin, *The West Indies*, p. 13.

11. MacMillan, *Warning from the West Indies*, p. 114.

12. *West India Royal Commission, 1938–39, Report*, pp. 174, 227.

13. Hearn, *Two Years*, p. 181.

14. Brereton, *Race Relations*, p. 77.

## 5

Colin A. Palmer

# Identity, Race, and Black Power in Independent Jamaica

When Jamaica became an independent nation in 1962, it adopted as its motto "Out of many, one people." Although many Jamaicans firmly believed that their motto was an accurate reflection of their social reality, more dispassionate observers were convinced that at best it was an expression of the national ideal and, at worst, a conscious exercise in self-delusion. Few could maintain with confidence that black Jamaicans who constituted a majority of the population wielded economic power, shared an abiding pride in their racial heritage, or even possessed a high degree of racial consciousness and identity.

It is clear, nevertheless, that one of the most agonizing and protracted struggles that the Jamaican people waged in the last half century has been that aimed at creating a racial identity. The majority of Jamaicans, probably as high as 90 percent, can make claim to an African ancestry. Yet many of these persons, particularly those who constitute the middle classes, or the more privileged sectors of society, find it difficult to come to terms with their possession of a black skin. On the other hand, many lower-class black Jamaicans have often espoused a fierce racial pride which provided them with psychic sustenance in spite of their awful material circumstances. The Rastafarians, who drew their inspiration in part from Marcus Garvey's slogan "Africa for the Africans, at home and abroad. One God, One Aim, One Destiny," have been most prominent in keeping alive the flame of a black consciousness in Jamaica and a strong identification with Africa.

This chapter examines the quest for a black racial identity in Jamaica, particularly after the achievement of universal adult suffrage in 1944 and as Jamaicans began the slow march to political independence in 1962. It focuses on the societal tensions that this search generated, analyzes the interplay between class and race, and demonstrates that a secure, confident racial identity has not yet been forged. In particular, the chapter addresses the nature of the Jamaican official and middle-class reaction to the Black Power ideology imported from the United States in the 1960s.

It is necessary to mention, albeit briefly, that the African slaves who labored in Jamaica, as did their counterparts in other parts of the hemisphere, created a culture that provided them with psychic sustenance and allowed them to survive as persons. This culture drew upon their variegated African heritage as well as upon that of their European masters. A dynamic creolization process or cultural fusion would form, in time, the essence of the society's Jamaicanness. Yet the African ingredients of that cultural mix were never generally accorded the same standing and occupied a decidedly inferior position.

Innumerable examples can be cited to show that any association with the cultural features ascribed to Africa was carefully avoided by Jamaicans, particularly racially mixed members of the middle class. Not only were African physical features denigrated but also the continent itself was often caricatured. Some African countries, particularly the Congo (as Zaire was then known), were deemed to be so "backward" and "barbaric" that "Congo" became a term of abuse in the island. Even members of the House of Representatives took umbrage at being characterized in the heat of debate as "Congos," as the following dialogue that occured in 1953 demonstrates:

> Mr. Bustamante: No. No. Roads must be considered development and that anyone who criticises—and the Gleaner is likely to criticize—some "Congo" over there. . . . I do not mean you on that side now.
> Mr. Glasspole: Mr. Speaker, is the minister entitled to use that kind of language in referring to members on this side?
> Mr. Speaker: He is not referring to members.
> Mr. Glasspole: He said over here.
> Mr. Speaker: The minister speaks to the Chair, and the Chair understands him.
> Mr. Hill: He said the press.
> Mr. Bustamante: Beyond over there, Sir. I was not referring to my friends and colleagues over there.
> Mr. Wilmot: The minister is not so rude as to call us "Congos."[1]

While members of the legislature disliked being called "Congos," other citizens used Africa and Africans as symbolic representations for much of what they viewed negatively in society. In a letter to the editor of *The Daily Gleaner*, for example, Mr. A. S. Clarke, the principal of St. Johns College, condemned the "introduction of Bantu education here and the corruption of everything educational." He knew that the new director of education would have "a gigantic task to change back from the Bantu Education introduced here to progress and literacy."[2] Along similar lines, one citizen who wrote to the editor to oppose any ethnic identification with Africa was certain that "the only race we belong to is the Human Race and our nationality is Jamaican, not African . . . what is our culture? What is our religion? Is it some African cult?"[3]

Other Jamaicans looked askance at any attempt to deemphasize cultural and political ties with England and to elevate those with Africa to positions of value and respectability. Mrs. H. E. Smith, a resident of Kingston, expressed this point of view very well in a letter to the editor in 1963:

From the time we attained our independence, we have gradually disassociated ourselves from England and have shown in our public and political life less and less respect for her. However, like it or not, England is our mother country, not Africa. We still need help and guidance and Africa can't give these to us as she needs help herself.[4]

It would be a mistake, however, to conclude that the aforementioned views reflected the sentiments of all Jamaicans. They revealed, however, the pernicious effect that centuries of European rule had had on the minds of sections of the Jamaican populace. A white bias had come to prevail and with it a concomitant devaluation of the sense of self of the citizens of African descent who, interestingly enough, comprised the vast majority of the people. The internal tensions and self-doubt that were undoubtedly the consequences of this racial and cultural devaluation made it difficult for a positive black identity to take root and flourish.

Despite the existence of these tensions, many privileged Jamaicans consciously, or unconsciously, exaggerated the degree of racial harmony that existed in society and promoted a form of Jamaican racial exceptionalism. Norman Manley, one of the island's most enlightened politicians, saw racial harmony "as one of the greatest and finest things we have ever tried to achieve."[5] William Strong, a columnist for the *Gleaner*, was sure that "Jamaicanism was raceless. . . . Jamaicanism is realization and acceptance of the fact that Jamaica is neither a black nor a white nor a pink country, but a country in which all men may dwell together in unity and good fellowship."[6] And Alexander Bustamante noted that Jamaica was a country where "races work and live in harmony with ever increasing respect for each other."[7] None of the exponents of the principle of Jamaican racial exceptionalism underscored the stark reality that poverty always wore a black face in the island and that racial harmony and equality could never be attained as long as that prevailed. The correlation between race and class made nonsense of any claims to racial exceptionalism.

While some individuals firmly believed that Jamaica was a land of racial harmony, many others were not so easily persuaded. Members of the Rastafarian movement, founded around 1930, were among the earliest groups to question the fundamental basis of society. The Rastafarians articulated a return to Africa by the brethren. To them Jamaica was Babylon, a land that held them in captivity. Africa, or more specifically, Ethiopia, represented the Promised Land that would provide them with a home. The Ethiopian emperor, Haile Selassie, was regarded as Divine. In spite of the general disdain with which members of the middle class viewed them, the Rastafarians clung to a fierce black nationalism and identified with Africa and its peoples at a time when this was not fashionable on the island. The victim of official disapprobation and persecution, the Rastafarian movement not only survived but increased the number of its adherents.

The source of their appeal appeared to rest on their rejection of Jamaican society with all of its social and economic inequities and the promise of a better life in Africa. They held the view that blacks were oppressed in society simply because of their race, an argument that the larger society could ill afford to ignore. During the late 1950s the Rastafarians became more aggressive in their demand for repatriation to Africa, and the government eventually dispatched a mission to the continent to explore the question.

There is no doubt that the Rastafarians' brand of black racial consciousness helped to force others to confront the fact that individuals who were phenotypically black were often discriminated against in society. Jamaicans had long been accustomed to the existence of "shade" prejudice whereby individuals who had a "lighter" skin color were favored for certain jobs, particularly at the managerial levels. Acting probably in response to public sentiment, the councillors of the Kingston and St. Andrew Corporation adopted a resolution in April 1950 urging commercial banks to employ black Jamaicans in such positions as clerks, ledger keepers, and cashiers. The resolution, which was moved by Councillor C. G. Walker, condemned job discrimination against black Jamaicans.

Interestingly enough, the banks did not deny these allegations of racial bigotry. The Royal Bank of Canada reported that a majority of its clerical employees were Jamaicans but "we note you refer particularly to dark Jamaicans and we shall keep the views of your Council before us." The Barclays Bank also promised that "your remarks will receive our most careful attention." Councillor Walker found such arrogant temporizing from the banks unacceptable, and Councillor Wills O. Issacs reminded his colleagues that oil companies and department stores engaged in similar racist practices. Councillor Rose Leon felt that the remedy for these practices resided in blacks deciding to "discriminate against the banks," presumably a call for a boycott of the offending businesses.[8]

The fact that the councillors were outraged by the unfair employment practices of the business interests attested to an emerging racial consciousness among members of the elite. In time, their ranks would be strengthened as they became influenced by the struggle for independence by the colonies in black Africa and by the civil rights movement in the United States. The struggle for social justice by black Americans had an enormous emotional appeal for Jamaicans, particularly those of African ancestry. Because many of these Jamaicans had been the victims of racist treatment in North America, the black struggle there had a special immediacy for them. Not surprisingly, events in the United States allowed some Jamaicans to take additional pride in what they believed to be their own racially harmonious society. It even allowed them to claim moral superiority over the Americans. Blissfully ignoring the treatment of the black poor in Jamaica, *The Daily Gleaner* in 1958, for example, characterized the residents of Alabama as "one of the world's backward peoples."[9]

Jamaicans followed the progress of the civil rights movement avidly and hailed its successes. When the famous march on Washington occurred in 1963, thousands of Jamaicans ranging from "scarlet robed University students to Rastafarian adherents in ceremonial dress" gathered and marched to express their solidarity with their black North American brothers. Several members of the crowd carried banners that advocated "Down with white supremacy," "Equal Justice for all," "Down with Imperialism," and "Up comes Socialism—liberation for Negro Peoples throughout the World."

The march provided an occasion for several Jamaican organizations that had individually promoted a black racial consciousness to join in a common cause. These organizations included the Political Academy, the Council for Afro-Jamaican Affairs, and the Afro-West Indian League. Given the tenor of the speeches delivered on that occasion and the nature of the resolutions that the crowd adopted, it is obvious that the Jamaican racial situation was also on their minds. One resolution urged that "the meeting should resolve itself into the Civil Rights Committee of Jamaica"; another demanded that at least 50 percent of the staff of several commercial and industrial firms be "staffed by persons of black complexion." Senator Dudley Thompson captured the essence of the crowd's mood when he described the occasion "as a march of the united black people of Jamaica."[10]

Undoubtedly the civil rights movement had a direct impact on the development of a black consciousness in Jamaica. Residents of the island held Martin Luther King in the highest esteem. They rejoiced when he was awarded the Nobel Peace Prize. The Jamaican Parliament unanimously adopted a motion moved by Norman Manley congratulating King, praising him "for his great service to the Negro People in the United States of America," and expressing "profound sympathy and respect for all the work that is being done in the fight against racial discrimination by him and his associates."[11] Shortly afterward, King visited Jamaica and declared "I am a Jamaican and in Jamaica I really feel like a human being," a statement that did not reflect a deep understanding of the circumstances of the black poor who heard that declaration.[12]

Jamaicans of African descent, it must be said, admired King because he spoke on behalf of racial justice everywhere. When he was felled by an assassin's bullet in 1968, the island felt a special sense of loss. The Jamaican Parliament observed two minutes of silence as a mark of respect, and recorded "its deep sorrow" at his untimely death and "profound appreciation for the great services rendered to mankind by this champion for the recognition of the principles of human rights and of the great role he played in the struggle for racial equality, justice, and human dignity."[13]

The popular reaction to the assassination showed the degree to which the black American struggle for justice was also a Jamaican struggle. Workers walked off their jobs at construction sites all over the island. Citizens of Runaway Bay, a rural community, wore "bits of black cloth on their dresses and shirts as a symbol of mourning." Many cars were draped in black, business places hoisted black flags, and churches tolled their bells. The *Gleaner* reported that in Kingston women dressed in somber colors and many men wore black arm bands. Those who attended the memorial service for the slain leader "sang in mournful tunes the anthem of the American Civil Rights Movement, We Shall Overcome . . . all bore vivid testimony of the sympathy felt by Jamaicans for the cause for which Dr. King fought and died." Rather ominously, in view of the social disturbances that would later strike the island, the newspaper noted that "there was also bitter racist reaction among the fringe sections of the city's community."[14]

The assassination provided Jamaicans with an opportunity to ask serious questions about racial justice in their own society but it was evidently not seized. Instead, official voices praised Martin Luther King and the cause he represented but failed to address the injustices that existed in their own homeland. Nevertheless, it can be maintained that the solidarity that many black Jamaicans expressed with black Americans in their struggle for racial justice was a healthy development. It manifested a heightened racial awareness and a recognition of a racial identity that transcended geographic boundaries. Much of the Jamaican official complacency and perhaps hypocrisy on issues of race and class would be revealed rather starkly a few months later when Prime Minister Shearer declared a young Guyanese lecturer in history at the University of the West Indies at Mona, Walter Rodney, as persona non grata. The popular lecturer had been giving public lectures espousing the ideology of Black Power, and he had established links with the poor in some of the ghetto areas of the city. On October 15, 1968, a frightened government prevented Rodney from reentering the island after a visit to Canada. The next day students at the university, as well as an amorphous group of the urban poor, took to the Kingston streets to express their disapproval of the prime minister's actions. When the government sought to prevent the demonstration from occurring, violence ensued for a day with considerable damage to property, stores, motor vehicles, and government buildings, and the loss of two lives.[15]

Our concern here, however, is not with the details of the riot but with the Black Power ideology that Rodney embraced and the nature of elite reactions to it—particularly after the events of October 16. It should be emphasized that Rodney's attempt to foster the development of pride in Africa through his lectures on African history and Black Power to Kingston's dispossessed was nothing particularly new. The Rastafarians, as has been noted earlier, and Marcus Garvey had long sought to educate the residents of the ghettos about their African past. But as Norman Girvan correctly observed, "Rodney's lectures in African history gave to black people a sense of past achievement and therefore of future purpose. They were, to people brainwashed for centuries in a sense of their own worthlessness, an indispensable psychological asset."[16]

What distinguished Rodney from most of his predecessors was that he sought to place the black condition everywhere within the framework of what he called the "Imperialist World."[17] Thus, according to Rodney, "Every country in the dominated colonial areas has an overwhelming majority of nonwhites, as in most of Asia, Africa and the West Indies. Power, therefore, resides in the white countries and is exercised over blacks."[18] It was not enough to recognize one's blackness, black people had to realize that to be black was to be power-less. As Rodney expressed it, "Conscious blacks cannot possibly fail to realise that in our own homelands we have no power, abroad we are discriminated against, and everywhere the black masses suffer in poverty."[19] His sense of history and his reading of contemporary realities led him to observe: "There is nothing with which poverty coincides so absolutely as with the colour black— small or large population, hot or cold climates, rich or poor in natural resources—poverty cuts across all of these factors in order to find black people."[20] White imperial power, then, must be held responsible for this state of affairs since it has "used black people to make whites stronger and richer and to make blacks relatively, and sometimes absolutely, weaker and poorer."[21]

Rodney's acute awareness of the international powerlessness of blacks led him to characterize Black Power as "a movement and an ideology springing from the reality of the oppression of black peoples within the imperialist world as a whole."[22] It was nothing less than a call to "black peoples to throw off white domination and resume the handling of their own destinies."[23] More broadly, Black Power would result in the destruction of an international capitalist system. Accordingly, Black Power must recognize both "the reality of black oppression and self negation as well as the potential for revolt."[24]

But Rodney did not apply his theories mechanistically. He knew that they had to be modified and fashioned in accordance with local realities. Consequently, he held that Black Power in the West Indies had three closely interrelated dimensions. First, it must "break with imperialism which is historically white racist"; second, it must "lead to the assumption of power by the black masses of the islands"; and third, it should produce a "cultural reconstruction of the society in the image of the blacks."[25] For Black Power to reach its fullest expression, however, it must include the peoples in the West Indies who are of Indian ancestry since they share a similar history of oppression in the islands. But mulattoes were in a different category altogether. Rodney saw the vast majority of these individuals as having succumbed "to the bribes of white imperialism, often outdoing the whites in their hatred and oppression of blacks." Yet such people had it in their power to change so "the movement can only keep the door open and leave it to those groups to make their choice."[26]

Contrary to the view propagated by his detractors, Rodney emphasized that Black Power would not lead to the persecution of other races. It must be understood, however, that Jamaica "is a black society—we should fly Garvey's Black Star banner and we will treat all other groups in the society on that understanding—they can have the basic right of all individuals but no privileges to exploit Africans as has been the pattern during slavery and ever since."[27] And, as he stressed, "the road to Black Power here in the West Indies and everywhere else must begin with a revaluation of ourselves as blacks with a redefinition of the world from our standpoint."[28]

Rodney's lectures on African history to the residents of West Kingston's ghettos bridged the gap between them and the intellectuals on the university campus. The young lecturer played an important role in raising the political consciousness of his hearers. His emphasis on the achievements of African civilizations, on the similarities in the black condition everywhere, and on the need to develop a strong racial consciousness appealed to those who knew they had no secure place in society. It was Rodney's vision that a knowledge of African history coupled with the growth of a strong racial identity and an understanding of contemporary social, political, and economic realities would provide the motive force for a thorough restructuring of Jamaican society.

Rodney's views were well received by the more progressive students at Mona, a few intellectuals, and the residents of Kingston's ghettos to whom he spoke. On the other hand, more than a few middle-class Jamaicans felt that such ideas threatened what they perceived to be a harmonious multiracial society. Prime Minister Hugh Shearer was of the opinion that "Black Power radicals are irrelevant. They are pushing causes and voicing slogans that they have adopted from elsewhere. We have a black government, we have votes for everyone, we have got rid of colour discrimination."[29] Shearer's failure to make fundamental distinctions between the phenotype of the elected officials and the exercise of power in all of its manifestations mirrored the perceptions of the more privileged classes in society. What is clear, however, is that Rodney's call for Black Power in all of its political, economic, and cultural dimensions served to exacerbate the tensions in a society that had failed to embrace its black masses and that did not wish to be reminded of that failure. Nor did the political leaders and the middle class wish to confront the racial implications of that failure. Not surprisingly, when the riot of October 16 occurred the politicians, the business interests, and the frightened members of the middle class blamed Rodney and the ideology of Black Power rather than the deeper structural problems that had given birth to Black Power in its Jamaican form.

There is no gainsaying the fact that many of those who participated in the October disturbances, particularly the students, were influenced by the Black Power ideology. Many of the protesting students carried banners identifying themselves as Black Power advocates and shouted "Black Power" as they marched. A sign stuck to the gate at the entrance to Irvine Hall, one of the dormitories, proclaimed: "Dictatorship government bans our lecturer and Black Brother."[30] When the students were joined by demonstrators from the ghetto areas and the violence erupted, the government identified the Black Power movement, Rodney, and the non-Jamaican students as the villains, and refused to recognize the horrendous problems of the urban poor and the depth of their alienation from the larger society.

In justifying the government's declaration of Rodney as a persona non grata, Prime Minister Shearer explained to an emergency session of the Jamaica Parliament on October 17, 1968, that Rodney was "carrying on activities which constituted a danger to the security of the nation." Quoting from a document prepared by the Security Authorities of Government, the prime minister noted Rodney's close association with "groups of people who claimed to be a part of the Rastafarian movement." The document charged that Rodney had "openly declared his belief that as Jamaica was predominantly a black country all brown skinned, mulatto people and their assets should be destroyed. He consistently told the groups with whom he associated that this could be only achieved by revolution and that no revolution had ever taken place without armed struggle and bloodshed."[31]

Shearer went on to accuse Rodney of organizing a Black Power movement on the Mona campus for the purpose of "hiding his subversive activities." He assured his fellow parliamentarians and the country that Rodney's definition of Black Power was "Castro Revolution." In denouncing the riots that had occurred in the aftermath of Rodney's exclusion, the prime minister explained that the violence had been organized "under the guise of a Black Power movement which to us and other well-thinking Jamaicans does not mean rebellion but rather the dignity of the black man."[32]

Shearer's clever attempt to link Black Power to subversion and communism evidently succeeded. Opposition leader Norman Manley, who had earlier condemned the government's exclusion of Rodney, was forced to admit that "it is good for Jamaica to know that the reason why Dr. Rodney was expelled from this country was because he was engaged in organizing activities which advocated violence and the overthrow of those things which are highly treasured in this country—our progress toward a multi-racial society in which a man is not as good as his skin but as good as his merit. And anything that tends to undermine our motto, in spite of our hardship, in spite of our suffering, in spite of our troubles . . . is bad for Jamaica."[33]

In his contribution to the debate, Victor Grant, the minister of legal affairs and attorney general, tried to convince his colleagues and probably himself that "in this country, there is neither black nor white nor pink. What we are interested in in this country is the quality of the individual, not the colour of his skin. That is the motto which keeps us and that is the motto which we strive for."[34] Edward Seaga, the minister of finance and planning, sought to blame the Black Power group on the campus for organizing the disturbances. Reading from an unidentified document, he charged that the Black Power group held a meeting in which the members urged "UWI students to wear gowns to act as decoys while Black Power non campus groups beat, burn and even kill . . . the real aim of Black Power is to overthrow the government."[35] Seaga came to the same conclusion as his prime minister had done before him: "These youths who are hiding under guise of a movement which has acquired dignity elsewhere, are patently not members of the Black Power Movement, but, rather of Red Power."[36]

Edwin Allen, the minister of education, saw Rodney as "one of the most dangerous men ever to set foot on Jamaican soil." He asked rhetorically:

> What did this man want to do? Let me remind you, Sir. All brownskin mulatto people and their assets should be destroyed. That man did not have to mention whites; did not have to mention the other races in Jamaica. He only said Jamaica was a black country; and in other words what he meant was that everybody who was not recognizably black should be destroyed in this country. . . . The most wicked thing anybody could do to a country like Jamaica whose motto is "Out of many-one people" is to come here and stir up racial troubles. We have enough of this in South Africa and elsewhere in the world. We don't want any of it in Jamaica.[37]

Given the fears that Black Power and Rodney engendered, it is not surprising that the Parliament passed, without dissent, a motion upholding the government's exclusion of Rodney "as an undesirable inhabitant of and visitor to the island" and approving "this action of the government in the interest of the security of Jamaica."[38]

While the politicians were vehemently denouncing Rodney and condemning what they perceived to be his version of the ideology of Black Power, members of the press and the general public spoke out. A majority of those who wrote letters to the press, for example, denied that Jamaica was a black country. Cora Anderson, who identified herself as a black woman, observed: "This 'making the black man feel he is a man' thought would suit a country like South Africa but not here in Jamaica where nobody is prevented from being a man . . . . Will some learned person kindly inform me how Jamaica comes to belong to the black man?"[39] Others were troubled by any association with Africa implied by the ideology of Black Power. Lucius Valerius (evidently a pseudonym), in an attack on Rodney, opposed the teaching of African history in the schools. He warned that "with our island sadly deficient in vital skills needed for our development we just cannot afford to spend the money of the West Indian taxpayer on such questionable luxuries as the study of African history."[40] Writing in the *Public Opinion*, the official voice of the People's National party, Perry Swope questioned the need for "a special course in African Studies." He maintained that "a dental faculty must be more important to us now than a law school or a department of African affairs. We have to consider the priorities and one of them is not African Studies."[41]

A number of other Jamaicans were disturbed by the ideology of Black Power because to them it was synonymous with black racism. These individuals shared the view that Jamaica was a color-blind society. The Reverend Richard Nelson expressed the position very well in a sermon that he delivered at the Duke Street Christian Church: "There is a great deal of talk now about Black Power. What it means to many is not the personal worth and dignity of the black man but Black Racism. In this sense, there is no room in Jamaican society for White Power, Black Power, Indian Power, or Chinese Power—there is a lot of room for Human Power—the recognition by all of the personal worth, inherent dignity and value of each man, be he white, black, Indian or Chinese."[42] The president of the Jamaica Association of Montreal, L. C. Morrison, echoed the view that Black Power fostered racism when he reported that his organization "will not ally itself with Black Power . . . nor will it associate itself with any racist organization."[43]

Reactions such as these avoided the issue of the economic powerlessness of blacks raised by the advocates of Black Power. In fact, a sizable section of the Jamaican population was convinced that black Jamaicans exercised complete control over their society. In an editorial, the afternoon tabloid, the *Star*, claimed that "in a country such as ours, where every Jamaican, regardless of colour has one vote, 'Black Power' concepts have no relevance and are just used by the left wing extremists to dupe and delude the uneducated. This is the 'treason of the intellect' that any responsible government must view with concern and vigilance."[44] In a letter to the editor of the *Star*, Jackie Estick saw no need for Black Power in Jamaica: "No! Certainly Not! For we have had it all along and did not realise it until the American Blacks found the necessity for something to spur them on, and invented this."[45]

The same positions were expressed by young high school students. In response to the question, "What do you think of the Black Power Movement?" Hazel Gibbon, a student at the Immaculate Conception High School, responded: "A Black Power movement here is totally unnecessary. We are already governed by a 'black government' so what purpose is there in going around shouting for Black Power or 'black supremacy?' Also Jamaica is a cosmopolitan country and it would be complete folly for a certain race to get up and start clamouring for particular power. I am afraid this will end in disorder and chaos. . . . Black Power is a foreign import, and, like women's fashions will soon fade into obscurity."[46] In a similar vein, Leroy Jackson of St. Georges

College confessed that "I see no purpose in having a Black Power Movement here. The Americans are justified in shouting for Black Power. What are our reasons? Isn't there already equality and equal rights for all in Jamaica?"[47]

The assault on the advocates of Black Power was frequently vituperative. Keith Chance, in a letter to *The Daily Gleaner*, unwittingly expressed considerable self-hatred when he bemoaned the fact that "the hearts of West Indian intellectuals are as Black as Black Art and Mau Mau and the hearts of the fetishistic worshippers of Africa."[48] Perry Swope, the *Public Opinion* columnist, was equally strident in his criticisms of them. He believed that "'Black Power' is for copycats and sheep, for mediocre minds and people suffering not so much from an inferiority complex as from the knowledge that they are inferior, for those who cannot really make the grade as people and so much [sic] settle for being Negroes by profession; it is for stooges and suckers, pseudo intellectuals and third rate journalists, rabble rousers and exhibitionists."[49]

While Swope dismissed Black Power advocates as having "mediocre minds," other Jamaicans were not so sure and perceived sinister motives behind the movement. The influential columnist who wrote under the byline of "The Political Reporter" was certain that "it was relatively easy for Dr. Rodney and others at the University to use 'Black Power' as a cloak for sinister activities leading many Jamaican students and others outside the University like so many sheep to the slaughter. The surprising thing about the Rodney affair, however, is that so many persons at the University and outside of it were deluded into believing that he was fighting for black man's rights and not advocating a Communist take over of the Jamaican State."[50] Wesley Powell, the respected headmaster of the Excelsior School, did not associate Black Power with communism but he felt that "the most dangerous appeal of Black Power . . . can destroy utterly the whole fabric of our civilized way of life."[51] P. V. Hall of Walderston, a rural community, had the answer to social disturbances and to Black Power. According to him, "Talking and tear gas alone will not stop the looting and destruction of property, also beating up of innocent people and Black Power. The only thing to stop them is to introduce Lead Power, that would stop them at once and for all times."[52]

It must not be concluded, however, that all of those whose views were reported in the newspapers expressed opposition to Black Power. In an editorial in *Catholic Opinion*, the organ of the Roman Catholic church, the ideology received a strong endorsement, at least in an abstract sense. The editorial concluded that "Black Power is real power. And the world is poorer for the fact that for so long a time the influence of Black Power has been nil. For the sake of self preservation, not to mention necessary progress, the world at large must accept Black Power and realize that there are so many black peoples in the world and their power will come."[53] Trevor Monroe, a lecturer at the university, felt that "Jamaica needs black power not only because black people are powerless here, more importantly because Jamaica is a black society."[54]

The question of political and economic power aside, some thoughtful Jamaicans realised that to be black was to be devalued in Jamaican society and that the advocates of Black Power were raising questions that could not be ignored. In a letter to *The Daily Gleaner*, Margaret Carter commented at length on this issue:

> Now don't let us fool ourselves, our multiracial society has functioned harmoniously because it is not only the white and brown man but the black man as well, who regards the black man as being an inferior being, hence meriting his status. Just listen to any quarrel between the white or brown man and the black man, and often the first words of abuse are "damn black nigger." Listen to black people quarrelling among themselves and, sooner or later we hear it "damn black nigger," "black bongo." Throughout the length and breadth of the island black is a known term of abuse. A black woman will tell another shade darker that she does not like "anything too black." The black domestic worker asserts vehemently "mi no work fe [for] black people," while the black housewife treats her black domestic helpers as if they were some inferior species of mankind. Has anyone ever wondered what damage this has been doing to the Jamaican personality?[55]

Frank Hill, chairman of the National Trust Commission and one of the island's most respected citizens, raised similar questions. He believed that the violence associated with the Rodney affair was being fed by class distinctions that were based primarily on skin color. Hill asserted: "It is hard for a black skin to adjust to a society that is still dominated by a white bias . . . when the black skin is well trained, educated, the neurosis and the frustrations tend to become deepened. So we get a growing, widening sense of alienation that is turning into a series of pools of isolation."[56]

These "pools of isolation," obviously, had not been created by Rodney and the Black Power movement. In fact, it may be doubted whether a "movement" in the sense that a structure, a recognized leadership, a clearly defined strategy, and a set of common goals ever existed. Norman Girvan saw the movement as merely a "loose coalescing of organizations, groups and individuals in different parts of the country."[57] Clearly, the Jamaican government and some of the island's citizens overreacted to what they thought the movement represented.

Rodney's role was exaggerated. He had been the most articulate spokesman for the ideology of Black Power, and had established links with some of Kingston's poor and alienated masses. But ultimately, the movement had been fed by Jamaica's severe socioeconomic problems, and the clear recognition by some that the society had to be reconstructed along fundamentally different lines. It was this reconstruction that many were unwilling to contemplate and to accept. The October riot gave the Shearer government an excuse to condemn Black Power and to stymie, at least temporarily, any movement toward structural changes.

The vitriolic response on the part of middle-class Jamaicans to the events of October 16 and to the ideology of Black Power reflected an unwillingness to come to terms with a black identity and consciousness. But it was more than that. Black Power, as Rodney and others promoted it, was frightening in its class implications because it threatened the precarious material existence of the privileged groups in society. Possessed of tremendous emotional appeal, particularly for the black dispossessed, the movement sought to elevate them to positions of economic and political power in society. Trevor Monroe explained this position clearly: "Black Power exists where the black man controls the social, political and economic institutions in his own collective interest."[58] Robert Hill, another university intellectual, echoed similar sentiments: "Black Power cannot coexist with White Power. One must go in this country."[59]

It was not only that the Jamaican elite feared the fundamental reordering of society that Black Power promised to bring in its wake. Members of that group were convinced that Black Power advocates were committed to the use of violence to achieve the societal redemption they wanted. One citizen, for example, complained in a letter to the editor of the *Gleaner* that "since the inception of Black Power doctrine in Jamaica, the incidence of certain types of crimes has escalated. Vicious attacks are made on people of all ranks, particularly the white and fair skinned."[60] The events of October 16 confirmed these fears and provided an alarmed elite with the ammunition it needed to discredit the movement. Conceivably, however, Black Power advocates would not have eschewed violence as a means of effecting change if that remained the only option at their disposal. Their belief that the existing institutions were incapable of cleansing themselves and generating systemic changes lend credence to this assertion. In fact, Rodney provided a moral justification for the use of violence by the oppressed when he noted: "Violence aimed at the recovery of human dignity and at equality cannot be judged by the same yardstick as violence aimed at the maintenance of discrimination and oppression."[61]

The profound Jamaican ambivalence to an essentially African racial heritage mirrors that of the other Caribbean societies. The events associated with the 1970 "February Revolution" in Trinidad (Chapter 6) provide another graphic example of this tendency. This ambivalence, to be sure, is another one of the unfortunate legacies of slavery and colonialism; its survival is due in part to the continuing poverty of the overwhelming majority of the peoples of African descent in all of the societies of this hemisphere. As long as there is a seemingly immutable correlation between a black skin and poverty, the development of a positive sense of self and of an enduring pride in a black racial heritage will remain elusive goals.

Under the circumstances, Rodney's exclusion from Jamaica did not produce social quiescence. The problems to which he drew attention remained to bedevil society and its successive governments. His observation that "there's bound to be an explosion whether I have anything to do with it or not" may still be painfully prophetic.[62] Jamaicans have yet to make their national motto a living reality and to create the kind of society that ascribes an equal place to all of Africa's children. That is at once Jamaica's promise and its challenge.

# Notes

1. *Jamaica Hansard*, Sessions 1953–54, p. 317.
2. *The Daily Gleaner*, Jan. 10, 1957, p. 8.
3. Ibid., Aug. 19, 1963, p. 10.
4. Ibid., Aug. 6, 1963, p. 21.
5. Ibid., Oct. 31, 1960, p. 12.
6. Ibid., Oct. 10, 1963, p. 8.
7. Ibid., Oct. 19, 1960, p. 10.
8. Ibid., May 13, 1950, p. 3.
9. Ibid., Sept. 30, 1958, p. 8.
10. Ibid., Aug. 29, 1963, p. 1.
11. Ibid., Apr. 11, 1968, p. 1.
12. Ibid., Apr. 5, 1968, p. 1.
13. *Jamaica Hansard*, Sessions 1963–64, p. 230.
14. *The Daily Gleaner*, Apr. 13, 1968, p. 12.
15. The riot lasted for only a day. Many buses were burned, cars overturned, and stores looted.
16. Girvan, "After Rodney," p. 59.
17. Rodney, *The Groundings with My Brothers*, p. 18.
18. Ibid.

19. Ibid., p. 19.
20. Ibid.
21. Ibid.
22. Ibid., p. 25.
23. Ibid.
24. Ibid.
25. Ibid., p. 28.
26. Ibid., p. 29. He saw the Chinese in the West Indies as part of an exploiting class. As he put it, the Chinese "will have either to relinquish or be deprived of that function before they can be re-integrated into a West Indian society where the black man walks in dignity."
27. Ibid.
28. Ibid.
29. *Guardian Weekly*, June 12, 1969, p. 12.
30. *The Daily Gleaner*: Oct. 17, 1968, p. 10; Oct. 18, 1968, p. 2.
31. *Jamaica Hansard*, Sessions 1968–69, p. 392.
32. Ibid.
33. Ibid., p. 396.
34. Ibid., p. 398.
35. Ibid., p. 406.
36. Ibid.
37. Ibid., p. 408.
38. Ibid., pp. 393, 410.
39. *The Daily Gleaner*, Oct. 28, 1968, p. 12.
40. Ibid., Nov. 11, 1968, p. 19.
41. *Public Opinion*, Nov. 15, 1968, p. 2.
42. Ibid., Dec. 13, 1968, p. 5.
43. *The Daily Gleaner*, Oct. 26, 1968, p. 1.
44. *The Star*, Oct. 19, 1968, p. 6.
45. Ibid., Nov. 8, 1968, p. 15.
46. *Catholic Opinion*, Dec. 6, 1968, p. 4.
47. Ibid., Dec. 6, 1968, p. 4.
48. *The Daily Gleaner*, Nov. 12, 1968, p. 12.
49. *Public Opinion*, Oct. 25, 1968, p. 12.
50. *The Daily Gleaner*, Oct. 20, 1968, p. 6.
51. *Public Opinion*, Dec. 20, 1968, p. 9.
52. *The Daily Gleaner*, Nov. 4, 1968, p. 8.
53. *Catholic Opinion*, Nov. 15, 1968, p. 8.
54. *Moko*, Oct. 16, 1970, p. 6.
55. *The Daily Gleaner*, Nov. 5, 1968, p. 19.
56. Ibid., Oct. 24, 1968, p. 31.
57. Girvan, "After Rodney," pp. 59–60.

58. *Moko*, Oct. 16, 1970, p. 6.
59. *Public Opinion*, Dec. 6, 1968, p. 7.
60. *The Daily Gleaner*, June 7, 1969, p. 8.
61. Rodney, *The Groundings with My Brothers*, p. 22.
62. *The Star*, Oct. 22, 1968, p. 1.

## 6

Herman L. Bennett

# The Challenge to the Post-Colonial State

A Case Study of the February Revolution in Trinidad

Threhe post-colonial history of the anglophone Caribbean lends itself to a fruitful analysis of the process of decolonization and the challenges that the new states confronted. During the first decades of their independence, Jamaica in 1968 and Trinidad in 1970 experienced social disturbances that took on a seemingly revolutionary character. In addition, several groups and individuals throughout the area issued demands for the elimination of colonial ties, habits, and institutions, as well as the redistribution of national wealth.

At the forefront of these demands were radical intellectuals and university students who criticized independence as a "flawed achievement." Many of these critics noted that a transformation in the social, political, and economic systems had not been effected in the post-colonial period. Criticism of the post-colonial order was not limited to university students and radical intellectuals, however. Among individuals in the general population who had hoped that independence would lead to improved material conditions, frustration prevailed when promised reforms and better socioeconomic conditions remained elusive goals. This frustration led to sporadic social unrest, antigovernment protests, and politically motivated violence directed against the expatriate as well as the indigenous elite. Yet, failed expectations alone cannot explain why Jamaicans in 1968 and Trinidadians in 1970 took to the streets to express their grievances.

By the mid-1960s, critics such as the university-based intellectuals who belonged to the New World Group, as well as an amorphous group of students, workers, the urban unemployed, and middle-class exponents of Trinidadian nationalism and Black Power who constituted the National Joint Action Committee (NJAC), concluded that decolonization had only initiated another phase of colonialism. Their criticisms, along with those of the noted Guayanese historian and Black Power advocate, Walter Rodney, were undoubtedly influential in shaping the character of the social disturbances that occurred in Trinidad. It can be maintained that the critics were also enormously effective in questioning the legitimacy of West Indian independence in general and in raising questions that the new leaders had to confront.

Primarily concerned with the issue of West Indian dependency on foreign capital, the radical intellectuals who comprised the New World Group were prominent critics of post-colonial development strategies. Trinidad's small size and dependence on preferential markets had convinced the ruling political elite that economic self-reliance was not feasible.[1] The inheritors of the colonial state were, consequently, persuaded to adopt the dependent development strategy advocated by the Saint Lucian economist, Sir Arthur Lewis. The Puerto Rican model, or "Industrialization by Invitation" as it was called, saw the government grant pioneer status to incoming firms, enabling them to enjoy tax holidays, accelerated depreciation, duty free imports, and other concessions. The government, in turn, hoped that industrialization would secure employment for the local population and that the local business elite would eventually acquire the capital and expertise to take over the industries. But members of the New World Group viewed the reliance on foreign capital as evidence that the West Indies remained economically dependent and underdeveloped, and that states such as Trinidad served the interests of the local and metropolitan elite.

The New World Group, therefore, concluded that the development of national economic and political structures was impeded by foreign capital and that unless ownership and investment patterns were changed colonial relations would persist. Seeking to eradicate the colonial legacy, the New World Group proposed an effective break with imperialism, the rise to power by the black masses, and the formulation of an indigenous political philosophy and culture. It also proposed a solution to underdevelopment and dependency. In the group's opinion, West Indian nations should "disengage" from international capitalism while initiating domestic capital accumulation. In the transition process, the state would play an active role by imposing import restrictions and other limitations on foreign capital. The state, moreover, would utilize local resources (labor, capital, and natural resources) to support the national bourgeoisie who, in turn, would foster independent development and ensure that West Indian economies operated from a position of strength and self-reliance in their interaction with international capitalism. Interestingly, the New World Group's alternative parallels the dependent development strategy of Sir Arthur

Lewis which also emphasized the necessity to generate local capital for development. Unlike Lewis's model, however, the New World Group rejected an alliance with foreign capital during the transition to economic self-reliance. It argued that precisely because Lewis's strategy relied on foreign capital, West Indian economies would remain structurally dependent on international capitalism.

Although they criticized the dependence on foreign capital and proposed solutions, members of the New World Group stressed the importance of intellectuals staying above active politics.[2] Lloyd Best, a spokesman for the group, summarized the members' objectives as eschewing established ideologies, providing an examination of Caribbean societies in their specificities, committing themselves to theorizing, and finally avoiding the political fray. Critics of the New World Group have suggested that its tactical stance reflected the organization's class composition and that this orientation eventually led to its demise.[3] Although its influence remained primarily academic, the New World Group, by criticizing the prevailing development strategies and proposing to transform the dependent West Indian economies into independent ones, posed an important challenge to the post-colonial order.

Not all intellectuals in the Caribbean avoided political activism, however. Walter Rodney, for example, bridged the divisions between radical intellectuals, university students, and the urban poor of West Kingston. Rodney's analysis of the post-colonial period in the Caribbean extended beyond the political and economic systems to include questions of identity, social classes, the role of intellectuals, the importance of African history, the Afro-Indian debate, and, most importantly, the deplorable socioeconomic conditions of the masses. As one of the more prominent Black Power proponents in the Caribbean, Walter Rodney brought "together class and racial issues precisely the way" the West Indian political systems "sought to prevent and to which [they were] most vulnerable."[4] Inspired by Rodney's ideas, many young radicals throughout the Caribbean embraced Black Power and raised probing questions about the political order. To the surprise of most observers, the most sustained expression of Black Power emerged in Trinidad where the ruling People's National Movement (PNM) had been characterized as the best example of black majority rule. James Millette, however, was most perspicacious when he noted that "black men in power do not connote Black Power." Black people in the West Indies, Millette maintained, were frustrated and felt "betrayed" by those blacks who claimed to rule in their name. Failed expectations, he suggested, was the primary reason why the confrontation emerged as a Black Power movement.[5]

At the forefront of the Trinidadian Black Power movement was the National Joint Action Committee. The organization first gained prominence in 1969 when its members barred the Canadian governor general from entering the University of the West Indies' Saint Augustine campus. NJAC's action was an expression of solidarity with the West Indian students arrested in Canada for their participation in the Sir George Williams University Affair.[6] Following the incident involving the Canadian governor general, NJAC broadened its appeal by concerning itself with community issues confronting workers, the unemployed, the poor, and other dispossessed elements in Trinidadian society.

In their political tracts, "Slavery to Slavery" and "Conventional Politics or Revolution," as well as in their news journal, *Liberation*, NJAC members established their reputation as critics of the post-colonial order. Between 1969 and 1970, the organization repeatedly addressed the linkage between the political order and the economy.[7] NJAC portrayed the economic system as being subservient to international capitalism. Its members argued that since the "white power structure" controlled the economy, it followed that black people were oppressed because they were victims of economic exploitation. Consequently, independence merely changed "imperial masters, the Maple, and the Stars and Stripes for the Union Jack. The decay of colonialism had heralded the dawn of neo-colonialism."[8] Thus, the destiny of the West Indies was still being determined by an external elite.

The indigenous elite, however, was held responsible for maintaining metropolitan interests, thereby ensuring that the exploitation of black people would continue. The so-called "Afro-Saxons," NJAC members argued, were cultural reflections of Europeans in terms of values, education, and orientation. NJAC, therefore, rejected independence as being an act of deception and suggested that no significant change would be forthcoming until the "black whites" were removed from political power.

Apparently, NJAC was not concerned with conventional politics or any goal short of revolutionary change. The organization's radicalism was evident in its proposal for economic reconstruction, which called for public ownership and control of the land, national ownership and control of the entire sugar industry, establishing a land use plan, linking both sectors of the economy to generate local capital, diversifying trade links to reduce dependency, eliminating unemployment in five years, and allowing trade unions to have strike privileges.[9] As one NJAC spokesman stated about the new order: "It is no point talking in terms of reform . . . we have always to think in terms of total rejection of the system which has so dehumanized and oppressed black people."[10]

Contrary to popular opinion, however, NJAC's program was not grounded in an Afro-Marxist framework. Within the leadership ranks there was open hostility to Marxism of any sort. The Workers Educational Association, a Marxist-Leninist organization, for example, which had joined the NJAC coalition at its inception, was later expelled for allegedly not understanding the problems of black people.[11] Although NJAC maintained ties with individual Marxists, the organization's main ideological thrust was an antiimperialism fused with ethnic nationalism. Responding to critics who charged that NJAC's appeal was overly racial, a spokesman remarked that the "emphasis on blackness . . . was a necessary prerequisite for the first phase of the Black Movement."[12]

NJAC's Black Power emphasis was somewhat injudicious in a racially heterogeneous society like Trinidad. Given the shrewd manipulation of hostilities between Afro- and East Indian Trinidadians (who respectively comprised 42 percent and .37 percent of the population), Black Power only exacerbated a potentially explosive relationship. During the events of 1970, NJAC grossly underestimated the level of hostility existing between both groups. Although both shared similar socioeconomic conditions, the years of racial tension and conflict in addition to cultural differences effectively prevented Afro-Indian unity.[13]

Despite the failure to incorporate East Indians into the Black Power movement, members of NJAC were outspoken ideological critics of the post-colonial state. Their analysis and solutions to the problems of dependency reflected a degree of political sophistication similar to that of the New World Group and Walter Rodney. It also appears that NJAC was able to raise the level of consciousness among the poor by arguing that independence had provided little or no change in the lives of most people. In the final analysis, however, the revolutionary objectives of NJAC frightened participants in the February revolt, causing some to reembrace the conventional political system.

The critics of the nature of independence agreed that colonial attitudes still prevailed everywhere in the West Indies. They charged, for example, that the substitution of a national flag, anthem, and motto was at best "symbol manipulation" initiated by the indigenous elite.[14] This elite, Rodney and NJAC pointed out, could not envision a self-reliant existence. Dependency, on the other hand, delayed societal reconstruction which would ensure popular and indigenous control; political, economic, and cultural autonomy; and a more equitable distribution of the nation's resources. Given the extent to which the West Indies were still dominated by foreign elements, the nature of this criticism can be described as nationalist. For as Norman Girvan observed, "a reaction against imperialism assumes a nationalist character."[15]

By the late 1960s, the nationalist ideologies, especially Black Power, appealed increasingly to the urban dispossessed. The source of this appeal was the deteriorating socioeconomic conditions that Black Power proponents addressed. The "black massa," it was argued, "pays greater attention to the representation of foreign investors and their domestic allies than to the needs of oppressed blacks."[16] Because of its racial and somewhat xenophobic dimensions, Black Power attracted the urban poor whose conditions were in part determined by their race and relation to foreign capital.

Yet to suggest that the ideological currents espoused by the New World Group, Rodney, or NJAC inspired the events of 1970 is to ignore the other causes of the disturbances in Trinidad. Whereas radical intellectuals and university students sought to eradicate dependent relations, the urban dispossessed wanted to improve their material conditions. The prevailing ideology of Black Power was important to the urban poor but employed only insofar as it articulated their social grievances. Commitment to changes beyond the redress of social grievances was essentially confined to organizations like NJAC and the New World Group in addition to individuals like Rodney. Limited in their demands, the majority of demonstrators placed restrictions on the content, the nature, and the eventual outcome of the social disturbances that occurred in Trinidad.

## Popular Mobilization

Inspired by the anniversary of the Sir George Williams University Affair, a group of two hundred students and their supporters participated in a protest demonstration denouncing Canadian imperialism and racism. Within days, the events of February 26, 1970, had escalated into a massive Black Power demonstration that paralyzed Trinidad and Tobago. The disturbances lasted until the declaration of a "State of Emergency" on April 21 when the authorities brought the situation under control, leaving the Trinidadian political system more or less intact.

The bitter confrontation between militant blacks and the post-colonial government of Trinidad was a surprise to most Caribbean observers. Even among Trinidadians aware of the growing political temper and an emerging black consciousness, surprise was expressed at the massive support Black Power advocates, especially NJAC, gained between February and April 1970. Although the disturbances did not constitute an incipient revolution, as many Trinidadians feared, they profoundly challenged the foundations of conventional Trinidadian politics. The events were initially a nationalist expression on the part of radical university students and intellectuals who demanded an end to metropolitan dominance over Trinidadian society. In order to attract supporters, however, the activists had to address issues relevant to the average Trinidadian, in particular unemployment, racism, and material dispossession. These considerations at once defined and limited the goals, content, and nature of the disturbances.

Given its limitations, it is more appropriate to characterize the events between February and April somewhat loosely as a "revolt." For revolts are basically angry or violent expressions by individuals or groups who refuse to continue in their present condition. Symbolizing reform for its participants, a revolt embraces various sectors of the population including the youth, the unemployed, and the dispossessed. The lack of a coherent ideology, moreover, places constraints on the objectives and outcome of a revolt. Mark Hagopian suggests that "the lack or weakness of ideology helps to explain why many revolts hesitate and then disintegrate after having [confronted] the forces of order. The revolt simply does not know what to do." In view of their limited objectives, revolts are basically "conservative or even retrograde" in nature since most participants only seek to better their socioeconomic condition. Thus the possibility of effecting fundamental changes does not exist.[17]

Between February and April, for example, NJAC failed to articulate a coherent ideological position or program. The ambiguities surrounding Black Power also suggest that the so-called "February Revolution" lacked the basis for fundamental change. If the conditions for a revolution were in fact present, what explains the apparent lack of participation by the industrial and agricultural workers who comprised a significant proportion of the population? The lack of interest among members of the population in general can be explained partly in terms of their ideological reservations about Black Power and what it appeared to represent. Most people were unwilling to support a movement that could jeopardize their existing status. Among industrial workers, "Industrialization by Invitation" had created a small "relatively well-paid unionized working-class elite" which was unwilling to support any radical departure from conventional politics.[18]

The same case can be made for the majority of the protesters, many of whom were primarily interested in improving their material conditions. When looting, burning, and bombing of businesses occurred, many of the marchers were appalled by the lack of discipline and abandoned the "revolutionary" movement. If the objective of most participants was to reform the political system in order to improve their socioeconomic conditions, the leadership of the February Revolution overestimated the importance of symbolic gestures pertaining to black pride and consciousness. In fact, the level of commitment among the demonstrators was misinterpreted. If the majority of protesters had been committed to revolution, the demonstrations would have maintained their intensity beyond the declaration of the State of Emergency. This was not the case. Yet the implications of the disturbances cannot be easily dismissed. The events between February 26 and April 21 strongly suggest that a fundamental dissatisfaction with the post-colonial order existed among young urban blacks, who were overrepresented among the unemployed and dispossessed. Black Power attracted young urban blacks because it spoke to their immediate needs.

The first portent of the challenge to the existing order occurred on the first day of Carnival, February 9, 1970, when Black Power themes and protest bands appeared alongside the traditional fantasy and historical costumes.[19] The political overtones were apparent, for example, in a depiction of the black experience, entitled "The Truth about Blacks—Past and Present," which portrayed slaves and indentured servants in addition to "massas" and the "stooges of the massas."[20]

Within seventeen days, the situation reached crisis proportions when NJAC set in motion the February revolt. Although it was viewed as a spontaneous Black Power demonstration in support of the West Indian students arrested in connection with the Sir George Williams University Affair, the events that followed were an outgrowth of the sociopolitical tensions permeating Trinidad. Motivated by the anniversary of the Canadian incident, demonstrators under the direction of NJAC directed their venom at Canadian authorities and Canadian-owned businesses in Trinidad's capital, Port of Spain. As the day proceeded, the focus of the demonstrators broadened to include the Roman Catholic church when a number of the demonstrators entered the Cathedral of the Immaculate Conception, gave speeches, and engaged in sharp exchanges with the priests. The crowd then proceeded to Woodford Square where demonstrators listened to speeches until 7:00 p.m.[21]

After the initial demonstration, the Sir George Williams University Affair became insignificant in relation to the events that followed. The affair was only important in that it enabled NJAC and other organizations to link racism in Canada to the realities in Trinidad. Organizational leaders like Geddes Granger, Dave D'Abreau, Alwdyn Primus, and Carl Blackwood repeatedly emphasized how racism and foreign capital were related to the systemic problems confronting Trinidad. For the majority of the participants, mainly university students, the linkage was made explicit by the fact that Canada was the largest foreign investor in Trinidad. One can, therefore, conclude that the initial demonstrators were inspired by antiimperialist sentiments.

The government reacted swiftly to the demonstration by arresting nine NJAC members for "unlawful assembling in the vicinity and within the Cathedral of the Immaculate Conception."[22] Instead of decapitating the movement with the arrests, however, the government's response served to exacerbate the situation. Intrigued by the events of February 26 and issues raised by NJAC, an estimated 10,000 people paralyzed Trinidad's capital when they gathered to greet the nine arrested NJAC spokesmen on March 4. Members of Black Power organizations from throughout Trinidad, including the Black Panthers, the African Unity Brothers, the African Cultural Association, the Afro-Turf Limers ("limers" refer to people who gather on street corners, generally unemployed), the Pine-toppers, the Southern Liberation Movement, and the National Freedom Organization, joined the assemblage of March 4 to express their solidarity with NJAC.[23]

Led by NJAC leader Geddes Granger, the demonstrators marched into Shanty Town, an urban ghetto in Port of Spain. In Shanty Town, the protesters asked the residents to join them. According to the *Guardian* reporter Raoul Pantin, "They came. Asked to talk, one did. She gave a very brief talk, attacking the government for the fact of Shanty Town."[24] NJAC spokesmen then criticized the "white racist power structure" and its "black tools" for oppressing black people.[25] The need for black unity was also repeatedly emphasized, while the mostly young demonstrators shouted "Power" accompanied by clenched-fist, Black Power salutes.

The March 4 demonstration marked a critical point in the revolt. NJAC leaders realized almost immediately that the crowd was only receptive to ideas that pertained to such local issues as unemployment, poverty, and racial discrimination. At this point, NJAC members altered their interpretation of Black Power so that it would focus specifically on local issues thereby de-emphasizing its initial antiimperialist and nationalist orientation. Throughout the two-month revolt, the central ideological content of Black Power would remain limited to practical issues relevant to the majority of the demonstrators.

The mood among protesters grew increasingly militant after the March 4 demonstration. In response to the shooting of John Gomez, an innocent bystander, an angry crowd, consisting of school children, young men and women, hurled objects at stores and the police. In the following days, the demonstration continued with an added dimension. Molotov cocktails were thrown into the home of the minister of education and culture, while the Bank of Nova Scotia, Kirpalanis (an East Indian-owned dry goods store), the Modern Wear Garment factory, and other businesses were victims of similar attacks.[26] Thus by March 8, police assaults, retaliatory violence, and the increasing militancy of the demonstrators had intensified the situation.

At this point, it is possible that Geddes Granger, the NJAC leader, began to sense the possibilities for more drastic action. Granger stated that "we are prepared to take over the country."[27] The government, in turn, felt threatened by the demonstrations and sporadic violence. The minister of industry, commerce, and petroleum claimed that the current crisis was being "engineered by communist agitators trained and paid by Fidel Castro" who "were using the Sir George Williams affair as a Red Herring in their revolutionary move aimed at the overthrowing of the ruling PNM Government."[28] In contrast, members of the East Indian-based parliamentary opposition, the Democratic Labour party (DLP), feeling less threatened, provided a more trenchant analysis: "[T]he protesters have taken to the streets to express . . . their disappointment and disenchantment with the present state of affairs. . . . Everyone knows that unemployment is compounding the economic as well as social ills of the country."[29] Although perceptive in its critique, the DLP—along with other observers—saw the February revolt simply as black pride manifesting itself in wanton violence against East Indians, whites, and private property.[30]

In response to claims that the Black Power movement was anti-East Indian, Geddes Granger announced that the demonstrators would proceed to the sugarcane areas populated largely by East Indians to express their solidarity with them. Aware of Trinidad's racially plural nature and the underlying tension that existed between blacks and East Indians, the NJAC leadership realized the boost the movement would receive if disillusioned East Indians united with Afro-Trinidadians. Granger stated that this symbolic march would give the demonstrators (who were primarily young, unemployed black youths) "an opportunity to share the work experience of the Indians and to witness the suffering of the people and the way they are exploited." "The experience," Granger argued, "would help us develop a new understanding that would further strengthen the bond, of brotherhood between black people—Indians and blacks."[31] In addition, the NJAC leader issued a formal statement inviting the Roman Catholic archbishop of Port of Spain to join the marchers on their historic trek into Caroni. On the morning of March 26, over 6,000 Afro-Trinidadians marched the twenty-six miles into the heart of the Indian belt, Caroni, to express solidarity with their Indian brothers and sisters.

Despite strong opposition from Bhadase Maraj, head of the All Trinidad Sugar Estates and Factory Workers Trade Union and the Democratic Labour party, who had threatened the marchers with violence if they entered the sugar belt, the march took place without incident.[32] While the march had shown that no conflict between the two races would materialize, it also demonstrated that the protesters could not expect substantial East Indian support. Suspicion between the two groups was widespread, and it would take more than a march to alleviate the tension that existed. The Black Power leaders underestimated the importance of these divisions, and failed to provide the necessary groundwork within the Indian community.[33]

The term "black," moreover, generally referred to persons of predominantly African descent. Most Indians did not regard themselves as being black. In a letter to the editor, for example, an Indian writer responded negatively to having been categorized as such by the Black Power movement: "I object to being called black . . . Indians belong to the Caucasian or "white" race . . . why then call Indians black?"[34] D. Jugmohan, in a more dispassionate letter, wrote, "You, the Black Power members are asking us to join you in your march for power. . . . Your sudden interest in the East Indian sugar worker is viewed with suspicion. . . . We are not prepared to support you."[35] Overall, the concept of Black Power had little appeal for the Indian population and throughout the period of unrest the majority of participants were of African descent.[36]

Opposition to Black Power was not limited to East Indians, however. A number of Afro-Trinidadians questioned the relevance of Black Power in a multiracial society like Trinidad. In a letter to the editor, Dr. R. K. Richardson observed that "Black Power seems unsuitable for application to the requirements of this multiracial, multi-coloured society because the term suggests a racist content." "Majority Power," he argued, was more applicable since it would facilitate the "elimination of unemployment and the achievement of rapid socio-economic re-orientation."[37] Another writer, Dr. T. K. Agbie, expressed contempt for a concept that would "spoil our peaceful and prosperous island." Rejecting Black Power on the grounds that it was incompatible with the existing "racial harmony, progressive Government and standard of living," he expressed hope that the government would "crush this ugly rebellion."[38] Similarly, Violent Purplint (a pseudonym) abstained from embracing Black Power. "It is dangerous," she wrote, "to sympathize with Black Power. The ideas they are propagating are much more dangerous than the violence."[39] Some letters were characterized by racial self-hatred in their criticism of Black Power. That of Charles Williams stated, "I am a dark Negro through no fault of mine. . . . In my opinion black is an ugly word to describe a person." "Black Power," he continued, "is no compliment."[40]

In general, the reactions to Black Power varied. Certain generalizations can be made, however. More affluent members of Trinidadian society, especially blacks, felt threatened by the concept of Black Power and the aims of the February revolt. The poor, on the other hand, particularly urban blacks, were sympathetic to the goals of the movement as long as it promised material improvement. This attitude among the urban poor reflected their limited interests and was ultimately responsible for the reformist nature and eventual disintegration of the February revolt.

Evidence of divisions within the movement first emerged on March 18 when the Black Panthers withdrew their support from the February revolt.[41] The division between the Panthers and NJAC arose out of ideological differences. Brian Meeks suggests that while "objectively the massive demonstrators stood for revolution, large sections of the demonstrators had hoped for reform from the PNM."[42] Ideologically, the Black Panthers stood with the reform-oriented demonstrators. At most, they saw the role of the demonstrations as a way of forcing the People's National Movement to democratize the society. The Panthers' departure, however, did not seriously affect the movement for at no point in their history had they been able to organize and recruit a large number of Trinidadians.

On March 23, sensing a moment of weakness in the revolt, Prime Minister Eric Williams addressed the nation. Attempting to regain his progressive image, Dr. Williams announced that several changes were taking place in the government. For one thing, he had fired the minister of industry, commerce, and petroleum, the same person who had charged that the Black Power demonstrations were Communist-inspired plots. Next, he stated that a 5 percent special tax would be levied on companies and the revenue used to combat unemployment. In addition, the prime minister warned the business community "to set its house in order with respect to discrimination in employment." He also mentioned that further government intervention in the private sector was being planned, including a proposal to purchase a 51 percent interest in the largest sugar producer, Caroni Ltd.[43]

To the surprise of many Trinidadians, the prime minister expressed his support for Black Power: "The fundamental feature of the demonstrators was the insistence on Black Dignity, the manifestation of Black consciousness and the demand for Black economic power. The entire population must understand that these demands are perfectly legitimate and are entirely in the interest of the community as a whole. If this is Black Power then I am for Black Power."[44]

Although all of these proposals were quite radical in the context of the PNM's official platform, they were incapable of pacifying the revolutionary movement. The next day, in fact, the police in an attempt to disperse angry protesters from the commercial district, where some were involved in the destruction of private property, released tear gas which only served to exacerbate an already tense situation. Thus, the expectation that government-initiated reforms would heal the division between the demonstrators and the ruling elite appeared to have been unfulfilled.

Several observers have concluded that March 24 was the critical point of the revolutionary movement, because many of the reform-oriented demonstrators were now looking for "a confrontation to bring the regime down as quickly as possible."[45] This interpretation is misleading, however, given the events that occurred between March 25 and April 21. Although the numerical strength of the protesters continued to increase, the reformist nature of the movement remained apparent, as reflected in the NJAC manifesto entitled "What the NJAC Wants Is What Any Poor Man in the Community Wants." Its demands included "food, shelter, employment, dignity to regain his manhood, having a place in the political structure; to be able to play some part in the economy and be able to contribute meaningfully to his family and community."[46]

The manifesto condemned "the evil society" that was oppressing poor black people. As such, the movement was "prepared to take any action in order to bring about the important changes."[47] Elaborating on the manifesto, Granger told a crowd in Woodford Square that "we are in the midst of a revolution" and that "it was a confrontation between the poor and the rich, the haves and the havenots."[48] Although Granger's rhetoric suggests the application of a class analysis, participants in the revolutionary movement and members of the NJAC shunned any references to Marxism. For example, when George Weekes, president of the Oil-field Workers Trade Union, addressed the demonstrators as "Comrades," the crowd shouted "None ah dat. . . . We are brothers and sisters."[49]

The final stage of the revolutionary movement began on April 9 with the funeral of Basil Davis, a twenty-two-year-old NJAC supporter who had been shot and killed by the police. In a spectacular display of strength, between 30,000 and 100,000 people joined the movement's procession for its first martyr.[50] In the aftermath of the funeral, A. N. R. Robinson, minister of external affairs and a likely successor to Eric Williams, announced his resignation from the cabinet. Explaining his move, Robinson stated that he did not feel that a "sufficiently serious attempt [has been] made by the government to remove the underlying causes of the present situation in the country."[51]

Following the funeral, the situation became increasingly explosive. The Black Power leaders were beginning to enhance their strength by forming loose alliances with various organizations and individuals who had traditionally supported the PNM, such as the National Association of Steelbandsmen, the Oil-field Workers Trade Union, the Trinidad and Tobago Electricity Commission Workers, and several progressive labor leaders from the transportation and sugar unions. Previously, Michael Als, leader of the Young Power organization, expressed his organization's support for the February revolt by issuing a statement calling on the government to stop granting pioneer status to foreign companies, to drop all charges against NJAC, and to lift the ban on the Trinidadian-born Black Power advocate, Stokely Carmichael.[52] The Young Power organization also called for a radical transformation of the political, economic, and educational structure.[53]

Collectively, the various organizations announced plans for a general strike that would take place on April 21 and 22. The significance of this alliance cannot be overstated. The organizations, especially the steelband movement and the Young Power organization, had been cultural and political outlets for a large section of the black population. The PNM, which in the past had derived its strength from a coalition of progressive intellectuals, students, workers, and unemployed, now found itself opposed by precisely those sectors.

In response to the impending strike, Prime Minister Williams declared a State of Emergency on April 21. The declaration imposed a dawn-to-dusk curfew and led to the arrest of fifteen Black Power leaders. In contrast to its past behavior, the government decapitated the revolutionary movement by arresting its leaders. Thus, after April 21 protest activities almost ceased. On April 21, however, one more incident occurred that paralyzed Trinidad. A section of the 750-man Defence Force, when called up to reinforce the State of Emergency, revolted against its superiors. While it is now clear that the linkage between the army's revolt and the Black Power movement was superficial, the event triggered the fear of a military coup. Fortunately for the government, the Coast Guard was able to contain the "mutineers" who were eventually arrested.[54]

The historical record surrounding the February revolt is in many respects incomplete. Even today, one can only speculate about the central objectives of the revolutionary movement. Although NJAC spoke emphatically about the "new man," the "new society," and the need to "regain black manhood," the pronouncements remained vague and ambiguous. The February revolt was not characterized by a coherent ideology, specific strategy, or definite objectives. Critics and supporters alike, for example, repeatedly questioned the aims of the Black Power movement. An editorial in the *Trinidad Guardian* on March 11, 1970, stated that "the dissenters have so far not been able to articulate quite properly the precise causes of their discontent."[55] Several days later, the *Guard-*

*ian* reiterated its criticism in addition to questioning the viability of constant demonstrations: "Further demonstrations would only tire out the demonstrators themselves and make protest seem pointless. It is necessary for the demonstrators to articulate their demands."[56] NJAC responded by rejecting suggestions to introduce specific demands into the movement, maintaining that the people wanted more demonstrations.

NJAC's Jacobinism and reluctance to organize the demonstrators around specific objectives, plus the fact that the majority of the demonstrators were narrowly focused on reforms within the conventional political system, were in part responsible for the February revolt's failure to effect change in Trinidad. Yet, the larger responsibility for the movement's failure rests with the fact that the revolt involved only a small segment of the population. The lack of participation suggests that discontent was not as pervasive or as intense as some observers argued. Moreover, even if NJAC had had a more coherent ideology, structure, and program of action, it is doubtful that the revolt could have brought the government down. Throughout the rebellion, the government forces were never seriously challenged. Nevertheless, the movement awakened the Trinidadian elite to the plight of young urban blacks who out of frustration embraced Black Power as a viable alternative to their deplorable predicament.

The urban unemployed, however, did more than just embrace Black Power. Whereas before the February revolt Black Power's orientation provided a far-reaching analysis and program of action (which included a dependency analysis conditioned by West Indian realities, explored the causes of underdevelopment, and emphasized a racial and class analysis in the context of the West Indian political economy), the objectives of the urban poor limited its demands to a redress of socioeconomic grievances.

NJAC members were, in turn, confronted with the option of making their analysis relevant to local conditions or being bypassed altogether. Out of political necessity, NJAC opted for the former despite its limited appeal. The reformist nature of the February revolt was illustrated, for example, at a rally several days before the State of Emergency at which NJAC recounted the movement's victories: "Pay increases for the police regiment, Coast Guard and allocations for the 'improvement' of the steelband movement . . . because of the Black Power Movement."[57] Although there was no mention of ameliorating the deplorable socioeconomic conditions, the above-mentioned gains give credence to the revolt's reformist orientation.

Finally, despite its limitations during the February revolt, Black Power called attention to the alarming socioeconomic conditions in Trinidad in addition to representing a nationalist expression on the part of radical intellectuals and students. In the Trinidadian context, social grievances and nationalist aspirations were not mutually exclusive. The class/color correlation and its connection to foreign capital provided NJAC with sufficient fuel to link both causes under the rubric of Black Power. Moreover, the various dimensions of Black Power served to raise questions about the social order and the role of foreign capital, and most importantly reminded the nation of its failure to alleviate, as promised, the deplorable socioeconomic conditions of most Trinidadians. When it was perceived that the People's National Movement had failed to transform Trinidad, radical intellectuals, students, and the urban dispossessed concluded that "Massa Day No Dun Yet."

## Notes

1. Ryan, *Race and Nationalism*, p. 384.
2. Gray, "State Power," pp. 347–52.
3. Ibid., p. 347.
4. Payne, "The Rodney Riots," p. 165.
5. James Millette, "The Black Revolution," Port of Spain (n.d.), pp. 6–9.
6. On February 11, 1969, a group of West Indian students attending Sir George Williams University began to complain about racist practices by a biology professor. Hoping to have their case heard, the students took their grievances to a university board. This was to no avail. Finally the students staged a sit-in at the university's $1.6 million computer center, after which followed a ten-hour battle with police resulting in the destruction of the computer center, school cafeteria, and faculty lounge. Consequently, the students were arrested and charged with conspiracy to commit arson and felonious mischief. See "Students Riot in Canada," *Trinidad Guardian*, February 13, 1969, p. 1.
7. Riviere, *Black Power*, p. 23.
8. Ibid., p. 14.
9. Ryan, *Race and Nationalism*, pp. 427–28.
10. Riviere, *Black Power*, p. 27.
11. Meeks, "The Development of the 1970 Revolution," p. 251.
12. Riviere, *Black Power*, p. 54.
13. David Nicholls suggests that throughout the Black Power movement less than one percent of the participants were of East Indian origin. "East Indians and Black Power," p. 447.
14. Carl Stone develops this concept in *Class, Race and Political Behaviour*, p. 98.
15. Girvan, *The Political Economy of Race*, p. 1.

16. Riviere, *Black Power*, p. 27.

17. Hagopian, *The Phenomenon of Revolution*, pp. 11–12, 317.

18. Ryan, *Race and Nationalism*, p. 363.

19. Meeks, "The Development of the 1970 Revolution," p. 194.

20. "Jour Ouvert 1970," *Trinidad Guardian*, February 10, 1970, p. 1.

21. Raoul Pantin and Hollis Boisselle, "Black Power March in City: Demonstrators Take Over Roman Catholic Cathedral," *Trinidad Guardian*, February 27, 1970, p. 1.

22. Raoul Pantin, "Bail Refused 8 Charged under Riot Ordinance," *Trinidad Guardian*, February 28, 1970, p. 1.

23. Raoul Pantin, "Marchers Go to Shanty Town—Groups Come to Town to Join Demonstrations," *Trinidad Guardian*, March 5, 1970, p. 1.

24. Ibid.

25. Ibid.

26. Raoul Pantin, "Black Power March to San Juan—14,000 at Cruisee Meeting," *Trinidad Guardian*, March 7, 1970, p. 1.

27. John Babb and Raoul Pantin, "Minister Blames Red Agitators," *Trinidad Guardian*, March 10, 1970, p. 1.

28. Ibid.

29. John Babb, "DLP Calls on Government to Break Silence," *Trinidad Guardian*, March 7, 1970, p. 1.

30. This was the general impression conveyed by the *Trinidad Guardian* between February and April 1970.

31. Raoul Pantin, "Archbishop Invited to Join 'Power' March to Caroni," *Trinidad Guardian*, March 11, 1970, p. 1.

32. Raoul Pantin, "March to Caroni Incident-Free," *Trinidad Guardian*, March 13, 1970, p. 1.

33. Nicholls, "East Indians and Black Power," p. 446.

34. Gasesh Hall, "Indians Are Not Black," Letter to the Editor, *Trinidad Guardian*, April 8, 1970, p. 10.

35. D. Jugmohan, "We Do Not Intend to Support You," Letter to the Editor, *Trinidad Guardian*, April 8, 1970, p. 8.

36. Nicholls, "East Indians and Black Power," p. 447.

37. R. K. Richardson, "'Majority Power' Would Be Better," Letter to the Editor, *Trinidad Guardian*, March 26, 1970.

38. T. K. Agbie, "We Do Not Need Black Power," Letter to the Editor, *Trinidad Guardian*, April 4, 1970, p. 8.

39. Violent Purplint, "Let's Have Poor Power, Not Black Power," Letter to the Editor, *Trinidad Guardian*, April 2, 1970, p. 8.

40. Charles Williams, "Black Power—Ridiculous Misnomer," Letter to the Editor, *Trinidad Guardian*, April 26, 1970, p. 10.

41. "Panthers Take Back Seat at Black Power Meeting," *Trinidad Guardian*, March 18, 1970, p. 1.

42. Meeks, "The Development of the 1970 Revolution," p. 212.

43. Eric Williams, "Prime Minister's Television Broadcast," *Trinidad Guardian*, March 23, 1970, pp. 3–10.

44. Ibid.

45. Lloyd Best, "The February Revolution," *Tapia*, December 1970, p. 1.

46. "Black Power: The Stirrings of an Integrative Society," *Trinidad Guardian*, March 21, 1970, p. 6.

47. "Black Power Goes West," *Trinidad Guardian*, March 26, 1970, p. 1.

48. Ibid.

49. John Babb, "Police Use Tear Gas on Crowd," *Trinidad Guardian*, March 25, 1970, p. 1.

50. "Power Funeral for Shot Youth," *Trinidad Guardian*, April 8, 1970, p. 1.

51. "Talk of War by NJAC," *Trinidad Guardian*, April 14, 1970, p. 1.

52. "Young Power March in the South," *Trinidad Guardian*, May 26, 1968, p. 3.

53. "Black Power Goes West," *Trinidad Guardian*, March 26, 1970, p. 1.

54. For a detailed discussion of the Trinidad mutiny, see "Peace Talks Going on at Chag.: Dissidence in Army Confirmed," *Trinidad Guardian*, April 23, 1970, p. 1, and "Situation Very Much under Control," *Trinidad Guardian*, April 25, 1970, p. 10.

55. "And Now to the Constructive Phase," *Trinidad Guardian*, March 11, 1970, p. 10.

56. "Showing Solidarity," *Trinidad Guardian*, March 14, 1970, p. 6.

57. "Gov't Planning Snap Elections, NJAC Claims," *Trinidad Guardian*, April 4, 1970, p. 1.

## 7

Blanca G. Silvestrini

# Contemporary Puerto Rico

## A Society of Contrasts

**P**uerto Rico, was swiftly incorporated into the United States' economic and political worlds after the American occupation in 1898. At the same time, Puerto Ricans were struggling to maintain their cultural symbols and world views and to resist the process of acculturation that began then. Now, two different basic systems of social organization coexist in Puerto Rico.

Poverty and abundance live side by side. High-technology industries bloom amid declining agriculture and unemployment. An urban society is splattered with the most traditional values. Why do these seeming cultural contradictions persist after nearly a century of close contact with the United States? Which historical processes have shaped the Puerto Rican experience in the twentieth century?

In an attempt to clarify these striking contrasts, this chapter first confronts the effects of social and economic change on the lives of Puerto Ricans. Second, it discusses ways in which Puerto Ricans have resisted the imposition of new sociopolitical values and economic forms. It thus explores some of the variables involved in the changes and portrays various social, economic, political, and cultural elements that have interacted to produce the present Puerto Rican society.

## Economic and Social Changes after the American Occupation

The Spanish-American War unleashed U.S. expansionism. The United States had to delineate a policy toward its newly acquired territories as well as to redefine its cultural and economic role in the Western Hemisphere. New markets and opportunities for capital investments opened up for American corporations in the Caribbean, and their new economic role then demanded more active political participation in the region by the U.S. government. Geopolitical concerns and a policy of protecting capital investments led to U.S. military interventions throughout the Caribbean—in Cuba, the Dominican Republic, Haiti, Panama, and Nicaragua. Puerto Rico was no exception.

From the moment Spain ceded Puerto Rico to the United States in 1898, Puerto Rico—in contrast to Cuba and the Philippines—became a possession of the United States.[1] Puerto Ricans, though, were not immediately granted U.S. citizenship, nor did they have representation in the United States Congress. The U.S. strategic and economic interests on the island were safeguarded by the acquisition of land for military purposes. Soon after the occupation, the government of the United States began to secure military bases and lands in neighboring Vieques and Culebra. The island thus acquired a significant role in the North American hemispheric defense policy toward Latin America.

In 1900 the United States Congress approved a new organic law for the island, the Foraker Act, which determined political and economic relations with Puerto Rico. Although the Foraker Act terminated the military government and provided a civil structure for the executive branch, the main decisions of government were retained in North American hands. The president of the United States appointed the governor and cabinet members. The latter in turn were also ex officio members of the elected legislature. Even the justices of the Supreme Court were presidential appointees. Through this appointive structure the United States controlled the three branches of government and the central decision-making process locally.

The Foraker Act had long-term economic consequences as well. It provided the legal framework for economic dependency through the incorporation of the Puerto Rican economy into the American scheme. In fact, although the political structure of the government was reformed in 1917 through the Jones Act, many of the provisions related to the economy have endured well into the 1980s. The North American tariff structure, the U.S. currency, and congressional commercial regulations were extended to the island. Puerto Rico could not negotiate commercial treaties with foreign nations or design an independent tariff structure. With the new regulations, all products shipped between the island and the United States had to be carried in American vessels. The peso, the Spanish currency in circulation in Puerto Rico, was recalled at a 60 percent devaluation. These measures affected prices, the availability of products, and accumulated wealth; stagnation in wages created an even more difficult economic situation for the workers.

The island's three main exports—coffee, sugar, and tobacco—were all affected. In the sugar industry, the process of mechanization and concentration of land in fewer hands, which had begun in the late nineteenth century, accelerated. Large American corporations, many of them with capital investments in other areas of the Caribbean such as Cuba and the Dominican Republic, bought land, establishing the land and factory units called *centrales*. By 1928 U.S.-owned centrales controlled approximately 80 percent of the sugar lands and processed more than 60 percent of the sugar exported.[2] The peso devaluation and scarcity of currency made it very difficult for the Puerto Rican *colonos*, the sugarcane growers who supplied the centrales, to expand or modernize their farms in competition with foreign investors.

Working conditions changed significantly on the plantations and centrales. Intensified sugar production promoted the decline of subsistence agriculture by taking land away from small farmers and increased the use of seasonal labor at lower and lower wages. The result was that by 1920, about 75 percent of the population depended in some way on the sugar industry. When labor began to organize, the sugar corporations adopted long-standing North American management tactics. They employed strikebreakers, closed shops, and overt coercion to counter the workers' demands. The workers steadily struggled against these tactics, and their resistance provided some of the most forceful confrontations with the American government at the beginning of the twentieth century.

During the first three decades of the American regime, tobacco production increased, although it never reached the level of sugar. Growing tobacco provided an alternative livelihood for some of the former coffee hacendados, who suffered bankruptcy as a result of the 1900 tariff regulations and subsequent adverse economic policies. With the decrease in labor-intensive coffee production, a new migratory movement from the rural mountain areas to lower lands and cities began. Tobacco processing and needlework provided alternative working opportunities. Although most of the tobacco cultivation as such remained in Puerto Rican hands, the processing and export phases of the industry became the domain of American investments. Factories were organized both near the cultivation sights and in San Juan to manufacture tobacco ready for exportation. Women became the favored work force in the industry; they were perceived as cheap labor with little possibility of challenging the working conditions.

The needlework industry flourished after World War I. American textile companies contracted with Puerto Rican intermediaries, who established needlework manufacturing centers. In this capitalist environment women were hired to work in rudimentary factories under squalid conditions. More than 60 percent of the needleworkers earned less than $0.02 per hour in extended workdays usually lasting more than twelve hours. Both tobacco and needlework products were geared toward the American market, where they were sold at impressive marked-up prices.[3] But contrary to industrialists' expectations, women in both the tobacco and the needlework industries soon began to mobilize. They either organized their own labor unions or joined already active organizations which struggled to improve the workers' living conditions.

Economic inequality spawned a social inequality that was reflected in the labor struggles of the early twentieth century. During the 1890s a trade union movement had begun to emerge in Puerto Rico. Although it attracted some sugar workers, its main constituency was artisans, particularly typographers and those who processed tobacco by hand. A labor federation was organized in 1899 as an attempt to unite artisans and agricultural workers. The establishment of an elaborate capitalist industrial structure geared toward export stimulated the emergence of a new kind of labor organization and a revived consciousness among sugar, tobacco, and textile workers. Although they still organized under the trade union structure, the issues discussed and their modes of struggle were closer to the industrial world. And while they still considered collective bargaining their major tool for attaining changes in their working conditions, labor legislation proposals were launched as alternatives. Therefore, workers began to participate more actively in politics, advancing new social measures. In search of more power, some of these groups affiliated with the American labor movement. They also organized the Socialist party in 1915. The labor struggles became a microcosm of some of the contradictions in Puerto Rico. On one hand, the movement severely criticized the practices of the American companies on the island; but on the other, its leadership supported the permanent incorporation of Puerto Rico into American society as a guarantee of broader liberties.

Gradually Puerto Rico became a valuable market for U.S. exports as well as an important supplier of commodities. Unemployment, the devaluation of currency, higher prices, and the decrease in subsistence agriculture created a greater dependence on imported goods. By 1910, the island was already the twelfth largest consumer of U.S. goods in the world. By 1938 almost 92 percent of Puerto Rican imports came from the United States, and 98 percent of its exports went to the mainland.[4]

U.S.-mandated restrictive trade policies and North American capital investments during the first three decades of the twentieth century transformed the Puerto Rican economy. It changed gradually from primarily subsistence agriculture to a cash-oriented structure dependent on U.S. markets. Urbanization, the consolidation of landholdings, and a growing gap between rich and poor were the predictable result.

Because of Puerto Rico's close ties to the U.S. economy, the economic depression of the 1930s had severe consequences on the island. It upset the scheme of heavy capital investments supporting the export of a few major agricultural products. As a result, Puerto Rico became even more dependent on U.S. markets. The value of all exports decreased substantially between 1927 and 1939, consonant with reduced demand in North America. Prices of imports increased, further affecting the adverse balance of trade. Moreover, industries tried to retrench by curtailing some operations in Puerto Rico in order to reduce expenses and increase profits. They also feared the effects of protective social legislation, such as minimum wages, the eight-hour workday, and workmen's compensation.

Puerto Rican working families suffered the most. Unemployment, the increase in prices, the lack of currency, and the scarcity of basic goods caused an intense economic crisis on the island. Income per capita decreased rapidly, from the already low level of $122 in 1929–30 to $86 in 1932–33. Import prices increased almost 65 percent in the twenty years before 1940. By 1935, the U.S. secretary of the interior, Harold Ickes, pointed out that Puerto Rico

has been the victim of the laissez faire economy which has developed the rapid growth of great absentee owned sugar corporations, which have absorbed much land formerly belonging to small independent growers and who in consequence have been reduced to virtual economic serfdom. While the inclusion of Puerto Rico within our tariff walls has been highly beneficial to the stockholders of those corporations, the benefits have not been passed down to the mass of Puerto Ricans. . . . There is today more widespread misery and destitution and far more unemployment in Puerto Rico than at any previous time in its history.[5]

The social consequences of these problems were immediately felt. Widespread unemployment was common. Seasonal work, low wages, and unsatisfactory working conditions existed for those fortunate enough to find work. Migration became an alternative for many. From the beginning of the century small numbers of workers had migrated to the United States and to other Caribbean areas. With the economic crisis of the 1930s, however, the number of migrants greatly increased; most went to North America. (See Table 7-1.) This was a temporary and inadequate solution to the island's unemployment problem, for many migrants lived in conditions in the United States worse than

**Table 7-1**

Puerto Rican Net Migration to the United States

| Year | Number of Migrants |
|------|-------------------|
| 1900–1909 | 2,000 |
| 1910–1919 | 11,000 |
| 1920–1929 | 42,000 |
| 1930–1939 | 18,000 |
| 1940–1949 | 151,000 |
| 1950–1959 | 430,000 |

Source: José L. Vázquez Calzada, *Las causas y efectos de la emigración puertorriqueña*, School of Public Health, University of Puerto Rico, mimeographed.

Note: Net migration means the number of persons who remained in the United States once those who returned to Puerto Rico are subtracted.

they had left in Puerto Rico. But as Frank Bonilla and Ricardo Campos have pointed out, "American citizenship, conveniently decreed during World War I by the Jones Act, allowed the already itinerant work force of Puerto Rican nationals to circulate freely through increasingly extended circuits within the U.S. labor market. Thereafter, workers and capital traversed closely-linked, though inverse, paths between the colony and metropolis."[6]

## Struggles for the Definition of Political Status

Since the beginning of American rule in Puerto Rico, the uneasy relationship between the two has been a constant source of friction and controversy. The struggles to end the military regime and later to amend the Foraker Act and clarify the relationship with the United States led to the demarcation of three major political positions that differed in their proposed response to the status question: independence, statehood, or autonomy. Advocates of the three positions coalesced into parties, which debated endlessly about access to the political structures. But with some structural modifications in the composition of the legislature and the appointment of certain functionaries, the U.S. government retained control of local affairs in Puerto Rico until the new constitution of 1952. Education, public health, and criminal justice, for example, remained directly in American hands for decades, since they were conceived as pivotal in the Americanization process.

Politicians thought that with access to government positions or seats in the legislature they could change the island's relationship with the United States. Meanwhile, the critical decisions that affected the lives of the Puerto Ricans continued to be made on the mainland—in federal agencies, the United States Congress, and the United States Supreme Court. Political strife surfaced and a string of seemingly contradictory political coalitions ensued in an effort to win elections and gain more control over issues affecting Puerto Ricans. On one hand, political parties wanted to win the elections, in hopes of solving the status question according to their individual preferences. On the other, political leaders representing the three different political-status alternatives looked for support in Washington and gradually began dancing to the tunes of American politics.

Even the Partido Socialista Puertorriqueño, founded in 1915 as the political arm of the organized labor movement, followed some of these trends. The basic platform of the party centered on labor-related social and economic reforms. The Socialist party struggled to obtain improved working conditions, more schools and health care centers for the poor, higher wages and the eight-hour workday. It also provided the first formal forum for women to voice their demands for improved living conditions. Later, though, the Socialist party also became involved in party politics and the quest for status.

In the 1930s the three main political factions better defined their expectations about the relationship with the United States. The Republican and Socialist parties united as the defenders of statehood in an apparent contradictory coalition. The Republicans had traditionally represented the interests of the large landowners and American corporations; the Socialists embodied the labor interests. Their pro-statehood interests, and the economic corollary of the promotion of the capitalists' interests, dominated their political action for the eight years that they jointly controlled the government. The Nationalist party, also reorganized after 1932, took a much more radical stand against the role of American corporations and government on the island. Turbulent demonstrations of workers, students, and small landowners challenged the colonial model that had dominated the first third of the twentieth century.

Workers' unrest flourished during the 1930s in spite of the Socialist party's efforts to minimize strikes and to project an image of governmental efficiency in the coalition. In the sugar and needlework industries, especially, great discontent surfaced, with both government decisions and the labor leadership's handling of workers' issues. Gradually, a new leadership emerged and began to organize groups of workers not affiliated with the traditional labor organizations.

The Nationalist party initiated a strong campaign to support both political and economic independence. Faced with the economic depression, it intensified its defense of the independence of Puerto Rico, gaining support from some workers and intellectuals. Government opposition, however, was energetic, producing several violent incidents with wide repercussions in the United States. Civil rights were denied to participants in the Nationalist movements. The severe retaliatory measures applied by the American government on the island further alienated a number of political groups.

The new incorporation of Puerto Rico within the United States' economic structure had dramatic political implications. Some New Deal legislation—for example, the establishment of agricultural quotas and of federal minimum wages—had a direct negative impact on exports. Some large corporations, fearful of increased government restraints, preferred to decrease their investments in Puerto Rico or to move elsewhere. Even nature seemed to make things worse, as two furious hurricanes in 1928 and 1932 blasted the island and severely curtailed agricultural exports. Recent calculations have indicated that in 1937 "Puerto Rico needed to export 36.2 percent more in volume . . . to purchase the same quantity of imports as it did in 1910–14."[7]

By 1940 Puerto Rico had become an economic dependency of the United States, with extremely limited possibilities of self-sustenance. American capital was the main source of finance for economic activities; therefore, the priorities for investments, market preferences, and prices were decided on the mainland. Subsistence agriculture had almost disappeared, leaving the population dependent on food imports from the United States. Government tried to develop a new role for itself in economic matters to alleviate the crisis. Despite the New Deal programs and some new social legislation, little was achieved in ameliorating poverty on the island during the depression.

## The Times of Hope, from the 1940s to the 1960s

The year 1941 opened a new direction in Puerto Rican politics. It led to a realignment of political parties, a reformed relationship with the United States, broad economic changes, a redefinition of the role of the government, and a sweeping social transformation. The roots of some of Puerto Rico's major problems in the 1980s—excessive consumerism, almost total dependence on the U.S. economy, widespread reliance on federal aid, deep social class differ-ences, among others—can also be traced to the policies in the early 1940s. Confronted with a stagnant economy and worsening living conditions, a new coalition of forces emerged with the foundation of the Partido Popular Democrático (PPD; Popular Democratic party) in 1938. Led by Luis Muñoz Marín, a group of dissenting members of the Liberal party (a party associated with autonomy under the American government) succeeded in attracting small landowners, workers, and professionals to the new party. Initially, its electoral campaign was geared toward the peasants' needs, although the PPD also sup-ported issues attractive to labor organizations. Nevertheless, the most impor-tant political decision of the party at its inception was to defer the status issue. The other political parties still debated the status question, but the *populares* postponed indefinitely in the electoral campaigns the direct discussion of the relationships with the United States. Although in many ways over the years the new social and economic policies launched by the party during its terms in government were actually defining these ties, for at least two elections the PPD claimed that status was not an issue. There was a strong emphasis on govern-ment control of the sugar industry, division of the large landholdings, and the reduction of unemployment through the promotion of industrialization.

Meanwhile, popular support for the Republican-Socialist Coalition, strong throughout the 1930s, had been waning. The Socialist voters were disen-chanted with the coalition's failure to support the measures of the Fair Labor Standards Act and its constant rejection of workers' demands. The Republicans were divided by internal struggles for personal political control. A new political style emerged in the 1940 elections. The campaign was taken to the small towns and rural areas in an attempt to obtain the support of groups of people not yet incorporated into the political life. In 1940 the Popular Democratic party won the elections. A year later it gained the support of some elected legislators, obtaining a working plurality in both houses.

The program of socioeconomic reforms proposed by the Popular Demo-cratic party initially included measures that gave more control of the economy to the local government. It created a Land Authority to guide agrarian reform and appointed a Minimum Wages Board to look into the best interests of workers and industry. A government-controlled electric company provided better service to consumers and promoted industrial use of electricity. Each of these measures responded to specific political interests of groups supporting the PPD. To carry out these reforms, major changes in the executive branch were essential. Since the beginning of the century, most of the American-appointed governors had little understanding of Puerto Rico's special needs.

With few exceptions, their previous knowledge of the island was scant, their administrative skills were negligible, and their efforts extended no farther than preventing political unrest and keeping the island as a U.S. possession.

In 1941 President Franklin D. Roosevelt appointed Rexford G. Tugwell governor of Puerto Rico. His stewardship marked a sharp break with past governors. He had been one of the framers of President Roosevelt's policy on the mainland, and had direct experience with the New Deal's program in Puerto Rico in the 1930s. Tugwell was able to establish a firm collaboration with the elected legislative branch at the same time that he strengthened the executive. His knowledge and attitudes cleared the way for a new program of reforms for Puerto Rico.

A priority of government in 1941 was the reorganization of agriculture. Large landholdings by American corporations were a serious problem. Since the beginning of the century the sugar corporations had been illegally acquiring land in excess of the 500-acre limit, combining large landholdings into a few absentee hands. The Puerto Rican colonos had been slowly losing their land and their independence because they could not compete for capital or technological advances with the sugar barons, who controlled most of the land and labor.

By 1940, however, Puerto Rico suffered from minifundism as well as agricultural consolidation. Seventy-five percent of the farmers cultivated less than 20 acres and occupied only 15 percent of the land. These small farms, most of them dedicated to food production, did not have enough resources to compete with the agricultural imports coming from the United States. At the same time, in 1940 there were 342 farms of more than 500 acres; they represented only 1 percent of the farms, but comprised more than 30 percent of the tilled land.

The political promise of the Popular Democratic party was to divide the large landholdings among the peasants. Therefore, the purpose of the agrarian reform, in giving away in perpetuity small plots of land, was to provide homes for the peasants. The reforms did not promote the development of commercial agriculture, since the small farmers seldom had the technical knowledge or the financial resources needed for intensive farming. In 1948, the Land Law was amended to provide for farms of 5 to 25 acres. But again the government did not provide the financial resources necessary for commercial exploitation of the land. There was no protection against the strong competition with American products.

Manufacturing began to increase slowly during the decade of the 1940s. The first industries supported by government were those manufacturing cement and glass. The rum industry experienced a notable growth, especially during the years of World War II. Direct government loans were approved for industry and technical assistance was provided. By 1946 the government decided that industrialization rather than agriculture should be the priority for economic growth. The economic policy also changed. Government would no longer own industries but would support private investment with favorable tax laws. The legislature approved a new tax exemption for industrial capital, hoping thereby to attract investments that would boost employment. In addition, the government used public funds to sponsor a promotional campaign in the United States, which met with immediate success.

In 1947 the Popular Democratic party launched Operation Bootstrap as the official economic policy of Puerto Rico. It included some of the measures mentioned above. Of particular importance was a ten-year tax holiday for certain new industries. To attract tourists, government invested directly in the construction of a big hotel in San Juan, the Caribe Hilton, which opened in 1949. The main thrust of Operation Bootstrap was to attract industries from the United States that would employ large numbers of workers, using imported goods and exporting finished products. The program of industrial development gradually attracted many new companies, and it radically transformed the economy and society of Puerto Rico.

The industrialization policy sponsored by the Popular Democratic party implied a basic change in its initial views of not discussing the political status of the island. In order to attract new industries and capital investments, Puerto Rico would have to remain permanently associated with the United States because some corporations refused to locate their plants in an independent Puerto Rico. To alleviate their fears, influential members of the PPD floated the idea of developing a third alternative to the status question, then hovering between full statehood and independence. Among them were many of the old supporters of autonomy. Not surprisingly, therefore, the new alternative had a familiar ring. The idea proposed was a *dominion*, in the British sense, like Australia, Canada, and New Zealand at the time. In the British system those colonies had achieved political and administrative changes while remaining under Commonwealth control. In the case of Puerto Rico, however, some political groups demanded at least the inclusion of an elective governor.

Meanwhile, during World War II, popular national movements began to demand the free self-determination of all peoples. The Atlantic Charter, signed in 1941 by the president of the United States and the British prime minister, recognized these rights. In Puerto Rico, the supporters of independence requested from the United States the application of the charter. Even the legislature, controlled by the PPD, asked for political reforms to take effect when the war ended. A bilateral commission was appointed in 1943 to study possible reforms of the Jones Act. After some years of debate on the island but little action, international pressures, brought through the United Nations, forced the United States to look at its relationship with Puerto Rico. The island was included, to the embarrassment of the United States, in the list of colonies that had to submit annual reports on the state of decolonization.

Actual reforms in Puerto Rico were few. The position of governor of the island was made elective and a new appointive post, Commissioner of the United States in Puerto Rico, was created. The United States wanted to keep a close eye on island affairs through indirect control of the executive. Meanwhile, the governor and heads of departments had to submit periodic reports to the commissioner, who became a general supervisor for the island.

In the 1948 elections, for the first time the three political ideologies, which had been in conflict since the beginning of the century, concurred in the electoral polls. The newly formed Partido Independentista Puertorriqueño (PIP) supported the pacific struggle for the organization of a republic in Puerto Rico. The pro-statehood groups rallied behind the Partido Estadista Republicano, which brought together the old Republicans and also gathered the votes of the Socialists and some Liberals. The Popular Democratic party reoriented its political platform to oppose both statehood and independence. In their place the party proposed a formula of *gobierno propio* (or self-government) under which the United States Congress would allow Puerto Ricans to create a constitution but would also preserve economic relations with the mainland. As Luis Muñoz Marín explained, the problem of political status was a problem of volume of production because autonomy under the American flag was the only alternative for economic growth.

The result of the election was a mandate for the Popular Democratic party formula. The PPD won all seats in the Senate and the House of Representatives. Luis Muñoz Marín was the first Puerto Rican elected governor. Since all three status alternatives were represented in the elections, the results were interpreted by the PPD as overwhelming support for the new type of autonomy it proposed.

The first step toward achieving autonomy was to draw up a constitution. In 1950 the United States Congress approved a measure that authorized the islanders to adopt an agreement "in the nature of a compact so that the people of Puerto Rico may organize a government pursuant to a constitution of their own adoption."[8] The act provided for a referendum to accept or reject this idea, and the U.S. president and Congress had to approve the final version of the constitution. Public Law 600 was passed to conform with the United Nations guidelines on decolonization. In practice, though, the last word on the Puerto Rican constitutional structure rested in the hands of the United States, although the final approval procedure provided for bilateral consultation in case of modifications to the political status of the island.

The Constitutional Assembly met from September 17, 1951, to February 6, 1952. The final document provided for a government structure with ample local autonomy. It recognized full civil rights that went beyond those provided by the U.S. Constitution, as for example in recognizing equal rights for women, the right to an elementary education, and the workers' right to strike. Finally it created the Estado Libre Asociado de Puerto Rico, later loosely translated as "Commonwealth."

Once approved by Puerto Ricans in a referendum, the document was submitted to President Harry S Truman, who delivered it to Congress. Heated debates in Congress showed that the idea of a compact was not readily accepted. Congress unilaterally wanted to change the drafted constitution. For example, the draft that initially recognized the rights of Puerto Ricans to free elementary and secondary education, guaranteed work, and adequate living conditions provoked much opposition in Congress. The clause was opposed mainly by those who thought it implied Socialist ideas. To ensure final approval by Congress, this clause was amended to include only a recognition of free public education at the elementary school level.

The controversy over the new constitution led to a review of the actual relations between Puerto Rico and the United States. Together with the constitution, the United States Congress approved an amendment—Public Law 600, known also as the Puerto Rican Federal Relations Act—which reserved for the federal government the same powers that the Foraker and Jones acts provided. All federal laws were made applicable in Puerto Rico with the exception of those designed to address issues that were clearly peculiar to the mainland. Puerto Ricans thought that with the enactment of the constitution a new status had been given to the island within the framework of the American Constitution. But the United States maintained control over the same areas covered under the Foraker Act: defense, migration, trade, the postal system, and international representation. Puerto Rico continued to be a nonincorporated territory of the United States. For international purposes, however, this control had the consent of the Puerto Rican people.

In practical terms, the constitution changed the structure of the government. The office of the elective governor provided control over the executive branch, in which all appointments would be made by the elected Puerto Rican governor. The members of both the Senate and the House of Representatives were elected, providing for a broad representation of all sectors. The appointment of the judicial branch was vested in the governor, with Senate confirmation. Aspects such as education, health, justice, and welfare that had been pivotal in the Americanization of the island were now under the direct control of Puerto Ricans.

One of the government's priorities had been to improve the working and living conditions of the working class. The industrialization program sponsored by the government gradually increased the percentage of workers in industry. Wages rose significantly with factory work. Puerto Rico, although exempted from the federal minimum-wage regulations, was able to impose its own minimum-wage scales. In the decade of the 1950s, for example, wages doubled for workers in industry. Agriculture did not experience the same trend, since after 1940 it faced severe troubles and continued to decline in productivity.

A significant change in Puerto Rican society after 1950 was the incorporation of women into the industrial labor force. In 1930 women represented 26 percent of the labor force. After 1940 they virtually abandoned homework or cottage industries for the industrial workplace. In 1935 almost 36 percent of the women did paid work in their homes. Twenty-five years later that figure decreased to only 3.8 percent. By 1960 more than 80 percent of women workers labored in factories not associated with needlework.

Another change was related to the role of the labor movement. After 1940 trade unions lost importance, giving way to the organization of industrial unions. Workers of the same industry, no matter what their tasks, became members of the same union. Confronted with the weakening of the traditional labor organizations, union leadership in 1940 established a new federation— the Confederación de Trabajadores Puertorriqueños, or Confederation of Puerto Rican Workers. Its relationship with the Popular Democratic party was close, and it depended increasingly on government agencies for the resolution of labor disputes and the negotiation of new collective agreements.

Industrial growth brought deep changes in the urban landscape. Large numbers of people left the rural areas, which provided fewer opportunities for gainful employment. They clustered in cities, near industrial zones, in hopes of getting better jobs. In 1940 two out of three Puerto Ricans lived in the rural areas; twenty years later approximately half of the population lived in urban communities. The style of life in the cities also changed dramatically. New urban conglomerates emerged. Some middle-class people lived in houses of *urbanizaciones*, or carefully designed suburbs; others moved into public housing projects developed by the government. Living in the new urban areas created life-styles and consumption patterns different from those of the rural areas. Consumption of imported goods increased. Television sets, refrigerators, and imported furniture became commonplace in Puerto Rican homes. Since houses were far from the workplace, private automobiles became a common means of transportation. These material goods began acquiring a significance sufficient to distinguish people by social classes. They also accentuated U.S. economic hegemony in Puerto Rico.

Dependency on the services provided by the government also expanded, resulting in a more complex government apparatus. Social welfare became more generalized. Public health needs were met mainly by government agencies, which established hospitals and health centers throughout the island. Education was financed by public funds, with more than 25 percent of the budget committed to the expansion of the educational system.

In the rural areas, life also changed dramatically. As a result of the land distribution more people had their own plot of land. Electrification, schools, and public health units reached the countryside, providing much-needed services and reducing illiteracy and disease. Even in the rural areas the consumption patterns were modified, with most of the food bought in general stores rather than produced on farms. Radios and television sets provided a wider contact with the outside world, and gradually reduced the gap between rural and urban Puerto Rico.

The debate on the status question did not end with the enactment of the constitution. Faced with the challenge of the new commonwealth status, the pro-statehood party designed a vigorous campaign. The Republicans proposed a tax reform, higher minimum wages, subsidies to coffee and sugar producers, ownership of the *parcelas* (the plots rented by small farmers), and more scholarships for students of low income. Together with its defense of independence, the Partido Independentista Puertorriqueño proposed innovative measures of social legislation. The PIP advocated agriculture as the foundation of any sound economic policy, in sharp contrast to both the pro-statehood and pro-commonwealth parties.

The Popular Democratic party suggested the evolution of the commonwealth within a permanent association with the United States. In 1959 the commissioner of Puerto Rico in Washington introduced a bill in the United States Congress that would clarify certain areas of the relationship with the United States. It was based on the old idea of association by consent, grounded in common citizenship, defense, international relations, and markets. Puerto

Rico would retain control of its customs and could negotiate its own commercial treaties. In Congress strong opposition developed, eventually forcing the bill to be withdrawn. This left open the status question.

The three political positions recognized that the commonwealth had to be reformed. After much discussion, a plebiscite was carried out in 1967. The three status alternatives were included, but neither the Partido Estadista Republicano nor the Partido Independentista participated. Statehood and independence were represented by organizations especially formed for the plebiscite purpose. The commonwealth formula won 60 percent of the votes; statehood, 39 percent; and independence, 6 percent. The plebiscite again left the status question open, for it did not achieve a consensus among all the parties.

The failure to resolve the political status question did not directly affect the economic policy of the commonwealth. Despite the political uncertainty, the industrialization program continued. Gross investment increased 219 percent from 1950 to 1960 and 295 percent from 1960 to 1970. Per capita income grew five times, from $342 in 1950 to $1,729 in 1970. Recently, however, it has been shown that "unambiguously . . . an increasing share of production and income created in Puerto Rico has been appropriated by external investors and has been unavailable as income or for consumption or for local investment."[9] In 1960 a fifth of the income from manufacturing went back as repatriated income, while twenty years later more than half of this income returned to the United States. The problems of integration with the U.S. economy began to emerge by the beginning of the 1970s.

## Success or Failure?

The hopes of the previous decades waned as the 1970s began. Finally, the "progressive" goals of the 1940s showed an unexpected underside. Economic growth, urbanization, education, technology, consumerism, capital investment, and excessive imports all affected Puerto Rican society in significant, but not necessarily similar, ways.

In the face of the uncertainties and difficulties of changing the relationship with the United States, a new trend emerged in Puerto Rican politics. Although the status of the island was and is still unresolved, elections have been decided mainly on issues of public administration. People knew that elections as such would not solve the status question. The independence movement suffered from severe blows. Internal and leadership crises divided the movement. Independence was not presented as a feasible alternative within the new economic framework, while many people feared possible alliances with Socialist movements. Leadership struggles have resulted in the formation of relatively small but active groups supporting independence. These groups often do not rely on electoral campaigns to achieve their major goals.

Voters have been divided almost evenly in their support of the commonwealth and statehood. Since 1968 the parties representing these positions have alternated in government without achieving a dramatic and significant shift of voters to their own sides. The pro-statehood leaders preach the *estadidad jíbara*, promising to preserve what they define essentially as the Puerto Rican culture, language, and values relatively untouched by their annexation to the United States. The commonwealth supporters strive to maintain the present status of permanent association with the United States within a framework of internal autonomy. This fragile equilibrium is, nevertheless, constantly challenged. The federal courts, administrative agencies, and federal programs have constantly expanded their sphere of action on the internal affairs of Puerto Rico, sometimes with commonwealth acquiescence.

Another noticeable trend has been the gradual incorporation of mainland and island politics. Through the years the dominant American political parties had established only formal relations with Puerto Rican politicians. Traditionally, the Democrats supported candidates of the PPD, and Republicans the advocates of statehood. In the 1970s, however, some Puerto Rican politicians began to look for support from their mainland counterparts on certain issues. Of particular importance were questions related to the definition of the relationship with the United States, federal assistance, and the differential treatment that certain laws of Congress gave to Puerto Ricans. Presidential candidates in the United States courted the support of Puerto Rican political leaders in the mainland primaries and electoral campaigns. Even when Puerto Ricans could not participate directly in the U.S. presidential elections, gradually some American political issues became significant to them. Thirty years after the adoption of the Puerto Rican constitution, the commonwealth in practice has evolved into a permanent association with the United States rather than in an autonomous direction.

The economic policies launched by the government after the 1940s boosted these political developments. Once the Puerto Rican economy was bound up with the United States, a complete dependence on American markets, capital investments, and regulations (or deregulation) developed. A permanent political association with the United States had to be maintained to support the economic order. But serious economic problems began to emerge. A study by the U.S. Department of Commerce published in 1979 warned of a dislocation of the local economy due to a gap that "consists almost entirely of profits and interest income remitted to firms and creditors on the mainland."[10] After almost forty years of industrialization and modernization, high rates of unemployment and partial employment persist and almost 60 percent of the population lives at the poverty level as defined by the U.S. government.

Puerto Rico faces today the contradiction that its high-cost technology industries do not provide the expanding employment opportunities necessary for long-term development. Bonilla and Campos have found that "between 1970 and 1979 the number of employed Puerto Ricans grew by only 17.6 percent, a sharp contrast to the numbers of unemployed or those counted as surplus population, which more than doubled (116.4%). During this same period, variable capital in industry more than doubled (149.5%), while industrial jobs advanced by only 15.1 percent."[11] The problem of the repatriation of income through the payment of profits, interests, and dividends to nonresidents has sharpened in the 1980s. The picture of the Puerto Rican economy darkens when we note that "in 1980, though manufacturing apparently produced about 48 percent of *total* GNP, its *net* contribution was only 19 percent—only slightly more than its contribution for the preceding twenty years. In 1982, the net contribution of manufacturing to GNP actually decreased and was once again near its 1950 level."[12] Although improvements occurred in 1986–87, the long-term trends are not very promising.

One of the serious problems of dependence in Puerto Rico has been the island's inability to generate its own sources for financing economic activities and long-range development. In the early 1950s Puerto Rico imported around 40 percent of its total capital funds, but by 1980 the imported capital had increased to 74 percent. When manufacturing is isolated, then over 90 percent of its financing came from external sources—mostly, of course, from the United States. This situation created severe problems that in the long run resulted in the loss of domestic control over the economy.

Early in the development of the commonwealth's economic policies, agriculture was abandoned as a practical alternative to industrial development. Already in decline, agriculture began to be supplanted by manufacturing in the 1940s. By the 1970s commercial agriculture had virtually collapsed. In addition to the direct economic impact of the decline of agriculture on employment and income, the lack of production for local consumption has resulted in the importation of large amounts of food. This change had immediate consequences for the lives of Puerto Ricans. Food prices have increased, the Puerto Rican diet has been modified, and the availability of products now depends on external factors.

The importation of food products has been facilitated by assistance from the U.S. government. Federal payments constituted 20 percent of personal income in 1970 and 30 percent ten years later. Although some of these funds represent social security taxes and veterans' benefits, a large proportion comes through federal food assistance to poor families. Since its inception, for example, the food stamp program or its equivalents affected from 25 to 50 percent of Puerto Rican families. Besides having a direct impact on the economy by pumping in money, the food assistance program is a good example of the contradictions in Puerto Rican society. The original purpose of the program was to assist needy families in improving their diet. But its long-term effects constrict the same economy that it intends to aid. On one hand, the open circulation of federal government money to buy food inhibits local agriculture, since it makes imported products much more accessible. It also promotes what economists call the illusion of an affluent economy because of its effects on the purchasing power of the people. On the other hand, the social consequences of this kind of program for families have been significant. Dependency attitudes are promoted at the same time that developing skills and abilities are ignored. The program accentuates the gap between social classes; it separates those who own their own resources from those who have to depend on government assistance.

At the same time, over the years, significant forms of resistance in Puerto Rican society developed against welfare programs. Subtle forms of social resistance rooted, for example, in the lives of welfare recipients have passed unnoticed because of the greater visibility of political and other more public forms of social action. In the early 1930s, at the inception of the New Deal programs, large groups of women and men organized protests demanding work instead of welfare. Later, the free food program of the Puerto Rican government was consistently boycotted because it represented an imposition of alien values. Providing food was considered the responsibility of the family and not of the government. Above all, Puerto Rican poor families did not accede to surplus products brought from the United States, because refusal signified their struggle against another phase of the Americanization process. Today, resistance may be found in the ways the *cupones*, as the federal food assistance is known, or the more recent PAN (Program for Nutritional Assistance) are cynically administered.

There are many other forms of subtle resistance to Americanization in contemporary Puerto Rico—strong ties with extended family or similar support groups, the special language of the public housing projects and shantytowns, the emergence of nonorthodox religious beliefs, the use of naturalistic or spiritual means of healing, the disregard for the graded school system, the apparent lack of interest in learning English or its use as an alternative choice in social communication, the rites of bereavement among the poor, the *salsa* and its varied rhythms. These forms represent at the same time continuities with departures from the traditional rural values that often are identified with Puerto Rican culture. Although they have changed from the cultural expressions of rural Puerto Rico at the beginning of the century, they are ingrained in the most traditional values on the island. They are, nevertheless, the creation of culture—culture that takes from the old, transforming it into something new; the product of the continuities with the traditional world as well as of the interactions with the sociopolitical and socioeconomic environment of the twentieth century.

Change thus should not only be viewed in the gradual or sudden acquisition of American "customs" often associated with urban life. Such acquisition does take place, especially among the more privileged groups, "but at the same time new cultural and institutional forms are shaped, drawing in part on the older, pre-imperial culture and partly created anew in adaptation and in opposition to foreign impositions."[13] Many times cultural resistance of this type—subtle, indirect, but powerful and recognizable—is understood as a contradiction or even an aberration in "modern Puerto Rico." It should be viewed as a transformation of the culture and a significant component of the creation of new cultural understandings.

The experience of the return migrants to Puerto Rico is perhaps one of the best examples of this process. After years of resisting "acculturation," of preserving and protecting their culture instead of adopting American ways, they return to Puerto Rico. But in spite of their own sense of being Puerto Ricans, they are considered different. While fighting to defend what they considered Puerto Rican, they created new ways of being Puerto Rican. Their ambiguity transformed their culture into something new, although based on continuity with the old:

> yo peleo por ti, puerto rico, sabes?
> yo me defiendo por tu nombre, sabes?
> entro a tu isla, me siento extraño, sabes?
> . . . . . . . . . . . . . . . . . . . . . . . . . . . . . . . .
> me desprecias, me miras mal, me atacas mi hablar,
> mientras comes mcdonalds en discotecas americanas,
> y no pude bailar la salsa en san juan, la que yo
> bailo en mis barrios llenos de todas tus costumbres[14]

I fight for you, Puerto Rico, do you know that?
I defend your name, do you know that?
When I come to the island, I feel like a stranger, do you know that?
. . . . . . . . . . . . . . . . . . . . . . . . . . . . . . . . . . . . . . . . . . . . . . . . . . . . .
You reject me, you look down on me, you question my word,
while you eat McDonalds in American discotheques,
and I couldn't dance salsa in San Juan, as I do
in my barrios full of your traditions.

The profound lament of the poet Tato Laviera, himself a product of this process, points to the contradictions in twentieth-century Puerto Rico. Some groups claim to defend Puerto Rican culture while promoting the incorporation of the island into the American world, but many other Puerto Ricans, often struggling to survive in the new socioeconomic order, resist with strength by creating alternative ways of being in the world. The rift may be widening in the 1980s, but in the long run it may produce a better understanding of the reasons why Puerto Rico has been able to survive the powerful process of Americanization that began in 1898.

# Notes

1. For a general discussion of the changes experienced in the sugar industry in Puerto Rico by the end of the nineteenth century, see A. Ramos Mattei, *La hacienda azucarera* (San Juan: CEREP, 1981).
2. Bailey and Diffie, *Porto Rico*, pp. 133, 135.
3. Silvestrini, "Women as Workers," pp. 247–60.
4. Dietz, *Economic History of Puerto Rico*, p. 291.
5. Mathews, *Puerto Rican Politics*, p. 215.
6. Bonilla and Campos, "A Wealth of Poor," p. 134.
7. Dietz, *Economic History of Puerto Rico*, p. 159.
8. *Documents on the Constitutional History of Puerto Rico*, p. 153.
9. Dietz, *Economic History of Puerto Rico*, p. 246.
10. U.S. Department of Commerce, *Economic Study of Puerto Rico*, 2 vols. (Washington, D.C.: Government Printing Office, 1979), 2:5.
11. Bonilla and Campos, "A Wealth of Poor," p. 135.
12. Dietz, *Economic History of Puerto Rico*, p. 257.
13. Caulfield, "Imperialism, the Family, and Cultures of Resistance," p. 75.
14. Laviera, *Ame Rícan*, p. 54.

## 8

Franklin W. Knight

# Cuba

Politics, Economy, and Society, 1898–1985

s Teresita Martínez Vergne shows in Chapter 9, the end of Spanish colonialism in Cuba found the island's elite sharply divided over the most acceptable form for the state and the nature of Cuban nationalism. Throughout the nineteenth century the strains between metropolis and colony grew worse, as Spain wavered between granting political concessions and increasing the political repression on the island. Meanwhile, the dominant and articulate groups could not agree on whether Cuba should be a free and independent state, a self-governing dominion under the Spanish Crown, or a part of the United States of America. Nor could they agree on whether all the component groups—whites and nonwhites—should be included within the definition of Cuban nationalism. The plural society was a difficult concept during that time.

Partly because of this the Ten Years' War (1868–78) ended in political stalemate. The wealthy, powerful sugar producers of the western part of the island supported the continuation of colonialism, not because they were predominantly Spanish, but because they felt that their slaves and their property were more secure under a Spanish government. The insurgent Nationalists divided into four antagonistic, but not necessarily mutually exclusive camps: those who supported the continuation of slavery, those who endorsed some form of abolition, those who preferred complete political independence from Spain, and those who favored annexation to the United States. To further complicate matters, the United States had already replaced Spain as the dominant trading partner of Cuba, receiving 83 percent of all Cuban exports (compared with 6 percent that went to Spain), selling the Cubans about $1 million worth of goods per year, and investing more than $50 million in Cuba, mainly in the sugar industry.

With such important economic interests at stake, the Cuban war of independence in 1895–98 could not be confined to a dispute between colony and metropolis. It broadened inevitably into a Cuban-Spanish-American war. Nor should it have been surprising that Cuba began its political independence on January 1, 1899, under the military occupation of the United States. Having entered the conflict in its third year by declaring war against Spain on April 25, 1898, the United States virtually dictated the peace treaty signed in Paris on December 10 of that year. The war eliminated Spanish colonialism in the Americas but failed to resolve the question of Cuban political sovereignty.

## The American Military Occupations, 1899–1902 and 1906–1909

The Americans did not find political disengagement from Cuba to be an easy task. On the one hand, they held definite views about how to restructure the island to make it compatible with their own political system. Despite their struggle for political independence Cubans would be recolonized. And the Americans mistakenly thought that would be a simple matter. On the other hand, the Americans unwittingly became an important dimension of the complex domestic political machinations of Conservatives, Liberals, and Nationalists, all of whom had conflicting views about how the new Cuban state should be constituted. Except for the Nationalists, the military followers of Máximo Gómez, and the intellectual heirs of José Martí, many Cubans did not seem to mind a new colonialism as long as it was indirect and they controlled the local instruments of government. But neither Cubans nor Americans could work out a satisfactory mechanism that reconciled their divergent aims. The first military government from 1899 to 1902 was designed precisely to achieve this end. It had mixed success.

General John Brooke, who had accepted the formal Spanish surrender, became the first military governor of Cuba under the U.S. flag. Brooke managed to disband the Cuban army, supervised the first detailed census of the island, and initiated the reconstruction of Cuba which had been extensively ravaged by the disastrous war of independence. Succeeded by General Leonard Wood who had been the military governor of Santiago de Cuba, the American occupation began a systematic transformation of the island. As the United States built schools, roads, and bridges, deepened the harbor at Havana, and installed waterworks, sewer works, and a telephone and telegraph system, the American presence penetrated almost every aspect of Cuban life. Some results, such as the advances made in the control of yellow fever and the organization of the public school system, were laudable. Others, such as the increase in racial discrimination and the crude attempts to exclude Afro-Cubans from political participation, were deplorable. And while the Americans did organize the first free elections in the new state, they forced the Cubans to accept the Platt Amendment to their constitution (passed by the United States Congress in 1901 and repealed in 1934) which allowed the United States to monopolize the economy, to intervene in domestic political affairs, and to approve international treaties, and which granted an indefinite lease to the area where they established the Guantánamo Bay naval station on the southern coast east of Santiago.

The reluctance of the Cubans to accept the Platt Amendment derived from its inherent threat to their sovereignty and their independence. Indeed, even within the United States Senate a number of members—mostly Democrats such as Benjamin Tillman of South Carolina, John Morgan of Alabama, Joseph Foraker of Ohio, and James Jones of Arkansas—declared that the amendment violated Cuban sovereignty. For their part, the Cubans, however much they admired the United States, felt that they ought to have the right to freely engage in commerce and other forms of dialogue with any nation without having to obtain prior approval from Washington. Thus the "manifest destiny" to incorporate Cuba into the United States, dreamed about by the North Americans since the expansion into Texas in the 1830s, was finally realized. Even more important, by having the Platt Amendment become both an integral part of the Cuban constitution as well as a part of the laws of the United States, the right of military intervention implied in the old, vague Monroe Doctrine of 1823 attained international legality and recognition. Faced with the Hobson's choice of accepting either the Platt Amendment or the continuation of military occupation, the Cubans finally gave in and accepted the amendment. It was the required precondition for their first experiment with a democratic republic. The Cuban Republic, which lasted from 1902 to 1959, could never extract itself from this pervasive and confining hegemony of its mainland neighbor.

Tomás Estrada Palma, the first popularly elected president of Cuba, had spent most of his life in the United States as an exile. An unabashed pro-American and annexationist, he thought that his main purpose was to prepare Cuba for eventual admission to the Union, an idea with considerable appeal among the upper echelons of the society and a segment of the U.S. government. Given the hegemony of the United States and the unsettled state of Cuba after the long war, Estrada Palma found his political options limited. But Estrada Palma's gravest error was to try to hold on to office at the end of his first term in 1905. Opposed by a loose coalition of Liberals, the political impasse brought on the second military occupation by the United States, although that gave way shortly to the civilian administration of Charles Magoon, a lawyer from the state of Minnesota, who had served as governor of the newly acquired Panama Canal Zone between 1905 and 1906. This second intervention, encouraged by several Cuban factions as well as the North American expatriate community, began the process by which Cuban politicians would use the threat of intervention as a political weapon either to get into office or to keep themselves there.

Unlike in the first intervention, the United States emphasized the civilian aspects of its administration. Magoon retained the Cuban constitution, kept the national flag flying on public buildings, and employed a number of Cubans in the upper levels of the administration. Indeed, he laid the foundation for a permanent civil service in 1908, but that quickly became recognized by Cubans as a public opportunity for private enrichment. The most significant achievement was the revision of the electoral laws which allowed the Liberals to accede to office under José Miguel Gómez in 1909, thus vindicating their revolt in 1905. The act of military intervention by itself did not comprise a precedent for future action. The United States had already been involved in Nicaragua, had only just completed the bloody war in the Philippines and the creation of the new state of Panama out of Colombia, and was on the threshold of military engagement in Haiti and the Dominican Republic. But by allowing the Liberals to accede to office after their revolt in 1906, the United States reinforced the notion that they were the determinants of political rules in Cuba. All politicians in Havana, until Fidel Castro's revolution in 1959, lived under this constraint. And by consistently exploiting the American connection, Cuban politicians unwittingly undermined their ability to develop their nationalism and repair the divisions created by slavery and colonialism. After 1906 Cuban interests became tied to the United States and their action would move in tandem with their perception of that reality. That both perception and reality would often diverge merely complicated the picture. The Americans, after all, remained ambivalent about what to do with Cuba, and how best to achieve its proper integration into their larger political and economic sphere.

## Politics and Society under the Republic

Between 1902 and 1959 Cuban politics varied between periods of modified democracy, most notably between 1933 and 1952, and outright repression, most notably during the regimes of Gerardo Machado (1925–33) and Fulgencio Batista (especially during Batista's later term after his coup d'état in 1952). Politicians were guided less by any concepts of national interest than by their sense of the greatest extent to which they could manipulate the system without being overthrown by their local opponents or attracting the hostility of the United States. Political parties represented a mere collection of personal followers whose fidelity was maintained uneasily by graft and corruption. Politicians like José Miguel Gómez, Gerardo Machado, and Fulgencio Batista used parties as political conveniences rather than legitimizing instruments. The institutions of government—the Congress, the courts, and the bureaucracy—served the head of state rather than the people and by so doing engendered neither autonomy, legitimacy, nor respectability.[1] Whenever the government was overthrown—in 1933, or 1952, or 1959—the entire instruments of administration came tumbling down as Jorge Domínguez details in his fine study, *Cuba: Order and Revolution.*

The enduring pattern of graft, corruption, maladministration, fiscal irresponsibility, and social insensitivity to minority groups may have been a legacy of the colonial period and the repressive slave system abolished only in 1886. But it achieved phenomenal proportions during the republic. It took a quantum leap under the Gómez administration (1909–13), when investment capital was flowing into Cuba and the sugar industry expanded further into Oriente Province. Indeed, by one report, foreign investment during the four years ending in 1913 amounted to more than $112,000,000: from England ($60,491,190), the United States ($35,000,000), France ($12,500,000), and Germany ($4,500,000). At the same time, the report estimated the increase in wealth around Havana and its environs at more than half a billion dollars.[2] By 1929 capital investment from the United States alone had increased to more than one billion dollars, and the island had passed through some heady days of prosperity in the 1920s called the "Dance of the Millions." The rapid economic expansion from 1902 to the 1920s masked the weak political base on which the actors in Havana sought to legitimize their occupancy of administrative power. Political mobilization, rather than being increasingly concentrated, tended to become increasingly fragmented and, in some cases, alienated. The Afro-Cubans were the first group to be isolated and alienated.

During 1912 some Afro-Cubans, led by Pedro Ivonet and Evaristo Esteñoz, organized themselves to secure better jobs, more political patronage, and a share of the wealth that was pouring into the island. They also protested against the law of 1909 which proscribed political associations based on race and color. The Gómez government responded by sending troops to Oriente, where the main body of Afro-Cubans was assembled, and savagely eliminated the demonstrators at a cost of more than 3,000 lives. That was the last major Afro-Cuban political protest in Cuba.

The pattern of political corruption set by Gómez continued during the administration of his successors, Mario García Menocal (1913–21), Alfredo Zayas (1921–25), Gerardo Machado (1925–1933), and Fulgencio Batista (1940–44, 1952–59). The Machado dictatorship had concentrated a great deal of political power in the hands of the chief executive, mainly by resorting to force and terror. But his administration could not deal with the great social, economic, and political changes of the times. At the social level, expanding educational opportunities had produced a lively, large, politicized generation of youths, mainly based at the newly reformed University of Havana, whose interest in their country and the rest of the hemisphere was as intense as it was idealistic. These students played an important role in the political affairs of the state between the 1930s and the 1950s. Machado's unimaginative response to student political activity was to murder or exile the leaders. On the economic front, Machado had to deal first with the aftereffects of the boom in the early 1920s and then with the devastating depression of the early 1930s. The sugar market plummeted, and, without the wherewithal for patronage, the government rapidly lost its fragile support base. During the 1933 revolution, when Machado tried to generate some national sentiment to counter pressure from the United States, he encountered a dismaying indifference in Cuba. Politically, Machado was also caught uncomfortably at the cutting edge of change. Under a new administration, Washington was beginning to change its policy in the hemisphere. Crude direct intervention was to be replaced by a carrot-and-stick approach, called the "Good Neighbor Policy." Old puppets, therefore, had to be sacrificed to create the veneer of change. The Americans did not overtly engineer the overthrow of President Machado, but, by visibly and vocally withdrawing their support of his administration, they removed the basis of his limited legitimacy thereby emboldening his opponents. Thereafter, in Cuba as elsewhere throughout the Caribbean, the United States would be less clear about its policies and goals, thus creating confusion and ambiguity. The revolution that overthrew Machado did not significantly alter the chaotic state of Cuban politics.

Between 1933, when Machado was overthrown, and 1940, when Batista achieved a sort of paramountcy with support and encouragement from the United States, Cuban governments fell with disconcerting rapidity. Nine individuals served as president between 1933 and 1936, some only for a few hours. Political power, formerly divided between Washington and Havana—or rather the Presidential Palace in Havana and the U.S. embassy—became further divided between the Presidential Palace, the U.S. embassy, and the Cuban military barracks, increasingly under the control of Sergeant Fulgencio Batista. Effectively, Batista remained the strongman in Cuba until 1958, overshadowing the constitutionally elected governments of Ramón Grau (1944–48) and Carlos Prío Socarrás (1948–52).

Politics during the republic was a continual struggle to establish legitimacy, popular support, and a degree of maneuverability within the hegemony of the United States. Successful politicians depended increasingly on patronage or military support to keep themselves in office. Obviously, periods of economic upturn favored the incumbents, while recession created problems. But the question of legitimacy remained closely tied to support from the United States. When that support was forthcoming, as in the case of Menocal in 1917, the president could successfully resist his opponents. On the other hand, when the United States withdrew its support, as in the cases of Machado in 1933 and Batista in 1958, their governments fell rapidly. Cuban presidents, therefore, had to be unusually sensitive not only to the ebb and flow of policy from Washington, but also to the ebb and flow of the economy—and in both cases, the price of sugar could be a good indicator.

The wealth of Cuba derived from the production of sugar. That had been true for more than a century before the Great Depression of 1929–33. Under the auspices of foreign capital, sugar production in Cuba virtually doubled every decade between 1900 and 1930. Between 1899 and 1927 sixty-three new sugar mills were built in Cuba, including some behemoth centrals constructed by the United Fruit Company, the Hershey Corporation, the Cuban American Sugar Company, and the Atlantic Sugar Company. No new sugar mill was constructed between 1927 and 1975,[3] but between 1925 and 1929, at the height of production before World War II, Cuban production averaged nearly 5 million tons of sugar. This was equal to nearly 30 percent of all cane sugar production and roughly 21 percent of the total sugar (cane and beet) produced in the world. In 1929 one Cuban Central factory could produce more sugar than the entire island did a century before. The six mills of the Cuban Atlantic Company produced nearly 200,000 tons of sugar in 1939. By contrast, the entire production of the island of Barbados was 133,000 tons; of Antigua, only 22,000 tons. All the British West Indies, including British Guiana, produced only 370,000 tons of sugar in 1928.[4]

The fluctuating income from sugar was augmented from other sources: construction of centrals, homes, businesses, roads, bridges, hotels, and casinos; and public works such as the deepening of Havana harbor and the expansion of sewer and other sanitation systems. More money in circulation meant more jobs and a greater distribution of income. The long period of general prosperity came to an end in 1929, but mini-booms reappeared in the 1940s and 1950s when both World War II and the Korean War gave sugar prices a boost.

Cuban wealth, however, was not equitably distributed. Although the island had one of the highest national per capita incomes in all Latin America and the Caribbean in 1958, the gap between the rich and the poor in Cuba remained enormous. So too did the contrast between Greater Havana, where nearly 40 percent of all Cubans lived, and the rest of the country, especially the rural areas. Even in sugar zones, unemploymnent and underemployment prevailed, driving the average annual rural wage down to approximately ninety-one dollars. More than 75 percent of rural dwellings were substandard in construction, and a high proportion lacked basic amenities such as running water, toilets, plumbing, electricity, or cooking stoves. The majority of peasants enjoyed neither a balanced, nutritious diet nor good health.

Nevertheless, it would be a serious mistake to credit either economic discontent or American imperialism for the revolution that ousted Batista in 1959. The Cuban political system had structural weaknesses which manifested themselves continually through the six decades of the republic. The legislature was neither independent nor representative. The bureaucracy was neither efficient nor honest; and the entire government lacked full legitimacy vested in the Cuban people. Rather, legitimacy derived from the perception of U.S. goodwill. From time to time attempts had been made to adjust the system, most notably in the heady days after the overthrow of Machado in 1933 when a great deal of social legislation was implemented, and the new 1940 constitution which formed the basis for Castro's legal challenge to Batista after 1952.

## The Castro Revolution

When Fidel Castro and his small band of revolutionaries ousted the Batista government, revolution was a popular concept throughout all of Latin America. After Batista staged his coup d'état in 1952, a number of groups had organized themselves in Cuba and declared themselves revolutionaries.[5] No consensus existed on what precisely they meant by a revolution. But every group thought that no revolution could begin without first overthrowing Batista by the ballot box if possible, or by force if necessary. Since very few entertained the immediate possibility of change in 1959, few had concrete programs in hand when the 26th of July Movement assumed the government on January 1—Batista and his government having collapsed the night before. Fidel Castro's definition of government emerged gradually, alienating many whose support went back to the suicidal attack on the Moncada military barracks in Santiago on July 26, 1953—hence the name of his movement.

The Castro revolution was not merely the replacement of one in-group by a faction of the out-group, as often occurs in so many Latin American impromptu political changes. After 1959 a series of fundamental changes took place in the structure of Cuban society, economy, and politics which, if they did not produce a new Cuban, at least produced a new Cuba.

Without some fundamental change and realignment in the social base of political power, there cannot be a revolution. By 1986 no aspect of the old Cuban society had remained untouched by the changes introduced by the energetic and idealistic young men who stormed into power with the dawn of New Year's Day, 1959. The permanent nature of this structural change in Cuba not only assured the revolution, but facilitated its perpetuation.

Few persons could have anticipated the extent of the changes about to be wrought on Cuba in 1959. Mario Llerena, an insider who opted to leave the 26th of July Movement in 1958 (thereby becoming one of the first of a substantial number of disenchanted), terms the Castro revolution "unsuspected." Perhaps not even Castro himself knew with any certainty the course the revolution would assume in the following years. In general, middle-class Cubans were divided in their appraisal, some talking disparagingly of the *barbudos*, or bearded ones, a reference to the healthy beards worn by the warriors in the Sierra Maestra Mountains in the struggle against Batista. Others, however, found the term endearing. Among the movement, informality was the order of the day. To all and sundry the leaders were "Fidel" (Fidel Castro), "Raúl" (Raúl Castro), "Che" (Ernesto Guevara), "Camilo" (Camilo Cienfuegos), "Frank" (Frank País), "Haydée" (Haydée Santamaría), and "Celia" (Celia Sánchez). Later, of course, those names would be modified by the appropriate variations of *compañero* (comrade) or *comandante* (chief). By that time the idealism and the euphoria of success had begun to wane. Equality succumbed to hierarchy. Pluralism gave way to increasing orthodoxy. The "guerrillas in power" were fashioning the socialist state. The revolution became "The Revolution": iconoclastic, eclectic, socialist, and defiant—although increasingly less so as time passed.

The course of the revolution is a study in contrasts. While ordinary Cubans enjoy a better general standard of material well-being than before 1959 and their government has a greater range of international contacts, they remain relatively isolated from most international communication and intercourse. They rank among the most literate people in the world (although less so than Barbadians and about on a par with Trinidadians), and possess a highly developed internal media network of radios, television, and newspapers. Cubans read more than 100 newspapers, magazines, and specialized journals designed for a popular clientele. Some 2,000,000 radio receivers and 880,000 television sets tune in not only to the local 122 radio and television transmitters (most of which are booster transmitters) on the island, but also to stations in Miami and other North American cities. Compared with the United States where each 100 inhabitants own 200 radios and 62 television sets, the Cuban media system might not appear impressive. Within the Caribbean and the wider world, however, the density is impressive. With their 20 radios and 9 television sets per 100 inhabitants, the Cubans compare favorably with Mexicans (30 radios and 8.4 television sets) and are well ahead of their island neighbors except for Puerto Rico. (Jamaica has 2.7 radios and 5.8 television sets per 100 inhabitants; the Dominican Republic, 8.2 radios and 4.7 televisions sets; whereas Puerto Rico has 54 radios and 16 television sets per 100 inhabitants).[6]

The Castro revolution has been marked by a series of overlapping and sometimes imprecisely delineated stages. Four of these may be discerned. The first, in which the inherited capitalist institutions of the state were dismantled and some socialist models were introduced, lasted from 1959 to 1963. The second was a period of indecision between 1963 and 1965, in which competition existed between the followers of Castro with their Soviet model and those of Guevara with their Chinese model. The third period began with the reassessment after the U.S. invasion of the Dominican Republic (1965) and was characterized by a period of radicalization both at home and abroad, with attempts to export the revolution and affiliate with all opponents of imperialism worldwide. This period lasted until 1970 and included the death of Guevara in Bolivia in 1967, the virulent campaign against bureaucrats at home, and the unsuccessful attempt to produce 10 million tons of sugar. The final period began in 1970 with an assessment of the revolution, and included the gradual institutionalization along orthodox Soviet lines, the convocation of the First Party Congress in 1975, and the publication of the new constitution. This was the maturing phase of the revolution. The army and the party became paramount while eclecticism and experimentation diminished considerably, although the introduction of free markets between 1980 and 1986 indicated a residue of the earlier spirit. These free markets were a tacit admission of economic failures, especially in domestic agricultural policies.

Political and economic policies have been characterized by equal components of idealism and pragmatism, by success and failure. After more than a
quarter of a century the revolution has not successfully exported its model to
Venezuela, Bolivia, the Dominican Republic, Grenada, or Suriname—all places
where the effort has been made. The extensive military and technical assistance
programs from Nicaragua to Ethiopia have reaped as much praise as fear, and
have complicated Cuban global foreign policy initiatives.[7]

The revolution has been dynamic, however. Conditions in Cuba have been
constantly changing. The picture of Cuba in 1962 at the time of the missile
crisis or in 1968 when the campaign against bureaucrats was at its most
disturbing extreme and the country had begun to mobilize itself for the 10-
million-ton sugar harvest was one of indecision, uncertainty, and insecurity.
During the 1970s the Cubans made dramatic changes. Cuba broke out of the
diplomatic isolation imposed during the 1960s, reestablishing diplomatic relations with most of the mainland Latin American states and a number of newly
independent Caribbean ones. Havana ranked second only to Washington as a
site for diplomatic missions. Cubans embarked on a new type of foreign policy,
with increased military assistance in several African countries, including Alge-
ria, Angola, the Congo, Ethiopia, Guinea, Guinea-Bissau, and Mozambique.

By the late 1970s and early 1980s the Cuban influence began to decline
among the Third-World states. In the Caribbean, in Latin America, and in
Africa, Cuban general support of the Soviet Union in the Horn of Africa in
1978 and in Afghanistan in 1980 reduced its credibility as a truly nonaligned
state—especially since Cuba headed the movement at that time. Nevertheless,
Cuban and Soviet foreign policies are not always synonymous, and accusations
that the Cubans are mere lackeys of the Soviets are largely without foundation.
Cuban and Soviet interests are closely related but not identical in every respect.

Friction developed with Barbados over the crash of a Cubana Airlines plane
there in 1976. In 1980, Fidel Castro's close friend, Michael Manley, lost the
general elections in Jamaica and was replaced by the conservative Edward
Seaga, a good friend of President Ronald Reagan of the United States. Seaga
expelled the Cuban ambassador to Jamaica, but retained the Cubana Airlines'
access to the Kingston international airport. In the spring of 1981, Colombia
broke diplomatic relations over alleged Cuban support for its own leftist
guerrillas. Then in 1983, Maurice Bishop, the very close friend of Castro, was
overthrown and assassinated by his fellow revolutionaries in Grenada. The
immediate consequence was an invasion by the United States which ended the
People's Revolutionary Government and Cuban influence in Grenada. Ironi-

cally, the airport which the Cubans were building, and which the United States had vigorously opposed for years, was rapidly completed after the invasion by the invaders. Later that year Suriname expelled the Cuban ambassador. Nicaragua remained the only North American state with close political and diplomatic ties to Cuba. But economic and diplomatic relations were better regionally than ever before.

On the domestic political front the state formally institutionalized a socialist form of government. In 1975 the previously six provinces were expanded to fourteen, each with its own provincial assembly. The following year a new constitution made the Communist party the sole political party and established the government along orthodox Soviet lines, giving the titles of "Head of State," "President of the Council of Ministers," "President of the Council of State," and "First Secretary of the Party" to Fidel Castro. Popular elections returned 481 members to a National Assembly, and the Politburo was expanded. Political organization is now streamlined from the local level to the national level.

For a few years commodity prices rose and the island tasted prosperity, but the decline of prices in the early 1980s brought back the economic problems reminiscent of the 1960s. One symptom of the economic recession was the exodus in 1980 of 125,000 Cubans through the port of Mariel for the United States. Notwithstanding, the availability of consumer items is far greater than at any time since 1959. In 1985 ration books accounted for only about 30 percent of individual consumer items. More important, nearly 60 percent of all food items had been "liberated" from rationing.

Hard currency availability still ranks as a major concern of the Cuban government. Despite enormous subsidies and generous financial and trade support from the Soviet Union, the overall economic condition of the island leaves no room for complacency. Cuba still remains essentially the sugar-producing island that it was in 1959. Sugarcane planting has been virtually mechanized and nearly 70 percent of the harvest is mechanically reaped. Sugar, with annual production of more than 8 million tons (compared with a little more than 5 million tons in the late 1950s) still accounts for more than 80 percent of the value of total exports from Cuba, most of which is committed in long-term contracts to the member states of the Council for Mutual Economic Assistance (COMECOM) at prices fixed above the free world market rates. This commitment insulates the Cubans from the worst consequences of price fluctuations, and has enabled them to continue with their modernization plan of building 11 new factories by 1990, which with the existing 151 would permit a handling capacity of more than 10 million tons of sugar per year. But with world sugar prices in 1985 being only about 40 percent of what they were in

1970, the emphasis on sugar production—even with a semiprotected market—does not promise economic improvements for the Cubans.

Not surprisingly, therefore, the overall economic situation for Cuba does not differ much from the other Latin American and Third-World countries. Between 1980 and 1982 the Cuban budgetary deficit increased from more than $311 million to more than $785 million, and is expected to continue to be out of balance for the rest of the decade. According to figures supplied by the Economic Commission for Latin America, the trade deficit passed $1 million in 1981.

The Cuban foreign debt has also been steadily increasing. In 1981 Cuba owed some $10.6 billion, with $7.3 billion owed to the Soviet Union, $1.8 billion to Western governments, and $1.5 billion to foreign commercial banks. On a per capita basis, this volume of public debt placed Cuba in the same ranks as Brazil, Argentina, Mexico, or the United States.

The Cuban economic experience constitutes a graphic example of the enormous problems resulting from the dependence on single exports and trade. In the early days of the revolution the government tried to diversify the economy without marked success. Then after 1968, reversing itself, the government decided that efficient production of what Cuba did best—that is, produce sugar—provided the best promise for future economic growth. The Cuban sugar industry ranks among the most efficient in the world, but the instability of world commodity prices has seriously undermined the expected rewards from increased productivity.

Nor has foreign aid done much to alleviate the national economic problem. Between 1960 and 1980 the Soviet Union supplied Cuba with more than $16 billion in economic aid. In 1979 alone that aid amounted to $3.1 billion, equivalent to a per capita subsidy of $315, or nearly 20 percent of the gross national product. By contrast, this level of aid is·more than fifteen times that promised to the eligible countries by the 1983 Caribbean Basin Initiative or the report of the 1984 Kissinger Commission on Central America. Despite this infusion of economic support, the perceived material conditions of life on the island by the 125,000 who chose to leave in 1980 inspired not hope but pessimism.

By the mid-1980s Cuba had the most disciplined, best fed, best housed, and best formally educated population throughout Latin America and the Caribbean. Although the state no longer provided completely free items such as cafeteria meals, school fees, telephones, transportation, electricity, and uniforms, the living conditions, as gauged by the ability of the wage earner to afford the necessities of life, were superior to those elsewhere. Infant mortality and general death rates are among the lowest in the hemisphere, and the former wide variation in the access to amenities between rural and urban areas has been considerably reduced.

All these observations do not make Cuba a paradise. Dissatisfaction, dissent, and some forms of discrimination exist. Heavy social and legal sanctions are imposed for loafing and other politically determined examples of socially deviant behavior, including what is defined as sexual deviance. And an unspecified number of political prisoners continue to linger in Cuban jails.

## Art and Culture

Art and culture have been among the priorities of the revolution since 1959, and the literacy campaign of the early 1960s expanded the market for publications of all sorts. The government-controlled Book Institute supervises the publication of tens of millions of books annually, mainly reference works and scientific texts for free distribution. The National Union of Cuban Writers, Artists, and Cinematographers (UNEAC) was one of the first creations of the revolution in 1961, along with other enduring institutions such as the Revolutionary Armed Forces (FAR), the Interior Ministry (MININ), and the National Association of Small Farmers (ANAP). Through the Casa de las Américas, UNEAC conducts annual writers' competitions for authors from all over the world in a number of languages. Although the political content of publications is high, censorship is largely self-imposed.

Academic journals include *Universidad de la Habana, Santiago, Revista de la Biblioteca José Martí, Islas,* and *Signos,* mostly devoted to the humanities and social sciences. Popular magazines include *La Gaceta de Cuba, Casa de las Américas, Conjunto,* and *El Caiman Barbudo.* The leading press publications are *Granma* ("Grandmother"), the official paper, named after the yacht that carried Fidel Castro and his companions from Mexico to Cuba in 1956, with a daily circulation of about 500,000; *Bohemia;* and *Juventud Rebelde* ("Rebel Youth"), the paper of the Young Communist Organization. While all have sections for open letters to the editor, and recent studies have indicated that most correspondence is neutral (although unfavorable letters exceed favorable ones), a 1979 policy statement warned that "effective criticism should be fraternal in spirit, constructive in objectives and precise in target."[8]

In 1959 the newly created Cuban Institute of Cinematic Art and Industry (ICAIC) began an aggressive development of films and documentaries that quickly propelled Cuba into the forefront of the industry worldwide. Films such as *The Adventures of Juan Quin Quin* (1968), *Death of a Bureaucrat* (1968), *Lucia* (1969), *The Other Francisco* (1975), *One Way or Another* (1977), and *The Last Supper* (1977) have demonstrated the superb skills of cinematographic technique that have brought international acclaim to some of the directors such as Tomás Gutiérrez Alea, Julio García Espinosa, Sergio Giral, and Sara Gómez.

Along with literature and the cinema, sports have also been an area of international distinction, with excellent performances in baseball, basketball, boxing, and track and field events. Enthusiasm for sports preceded the revolution, of course, but in 1971 the government created the National Institute for Sports, Physical Education, and Recreation which organized sports competitions from the local level to international participation. While professionalism is not recognized, athletes, as in other socialist countries—and in common with writers and artists—are considered full-time workers for the state and are so treated.

One of the most difficult areas for the revolution was the question of religion. In the early phase relations between church and state were difficult, often antagonistic, and the mutual suspicion prevailed until the late 1970s. This resulted from the large number of foreign priests, the close ties of many Cuban religious organizations to similar ones in the United States, and the increasingly radical rhetoric of Cuban officials. Relations have improved considerably, with the state no longer officially regarding religion and Marxism as incompatible; and since Fidel Castro's complimentary statements of 1984 to the Brazilian Dominican priest, Father Betto, religious adherents have felt much more comfortable in Cuba.[9] The 1976 constitution considered religion a private matter. Article 54 stated: "The Socialist State, which bases its activity and educates its peoples in the scientific materialist concept of the universe, recognizes and guarantees freedom of conscience and the right of everyone to profess any religious belief and to practice within the framework of respect for the law, the belief of his preference."

Ministers of religion, like athletes (but without their aura and the material rewards), are considered full-time state employees. While most churches in Cuba convey the impression of neglect, and audiences tend to be small, preponderantly old, and female, the newer, more evangelical sects such as Jehovah's Witnesses, Seventh Day Adventists, and other fundamentalists have been expanding their membership. Older, more conventional denominations such as Baptists, Episcopalians, Methodists, and Presbyterians have been holding their numbers whereas the Roman Catholics have suffered a small decline.

The revolution has consolidated itself at home. But in so doing, it has created a permanent exile community scattered throughout Europe and the Americas, with the largest concentration of nearly a million persons in Miami, Florida. Although the implacable hostility of these exiles has abated, their presence is yet another factor in any assessment of the revolution. But the continued existence of a growing body of exiles cannot overshadow the successes of the revolution. While the Castroites may not have succeeded in creating a new Cuban, they have definitely created a new Cuba. And the new Cuba is more than the introduction of socialist methods of government and economic regulation. The revolution has boosted nationalism, reduced considerably the vitiating frictions of race and class, and projected an international image that ability to compete on an international scale is not narrowly related to large physical size, industrial development, and advanced technology. Cuban achievements since 1959 have been an inspiration to many small, Third-World states.

## Notes

1. Leonard Wood Papers, Cuba 1899–1902, Box 202, AC 4488, Manuscript Division, Library of Congress, Washington, D.C.

2. Domínguez, Cuba: Order and Revolution, pp. 80–84.

3. The last sugar mill built in Cuba before the revolution was Central Santa María, near Santa Cruz del Sur, Camaguey Province. See Hugh Thomas, Cuba, p. 558.

4. British West Indian sugar production increased through the 1930s, aided by preferential price supports from the metropolis, to about 620,000 tons in 1938. At the same time, Cuban producers had agreed to withdraw 60 percent of their cane fields, and to keep production to about 3 million tons of sugar per year, just about what they could sell on the increasingly competitive U.S. market.

5. Domínguez, Cuba: Order and Revolution, pp. 123–33; Hugh Thomas, Cuba, pp. 950–55.

6. Nichols, "The Mass Media."

7. Moreira and Bissio, "The Cubans in Africa"; Weinstein, Revolutionary Cuba; Blasier and Mesa-Lago, Cuba in the World.

8. From a Party Central Committee document of November 1979, cited in Nichols, "The Mass Media," p. 103.

9. Fidel y la religión. Betto points out that Fidel had celebrated meetings with Catholic clergymen on his visit to Chile in 1971, and with Jamaican clergymen while he was in that island in 1977—a point also repeated by Armando Hart in his short introduction. Some Cubans say that after the visit of the Reverend Jesse Jackson to Cuba in 1984 the official attitude toward the churches improved significantly.

## 9

Teresita Martínez Vergne

# Politics and Society in the Spanish Caribbean during the Nineteenth Century

Social scientists of today's Caribbean continue to explore the question of the development of a sense of national identity in each of the three Spanish territories during the nineteenth century. Cuban historians ask themselves why their glorious struggle for independence concluded in negotiations over their political status with the United States. Political scientists writing on Puerto Rico struggle to understand the population's almost total indifference to separation from Spain as a political alternative. Spanish-speaking Dominicans—not to be confused with citizens from English-speaking Dominica—are frankly bewildered by their leaders' annexation schemes and the political instability that ensued as they sought personal aggrandizement. In all three places, the social and economic forces that constantly influenced the development of a national consciousness seem to have predominated. Ultimately, revolutionary Cuba became a protectorate of the United States, conciliatory Puerto Rico changed masters; and the annexationist Dominican Republic succeeded at independence.

The question of how nationalism developed in the Spanish colonial possessions—Cuba, Puerto Rico, and the Dominican Republic—is central to their nineteenth-century enigma. The extent to which Puerto Ricans, Cubans, and Dominicans thought, felt, and acted differently from their metropolitan counterparts had much to do with local political and economic considerations. It was easier for the elite in each of the three Spanish territories to identify their grievances than to reach a consensus—with the rest of the population—on the nature of a new order. Cuban separatists remained divided on the issue of slavery; progressive landowners, professionals, and intellectuals in Puerto Rico worked strictly within the framework of national parties to obtain reforms;

Dominican caudillos were both victims and perpetrators of the existing regime of economic backwardness and foreign domination. As the practices it sought to eliminate affected only minimally other segments of society, the political leadership of the Spanish Caribbean islands sought independence based on a naive understanding of nationhood and an illusory assessment of the viability of the state.

## Cuba

Cuba's transformation into a society prepared to pursue its own objectives was a slow and painful process. Even as wealthy, powerful, and determined sugar planters dominated the scene in the first decades of the nineteenth century, many forces militated against the definition of local interests as separate from those of the mother country. The effectiveness of lobbies before metropolitan decision makers convinced many that association with Spain secured Cuba's privileged position as the world's largest sugar producer. On the island, the needs of the elite were met by a regime that discouraged activism. Plans to enter the North American union as a slave state—as well as the movement for reform that followed—were de facto negations of an identity of interests separate from a metropolitan power, which served only to maintain the economic status quo. The fear of abolition—to many, synonymous with bankruptcy—defeated Cuban unity of purpose during the Ten Years' War, a violent and protracted conflict over Cuba's political destiny. When the fight for political independence and national definition erupted in 1895, the intervention of a still greater power—the United States—prevented the establishment of a nation-state as envisioned by revolutionary leaders.

Cuban prosperity required and reinforced the colonial connection during the nineteenth century. Initially stimulated by the collapse of Haiti as the world's largest producer of sugar, traditional planter families invested in the expansion of their mills, in equipment, and in slave labor. With the wealth accumulated for generations, merchants—traditional purveyors of slaves and monopoly consumer goods—and financiers also invaded the sphere of production. In the name of the existing order, these groups—together with the mainland bureaucratic and military contingent—constituted the most loyal defenders of Spanish rule on the island. The maintenance of a favorable business climate was a powerful incentive for acquiescing to Spanish rule.

This is not to say, of course, that differences of opinion did not exist between the creole elite and the Spanish. The relationship between colony and metropolis, to be sure, rested on Spain's continued exploitation of Cuban wealth. That Spain was enlightened enough to sponsor and participate in agricultural and commercial development does not mean that the imposition of taxes responded to considerations other than the needs of the Spanish treasury. Large sugar planters were likely to suffer on two grounds: indirect taxes on agricultural production and duties on exports hiked the price of Cuban sugar in the increasingly competitive international market, and import duties on machinery and consumer goods raised the cost of operations tremendously. Plantation owners were quick to realize that Spain's policies aimed to meet metropolitan fiscal needs rather than economic development objectives for the island.

Cuba's captains-general—in open defiance of metropolitan guidelines—cooperated with, redirected, or sabotaged the efforts of sugar planters to define their interests. In the 1820s and 1830s, captains-general Dionisio Vives (1823–32), Mariano Rocafort (1832–34), and Miguel Tacón (1834–38) ruled the island in the Bourbon tradition with the absolute authority granted to colonial governors by a royal decree of 1825. Generally inclined to take advantage of the economic boom in the island, they cooperated with both saccharocracy and slave merchants in an intricate system of favor and interest. Gerónimo Valdés (1841–43), Leopoldo O'Donnell (1843–48), and Juan de la Pezuela (1853–54) translated metropolitan objectives—namely, the economic prosperity of Cuba and the appeasement of Great Britain over the continuation of the slave trade—into policies they considered appropriate for particular situations in the colony during the 1840s and 1850s. White immigration schemes, measures to end the slave trade, and violent curtailment of slave activity succeeded each other as colonial policy in this period. Francisco Serrano (1859–62) and Domingo Dulce (1862–66), island governors in the 1860s, established yet another style of government as they encouraged discussion of Cuba's political, economic, and social problems. The contradictions that resulted from the rule of autocratic governors convinced many planters that cooperation (when convenient) and adjustment through bribes (when necessary) paid off as sure ways of escaping some of the difficulties of colonial life.

Yet the actions of island bureaucrats, as they participated in the island's society and economy or hindered their development, must have contributed to Cuban self-definition. Claudio de Martínez, Conde de Villanueva, president of the Real Consulado de Agricultura y Comercio and intendant from 1825 to 1852, was also a sugar financier and railway promoter. He served the sugar interest well when he refused to publish an 1841 order to free slaves who arrived after the formal abolition of the slave trade in 1820. Captain-general

Tacón may have won a few friends with the expulsion of the abolitionist José Antonio Saco from the island, but he alienated others by refusing to call elections for representatives to the liberal Spanish Cortes in 1836. Governor Pezuela's decrees proclaiming *emancipados* (blacks seized in slave ships after 1820) free, punishing slave importers, and encouraging interracial marriages threatened to shake the very foundations of Cuba's caste and class structure, and, by so doing, radicalized planter thought.

The movement for annexation to the United States and its corollary, the reform movement, tacitly expressed Cuba's ambivalence with respect to its political—that is, economic—future. The preservation of their concerns—the force behind planter action and inertia—had so obsessed Cuban landowners that many considered joining the Union to prevent the liberation of their slaves through British pressure. Gathered in the Havana Club, these men had advocated the introduction of new technology and welcomed the opportunity to compete in British and U.S. markets since the late 1840s, but were conservative insofar as they feared the destruction of the world they had grown used to by either abolition or a slave revolt. Their faith in the mother country's ability to safeguard the future against England had waned considerably. The United States, in contrast, relied on a vastly greater power to deal with these problems; it also symbolized the spirit of capitalist enterprise and was fast becoming Cuba's largest trading partner. Convinced that their interests were better served by the North American giant, some Cuban planters supported overtures to become a U.S. protectorate.

Despite the forceful efforts of annexationists in the late 1840s and 1850s, Cuba did not become part of the United States during this period. Repeated military invasions of the island by exiles in the United States never met with popular support. Frequent U.S. attempts to purchase Cuba—either outright or as security on a loan to Spain—failed when diplomatic missions blundered at the negotiating table. Ultimately, a reversal in Spain's policy toward Great Britain's demands to declare the slave trade piracy and the defeat of U.S. slaveholders in the Civil War removed all annexationist sentiment on the island. The appointment of a new captain-general quieted planter unrest, as it brought assurances of white domination over a slave labor force. Once assured of a favorable business climate, Cuban landowners were happy to comply with Spanish rule on the island.

The movement for reform in the 1860s was similarly predicated on the maintenance of Cuba's prosperity through a colonial relationship. Members of the Havana Reform Club (composed mostly of ex-annexationists and planters) responded to the chronic ills of the island's economy: uncertainty over abolition, an exacting tax system, and unfavorable market conditions. They hoped for a reduction in the authority of the captain-general and the extension to Cuba of such political rights as existed in Spain. In the economic sphere, they favored mechanization and centralization, convinced as they were of the imminent end of the slave trade and, eventually, of slavery. Because the objectives adopted were designed to correct decades of institutionalized abuses, these efforts were doomed to fail.

The reformist movement suffered a violent death after the Junta de Información of 1866 had auspiciously announced the arrival of reforms. Elected colonial representatives were greeted in the metropolis with the news of the fall from power of Progressive liberals. Discussion of the much-awaited special laws that were to apply to the colonies was replaced by questionnaires addressed to each participant. The appointment of a reactionary captain-general and the resignation of the new overseas minister, Alejandro de Castro, dealt a deathblow to the movement. The absence of consensus among the moderate men and rich planters who clamored for change translated into ineffectiveness in the face of the powerful external circumstances that militated against reform. A Cuban commonality of interests, if it had existed at all, had failed in redefining the colonial relationship.

Subsequent metropolitan indifference convinced many that modifications in existing social, economic, and political structures were hard to obtain. The sugar industry entered a period of crisis, caused by its growing sensitivity to international financial movements and by misdirected and partial efforts at modernization. Ignoring the plight of Cuban planters, the mother country further burdened the landowning classes by adding a direct tax onto the existing regime of import and export duties. In the east, those hacendados unable to participate in the frenzied growth of the plantation economy due to the lack of capital to invest in machinery and slaves began to discuss a redress to their grievances in Masonic lodges. Under the leadership of Carlos Manuel de Céspedes, they obtained the financial support of the powerful western planters, also alienated by the mother country's callous response to their urgent needs. The Ten Years' War brought to a head the cumulative grievances of the Cuban cane industry.

The fight that followed violently exposed regional differences in Cuba's economy. In the eastern countryside, Antonio Maceo and Máximo Gómez led guerrilla bands rendered superior to the Spanish forces by their immunity to disease, high mobility, and familiarity with the local terrain and population. Their strategy centered on garnering planter support from the west and destroying the economic wherewithal of the opposition by burning cane fields.

Spanish generals responded to guerrilla warfare by containing the revolution in the rebel-held territory to the east by means of a fortified ditch running the width of the island and by establishing martial law in loyal cities. By the time the rebels laid down their arms in 1878, the eastern part of the island, especially Puerto Príncipe, was devastated; the west was left almost untouched.

The reasons for the rebel defeat were many and varied. In the first place, the obsession of the insurgents with obtaining the imprimatur of the United States as legitimate belligerents prevented them from making bold decisions, such as marching west in the early years of the revolt. The United States would not be moved to support violence: it sought to buy the independence of Cuba through a cash payment to Spain, to be made by U.S. bankers as a loan to the Cubans for $100 million. That the United States remained Spain's ally and considered the independence struggle unjustifiable became abundantly clear in 1873, when it accepted an apology, indemnity, and a promise to punish the Spanish officer responsible for the summary execution of fifty-three rebel supporters, some of them Americans, on board the *Virginius*, a Cuban supply ship sailing under the U.S. flag.

A second factor that prevented a successful revolt was the lack of support from the west, as the controversial question of abolition divided the landowning classes. The small planters of the eastern sector relied only marginally on slave labor for their agricultural operations; they had even begun to rent their slaves for wages. The prosperous western planters, although embracing technological innovation, refused to discard slavery, an economic system many now see as anachronistic. In its defense of slavery, the west had been supported both by the mother country against British efforts to abolish the slave trade and by local Spanish merchants. After Céspedes freed his slaves and the councillors of the eastern town of Bayamo proclaimed complete abolition there, prosperous *habaneros* of Spanish origin retaliated by organizing groups of "volunteers" to oppose the eastern rebels. Conciliation between east and west became impossible.

The race issue posed an obstacle to success in yet another way. The charismatic figure of one of Cuba's most brilliant military men, the mulatto Antonio Maceo, stirred in some fears of social dislocation caused by racial conflict. The presence of Maceo among the revolutionary leadership became even more suspect when he refused to accept the generous conditions for peace proposed by Spanish general Arsenio Martínez Campos on the grounds that they excluded the abolition of slavery and the independence of Cuba. As if to confirm that the rich western planters who supported the war effort distrusted the aims of the mulatto leader and his mambí army, Maceo was not given the command he was promised during the short-lived revolt called the Guerra Chiquita.

The Ten Years' War, however, crystallized Cuban nationalist feeling as nothing else had before. Although social and economic motivations to participate may have varied by group, certain political attitudes grew and became established as a result of the example set by the financial contributions of wealthy men, the cooperation of small farmers in the war effort, and the support of slaves as fighting men. In addition, the Ten Years' War forced Spain—and so, Cuba—to resolve the divisive question of slavery: under pressure from France and Great Britain, Spain declared free the children of slaves born after September 1868. Coupled with the chronic ailments of the sugar industry (worsened by the international depression and low prices of 1874–75), the Ten Years' War also made possible the rebirth of the Cuban cane industry: a new aristocracy of money arose from the war business, the slave regime was rejected as unprofitable, and the destruction of heavily mortgaged properties in the east allowed the establishment of *centrales* (sugar factories) and *colonias* (agricultural settlements that grew cane for the mills) with U.S. capital beginning in the early 1880s. The social transformations these sudden dislocations brought about permitted Cuban revolutionaries to dismiss the old sugar oligarchy as a basis for support and to embark upon a much bolder independence effort beginning in 1895.

Cuba's 1895 call to arms was destined for success. José Martí articulated elite discontent over Spanish taxation and planter tribulations over U.S. tariff policy. Within six months of the declaration of hostilities, Gómez took the critical step of extending the war to the west, burning every plantation that was producing sugar, including U.S.-owned ones. The Cuban revolutionary junta in New York took extreme care in feeding newspapers stories about war atrocities allegedly committed by Spanish troops, while international circles deplored Spain's policy of winning first and negotiating later. Spurred on by favorable circumstances in and out of Cuba, the revolutionary leadership would not settle for anything less than independence.

This situation changed considerably when the United States intervened. Cubans and their fight for freedom were almost irrelevant in what became the Spanish-American War. U.S. troops found they had more in common with the disciplined white Spanish forces than with the mulatto guerrillas that made up the Cuban army. The Cuban cause had lost the critical support of U.S. newspapers, its military officers their drive, and many of the outstanding leaders their lives. Although the Teller amendment assured some that territorial expansion was not a consideration for the northern giant, U.S. economic interests—in terms of trade and investment—appeared powerful enough to merit annexation. Ultimately, the nation-in-the-making gave way to a quasi-state established to conform to U.S. business and political directives, as embodied in the Platt amendment to Cuba's constitution.

The case of Cuba, then, brings to the fore many of the forces that shaped Hispanic Caribbean nationalism. For the longest time, Cuba's prosperity and Spanish colonial policy were inextricably and profitably bound together. As the sugar economy grew, the island's planters discovered their interests conflicted with the mother country's. More importantly, their strong economic position made possible a showdown, in which all classes of society were eventually included. The efforts of Cubans who united for independence, though, were interrupted by the unquestionably more powerful forces of Cuba's northern neighbor. The establishment of a de facto U.S. protectorate stymied the emergence of a politically autonomous nation.

## Puerto Rico

Political developments in nineteenth-century Puerto Rico reflected in large part two outstanding features of colonial rule on the island: the all-encompassing authority of the captain-general and the limited development of the sugar industry. Constrained in ways Cuba was not, Puerto Rico's landowning, merchant, professional, and intellectual groups participated in politics only through the formulation of very localized demands consonant with circumstances in the mother country. It is not surprising, then, that the constant attempt at reform culminated in plans for autonomy, and not independence. The acquisition of the island by the United States as war booty at the end of the Spanish-American War proved further that Puerto Rico's fate was inexorably tied to Spanish internal politics.

The patterns of political activity in nineteenth-century Puerto Rico conformed largely to the directives established by all-powerful captains-general. Beginning in the 1820s, repressive measures designed to protect the colony from the influence of the Latin American independence movements reflected the captain-general's supreme authority. The infamous *facultades omnímodas* made Puerto Rico's governor virtually omnipotent: besides exerting broad executive and legislative powers, he was supreme commander of the island's military forces as captain-general, controlled the royal treasury as intendant, exercised power over the church as vice-regal patron, and acted as superior judge under the *audiencia* system. The centralizing and absolutist tendencies of late Bourbon rulers in Spain were thus revived in the colonial context.

Puerto Rico's economic development was equally affected by metropolitan considerations. The sugar industry, initially stimulated by the elimination of Haiti as a major competitor in the 1790s, flourished during the first decades of the nineteenth century because of favorable legislation with respect to credit and foreign imports, and special treatment of the colonial product in the home market. Machinery entered the colony duty-free; export and customs duties were minimal. The happy coincidence of increased demand, high prices, financial incentives, and protection at home made possible the growth of a modest export economy by mid-century.

The privileged position of Puerto Rican planters vis-à-vis importers and exporters, however, was seriously undermined by 1850. Spain began to protect metropolitan manufactures by raising customs duties on U.S. goods—also imported by the colony—and taxed island sugar exported to the mother country. It was an unfortunate coincidence that the drastic drop in market prices caused by the introduction of subsidized beet sugar also began in 1850. Those who could afford it tried to modernize their mills. Most avoided disaster simply by increasing output. All were equally aware of their vulnerable position in the face of factors they could not control.

These early political and economic developments resulted in the formation of a weak national bourgeoisie. Merchants and planters dominated the economic life of the colony in a mutually dependent relationship: both were involved—at opposite ends—in the business of placing agricultural commodities in international markets in exchange for manufactured goods not available on the island. They also controlled—by their participation in colonial institutions—the instruments for preserving or shaking the foundations of the island's social, economic, and political structures. A basically solid, but uneasy, alliance held Puerto Rico's upper class together, its primary objective reduced to preserving the limited returns on its early investment.

But, as dominant and cohesive as it seemed, this incipient bourgeoisie—unlike Cuba's—remained ineffective in tracing and pursuing the course the island was to follow. The business partnership of planters and merchants remained unequal and laden with uncertainty: the landowner could only borrow money at high interest rates to finance his operations and import expensive machinery, while the merchant, dependent on overseas market conditions, hoped for a high return on investment in sugar exports and imported consumer goods to compensate for perceived risks. Commercial groups opposed the creation of banks as rival institutions in granting credit, while planters vehemently proclaimed the necessity for mechanisms that would provide investment capital. Neither agricultural nor commercial groups operated in a context that permitted the emergence of carefully articulated class interests. Their incapacity to establish more-than-immediate goals rendered their objectives vague and their efforts weak.

The differences of opinion among commercial and landowning classes on the issue of their economic well-being spilled onto the political arena. Puerto Rico's elite split into those whose interests and inclinations bound them to the metropolis and the preservation of the status quo (Liberal Conservatives) and those who sought to change the colonial relationship in order to accommodate local interests (Liberal Reformists). Merchants—traditionally identified with peninsular Spaniards—thought Spanish domination provided the highest security for their prosperity; landowners—island-born Spaniards—bent toward demanding broader autonomy. Unconditionally pro-Spanish conservatives allegedly trusted the mother country's instincts blindly and clamored for more state intervention in local matters, especially economic ones. The more liberal thinkers aspired to greater individual freedom, based on concepts of popular sovereignty and obtained through legal reforms by peaceful means. Both classes-in-the-making, though, were unable to recognize that their views not only reflected, but also made possible their domination.

The activities of political groupings were further limited by the boundaries within which they operated. Because Puerto Ricans did not carry much clout with the metropolis in economic terms, they were forced to react at every chance provided by changes in Spanish internal politics. Progressive thinkers on the island had no choice but to believe that Spain would one day establish the special laws promised in 1837. Liberal governments had, after all, revitalized local town councils at different moments and institutionalized the Provincial Deputation beginning in the 1870s. Even the establishment of a high court of appeals in 1831 convinced many of the inevitable movement toward a liberalization of the political regime. The conviction that metropolitan parties in Madrid would acquiesce to island demands remained the underlying assumption of the strategy of reform.

The advocates of reform, then, identified themselves with political and economic liberalism within the boundaries drawn by the colonial relationship. Not failing to condemn the existing political regime as absolutist, despotic, and unfair, activists listed among island wants and demands the recognition of Puerto Rico as a Spanish province; permanent representation to the Cortes; freedom of petition, speech, and association; and free trade. The movement, not surprisingly, focused also on the sugar industry, denouncing the use of slaves and deploring the absence of modern methods in the cultivation and manufacturing processes. Reformists asked the metropolis to establish banks for agricultural credit and to facilitate the introduction of sophisticated machinery for sugar production. Although outspoken, nineteenth-century Puerto Rican reformers raised issues that highlighted more the bases for consensus than the potential for conflict.

The generalized desire for abolition also contributed to a certain degree of harmony between insular and metropolitan objectives. The reluctance of Spain to abolish slavery on the island resulted only from metropolitan fears that such a move would encourage undecided Cuban planters to support the rebels during the Ten Years' War. As far as Puerto Rico was concerned, the objective of establishing a "modern" wage labor system took precedence over possible losses of previous investment, if any, in slaves. Although cane planters depended on slaves for sugar manufacturing, the use of slaves in other agricultural tasks was limited due to the lack of capital during the period of expansion. Since the reduced numbers also removed the threat of a slave revolt or racial unrest, the fight against slavery became one with the struggle against political authoritarianism and commercial monopoly.

Due to the accommodating nature of island politics, then, it is not surprising that the culmination of the reformist trend was the assimilationist and autonomist currents. *Asimilistas* sought full organic unity with the metropolis and all the constitutional rights due Spanish citizens. They demanded equality with all other Spanish provinces, with the understanding that special institutions would recognize that Puerto Rico had particular needs and problems. The rival *autonomista* group based its program on self-government principles consonant with political union with Spain. Although administrative decentralization was the primary objective, control over immigration, the mail system, the insular budget, taxes, and trade negotiations was also included in the ambitious platform.

Luis Muñoz Rivera, the able Puerto Rican autonomist, and Mateo Práxedes Sagasta, the old Liberal Spanish politician, negotiated the new working relationship between Spain and Puerto Rico. It required, not surprisingly, the autonomista's pledge to affiliate with Sagasta's party. In exchange, Puerto Rico was granted self-government in the form of a fifteen-member Council of Administration, a Chamber of Deputies, and representation to the Cortes. The regulation of tariffs was irrefutable proof that the mother country ceased to consider the two Antilles, Cuba and Puerto Rico, as one entity. Following Prime Minister Cánovas del Castillo's assassination, the incoming administration granted Puerto Rico autonomy.

The embarrassing denouement of decades of intellectual and political work had little to do with the actions of Puerto Ricans. Both autonomy in 1897 and possession by the United States after the Spanish-American War resulted—ironically enough—more from association with Cuba than from either spontaneous or coherent policy on the part of the powers involved. Home rule was part of a "package deal in a last-minute bid to save Cuba for Spain."[1] U.S. pressure to end the war in Cuba and Spain's realization that military victory was no longer an option forced the mother country into granting autonomy to both islands. Similarly, the acquisition of Puerto Rico was a happy accident from the perspective of U.S. naval interests, intent on keeping European powers out of the American continent. It had little to do with elaborate plans to exploit the island as a colonial market, although Puerto Rico—as war booty—represented an attractive business proposition once in the hands of the United States.

The valiant efforts of Puerto Ricans to define their interests as different from those of Spain failed. Although cultural, racial, and political manifestations of nationalist sentiment were common throughout the century, the Puerto Rican elite could only take its cues from the political situation in the metropolis as a means to effect change. Both the autocratic figure of the captain-general and the limited leverage of Puerto Ricans in the mother country forced a potential political elite to cast its demands within the framework provided by Spanish internal politics. Consolidation of interests, as happened fleetingly at Lares, became almost impossible. Ultimately, Puerto Rico sought only a liberalization of Spanish administrative and trade restrictions, not separation from the mother country. Eager to protect their economic interests, reformists preferred autonomy; they received instead a new metropolis.

## The Dominican Republic

The growth of Dominican nationalism was fueled by adversity. In the days of the early colony, the constant presence of French settlers—civil and military—reinforced the poor and sparsely populated colony's tenuous relationship with Spain. Haitian attacks, beginning early in the nineteenth century and culminating with Dominican independence in 1844, fostered a Dominican sense of community. Ironically enough, these incursions served to convince the island's leaders—self-seeking local caudillos—to promote annexation schemes to the United States and Spain. That the Dominican Republic was able to obtain its independence from Haiti in 1844 and from Spain (for the second time) in 1865 remains—in the context of the regional and personal nature of politics—a phenomenal achievement. By century's end, not only independence, but also elite consensus on political and economic development issues presented themselves as colonial legacies on which to build the new nation-state.

Identification with the mother country stands out as characteristic of Hispaniola settlers during the Spanish possession of the island. Continuous conflicts with French squatters on the western end promoted unconditional loyalty to Spain, even as the mother country turned its back on the community, ceding its part of the island to France in the Treaty of Ryswick in 1697. Returning to the Spanish fold in a valiant show of force, Dominicans defeated the French in 1808 and proclaimed their support of the deposed Ferdinand VII and of the activities of the Junta Central Suprema in Spain.

As a by-product of self-defense efforts, a more coherent understanding of themselves as a community of settlers struggling to survive accompanied the chronic preservation of Spanish rule on the island. Protection against French attacks—especially after Spain withdrew its fleet from the area—took the form of local skirmishes, in which life and property—not state loyalties—were at stake. The same was true of incursions by various leaders of the ex-slave armies to the west during the revolutionary struggle: when Haitian emperor Jean-Jacques Dessalines threatened to take over Santiago in 1805, French and local troops united to repel the attack and protect their material possessions, not necessarily to preserve their political ties.

From 1822 to 1844, ad hoc resistance to the organized attack implicit in the Haitian domination contributed to the as yet vague effort at self-definition. The imposition of the alien regime was rejected on all fronts: race, language, culture, legal system, and economic organization. The abolition of slavery and the introduction of the Code Napoleon (which permitted expropriation of corporate lands) promoted the destruction of traditional landholding patterns dependent on privilege and a sparse population. The establishment of an unpopular rural code to provide labor to western plantations and eastern cattle ranches accompanied the new emphasis on production for export. The 1825 ordinance requiring both eastern and western ends to indemnify France for independence, the regulation of the rich eastern mahogany trade, and the closing of five western ports crystallized opposition to Haitian strongman Henri Boyer. In the eastern part, merchant Juan Pablo Duarte led the young Trinitarian intellectuals to proclaim—almost in a vacuum—the ascendancy of the trilogy "fatherland, man, and law." But the powerful Haitian opposition—La Réforme—intended merely to replace Boyer with Charles Hérard.

For the next ten years, Dominican military strongmen fought to preserve their country's independence from their Haitian neighbors. In 1844, a 30,000-strong two-pronged attack was successfully repelled in both north and south. Four years later, it took a Dominican flotilla harassing Haitian coastal villages, land reinforcements in the south, and a British and French naval blockade to force the determined Haitian emperor into a one-year truce. In the most thorough and intense encounter of all, Dominican guerrillas armed with machetes sent Haitian troops into flight on all three fronts in 1855. Success in the protracted defense of what already was a national territory developed in Dominicans a sense of self-accomplishment not found elsewhere in the Spanish Caribbean.

Buenaventura Báez and Pedro Santana, the two local caudillos under whose rule the independent state struggled to become a nation after 1844, had as a vague design—besides personal enrichment—the development of close ties with a foreign protector as a means to achieve political stability and economic prosperity in the face of constant invasions from Haiti. Their untiring efforts to obtain protectorate status included offers to already interested parties: France, the United States, and finally Spain.

Buenaventura Báez, the leader of the pro-French faction, was the first to act upon his convictions. Plotting in 1844 with French minister André Nicolas Levassour, he intended to turn over the Dominican Republic to France immediately after independence. Once the Dominicans repelled the Haitian enemy, however, France could no longer justify the acquisition of the territory: Great Britain would be outraged at French control of the Samaná peninsula, that is, of Dominican commerce. The French resigned themselves to intercede in favor of the new state in its negotiations with its bellicose neighbor. Both wartime diplomacy and cooperation with other European powers in shows of naval force against Haiti assured France of at least keeping the country as a trading partner.

The traditional champion of the U.S. protectorate was Pedro Santana. Impressed by the northern neighbor's military and economic might, the Dominican leader sought U.S. support during the independence struggle. The United States—interested as it was in the commercial potential of the island—was cautious in its involvement in the area: like England, which was satisfied with being the Dominican Republic's largest trading partner, it limited its support of the new state to sending some ammunition and clothing for the army and a commercial agent to evaluate the political and business climate. Even as U.S. military and business interests eyed the Dominican Republic, the thirst for territorial expansion surfaced slowly. Attempts to rent land for a naval base in the Samaná peninsula in 1855 and the short possession of the guano-rich Isla de Alta Vela by a group of North American adventurers in 1860 were isolated instances of the desire for outright territorial expansion. The Dominican Republic's formal bid for protection in exchange for the use of Samaná—a treaty of annexation—was finally turned down by the United States Senate in 1867.

Actively pursuing annexation or not, the great powers controlled the destiny of the Dominican Republic. Báez and Santana courted them and received their personal favors through simplistic machinations that responded to strategic and commercial considerations. Spain recognized Dominican independence in 1855 only after President Franklin Pierce showed an interest in leasing Samaná. Similarly, a treaty of friendship, commerce, and navigation with the United States threatened Spain enough to plot against Santana in 1855. In a rare instance of agreement, angry consuls accompanied by warships forced the Dominican Republic to establish exchange rates favorable to foreign merchants in 1859. The fate of the new state, for better and for worse, was in great measure tied to the goodwill and interests of these giants.

After seemingly endless searches, generous propositions, and tough negotiations, the Dominican Republic became Spain's protectorate in 1861. The agreement between the Iberian metropolis and the former colony safeguarded the autonomy and integrity of the Dominican Republic and offered protection from foreign attack, money for fortifications, the reorganization of the army, and the immigration of Spanish settlers. In exchange, the Dominican Republic would not enter treaties or alliances with other nations or alienate territory.

Spanish domination confirmed how little control the Dominicans had over their own affairs. The military commander sent from Cuba to coordinate administrative details perceived the situation as an opportunity to establish another colonial government in the area. None of the promises of the Spanish government were fulfilled: peninsulars were assigned to bureaucratic posts, new taxes were imposed, commerce was restricted, and investment capital did not arrive. Many of the policies established were openly resented: the Roman Catholic church regained its hegemonic social role, slavery was restored, and the devalued Dominican currency was not redeemed but only replaced by more paper money.

In the Cibao, a group of men rose in the name of independence, even if just from the abuses committed by Spanish troops in the region. In an almost intuitive rejection of what was Spanish and in defense of what was Dominican, southern cattle ranchers proclaimed themselves leaders of the country. The War of Restoration—a guerrilla fight such as became common in the Caribbean—ended with Spain's abrogation of the annexation treaty in 1865.

The highly personalistic nature of politics, however, made difficult the consolidation of the state and the definition of a nation for most of the century. The factions formed under the auspices of leaders who had effectively garnered support for the revolutionary cause were reduced to two shortly after independence. Tomás Bobadilla, recruited into the early independence effort because of his upper-class connections, plotted against Duarte, the leader of the Trinitarians, who was sent into exile with many of his followers. Santana, whose *seibanos* provided the military resistance against the Haitian menace, rose against Bobadilla on gaining the presidency and successfully persecuted all opposition, including the families of the exiled Trinitarians and the man responsible for the favorable colored response to the revolution. Santana's ruthless and arbitrary behavior then focused on the person of Buenaventura Báez.

From 1844 to 1873 (except for the four-year period of Spanish rule in the sixties), Santana and Báez struggled for the presidency. Although Báez, a merchant from Azua with some legislative experience, reached the highest office with the support of Santana, he soon alienated his mentor by challenging his military authority and by opposing Santana's efforts to bring about a U.S. protectorate. Exiled in perpetuity, Báez returned to the Dominican Republic under the patronage of the Spanish consul and became president in 1856. When *cibaeño* resistance against Báez crystallized in 1857, Santana joined the rebels and—within a few years of his victory—carried out his lifelong dream of establishing a protectorate, not under the United States, but under Spain. After Santana's Spanish allies left the country, the nation turned once more to Báez, who—for better or for worse—was a known quantity.

The absence of a political tradition against which to evaluate state leaders permitted Santana to pursue his quest for power and Báez to enrich himself in this period. Santana continually intervened in the workings of constitutional bodies. He forced the adoption of Article 210, which gave the president unrestricted control over the armed forces and the powers necessary for national security for the duration of the war with Haiti, on the representatives at San Cristóbal in 1844. In 1854, he simply created a new document, which assured the executive of supremacy over other branches of government and over the provinces. In his obsession with power, Santana required unconditional loyalty: he attacked the archbishop who had praised Báez's concordat with the pope and insisted that he swear loyalty to the constitution.

Báez's blunders revolved around money matters. In the face of chronic shortages of cash throughout his administrations, Báez simply had more paper money printed, so the peso dropped to 2 percent of its nominal value. Tobacco producers had reason to complain when Báez ordered them to sell their crops to the government in exchange for paper money and then resold it in the international market for hard currency. In flagrant violation of state interests, Báez had 24 million pesos printed in 1856 and 1857; only his friends and political relatives were allowed to redeem their paper money at the going rate before the emission and subsequent drastic devaluation. Using these tactics, Báez not only made 50,000 pesos for himself, but also accumulated in the national treasury enough money to meet the costs to be incurred in fighting his enemies. Both he and Santana operated from an instinct for self-preservation that did not make room for national unity considerations.

Regional economic divisions also stood in the way of national development. The Dominican Republic had little hope for unification as it suffered the consequences of the rise of local caudillos in the context of isolated resistance to foreign incursions. Báez and Santana, men from the southern cattle-growing and mahogany region, managed to exclude—for most of the nineteenth century—northern tobacco growers and merchants from political participation. Both in 1857 and 1865, the military elements entrenched in the south overpowered the northern movements against the fraudulent measures taken by Báez and the abuse of the Spaniards. Southern-based governments built oligarchical power structures based on large landholdings and on the temporary will of one person. Northerners thought more along lines of consensus among medium-sized property holders.

Out of these personal and regional conflicts and long after the achievement of independence, however, rose the Dominican nation. The unification of political groupings against Báez in 1878 was a declaration against arbitrary power, as liberal intellectuals and a new generation of politicians aspired to progress and order. The century-old movement directed at freeing the individual from economic and political restrictions, however, culminated in the rule of the dictator Ulises Heureaux.

## Conclusion

The three Spanish Caribbean territories aspired to autonomous status in the nineteenth century. Cuba, although self-assured in its wealth, had considerable difficulty in achieving independence. By contrast, Puerto Rico lacked the means to fight for it. The Dominican Republic, poor and divided, continuously sought foreign protection through most of the nineteenth century.

The tables turned by the end of the century. Cuba, closest of the three to establishing a popular national government, became a puppet of the United States. Puerto Rico's constant accommodations to metropolitan considerations were hardly appreciated and ultimately constituted only a preparation for a similar relationship with a new owner. The Dominican Republic's struggles against Haiti and Spain helped mold a national identity. In the final analysis, the establishment of states—or the separatist sentiment that is their basis— preceded the birth of nations in all three cases. None of the governments installed by the end of the century could count on parallel social developments to solidify the nation. Cuba's independence was a strictly artificial affair. Puerto Rico continued to frame its needs within the demands of empire. Even the Dominican Republic's hope-filled adventure with Heureaux turned sour as the apparatus of state failed to respond to the needs of society. Twentieth-century developments in these islands have largely conformed to the patterns established one hundred years ago.

## Note

1. Carr, *Puerto Rico*, p. 19.

## 10

Bonham C. Richardson

# Caribbean Migrations, 1838–1985

D r. Lloyd Greig, a physician who resides in Beverly Hills, California, visits Jamaica twice each year. His travels to the Caribbean, however, have nothing to do with Jamaica's advertised reputation as a friendly, salubrious tourist spa for vacationing North Americans. Greig is a native of Jamaica who moved away from his home island twenty years ago to receive his medical training at Meharry Medical College in Nashville, Tennessee, and who now practices medicine in the Los Angeles area. Recently he organized a group of West Indian-born physicians, who, like Greig, now reside and practice in the United States, to return to the Caribbean periodically to provide free medical care for island residents.[1]

Lloyd Greig is not, in terms of job definition, a typical West Indian migrant. A visible and growing number of West Indian-born professionals indeed live in Montreal, Toronto, New York, Philadelphia, Miami, London, Paris, and Amsterdam. More often, however, the Caribbean peoples who recently migrated—legally and otherwise—to these and many other urban centers in Europe and North America work as skilled and unskilled laborers. Yet Greig and working-class West Indians who live abroad have much in common because very few of them have lost touch with the peoples and places they have left behind. Whereas Greig donates his valuable medical skills to his home island, emigrant West Indian laborers routinely send money home. The taxi driver from Barbados in New York, the laundry worker from Aruba in The Hague, the street vendor from Guadeloupe in Paris—not to mention the cane cutter from Saint Vincent in Trinidad—all contribute materially to their home societies by remitting gifts or money or by paving the way for friends and relatives back home who may decide to migrate themselves in the future.

In many ways, the current generation of West Indian migrants is simply doing what earlier generations have done for one and one-half centuries. Since British slave emancipation in 1834, men and women of the Caribbean islands and rimlands have ventured abroad in order to compensate for a lack of resources and opportunities at home. They have thus broadened their livelihood possibilities by extending their travel patterns ("migrating") through extraordinary and costly individual efforts. Each successive generation of West Indian peoples has identified and traveled to nearby and distant locales. So a successful migration tradition characterizes much of the Caribbean region in the late twentieth century. In some of the smaller islands of the Caribbean, human migration sustains the local societies which would collapse without it.

Today's news media take little, if any, notice of the historical background of Caribbean migration, adopting instead an ahistorical slant that inevitably obscures understanding. Massive human movements from West Indian locales are, of course, events of contemporary international significance, not simply arcane academic topics, and these migratory movements are duly reported in metropolitan newspapers and on television. Even the most casual TV viewers, for example, are aware of the Mariel boatlift from Cuba to southern Florida, the ongoing "coloured question" in the United Kingdom, and a perceived political shift to the right in France, said to be partly a reaction to the metropolitan presence of immigrant guest workers from the former French Empire. But a thirty-second TV spot on the nightly news describing the close physical proximity of Haitian poverty and Miami's bright lights frames the issue of Caribbean migration entirely in the present; such a perspective ignores the fact that Haitians and other Caribbean peoples have been migrating and returning home for decades. Furthermore, metropolitan perspectives on Caribbean migration often carry with them an obscurantist, condescending, uninformed bias; academic seminars, congressional hearings, or symposia that deal with the "problems" of Caribbean migration thereby hold the assumption that such problems are aberrations. In this case, the norm, of course, is the uniquely bounded, sedentary affluence of Western society.

## Migration History

The roots of Caribbean migration go much deeper than the earliest outmigrations from the islands themselves and are far more fundamental than the human movements from and within the West Indies that have been going on longer than most of us realize. Unique among former colonial regions, the Caribbean was transformed from its aboriginal condition and re-created into a remarkably different—yet still "underdeveloped"—region within two centuries after Columbus's arrival. The decline of the Caribs and Arawaks, the modification of insular ecosystems, and the substitution of imported plants—predominantly sugarcane—for native food crops and natural biota all accompanied the creation of West Indian plantation societies whose physical environments were eventually geared toward the production of tropical staple crops for an impersonal and growing world market.

The key to sustaining an enduring flow of sugar, cotton, and cocoa from the Caribbean plantations to Europe in a preindustrial era, was, of course, the importation of a labor force to replace the decimated aboriginal stock. The solution came in the form of millions of African slaves who survived the Middle Passage and who came to populate the Caribbean region. Perhaps nearly half of the roughly 10 million African slaves imported to the New World from Africa during the slave era went to Spanish, British, French, Dutch, and Danish Caribbean colonies.

This calculated colonial transformation of Caribbean lands and a demographic policy of introduced overpopulation created local conditions with which West Indians have had to cope ever since. Imported food usually was necessary to feed slave populations whose main activities were devoted to producing tropical staples for export, not food for their own consumption. Planters' land-use decisions were responses to European market demands, not to insular environmental characteristics. The results of these early policies have left the Caribbean region a legacy of eroded landscapes exacerbated by continuous human population pressures. A cumulative historical incongruity between people and land in the Caribbean, moreover, has many implications. It is the reason why ecological "man-land" or "carrying capacity" studies by social scientists, presuming essential relationships between "native" peoples and the immediate environments they occupy, never have been widely practiced in the Caribbean as they have, for example, in the Pacific. It also helps explain why human migration has been an enduring livelihood strategy in the Caribbean region ever since its people have been free to leave.

Uncertainty about food rations was one of the many precarious elements of Afro-Caribbean slave life. Overwork, exhaustion, and disease also haunted the generations of men, women, and children held in captivity by European planters. One of the reasons for the surprisingly large numbers of slaves taken to the Caribbean during the slave era was that the tragically high death rate among slaves called for annual replenishment of slave labor forces, especially during the decades of the seventeenth century when slaves removed much of the forest cover of the eastern Caribbean to make way for sugarcane. Jamaican sociologist Orlando Patterson argues that it was during the Caribbean slave era that migration first became a powerful symbolic force among Afro-Caribbean peoples.[2] All slaves, or their ancestors, had experienced a forced migration from their West African homelands to the New World. Perhaps more important, migration to clandestine maroon encampments in forested interiors in larger islands and the backlands of the Guianas was one of the few means of escape. Actual migration from the islands themselves, however, with a few isolated exceptions, would have to await freedom.

Slave emancipation in the British Caribbean represented perhaps less a sharp break with the past than it did a continuity of oppression. Planters continued to monopolize the best lands. And local legislatures, dominated by planters, enacted a series of harsh, repressive post-emancipation laws designed to immobilize former slaves and to ensure the availability of an abundant, and therefore cheap, local labor pool. Resistance to ongoing post-emancipation plantation repression was notable throughout the Caribbean. Free villages of former slaves developed in the interiors of the larger islands, communities of peoples who had partially removed themselves from the plantations. Anthropologist Sidney Mintz has described this post-slavery era of the Caribbean as one in which "reconstituted peasantries" emerged throughout the region.[3]

Interisland migration by freedmen at emancipation was most notable on the smaller islands of the British Caribbean. On Barbados, for example, the fertile soil and comparatively level terrain of the entire island remained monopolized by sugarcane planters; black Barbadian freedmen had few local opportunities other than remaining on estates as poorly paid "located laborers." It is therefore not surprising that many Barbadians opted to emigrate, often in a semi-clandestine manner, to neighboring Trinidad and also to British Guiana (now Guyana) where planters offered higher wages than at home. By 1842, Barbadian colonial officials estimated that perhaps 4,000 Barbadians already had traveled away and that probably 10 percent of those had returned to Barbados. But colonial censuses in Barbados and other Caribbean colonies of the nineteenth century were generally unreliable. We know that migration and return from and to several of the islands was extensive before 1850 because planters and colonial officials continuously grumbled about it, but the precise numbers of migrants will probably never be known.

Similar to Barbados, the other small British Caribbean islands were ruled at emancipation by plantocracies determined to limit freedmen's access to local lands. Leeward Islands planters, for example, enacted trespassing and vagrancy laws to keep freedmen rooted to the estates. Within months after emancipation, however, hundreds of free men and women from Saint Kitts, Nevis, Montserrat, Antigua, and the Windward Caribbean had sailed south in response to wages offered by Trinidadian planters that were double those paid at home. By 1845, more than 10,000 migrants from small West Indian islands had traveled to Trinidad; over 8,000 others had gone all the way to British Guiana. The majority accomplished their journeys on the decks of tiny fishing sloops and schooners over hundreds of miles of tropical ocean interrupted by stormy interisland passages and unmarked rocks and shoals.

Perhaps the most remarkable dimension of this early migration adaptation in the small islands of the eastern Caribbean was that many of the emigrants eventually returned. Again, accurate records never were maintained. By 1848, however, Trinidadian officials complained that thousands of the "old islanders" (those from the smaller islands to the north) had gone home. The returnees took money back to friends and kinsmen who had stayed behind. And as early as 1854, colonial officials on Saint Kitts-Nevis reported that travelers had returned from Trinidad arrayed in "gaudy" and distinctive clothing. Successful Caribbean migrants of the mid-nineteenth century, interestingly, seem to have adorned themselves back home in modern, fashionable clothing they had purchased at their destinations. This distinctive clothing signified to those staying behind (just as it does among returned West Indian migrants of the late twentieth century) that the migrants had traveled far and prospered abroad.

The migration and return of freedmen from the small islands of the eastern Caribbean in the 1840s were intertwined, as they always have been, with world and regional economic trends and adjustments. At emancipation, the center of gravity of the British Caribbean sugarcane industry was shifting to the south, away from the eroded soils and antiquated infrastructures of the "old islands" toward the "new" southern colonies. Steam engines already had been used to crush canes in Spanish Cuba by 1796, and the new British colonies of Trinidad (recently Spanish) and British Guiana (recently Dutch) soon followed with the adoption of similar modern production equipment. Producing canes during the new industrial era, however, would, according to Trinidadian and Guianese planters, call for a great deal more labor than resided in their colonies at emancipation.

Migration of another kind, however, eventually "solved" the perceived post-emancipation labor shortages of southern Caribbean planters. At emancipation the British government approved the passage from India of indentured workers under five-year contracts to the Caribbean, the first boatload arriving in British Guiana in early 1838. From that year until the termination of the indenture system in 1917, nearly 240,000 men and women crossed the "black waters" from their native India to British Guiana, 135,000 were sent to Trinidad, and over 33,000 went to Jamaica. Lesser numbers ended up in several of the smaller British Caribbean islands. The use of indentured workers in the British

Caribbean was a single dimension of a worldwide system of exporting Indians to serve tropical labor needs in the British Empire. Before Indians went to the Caribbean, British and French planters had sent them to Mauritius in the Indian Ocean. And later in the nineteenth century, and into the twentieth, thousands more were shipped to the cane fields of South Africa and Fiji.

Indians arriving in the Caribbean were not always greeted warmly by black freedmen, who often saw the new estate residents as rivals for cash wages on the plantations. By flooding the labor market with indentured workers from India, planters were able to drive down labor costs; at the same time, they also ensured the incipient development of ethnic rivalries among different working-class groups in the region, rivalries that persist into the late twentieth century. The first imported Indians were housed in barracks or "ranges" on the Caribbean sugarcane plantations for the duration of their indenture periods. In several cases, their treatment was so harsh as to warrant investigation by the British Anti-Slavery Society, which supplied bitter accusations that slavery had been reinstituted in a new form. The Indians brought to the West Indies, moreover, were by no means a homogeneous group. Although the great majority had come from the recruiting terminals at Calcutta and Madras and were lumped together as "coolies" by outside observers, these new immigrants had come from all over India. They were separated in actuality by differences in language, religion, and caste. Even among Hindus, confusion prevailed among these new Asian residents of the Caribbean owing to the vast differences in cultural practices they had brought with them from different parts of India. Trinidadian historian Kusha Haraksingh feels that a good deal of the confusion and intragroup rivalry among Indians brought to the Caribbean was a function of "collapsing space," which saw disparate cultural practices from the whole of India compressed into tiny insular habitats.[4]

The British were not the only Caribbean planters to tap southern Asia for indentured laborers to compensate for the loss of a captive slave labor force. France abolished slavery in 1848, the Netherlands in 1863; Spain ended slavery in Puerto Rico in 1873 and in Cuba in 1886. Indians from French India went to the French West Indies for the first time in 1852. Within the next decade over 10,000 arrived, mainly from the French Indian enclave of Pondicherry. By 1885 another 87,000 Indians were in Martinique, Guadeloupe, and French Guiana, most of them transported in British ships. The planters of Dutch Surinam imported 35,000 men and women from British India between 1872 and 1917, and by 1924 roughly 22,000 Javanese had also arrived in Surinam. By the turn of the century, the importation of indentured Asians, combined with the (mainly African) inhabitants of the islands, had formed an ethnic mosaic of peoples and languages stretching from the eastern Caribbean into northern South America, a pattern created by cumulative, planter-sponsored in-migrations of peoples from throughout the world.

As some small colonial territories of the southern and eastern Caribbean attempted to resuscitate their sugarcane industry with massive infusions of migrant Asian labor, the Greater Antilles were beginning to dominate the production of Caribbean sugarcane. By 1860, Cuba, many times larger than any of the British, French, or Dutch islands, but which had not undergone the earlier plantation transformations as the others, was the world's largest producer of cane sugar. Cuba had continued to import large numbers of African slaves into the 1850s, but external economic and political pressures essentially blocked the trade thereafter. Cuban planters also had introduced tens of thousands of Chinese laborers beginning in the 1840s, a number that may have reached 100,000 in the next few decades. The Chinese brought across the Pacific to work in Cuban sugarcane fields and Peruvian guano beds were, formally, "indentured" laborers, although their living and working conditions differed little from those of slaves. And the transportation of these Chinese into the Caribbean, interrelated as it was with so-called "blackbirding" in the Pacific, marks a period in Caribbean migration history nearly as unsavory as that of slavery.

The accelerating importance of the sugarcane industries of the Greater Antilles during the latter half of the nineteenth century was due to technical changes, intensified internal capital investments, and, perhaps most of all, the presence of the U.S. sugar market. And just as the political and economic presence of the United States came to overshadow and direct activities on the plantations of Cuba, Santo Domingo, and Puerto Rico as the nineteenth century was drawing to a close, the dawn of a new century saw U.S. economic domination of the entire circum-Caribbean. Accordingly, the movement of tens of thousands of labor migrants throughout the Caribbean region early in the twentieth century was almost exclusively associated with—in some cases nearly mandated by—U.S. labor needs.

Construction of the Panama Canal (1904–14) by the United States uprooted and dislocated tens of thousands of West Indian men and women who traveled to Panama for jobs. The failed French attempt two decades earlier also had attracted perhaps 50,000 West Indians, mainly from Jamaica. Jamaicans had traveled to Panama even before that, many working on the isthmian railroad in the 1850s. So when officials of the Isthmian Canal Commission (the U.S. governmental agency responsible for canal construction) sought labor for the blasting and earth-moving, it is not surprising that they turned to Jamaica. To their disappointment, however, Jamaica denied the commission a labor recruiting terminal in Kingston, claiming that too many Jamaicans already had died and suffered working for the French.

The Americans eventually established their principal labor-recruiting station for canal workers in Barbados. From 1905 to 1913, U.S. officials shipped 20,000 Barbadian male contract laborers—as well as hundreds of others from nearby islands—from Bridgetown to Panama. But men and women traveling informally from their home islands to the Canal Zone far outnumbered contract workers during the construction decade. Barbadian historian Velma Newton estimates that as many as 40,000 Barbadians (besides the 20,000 contract workers) traveled informally to the Panamanian isthmus before the canal was completed, and that between 80,000 and 90,000 Jamaicans did so as well.[5] British West Indians were not the only Caribbean peoples traveling to the Canal Zone. Men and women from Danish, Dutch, and French islands went too. Between 1905 and 1907 U.S. labor recruiters shipped 7,600 contract laborers from Guadeloupe and Martinique to Panama before the continental French government ended the recruiting.

Whatever the total number (insular demographic data were still notoriously vague and unreliable), the West Indians who traveled from their home islands to Panama—and often back again—set in motion demographic trends that reverberated throughout the region. Thousands of West Indians perished on the isthmus from exhaustion, disease, and landslides; nearly 6,000 Barbadians alone died of all causes from 1906 to 1920 in Panama. Probably over 15,000 British West Indians altogether died in Panama before 1920. Others never returned home but drifted west to new destinations such as the new American banana plantations in Honduras and the Limón district of eastern Costa Rica. Hundreds joined the British West Indies regiment of World War I and fought against the Turks in Palestine. Thousands stayed in Panama and became the black "Zonians" whose presence would become a treaty issue between the United States and Panama decades later.

The flow of British West Indian laborers to the Panama Canal Zone in the first two decades of the twentieth century was paralleled by a countercurrent of money that workers sent home to their families and friends. The "Panama money" softened the effects of a severe economic depression in the British Caribbean that could be traced to competition with European beet sugar for the London market. Wives and mothers on the home islands used the wages sent from Panama to purchase foodstuffs, clothing, and membership in local burial societies. In thousands of cases, money from Panama also purchased land plots, fishing sloops, and shops throughout the islands, thereby affording working-class blacks a measure of independence from local plantocracies. This was not the first time small-island West Indians had prospered from money sent and brought home from a wage destination, but Panama money intensified the search for wages abroad by migrants from small Caribbean islands because it represented a volume and continuity of remittances that had never been known before.

When it became obvious to American officials that the canal project would soon be finished, they began to repatriate many of the West Indians to their home islands. Thousands of the labor migrants, now accustomed to receiving American wages, traveled on to Cuba and the Dominican Republic where U.S. capital had helped expand sugarcane acreage in both countries after the beginning of the century. The further "development" of the sugarcane industries of the Greater Antilles represented, in a broad sense, the same sort of challenge to American engineers that the Panamanian isthmus had; any economic problem, it was thought, could be solved with a lavish application of modern North American technology. Cuban sugar-processing techniques and field methods were thereby modernized by the turn of the century. Similarly, the "idle" lands of the southeastern quadrant of Hispaniola were rapidly converted from tropical forests and scrublands into enormous fields of sugarcane intersected by cog rails and commanded by the towering smokestacks of newly constructed grinding factories, built mainly with U.S. money.

The attraction of wage jobs in modernizing and constructing new agricultural facilities, and eventually harvesting the sugarcane, in Cuba and the Dominican Republic drew thousands of migrating black "Antillanos." Some were veterans from Panama. Many came directly from the English-speaking islands. Thousands of Haitians came too, mainly as seasonal cane cutters. Sailing schooners, and later steamers, had taken men from the English-speaking islands of the Leeward Caribbean to San Pedro de Macoris—in the heart of the Dominican Republic's sugarcane belt—since before the turn of the century. And Jamaican workers traveled to Cuba, mainly on steamships, in ever larger numbers as the Panama Canal construction wound down. In 1919 and 1920, the peak years for Jamaican migration to Cuba, nearly 50,000 Jamaicans sought work on the larger island. As a linguistically alien, dark-skinned, Protestant, and mostly male labor force, black West Indians were not always welcome in the large Roman Catholic, Spanish-speaking island. In Santo Domingo they were derided as *cocolos* by native Dominicans. Authorities in both countries insisted that these migrants—many of whom arrived for the annual cane harvest in January and departed after the crop was in in July—were holding jobs that should be performed by locals.

The application and withdrawal of U.S. capital at various locations throughout the circum-Caribbean region thus pulled and pushed labor migrants here and there. Accordingly, insular demographic patterns continued to reflect the familiar characteristics that migration societies have been known for before and since. Females, children, and old people had tended to predominate in the small Caribbean islands ever since principally male laborers had traveled away after slavery. But by the early twentieth century insular populations had become even more mobile and fluid from season to season and from year to year as external job opportunities appeared, disappeared, and reappeared. For instance, the massive exodus of men from Saint Kitts, Nevis, Anguilla, and Antigua to Santo Domingo at the beginning of each year in the first decades of the twentieth century began a six-month period in which mothers, wives, and children back home waited, hoping for remittances through the mail. Colonial officials in the same islands dreaded the men's return in the late summer because, for the next few months, unemployment always became a problem on the local sugarcane plantations, incipient labor protests and disturbances surfaced, and burglary rates rose. The population characteristics, economic opportunities, and even cultural attributes of these small Leeward Islands in the early twentieth century were influenced not so much by local events as by the rhythms of the sugarcane harvests in the Greater Antilles.

Although migration-induced demographic patterns had become intensified, Caribbean migration in the early twentieth century had changed in at least two ways from what it had been like in the decades immediately following emancipation. First, the number of people moving about became much larger as U.S. capital investment was concentrated in selected places, creating thousands of ephemeral work opportunities for multi-skilled laborers and their families. Second, migration was no longer simply a matter of traveling from one neighboring island to the next. Rather, it often involved journeys to the far edges of the circum-Caribbean zone.

It is therefore not surprising that more and more West Indians traveling farther and farther from home discovered the eastern United States, mainly the New York City area, as a migration destination. Some already had taken up residence in New York and Boston in the late nineteenth century as steamer lines expanded individual travel possibilities. But from 1901, when 520 "Negro Immigrant Aliens" were admitted from the West Indies, until 1924 when 10,630 arrived, 102,000 black West Indians entered the United States. Data were not maintained as to island of origin; some came from French, Dutch, and Danish Caribbean islands, but the great majority were British West Indians.

What were the general characteristics of these new black residents of the eastern United States? British West Indian newspaper reports of the time suggested that this migration had taken away disproportionately high numbers of brown-skinned, middle-class islanders. However, a large number of black Panama Canal veterans had also traveled to New York. These crucial color distinctions that immigrant West Indians noted among themselves and among American blacks went largely unnoticed by white American employers, who saw the West Indian migrants as an undifferentiated, dark-skinned group. Some immigrant West Indians who had regarded themselves as middle class at home were therefore often forced to accept menial, working-class positions in the United States.

But West Indian immigrants were by no means homogenized into U.S. culture. They maintained their insular identities in new surroundings, distinguishing themselves from American blacks as well as from each other in a number of ways. Many, for example, were Anglicans, not the Methodists, Baptists, and Fundamentalists usually predominating among black American churchgoers. West Indians also maintained their own cricket clubs and reading societies, behavior regarded as "aloof" by blacks who recently had come north from the southern United States. Many of the West Indian arrivals—perhaps as many as one-third—eventually returned to their home islands. Those who remained in the United States mailed increasing sums of money back to those who stayed behind, continuing a tradition of remittance payments that their fathers and grandfathers had begun in the nineteenth century.

The influences of West Indian migrants in the New York area went far beyond the establishment of cultural enclaves in a new environment. Jervis Anderson has pointed out that Caribbean migrants to New York were particularly vocal and assertive in the early twentieth century, often paving the way for new black professional opportunities that had previously been open only to whites. Influential West Indians, moreover, demanded greater personal respect and established new standards of black self-identity.[6] Jamaican Marcus Garvey arrived in Harlem in 1916 and transferred the headquarters of the Universal Negro Improvement Association (UNIA) the following year. The UNIA's newspaper, *Negro World*, indeed had an international circulation; among other things, this weekly stressed black pride and the importance of Africa as the original black homeland. Garvey's influence therefore extended well beyond the Caribbean. For a brief time, he played an extremely important role in the evolution of black consciousness in the United States.

Other West Indians had contributed significantly to the black community in the United States by the 1930s. They included writers Claude McKay (Jamaica) and Eric Walrond (British Guiana); Richard B. Moore (Barbados) and W. A.

Domingo (Jamaica), as leaders of black nationalist movements; and laborer organizers Ashley Totten and Frank Crosswaith (both of the Virgin Islands). W. E. B. Du Bois, historian, sociologist, and black American advocate of Pan-Africanism, also claimed West Indian parentage. The stream of West Indian migrants to the United States was abruptly curtailed on July 1, 1924, when the U.S. national origins immigrant quota law went into effect. In part a reaction to the massive influx of eastern Europeans and Chinese, the new law essentially closed the United States as a viable migration destination for men and women from the Caribbean region. During the first half of 1924, over 10,000 black West Indians had come to the United States. In the following year, only 308 arrived. The external sanctions against West Indian migration were thus similar to those that had occurred elsewhere in the past and would reoccur. Individual migration was by no means simply locating a suitable travel destination; the reception at the other end was likely to vary as a function of changing social and economic circumstances. Potential Caribbean migrants of the 1920s, however, were not soothed by noting that discrimination against Caribbean migrants was a recurring fact of life. Caribbean blacks in both the United States and the Caribbean spoke out against the recent ruling, arguing that intergovernmental conspiracy might be to blame.

In the Caribbean itself, destinations for migrating men and women were also changing, as macroeconomic controls over local events created boom-and-bust labor markets, sending workers home from some islands and attracting them to others. The high world sugar prices, buoyed by shortages created during World War I, plummeted in the early 1920s. Accordingly, the volume of seasonal labor migration to the Greater Antilles by cane cutters from smaller islands was sharply reduced. At almost the same time, the construction of oil refineries elsewhere attracted some former cane cutters who now became carpenters and masons. The Royal Dutch Shell refinery on the Dutch island of Curaçao began refining petroleum from Lake Maracaibo in 1918. The Standard Oil of New Jersey refinery on nearby Dutch Aruba began to process Maracaibo oil in 1929. Thousands of laborers from the British and Dutch Caribbean went to Curaçao and Aruba to build factories, warehouses, roads, piers, and barracks. The construction of the Lake Maracaibo derricks by American engineers had earlier attracted hundreds of workers from Trinidad, Grenada, and Saint Vincent—English-speaking labor migrants who had experience working in and around the water—to the large estuarine lake of northern Venezuela. Some of these same workers manned shallow-draft oil barges between Maracaibo and the small Dutch islands where the petroleum was refined.

Except in Curaçao and Aruba, however, bust replaced boom throughout the Caribbean region during the depression decade of the 1930s. A dearth of migration possibilities was not limited simply to one economic sector; migrant workers were laid off everywhere, and thousands were sent home. On the smallest islands, where jobs were scarce in the first place, returning migrants overloaded local labor supplies, creating underemployment that was no longer compensated for by remittances from abroad. Despair inevitably led to violence. An estate workers' dispute on Saint Kitts in January 1935 flared into riot and bloodshed: local police quelled the disturbance after shooting three rioters dead and wounding others. Official investigations attributed the riots to economic frustrations felt by a pent-up work force with few migration outlets. The Saint Kitts riot detonated an uneven chain reaction of similar disturbances throughout the eastern Caribbean. The urban poor in Barbados and Jamaica, coal carriers in Saint Lucia, oil field workers in Trinidad, and others rioted for higher wages. The disturbances of the 1930s led to economic and political reforms in several of the islands. And migration—or, more specifically, the lack of migration possibilities for what were, by this time, veteran migrant work forces—underpinned the rioting in each case.

The economic depression of the 1930s also intensified rivalries between host peoples of some Caribbean states and those who had come from neighboring islands to work. For years, for example, Dominicans had complained bitterly that migrant workers had taken jobs that locals should perform. In 1929, owing partly to economic depression, the Dominican Republic severely restricted seasonal immigration into the country, a law aimed in part at the sugar estate laborers who arrived every January from the eastern Caribbean. Tragedy in the Dominican Republic was also related to curbing immigration; it came in 1937 with the slaughter of between 15,000 and 20,000 Haitians who lived and worked in the western and central part of the country. The so-called "Trujillo massacre" was directed by the Dominican dictator and accomplished by those who resented the presence of Haitian migrants who had traditionally crossed over the border to work on Dominican sugar estates.

World War II provided short-lived relief for labor migrants in the West Indies. In 1940 the United States took control of military bases on several British Caribbean islands in exchange for fifty American naval destroyers sent to Britain. Jobs in Trinidad, Antigua, British Guiana, and also on Saint Thomas suddenly became available on the U.S. bases. Tens of thousands of West Indians—many sailing from nearby islands aboard schooners—extended airplane runways, fortified harbors, constructed military barracks, and worked as messengers, cooks, and maids. But, according to older West Indians who recall working for the Americans during the war, these jobs, as so many other jobs had been for Caribbean migrants in the past, seem to have been over nearly as quickly as they appeared. To make matters worse, economic conditions on some of the smaller islands after World War II had deteriorated even from where they stood during the depression. On the British islands, the sudden devaluation of the British pound in 1949 had the immediate effect of increasing prices for items imported from outside the British realm.

A momentous consequence of the aftermath of World War II in Britain—the need for unskilled labor to repair and rebuild the country after a war that had reduced British manpower—led to the massive migration of British West Indians to the United Kingdom in the 1950s. Caribbean blacks traveled to England on British passports so that reliable data were never available as to how many had gone to Britain or had left a particular island; estimates of total Caribbean migration to Britain between 1951 and 1961 vary from 230,000 to 280,000. The corresponding loss of people from some of the smaller islands during the decade was astonishing. The tiny British island of Montserrat in the northeastern Caribbean, for example, is said to have lost over 30 percent of its people to Britain during the 1950s. The travel itself was accomplished on steamers and charter flights. Husbands and fathers often went alone and established an economic foothold in England before sending for the rest of their families. A disproportionately large number of skilled workers—carpenters, masons, plumbers, electricians—left the islands for higher-paying British jobs, thereby depleting insular work forces and, according to some spokesmen, draining away the most capable and productive local inhabitants.

The Caribbean immigrants to Britain concentrated themselves heavily in some parts of the country where jobs were available—in the London area and in the industrial towns and cities of the British midlands. Far from being greeted warmly in the "mother country," however, British West Indians often were subjected to racial slurs and insults on the job and relegated to the worst housing conditions in the unfamiliar British cities. Coal dust, snow, and cold-water flats provided an inhospitable environment for Britain's newest residents, but these conditions were tolerable if the jobs held out.

In the early 1960s, amid widespread white British suspicion and resentment toward an accelerating volume of immigration from the former British Empire, the Commonwealth Immigrants Act was passed. The law, approved after acrimonious parliamentary debate in April 1962, took effect three months later: it specified that those West Indians already residing in the United Kingdom on July 1, 1962, could thereafter bring only wives, husbands, or children under sixteen from abroad to live with them. All others were essentially barred from living in Britain. The British government pointed to a saturated labor market, claiming that unrestricted immigration would create severe unemployment (long a problem in the British Caribbean islands) in the home country. Many West Indians condemned the British action as hypocrisy. And the new British law represented yet another external sanction against Caribbean migrants.

Britain in the mid-1980s had roughly 650,000 black citizens who continued to be concentrated in the nation's industrial slums. Most black Britons are those who immigrated from the Caribbean three decades ago plus an increasingly restive younger generation born in the United Kingdom. British blacks never have been truly assimilated into white Britain and a stagnant British economy has sent unemployment rates soaring among its black populace. The general economic disenchantment of Britain's blacks was mirrored in the Brixton riots in south London in April 1981: a large black mob rioted, looted, and confronted local police in disturbances said to be provoked by police harassment. An official report issued in late 1981 outlined the economic and social malaise of Britain's blacks and vowed improvement. But the white British population has not expressed unanimity in seeking a compassionate solution for former West Indians and their children who now reside in the United Kingdom. After the Brixton disturbances, a handful of British members of Parliament called for a "vigorous policy" of subsidized repatriation of nonwhite immigrants from the United Kingdom to their former colonial homelands.

Unlike the rush to the United Kingdom in the 1950s, the movement of French Antilleans to France was one of modest proportions after World War II. In 1954, those born in Guadeloupe and Martinique residing in France numbered only 15,620, a combined total increasing to 38,740 by 1962. Travel to metropolitan France by citizens of the country's overseas departments (Guadeloupe, Martinique, French Guiana, and the island of Reunion in the Indian Ocean) is currently facilitated by a quasi-governmental travel agency that also attempts to place new arrivals from the overseas departments in working-class jobs. During the 1970s and 1980s, an increasing number of French West Indians went to the metropole via similar travel arrangements. The 1982 census shows that over 190,000 French citizens residing in metropolitan France were born in the overseas departments of the Caribbean: 9,180 from French Guiana, 87,320 from Guadeloupe, and 94,940 from Martinique. Occupationally, French West Indians in France traditionally have held low-level positions in industry and the civil service. They live mainly in Paris but an equal number are scattered throughout other cities.

West Indians from the French Caribbean have sometimes experienced discrimination—similar to that leveled at their British West Indian counterparts—on arrival in Paris and other French cities. In his *Black Skin, White Masks*, Martinican Frantz Fanon points out that those French West Indians who consider themselves French (as, indeed, they legally are) have often been shocked and disappointed by the treatment they have received in France, although such discrimination is illegal there.[7] Yet despite the general similarities in the abusive treatment experienced in both England and France by West Indian immigrants going "home," West Indians in the latter country probably have fared better. This relatively better treatment is perhaps because the West Indian (and African and Haitian) black presence in metropolitan France is overshadowed by the hundreds of thousands of North Africans—Algerians, Tunisians, Moroccans—who have migrated to France since World War II. Guest workers from Portugal, Italy, and Turkey also have gone to France. The North Africans—who inhabit run-down sections of nearly every large French city—have been special targets of French working-class frustrations during the recent economic recession.

A tiny number of Haitians also reside in France. The great majority of them are from the urban area in and around Port-au-Prince, and they are principally students, professionals, and members of the diplomatic corps. Middle- and upper-class Haitians, a number of whom are political refugees, still consider France the ultimate source of their cultural heritage. The impoverished tide of Haitian political and economic refugees, on the other hand, cannot afford the luxury of even considering France as a migration destination and have turned instead to North America—especially French-speaking Quebec and nearby Caribbean states, principally the Bahamas and the Dominican Republic.

The most numerous influx of Caribbean peoples to Western Europe in recent years has been to the Netherlands from the Dutch West Indies, mainly from Suriname which is culturally Caribbean although located in northeastern South America. Smaller numbers have come from the Dutch affiliated islands, principally Curaçao and Aruba. Although earlier migrations from the Dutch Caribbean to the metropole were for traditional reasons such as the desire for education, job opportunities, or chances for upward mobility, the huge number of Surinamese immigrating to Europe in the past decade has been principally because of political push factors. Fearing ethnic rivalry and worse when the South American country gained political independence in November 1975, tens of thousands of Surinamese of Indian and Javanese descent rushed to Holland in the preceding months. A total of 40,000—10 percent of Suriname's populace—emigrated to the Netherlands in 1975 alone. More have left Suriname since the military coup there in 1980. In that year the population of

Suriname was estimated as roughly 350,000, with another 250,000 living abroad, including 180,000 in the Netherlands. Perhaps 30,000 Dutch Antilleans now live in the Netherlands.

As in Britain and France, the principal Dutch urban areas have been the destinations of the vast majority of Dutch West Indians, the Surinamese residing mainly in Amsterdam and many Antilleans in The Hague. And similar problems of discrimination and lack of assimilation have been reported by recent West Indian arrivals in the Netherlands, especially as their numbers have increased. In recent years events in both the Netherlands and the Dutch West Indies have also been influenced by the intimate interrelationships between the mother country and its former colonial possessions, interrelationships created by back-and-forth movements of Caribbean migrants. Antilleans in The Hague, for example, demonstrated against the use of Dutch marines to help quell the riots in Willemstad, Curaçao, in 1969, and several West Indian protesters in the Dutch city were arrested and jailed. Moreover, the "sergeants' coup" in Paramaribo, Suriname, in 1980 is suggested to have been indirectly related to the dissatisfaction of some noncommissioned officers in the Suriname army in contrast to the egalitarian treatment they had received during their earlier military training in the Netherlands.

Whereas hundreds of thousands of Caribbean migrants and those whose parents are West Indians live in Western Europe, Caribbean peoples now residing in North America (mainly the United States) can be counted in the millions. In the past twenty years, ever since the U.S. Immigration Act of 1965 modified the "national origins" system that favored Europeans, Caribbean migrants and others have poured into the United States. These voluminous movements of people are only partly because of changed immigration laws in the United States. Stories from returned friends and relatives, combined with extraordinary advances in communications and transportation technology, have made migration seem altogether less risky than staying home to face relative poverty on a West Indian island.

The effects of the recent Caribbean migration on the United States have been profound, creating irrevocable changes in the American landscape and in American culture. The most obvious effects, perhaps, are the visible results of so many peoples who recently have come north from the islands and rimlands of the Caribbean; such manifestations are Miami's "Little Havana," the Caribbean ethnic enclaves in the New York City area, and Brooklyn's Labor Day parade which has become an annual West Indian carnival. But Caribbean influences are not confined to exotic phenomena grafted onto, but really apart, from the American mainstream. The recent rush by Caribbean peoples and others to the United States has also helped to create a fortress mentality among some Americans, inspiring congressional debate about immigration reform. In the mid-1980s these debates aroused much interest although there was little agreement as to whether more immigration would produce positive or negative effects, and whether stringent new laws could work even if they were passed.

Debate, not to mention suggested legislation, concerning American immigration policy has been confounded by varying and contradictory immigration data. The United States admits over 600,000 persons from abroad per year, of whom roughly 15 percent are West Indians. But these data do not include, for example, the estimated 2 million Puerto Ricans who now reside in the continental United States but who leave no trace in immigration statistics. The U.S. citizenship granted Puerto Ricans in 1917 does not change how many other Americans perceive Puerto Rican "immigrants." Often they are lumped together with "Hispanics" and treated by employers in the same rough way as, say, undocumented workers from Central America. Puerto Rico itself is a society of return immigrants. The commonwealth government estimates that one-fifth of Puerto Rico's people have resided in the continental United States at one time or another. The ambivalent character of the Puerto Rican situation (are they or are they not "migrants"?) helps explain the relatively disappointing and impoverished conditions that many of them experience in the United States. With one foot on the mainland and another at "home," Puerto Ricans coming north have sometimes not carried with them the commitment found among would-be permanent immigrants.

If 600,000 come annually to the United States legally from all other countries, how many enter illegally? The estimated numbers vary from as low as 100,000 to 500,000 each year. Estimates of the total number of illegals, most of whom are acknowledged to be from Latin America and the Caribbean, presently in the United States range from 2 to 6 million. There is perhaps no better (or worse) example available to illustrate the vexing lack of hard data concerning U.S. immigration than that of trying to enumerate Haitians now resident in the United States. Michel Laguerre estimates that the number is perhaps 800,000: 150,000 American citizens, 50,000 students, 400,000 "undocumented entrants," and the remaining 200,000 children of both legals and illegals.[8] Other estimates are higher and many lower. Moreover, to group "Haitians" in the United States into a single category is deceiving at best. Early Haitian migration to the New York City area, a movement that began to increase in the 1950s, was noticeably of upper-class and middle-class professionals fleeing the Duvalier regime. Since 1972, however, the large numbers of black Haitians coming to the United States have been the impoverished boat people escaping political and economic desperation at home, whose sailing odysseys have brought them to Florida. Perhaps half of the estimated 70,000 Haitians now living in southern Florida resided at one time or another in the Bahamas, and the latter country's recent crackdown on its own "Haitian problem" sent many Haitians on to the United States. The great majority of New York City's estimated 300,000 Haitians are working-class blacks, many of whom are there illegally.

According to Jamaican anthropologist Charles Carnegie, the rules distinguishing "legal" and "illegal" migration, categories unquestioned by most Americans, are seen by migrants from the Commonwealth Caribbean as hurdles to cross in their quest to obtain a living.[9] Contemporary migration rules are therefore considered ephemeral obstacles that must be overcome, whether by "legal" means or otherwise. Migrants from the Commonwealth Caribbean have indeed been intimately involved in the U.S. economy for years. British West Indians were leaders in Harlem early in the century, and thousands more have worked in the United States as seasonal farm laborers in intervening decades. Thus, the migration to the United States from the states of the Commonwealth Caribbean since 1965 has represented a recent surge to some Americans but continuity to many West Indians. The great majority of the estimated 600,000 British West Indians now in the United States reside in the New York City area. Their desire to locate on arrival near kinsmen and friends of the same islands results, moreover, in some unlikely residential concentrations within the New York conurbation: the highest concentrations of Nevisians in the United States are probably in New Haven, Connecticut; Perth Amboy, New Jersey, is the home of many Anguillians. The largest numbers of English-speaking West Indians in New York are the roughly 275,000 Jamaicans there. Aggressive, hardworking, and increasingly prosperous, most of the recent immigrants from the Commonwealth Caribbean are referred to collectively as "Jamaicans" by many Americans, whether or not they are from Jamaica.

The same lack of distinction is applied to recent Cuban and Dominican arrivals, who, together with Puerto Ricans, are often considered simply "Hispanics." Furthermore, many Americans associate Cuban immigrants exclusively with those roughly 125,000 Cubans who came to Florida via the Mariel flotilla in 1980. Among the approximately 1 million Cubans (750,000 in southern Florida) who now live in the United States, many are those who left in response to Fidel Castro's takeover of the island a generation ago. The pejorative term "Marielito" is considered an insult in Cuban-American circles, especially among those people who left everything they had in Cuba two decades ago and have regained a measure of prosperity in the United States only after starting all over again. The estimated 350,000 persons from the Dominican Republic now residing in the United States have settled chiefly in the New York metropolitan area. By now a traditional ploy by "undocumented" Dominicans coming to the United States is to travel by boat to nearby Puerto Rico and then to fly directly to the United States where they are virtually indistinguishable from Puerto Ricans as far as U.S. immigration authorities are concerned.

The United States is not the only contemporary North American destination for Caribbean migrants. The 1981 Canadian census enumerated 172,245 immigrants whose previous habitat was "Caribbean Islands," which, in this case, usually meant the Commonwealth Caribbean. Canadian immigration policies, based on a "point" system stressing education and skills, is said to have drained off many of the more capable and energetic residents from the islands to Canada's benefit. But, according to Canadian anthropologist Frances Henry, black West Indians, regardless of their educational backgrounds, face a rising tide of racism in the cities of eastern Canada where most of them reside.[10] The overall number of black West Indians living in Canada in the mid-1980s is probably twice the number given in census reports because thousands of black Britons with Caribbean backgrounds recently have immigrated to Canada and are officially reported as "British" owing to their most recent country of residence. Among the roughly 350,000 peoples of Caribbean birth and descent now living in Canada are an estimated 40,000 Haitians, most in the greater Montreal area.

Despite the massive outflow of Caribbean peoples to metropolitan areas in Western Europe and North America during the latter half of the twentieth century, an even larger number continues weekly, monthly, and annually to travel from place to place within the Caribbean region. The great variety of reasons for these intraregional movements—to obtain part-time work, to seek medical attention, to shop, to sell, to return home, to escape authorities in either one's home or an adopted place of residence, and so forth—makes it extraordinarily difficult to classify these movements in any meaningful way. Yet enclaves of recent immigrants inhabit every West Indian state of any size or prosperity; examples include the Haitians in the Dominican Republic and the Bahamas, "down islanders" from the Leeward Caribbean in the U.S. Virgin Islands, Dominicans (from Dominica) in Guadeloupe, and Windward islanders and Guyanese in Trinidad. The contemporary movements of these peoples and hundreds of thousands of others around the Caribbean every year remind us that similar migrations have been occurring there for one and one-half centuries.

## Migration's Effects in the Caribbean Region

Caribbean migration is usually discussed from the point of view of the metropolitan destinations to which Caribbean peoples have traveled. For this reason
questions of migration "policy" debated by U.S. authorities give little, if any,
thought to impacts in the Caribbean region itself. In the instances when
migration's effects on Caribbean homelands are considered, however, the interrelated complexities of different time scales must be acknowledged because
Caribbean migration is at once a traditional means of getting by and an
irresistible contemporary fad. The giant Coca-Cola sign, for example, between
Santo Domingo and the city's international airport featuring Pedro Guerrero
(fellow countryman and St. Louis Cardinal baseball sensation) is particularly
appealing to young Dominicans because tens of thousands from the Dominican Republic have rushed to the United States in recent years. And the adver-
tisement is doubly effective because many Dominicans have sought money and
success in the United States since early in this century. The billboard also
suggests that the movement—one way and back and forth—of Caribbean
peoples affects and alters both migration origins and destinations at the same
time.

Demographically, the most popular explanation for Caribbean migration is
that the migrants are fleeing the local effects of overpopulation at home, an
"explanation" that is oversimplified at best. Indeed, the historically imposed
overpopulation in some islands has led to some of the highest human densities
in the world. The 1,500 Barbadians per square mile, for example, gives Barbados an island-wide human population density comparable to that of many U.S.
suburbs. The fact that nearly all of Barbados's 166 square miles are cultivated in
sugarcane gives some idea of how crowded the island's villages, towns, and
cities are. And Barbados's relative prosperity is, in part, evidence of how
effective migration and return has been as a traditional livelihood strategy
there. External migration, however, has actually led to dramatic declines during Barbados's recent demographic history, specifically in the Panama Canal
decade and during the exodus to Britain at mid-century. Small island size,
therefore, influences population volatility. Overpopulation suddenly can become underpopulation given attractive migration possibilities elsewhere. In
some of the islands that are smaller than Barbados, a sudden exodus of so many
young and middle-aged island residents is said to have created a malaise
among those remaining behind, mostly old people who lament the loss of
better times in the past when the home island bustled with people and activity.

Skewed demographic patterns with a preponderance of the very old and very young (because the people of working age have left) have characterized the region for decades. School administrators throughout the Caribbean invariably complain that rowdy children cannot be controlled by grandparents who are attempting to raise them in the absence of distant parents. In the late twentieth century both Caribbean men and women emigrate in roughly equal numbers. In times past, men were the more likely migrants, helping to create the mother-centered family of the region of which so much has been written. Yet emigrant fathers have served as role models for children who themselves leave home when they reach adulthood.

The volatile insular populations and ever-changing demographic patterns in the Caribbean mirror the external conditions that affect human populations of potential migrants. Geographer Bernard Nietschmann, who has worked among the Miskito Indians of Nicaragua on the rim of the far western Caribbean, explains the fluidity of Miskito demography as a function of traveling away during some periods and returning home in others in order to adapt to altered local economic conditions which are, in turn, affected by external economic cycles.[11] The conditions that affect the Miskito also hold true for most of the Caribbean region.

As it has so often in the past, money sent home by migrants helps sustain insular West Indian societies. Whereas a "brain drain" may siphon off many of the best educated of the region, a money flow heading back in the other direction helps cushion the loss. Scholars who study Caribbean migration patterns have devoted a good deal of time and energy to accumulating remittance data because these numbers are tangible, quantifiable representations of one of migration's most important effects. In the past, much of the money sent home was mailed by postal money order and therefore recorded in official government data sources. But in more recent decades, Caribbean migrants abroad have sent the majority of their remittances through private banks. In 1973 in the tiny island of Carriacou (resident population 6,000) in the Grenadines I learned that over $500,000 in U.S. currency was sent home the year before both by postal order and through the island's single bank. Most bankers are reluctant to divulge these data, although it is certain that remittances to the larger Caribbean islands run into the tens of millions of U.S. dollars annually per island.

Goods and commodities from metropolitan migration destinations also pour into the Caribbean region every day. Material goods from abroad sent and brought back by migrating men and women help to reduce spot shortages of staple items at home but, more often, represent a quality and diversity of commodities otherwise unavailable or prohibitively expensive in the islands.

The carry-on luggage on commercial airline flights alone hauled by West Indian returnees to their homelands reveals a wondrous array of goods: blaster radios, toaster ovens, spark plugs, television sets, potato chips, clothing, groceries, razor blades, and nearly every other item imaginable. The use and display of these goods back home—either by the returnees or their families—signify migration's success, thereby reinforcing its importance in local Caribbean cultures.

The faithful sending home of money and gifts from Caribbean peoples abroad is neither an irrational fetish nor indicative of a preoccupation with the commercial gimcrackery available in North American department stores. Remittances of money and gifts play a functional role for the migrants themselves, especially if external circumstances force them to return. Young men or women who have regularly remitted money in their absence invariably receive warmer homecomings than those who have not. The legendary faithfulness of migrants is, moreover, spread by stories circulated at home, stories that reinforce such faithfulness. Every small Caribbean island has similar anecdotal "treasure tales," which often tell of loyal returning migrants sewing money into their clothing to avoid currency regulations or smuggling expensive goods home to benefit their families.

It is not surprising that local prestige often is accorded those who have migrated successfully and returned. In the small British Caribbean islands nearly every shop, taxi, or house of any substance may be traced to the owner or family members having traveled away earlier to a destination where wages were higher and more reliable than at home. Old men who traveled to the Netherlands Antilles from the Grenadines in the 1940s and 1950s returned home to construct elaborate concrete "Aruba houses" with money earned abroad. "Curaçao houses," named for similar reasons but a different migration destination, are found on Montserrat. Often, rum shops and fishing boats also bear names related to their owners' migration experiences. Many political and business leaders of the Commonwealth Caribbean have resided abroad for extended periods of time.

But support and enthusiasm for those going away is not always unequivocal. The popularity of goods and ideas brought home from abroad, according to some disgruntled observers, can be detrimental to local Caribbean societies, invariably causing young persons to look elsewhere for success and prestige. And a backlash of sorts against those who have emigrated and returned is not unknown. Some of the residents of Suriname have observed with disdain returnees parading through tropical Paramaribo sporting winter European clothing so that no one can mistake that they recently have returned from

Amsterdam. In the towns and villages of Puerto Rico, the term "Nuyorican" is not always used to connote awe and respect. Older Barbadians recall with amusement the images conveyed by "Panama men" who returned from the Canal Zone with a strutting self-consciousness, bedecked with the latest fashions from Colón. The character of Caribbean migrants has even become grist for contemporary international propaganda. The Cubans who arrived in Florida in 1980 came via "a freedom flotilla," according to American spokesmen, because they were fleeing Cuban communism. Cuban representatives, on the other hand, designated the movement as the "scum shuttle" to alert the world that those on board the Mariel boats were selfish, lazy, and the dregs of Cuban society.

Migration also influences personality traits in some Caribbean areas. In the islands where working-class men and women have had to migrate—to escape poverty and joblessness at home—and then return in the wake of changing global conditions, personal characteristics of picaresque resilience and economic underspecialization have paid dividends. The outside world has presented an ever-changing array of obstacles, hazards, and rewards. And successful exploitation of the outside world has called for physical strength in some cases or the ability to haggle successfully with immigration officials in others. Economic specialization has held few long-term rewards. In the face of continuing uncertainty, migrating men and women have usually foregone permanent commitments in any one direction except for eventually returning home. Because coping successfully with the variety of hazards facing these migrants requires them to display many talents to survive, those who return are understandably proud of their achievements, a pride that some interpret as bravado. Along the island arc of the eastern Caribbean, men travel aboard rickety sailing schooners from island to island smuggling whiskey, an occupation requiring a good deal of courage in the face of danger. For these men, "A man is either brave or cowardly, and a coward only invites disdain. The desire to be thought of as brave is so strong that expressions such as 'please' and 'thank you' are seldom used because they indicate weakness."[12] Similarly, far across the Caribbean realm, in the English-speaking island of Providencia (owned by Colombia) men who have traveled away prefer one another's company to that of others and consider themselves courageous, successful, and brave: "So when men gather together in rum shops or beneath the palm trees on the beach much of their conversation is taken up with stories of their exploits—mostly those that occurred abroad."[13]

The physical environments of the Caribbean region continue to be intimately related to human migration. Local lands rarely support the people who reside in particular places. The awesome and tragic physical devastation of Haiti—featuring soil erosion that almost guarantees local malnutrition and starvation—is also found to some degree on all of the smaller islands in the Caribbean. The origins of this regional ecological ruin may be traced historically, of course, to the region's plantation past, a past that also introduced a human population unrelated to insular carrying capacities. But migration and ecological change have now become interrelated in the Caribbean, not simply the former following on the heels of the latter. In times of peak migration, depleted labor forces have made livestock-keeping economically attractive, expecially on lands already scarred from years of cane and cotton cultivation. During the 1950s' rush to Britain, livestock populations in the drought-prone Leeward Caribbean boomed to the point that sheep and goats overran the properties of those who had traveled away. Emigration itself has thus indirectly fed the ongoing devastation of some island environments, and some of the changes seem irreversible. Parts of some of the smaller islands already resemble moonscapes. They seem simply unable to sustain their local resident populations, not to mention future generations or those working abroad who may someday be forced to return for good.

It is appropriate that an understanding of Caribbean migration, a topic of immense contemporary significance, should depend so heavily on the past. The forced immigration into the region, which provided the Caribbean's "native" peoples, combined with the systematic alteration of the region's physical environment have produced local conditions with which the inhabitants subsequently have had to cope. One means of coping has been through individual and group mobility, which has brought hundreds of thousands of Caribbean peoples to the doorsteps of the colonial and neocolonial nations that have historically created the conditions encouraging these migrations in the first place. The meaning of the voluminous and recent movements of Caribbean peoples is not confined simply, as some would have it, to a case of the empire striking back. But the presence of ever-growing numbers of Caribbean peoples in North Atlantic metropoles provides the basis for serious self-reflection. For Americans, who ostensibly pride themselves on their historic assimilation of peoples from throughout the world, the immigration of hundreds of thousands of Afro-Caribbean peoples into the United States represents at once a test of ability truly to welcome and assimilate as well as an extension of a more numerous Afro-American presence that is centuries old. For Europeans, Caribbean migration represents a geographic reversal of an issue as old as empire itself: the associations between ruler and ruled, abstractions formerly confined to the far corners of the globe, are now local issues of immediate significance.

Even if those who already have traveled away from the Caribbean prosper in a relative sense and are somehow taken in elsewhere, local West Indian conditions and tradition will continue to send migrants away from the region in the future. And although predictions about the disastrous circumstances that lie ahead for Caribbean migrants have been fashionable for years, the future for these peoples is perhaps not as gloomy as one might think. Most Caribbean peoples are flexible, innovative, and responsive to immediate change. These characteristics—learned through their many travels and the travels of their parents and grandparents—provide insurance against the unknown though certainly precarious events that lie ahead. A combination of local and external factors, of course, will continue to influence Caribbean migration. It is also certain that Caribbean migration trajectories will be influenced by a blend of cumulative historical experiences and the immediate urgency of contemporary events. A quotation attributed to Jack Kerouac might well be part of a conversation overheard between two Caribbean migrants and at the same time a prediction for the future of migration from and within the Caribbean region: "Where are we going, man? I don't know, but we gotta go."

## Notes

1. Edward J. Boyer, "Caribbean's Driven Immigrants," *Los Angeles Times*, April 25, 1985.

2. Patterson, "Migration in Caribbean Societies."

3. Mintz, *Caribbean Transformations* (Chicago: Aldine, 1974), pp. 146–56.

4. Haraksingh, "Culture, Religion, and Resistance," pp. 223–37.

5. Newton, *The Silver Men*.

6. Anderson, *This Was Harlem*.

7. Fanon, *Black Skin, White Masks*, pp. 9–40.

8. Laguerre, *American Odyssey*, pp. 24–25.

9. Carnegie, "If You Lose the Dog, Grab the Cat."

10. Frances Henry, "West Indians in Canada: The 'Victims' of Racism?" Paper presented at a conference on "Caribbean Migration and the Black Diaspora," University of London, June 17–19, 1987.

11. Nietschmann, "Ecological Change, Inflation, and Migration."

12. Beck, "The Bubble Trade," p. 41.

13. Wilson, *Crab Antics*, p. 155.

Jay R. Mandle

# British Caribbean Economic History

## An Interpretation

he process of economic development centers on the application of
scientific, engineering, and technical knowledge to production.
Simon Kuznets writes that the "mass application of technical innovations constitutes much of the distinctive substance of that process." When this occurs, new sectors of economic activity appear and overall
levels of productivity increase. As a result per capita output rises. But Kuznets
also emphasizes that the process of technical change is itself socially determined. He writes that for new technology "to be employed efficiently and
widely, and indeed, for its own progress to be stimulated, institutional and
ideological adjustments must be made."[1] Seen in this way, advances in production methods and the establishment of new sectors of economic activity represent only the proximate sources of growth. The fundamental sources of development are to be found in society's institutions and the role they play in either
facilitating or limiting technical innovation.

The same approach is fruitful in the study of underdevelopment. A nation's
underdevelopment exists because it has not experienced wide or substantial
innovation in production. The focus of analysis in accounting for its poverty,
therefore, should be on how society's institutions acted to limit technological
change. Such institutions might have acted to constrain either the capacity or
the incentive to be innovative or both. But whatever the explanation appropriate to a specific country, the analysis of underdevelopment, like the study of
development, should center on the impact of social institutions on the pace of
change in production methods and the introduction of new products.

This study of the historical origins of Caribbean underdevelopment thus
emphasizes how the region's institutions constrained its economic development. In this way it adopts a method in examining West Indian economic

history similar to that used by Lloyd Best for the contemporary Caribbean. Best insists that Caribbean poverty is not caused by weaknesses in its social institutions, but rather by the way they function. Indeed, he underlines the deep-rooted nature and strength of those institutions, arguing that it is their strength which perpetuates underdevelopment and produces perverse effects. Best writes: "I can't see any way in which the Caribbean countries that I know are less developed than the more developed countries. What I see is that they're highly developed for poverty, which is something else. But the institutions are as deeply implanted: they are just as old. Barbados is just as old as the United States and as highly organized . . . the structures are deeply implanted, are highly developed mechanisms for doing whatever they are doing." The task of analysis, observes Best, is to explain how those institutions are "holding up the process of economic transformation."[2] That same problem, addressed historically, is the subject of this chapter. To that end it is necessary first to identify the salient institutions in the region's political economy and then examine how those institutions effected the emergence of a regional technological capability. With such an analytic framework established, it is possible to interpret the course of the region's economic history and explain the Commonwealth Caribbean's underdevelopment.

In summary form, the argument is that the institutional limiting of the West Indies' economic development occurred in three different forms corresponding to three different periods in the region's history. Until well into the twentieth century, West Indian economic history was decisively influenced by its plantation economy. With it, Caribbean social institutions were promotive of large-scale, labor-intensive export agriculture. As a result, a deep bias away from technological progressivity was present, profoundly inhibiting British West Indian economic development. When finally the plantation mode of production was dismantled, an effort to industrialize was mounted after World War II. But this attempt took the form of importing industrial capital and management from abroad. Little was done to promote local technical competence and entrepreneurship. The consequence was that indigenous development did not take root, even as a limited degree of externally sponsored industrialization did occur. Finally, this same limited technological competence persisted in the 1970s and 1980s despite the fact that in these years the governments of the region came to play an enhanced role in the economies of their countries. While they increasingly created public sector employment, they did not do much to enhance the technical and scientific prowess of the West Indian people. Economic development, therefore, continued to lag. Overall, then, the argument is that even as the Caribbean moved from a plantation mode of production to a dependent capitalism, and then to a system in which the public sector assumed greater importance, there did not emerge those social institutions that would be promotive of a domestic technical competence. The West Indies, in short, remains underdeveloped.

## The Plantation Economy

The quantitative dimensions of the pre-World War II failure of economic development are available for examination for only one territory in the region. Gisela Eisner's meticulously documented national income accounts study of Jamaica encompasses the years 1830–1930, and it stands as the only long-term study of the kind that exists. Generalizations from this one case study to the entire region are dangerous because of the possibility, indeed the likelihood, that Jamaica's experience was atypical. If anything, Jamaica was more developed and probably grew more rapidly than most of the other islands and British Guiana. It is, however, because Jamaica probably was relatively advanced that the bias involved in extrapolating from its history is not as damaging as it might otherwise be. The fact that Jamaica was more developed than other territories suggests that whatever retarded development there probably was also present, only even more so, elsewhere.

Table 11-1 reports Eisner's estimates of Jamaica's per capita output experience. The results are startling. The island's output per person was about the same in 1930 as it had been in 1832. To be sure, this stability masks the fact that the low point in this measure was reached in 1870 and that thereafter per capita output continuously increased. Even so, however, that growth was quite slow, averaging only about 0.4 percent per year over the sixty-year period 1870–1930. Such a growth rate was only about one fifth the level found in countries experiencing development at that time.

Eisner's data with regard both to productivity and structural change in the economy tell a comparably sad story. Labor productivity in Jamaican agriculture in 1890 stood at a level 22 percent below that of 1832, a year in which slavery still prevailed. Most of this decline, in fact, occurred in the aftermath of emancipation. But even so, labor productivity in Jamaica's agriculture increased by only about 11 percent over the forty-year period 1850–90. The productivity performance in the nonagricultural sectors was also poor. In this case, emancipation was not associated with a decline. But in the period 1850–90 productivity fell by 18 percent. Only in the 1890–1930 period did productivity in both sectors increase. Nonetheless, output per worker in agriculture in

**Table 11-1**

Jamaica's Per Capita Gross Domestic Product in 1910 Prices (£), 1832–1930

| | |
|---|---|
| 1832 | 15.6 |
| 1850 | 12.2 |
| 1870 | 11.9 |
| 1890 | 12.4 |
| 1910 | 13.7 |
| 1930 | 15.7 |

Source: Gisela Eisner, *Jamaica, 1830–1930: A Study of Economic Growth* (Manchester: The University Press, 1961), p. 289.

1930 was only 18 percent higher than it had been at the end of the slave era. In the rest of the economy the level achieved in 1930 had not yet reached that of 1832.[3]

The only indication of a structural change in the Jamaican economy occurred between 1832 and 1850. It was centered on the relative decline in export agriculture and increase in domestic food production. Thereafter, however, further change was generally limited to the export sector's reclaiming, between 1890 and 1930, some of the ground it had lost earlier. The sectors representing industrialization—building and construction, and manufacturing—in particular showed very little growth. This stability means that these sectors grew at rates comparable to that of the economy as a whole, a rate which, as we have seen, was quite low compared to what was required to keep pace with those countries experiencing development.

The plantation economy framework provides a theory of the failure of economic development symbolized by Eisner's data. This institutional explanation of underdevelopment was pioneered by Edgar T. Thompson and was articulated for the region by George Beckford, Lloyd Best, and in my own work.[4] There are differences among these authors. But they all agree that the dominance of plantation agriculture in society inhibited development and that its legacy continues to impede the region's economic expansion.

Concentrated control of land in large producing units and market power with regard to the hiring of labor were the basic attributes of plantation economies. On one hand, estates placed the best quality land under crops designated for overseas markets. On the other hand, the extensive size of those markets in combination with the labor-intensive technology available for the production of tropical staples dictated that, for planters to be commercially successful, they required access to large numbers of low-wage workers. The seventeenth- and eighteenth-century response to these structural circumstances was slavery, an institution which, despite all of its immorality, served the planters' economic interests well. It provided the basis for their achieving profits and accumulating fortunes. It did so because it supplied the estates with just what was needed: labor in numbers greater and at costs lower than would have been the case if a free labor market had been active.

Emancipation presented the planters with a crisis of the most fundamental nature. Immediately after the period of apprenticeship ended in 1838, labor costs rose dramatically while the number of workers willing to offer themselves to the estates declined. When this labor problem was joined at mid-century with the region's loss of preferential access to the British market, the sugar industry of the West Indies colonies, and with it an entire way of life, was severely jeopardized. The fact that despite all of this the industry survived, and by the 1870s even flourished, is testimony to the adaptability of the planter class within the confines of the plantation economy. That the salvation of the planters' world did not involve scientific and technological modernization makes their achievement no less impressive and certainly does not represent entrepreneurial failure. After all, their intent was to preserve their way of life as symbolized by the plantation society, not to create a new social order.

Decisive to the success of their survival efforts was once again the labor question. Needed were numbers; but just as important was a means to contain labor costs. The demise of slavery had deprived the planters of an institution that had simultaneously controlled costs and adequately supplied workers. But that demise did not mean that there were no alternative arrangements to accomplish the same goals. To be viable under alternative arrangements, the planters had to make certain that labor's opportunity costs were kept low. If that were accomplished even free labor would have to make itself available to the estates at wage levels the planters were willing to pay. Thus it was not necessary, as under slavery, to require that no alternatives to plantation labor be permitted. All that was needed was that these alternatives yield only very low levels of income. If small farmers could earn only a pittance cultivating their own land, they would have to make themselves available to the estates at low wages. As a result the plantations would have access to workers in numbers and at costs that would allow large-scale, labor-intensive export agriculture to be profitable. In short, the plantation economy could survive emancipation.

Conversely, if the peasantry had been allowed to become more productive, the small farmers might have reached the stage where they no longer would have supplied their labor to the estates. If that had occurred the continued existence of the plantation sector would have been placed at risk. What therefore at first seem to be missed opportunities to help small farmers, and in the process promote development, on closer examination turn out to be the means used to resuscitate the plantations. In his introduction to Eisner's study, W. Arthur Lewis lists a number of activities that should have been undertaken, but were not and mourns this failure. Irrigation, reclamation, drainage, terracing, conservation, the construction of feeder roads, and land settlement all should have been carried out. They would have helped "to make small farmers more productive," a goal that retrospectively he endorses.[5] But that precisely was the problem with such programs. If the peasants had been allowed to become more productive, they might have reached the stage where they no longer would have supplied their labor to the estates.

The same is true with regard to education. Everywhere in the region literacy rates were low, with Eisner reporting that as late as 1911 less than half of the Jamaican population could both read and write.[6] Far from this low figure representing a policy failure, however, the suppression of education should be seen as functional to the plantation economy. Education results in a widening of opportunities, and that precisely was what the society was organized to constrain.

In some cases simply denying resources to the nonplantation sector was not sufficient to ensure the viability of the estates. In those circumstances the British and the planters turned to a more active policy. On the region's southern frontier, in Trinidad and British Guiana, the person/land ratio was still quite low by the mid-nineteenth century. This meant that it was extremely difficult to maintain adequate levels of control over the peasant sector. In those territories the rise of the peasantry—an independent peasantry—seemed likely to threaten the labor lifeblood of the estates. In both cases, however, an active official policy came to the rescue. An administratively sophisticated and publicly financed indentured immigration system was put in place. Its purpose was to supply the hard-pressed plantations with the labor they could no longer attract at wages they were willing to pay. Between 1838 and 1916 Trinidad and British Guiana between them were supplied with over 450,000 indentured immigrants. The huge relative scale of this migration is suggested by the fact that at the turn of the nineteenth century the combined total populations of Trinidad and British Guiana came only to a little more than 500,000. Contracted to work on specified plantations for a period of at least five years and at very low wages, these workers provided the means by which the plantation sector was given new life. This "new system of slavery" too represented official policy triumphant.

Thus the peasantry that emerged in the region did so despite official discouragement and only, in Sidney Mintz's phrase, "in the crevices of their societies."[7] Government, responsive to plantation interests, did not jeopardize the plantation system by allowing small farm incomes to rise to the level where they would allow peasants to establish their independence from the estates. The peasantry that emerged possessed access only to a limited supply of land and human capital in the form of education. Furthermore, the peasant sector suffered from neglect by public officials with regard to activities such as research on the food crops they produced, and the provision of facilities essential for efficient marketing, distribution, and storage of that output. Thus it was that even landholding small farmers were usually forced to provide labor to the estates—the consequence of the low level of income they were able to secure from their own holdings.

George Beckford argues that, despite all of these handicaps, the peasant sector more than the plantations "generated internal linkages . . . and laid the foundation for the growth and diffusion of national income." It was the peasantry that pioneered the cultivation of new crops, some of which, as we have seen, like bananas, became estate staples. Because of the peasantry's activities, Beckford maintains that "a measure of independent economic development was achieved."[8] The argument is that it will not do to view the peasant sector exclusively as an appendage of the plantations. Despite the official hostility it experienced, the peasantry did manage to retain a vitality of its own. This argument is sound. Indeed, it was because of this vitality and the threat that it represented that there was a need for policy to constrain it in the first place. Nonetheless, the West Indian peasantry never decisively broke with the estates. Well into the twentieth century it continued to represent a supplementary source of labor to them. In this sense it should be conceded that public policy supporting the plantation sector in its struggle to deny viability to the peasantry was successful and that the resistance of the small farmers remained a defensive and rear-guard struggle.

The emergence of viable alternatives to plantation work would have placed plantation agriculture in jeopardy. It, therefore, was not irrational for the planters, the elite of local society, to resist such a process of diversification. Indeed, it is not even surprising, when seen in this light, that the British—with perhaps less of a vested interest in the traditional plantation structure than the planters themselves—might at least on some issues, as noted by Lewis, have been the less recalcitrant of the two. Nonetheless, the planters and the colonial officials continued in effective alliance, an alliance that conspired to preserve the old mode of production by constraining the emergence of a new one.

But in preserving the old plantation mode of production and preventing an embryonic but indigenous capitalism from emerging in the aftermath of slavery, the planter/Colonial Office alliance also denied to the region the opportunity to participate in the modern world of technological change and economic development. Preventing an independent peasantry from coming into existence meant the continued availability of inexpensive labor to the estates, in effect encouraging the latter to continue to use labor-intensive methods of cultivation and harvesting. Unlike in Cuba and Puerto Rico, this bias away from the use of capital and to labor in production reinforced the estates' technological stagnation since productivity-raising innovations typically are embodied in new tools and equipment. At the same time the diversification in production that an independent peasantry would have represented also was denied the region's economy. Thus, the policies that gave new life to the post-emancipation plantation economy both limited technological advance in the region's export sector and retarded the extent to which a widening of the structure of output occurred. Support of plantation agriculture, in short, was the vehicle for the continued economic backwardness of the region.

## The Breakdown of the Plantation Economy

One thing that the ready availability of inexpensive labor could not do was to protect the sugar producers from changes in the world market for their product. When, therefore, in the 1880s the European beet sugar industry, with government encouragement and subsidies, substantially increased its output, the world price for the commodity declined precipitously. Sugar prices in 1896 were almost exactly one-half the level reached in 1881. At these low prices European bounties and subsidies allowed the beet producers to displace the Caribbean cane exporters even in the British market.

The distress caused by these developments resulted in the colonial secretary, Joseph Chamberlain, appointing in 1897 a royal commission to investigate whether the region's sugar industry possessed a viable future. The commission came precariously close to answering this question in the negative. But instead of recommending the dismantling of the plantations, it pulled back and called for the presence of "two systems of large estates and peasant holdings to exist side by side with mutual advantage." The bitter irony of this recommendation is that the commission itself knew that a viable plantation system could not coexist with a strong peasant sector. In the paragraph immediately preceding its recommendation, the commission had acknowledged that "what suits them [the sugar estates] best was a large supply of labourers, entirely dependent on being able to find work on the estates and, consequently, subject to their control and willing to work at low rates of wages."[9] By raising the opportunity cost of estate work, the creation of a strong peasantry would destroy that dependency as well as undermine the traditional plantation. But by the same logic if a recovery in sugar occurred, that industry could benefit best only if a peasantry, and the income opportunities that it represented, were minimal. The estate sector and the peasantry were involved in a zero-sum game: a two-system solution was not viable.

Again in this case the plantation sector was victorious. The Brussels Convention of 1902 resulted in the abolition of the European bounty system which had subsidized the beet producers. The recovery in the region which resulted from that agreement, in combination with a substantial grant made by the colonial government to the region's sugar industry, but not to the peasantry, meant life to one sector and continued weakness for the other.

The experience with beet sugar seems to have revealed to the region's cane producers that the maintenance of low wages alone no longer was sufficient to ensure profitability. In a world in which the supply potential was increasing even more rapidly than was demand, viability now required increased attention to technical efficiency. A dependent labor force no longer was sufficient to contain costs. Furthermore, there were limits to which the industry could go. The 1897 commission in reviewing the situation believed that in light of the decline in wages which had recently occurred, "further reductions of salaries or wages was impracticable."[10] The industry's increased attention to efficiency can be traced to this period. Productivity advances took the form of higher-yielding varieties of cane as well as increased efficiency of the grinding process. The latter was achieved through a centralization of factories, resulting in economies of scale and the introduction of new equipment. Even in field operations, where methods of production changed least, employment grew proportionately less than did output. Especially in the years after World War I, as the Moyne Commission reported in 1938, "a big reduction in the costs of production . . . has enabled the industry to supply a steadily increasing quantity of sugar to the British consumer at a falling price."[11]

Thus it was that the West Indian plantation economy approached its demise. No longer could it function as a means to supply staples profitably on international commodity markets. Reliance on labor made inexpensive because it was denied effective employment alternatives now proved to be insufficient to provide owners with adequate returns. Increasingly the planters were compelled to turn to science and technology as the basis of production rather than their traditional approach of simply using brawn power. In turning away from the latter, however, the planters signaled that the traditional mode of production had outlived its viability.

But what was to replace it? The fact that the institutions which historically had constrained regional development were now being dismantled did not mean that new development-promoting ones necessarily were under construction. Economic development required technological advance to extend over new sectors of activity, and not be confined to sugar. But in the West Indian context the estates' continued domination of land ownership prevented such diversification in agriculture. Nor could manufacturing develop, since colonial policy opposed its encouragement. Thus the interwar years saw the ending of an era in which labor-intensive and large-scale agriculture had been hegemonic. But with the ending of the plantation economy no new structure, stimulative of development, was put in place. This failure to construct new development-promoting institutions came at a heavy cost. Not only would the region continue to be denied modern growth; but also for the first time the Caribbean was required to face the problem of excess labor.

Unemployment in the West Indies emerged because the years after World War I also saw the region enter a new phase of demographic history. These years witnessed the first significant downward trend in the West Indies' mortality rate. The resulting excess of births over deaths meant that for the first time immigration was not the major source of the region's growing numbers. At the same time it is clear that this decreased level of mortality did not occur because of rising income levels. Generally it was the result of improvements in public health facilities, which had important demographic consequences. In Guyana, such programs addressed the colony's waste disposal problems, potable drinking water availability, mosquito and therefore malaria control, and pre- and postnatal care availability—many of the factors that lay behind the colony's high mortality rate. In combination they seem gradually to have been responsible for a substantial reduction in its high level of mortality. Guyana's death rate averaged 21.7 per 1,000 of the population between 1929 and 1940, compared to 28.4 per 1,000 for the years 1911–28. By the end of the 1930s, population growth had reached a level of between 1.5 percent and 2.0 percent a year.

Always in the past, of course, an increase in the region's population was warmly welcomed by the planters and colonial administrators. More people meant more plantation workers, and that, in turn, meant more output and profits. But in the new era of increased attention to technical efficiency, the industry could or would no longer absorb virtually unlimited supplies of labor.

Population growth threatened to create a labor force beyond the absorptive power of the region's economy. The tragedy was profound. Now, when for the first time the health of the people had improved to the point where they could expand their numbers, it was also the first time in which such an increase in the population and labor force was not in demand by the plantations.

It seems reasonable to assume that a causal relationship exists between these demographic and technological changes and the "disturbances" that spread throughout the region between 1935 and 1938. In response to them the Moyne Commission was appointed to look into the causes of the regionwide violence and semi-insurrections that broke out in these years and to make recommendations. The commission was exhaustive in its portrayal of the life of the region but cautious in its policy recommendations. So devastating was its depiction of conditions that the Colonial Office withheld publication of the report itself in order to prevent its use against the British during World War II. Nonetheless its recommendations were issued, and soon afterward the program of Colonial Development and Welfare (CDW) was established. But Moyne had not laid out a strategy to transform the region, nor was the aid supplied by CDW a move in that direction. Although the commission acknowledged that the region needed "a substantial and steady increase in the volume of economic activity" to avoid rising unemployment, it found that "the majority of the population must continue to depend, for a long period, if not indefinitely, on export agriculture." This was because "West Indian manufacturing industries must necessarily be small and weak." Prospects for creating a prosperous peasantry were doomed to disappointment. The commission recommended that each of the West Indian governments "should have easily applied power to enable them to acquire compulsorily agricultural land when it is needed for such purpose as land settlement," but noted that such schemes "are expensive and throw a charge on the finances of the Colonies concerned that is heavy in relation to the number of persons settled." As a result an extensive program of land settlement was ruled out.[12] This meant, finally, the continued need to rely on export agriculture. To that end the commission proposed an expansion of the export quota that was assigned the region in the British market. In short, the basic structure of the region's economy was to remain intact.

What the region needed, but the Moyne Commission had not provided, was a strategy to deal with its long-term failure to develop while simultaneously addressing the emerging problems of unemployment and underemployment. The plantation sector continued to possess a concentrated control of the best agricultural land. Thus, even as the estates reduced the level of their labor demand they continued to act as an obstacle to the creation of new sectors of economic activity. On one hand, the land constraint continued to foreclose the emergence of independent farming; on the other, the low incomes still received on the estates limited the extent to which a market for local manufactured goods developed. But such a domestic market to which local businesses could devote their initial efforts was (and is) critical to regional development. Obviously the small size of the Caribbean's population, not to say that of any one of the territories, means that the domestic markets would be small in any case. Ultimately industrialization in the West Indies requires exports. But the ability to produce export quality goods at competitive prices requires business expertise. Such competence develops as a result of coping, initially on a small scale, with both failures as well as successes in the marketplace. A local market is a necessary training ground for businesses that must advance to world markets. However, the skewed income distribution associated with plantation dominance and the low levels of income received by the bulk of the population limited the extent to which that training ground was provided. Because of its failure to address the land question, the commission had left in place the principal basis of the region's underdevelopment.

The Moyne Commission's rejection of industrialization was unqualified. It came despite the upholding of the need to develop manufacturing by a young Saint Lucian-born postgraduate student whose offer to testify before the commission was rejected. In his paper, W. Arthur Lewis, the future Nobel Prize–winning economist, reviewed the desperate plight in which the West Indies found itself. His judgment was that the "gloomy prospects for agriculture the world over" required that the Caribbean look to industrialization. Lewis may not have been literally the first person to suggest this route for the region, but his 1938 position was intellectually pathbreaking. He even provided a list of possible products such as refined sugar, chocolate, copra, and dairy products as the kinds of industries which "the Commission would do well to consider."[13] There is no evidence that the commission seriously did so. The submission by Lewis, however, is the obvious precursor of the work he did after the war and the industrialization effort that was then undertaken.

In the meantime, however, the period of the war itself did see new departures in production. Particularly Trinidad and British Guiana were the beneficiaries of heightened economic activity as a result of the construction of U.S. military bases in those countries. Construction employment was extremely heavy and as result unemployment rates decreased there markedly. In addition, the fact that the region was substantially cut off from international trade meant that it had to become increasingly self-sufficient at least in agricultural foodstuffs. Throughout the area, "Grow More Food" and related programs were initiated. In these campaigns assistance was provided to the region's farmers in order to increase their output of food crops. This assistance ranged from the subsidized provision of planting material to the arrangement for special facilities to be made available to farmers so they could market their output efficiently. Most significantly, the governments of the territories required the plantations themselves to devote a specified fraction of their agricultural acreage to food crop production. Universally it appears that these programs were effective, with several of the islands, as well as British Guiana, so expanding their output that they were able to export their surplus to their neighbors.

Even with the diversification that "Grow More Food" represented, however, the Caribbean had not at last come to grips with the land question. To be sure, the demonstrated ability of the West Indies to feed itself was a refreshing departure from past practice. If considered as part of a comprehensive development program the increase in food crop production could have been conceived as freeing foreign exchange for the purchase of essential capital goods. It thereby could have been seen as development promoting. But "Grow More Food" never was viewed in that light. It always was considered as only a wartime expedient to be discarded once the war was over. Even with "Grow More Food," the basic structure of agriculture in the Caribbean remained intact. Estate land ownership continued to be dominant. As a result when trade resumed, there was nothing to prevent the familiar pattern of export specialization from reestablishing itself.

Table 11-2 shows the size distribution of landholdings and the distribution of agricultural acreage in the region during the 1960s. With regard to landholding, the vestiges of the plantation economy clearly persisted. Everywhere, except in Trinidad and Tobago, farmers cultivating less than 5 acres represented three-quarters or more of the units in production. But nowhere did these small farmers cultivate more than one-quarter of the land in production and, as in the case of Barbados and Jamaica, this share frequently was much less. At the same time, holdings of over 500 acres in all territories represented less than 1 percent of farms; yet they controlled, typically, one-third, and in the case of Saint Kitts more than one-half, of the land in production.

When the war ended the familiar pattern of production reasserted itself. The very large number of small farms primarily produced food crops for domestic consumption, and the large estates continued to produce export staples. But nowhere did this structure result in agricultural dynamism. Although the small farmers cultivated intensively, the resource constraint they faced prevented them from increasing their output significantly. The large holdings, however,

**Table 11-2**

Size Distribution of Farms and Share of Agricultural Land in Caribbean
Countries by Size of Holding, 1960 or 1970

|  | Percentage of All Farms | | Percentage of All Farm Land | |
|---|---|---|---|---|
|  | Less than 5 Acres | More than 500 Acres | Less than 5 Acres | More than 500 Acres |
| Barbados | 98.3 | 0.2 | 13.4 | 31.3 |
| Guyana | — | — | — | — |
| Jamaica | 78.6 | 0.2 | 14.9 | 44.9 |
| Antigua | 91.1 | 0.3 | 26.7 | 42.2 |
| Montserrat | 92.7 | 0.7 | — | — |
| St. Kitts | 94.5 | 0.4 | 15.0 | 56.6 |
| Trinidad and Tobago | 46.5 | 0.3 | 6.9 | 31.1 |
| Grenada | 89.7 | 0.1 | 23.9 | 15.0 |
| Dominica | 75.2 | 0.3 | 13.2 | 32.2 |
| St. Lucia | 82.5 | 0.2 | 18.0 | 33.8 |
| St. Vincent | 89.0 | 0.1 | 27.0 | 24.2 |

Source: George L. Beckford, "Caribbean Rural Economy," in George L. Beckford, ed.,
*Caribbean Economy* (Mona, Jamaica: Institute of Social and Economic Research, University of the West Indies, 1975), p. 87.

were often undercultivated and characterized by crop choice inflexibility, continuing to produce, for example, cane, despite the fact that with the passage of time that crop became decreasingly profitable. During the entire postwar period, therefore, the agricultural sector in the Caribbean lagged behind the rest of the region's economy. By 1973 even the nonindustrialized Leeward and Windward islands saw their agricultural sectors produce less than one-fifth of their economy's total output. This represented a decrease of more than one-third in the early 1960s. For the region as a whole the relative stagnation meant that, by the 1970s, the agricultural share of total output had fallen to less than 9 percent of total output.

# Industrialization by Invitation

In the aftermath of World War II the Caribbean economy faced a decisive turning point. The population and labor force were growing, but in the absence of a fundamental agrarian reform that growth could not be absorbed by agriculture. Moyne had not supported industrialization, and, in any case, thus far only a little activity had occurred in this regard. And yet there was an urgency to establish new sectors of economic activity, simply on the grounds of the need for employment creation, not to mention development. In this policy vacuum emerged the strategy of industrialization associated regionally with the name of W. Arthur Lewis. With it the West Indies entered a new period in its economic history.

It is commonplace to credit Lewis with first recognizing the need for the development of manufacturing in the region. His 1950 article, "The Industrialization of the British West Indies," built upon his Moyne Commission statement with a sophisticated defense of the need for industrialization. The article originally appeared in the *Caribbean Economic Review*, but was issued in several subsequent pamphlet editions and became a focal point of discussion.[14] However, as Terrence Farrell has pointed out, Lewis was not the region's sole spokesperson for industrialization. Jamaica's People's National party in the late 1940s was calling for industrial development based on the Puerto Rican model, as was the trade union movement. Furthermore, official British policy no longer opposed such development though in this regard it remained equivocal.

Lewis's vision was that industrialization could occur in the Caribbean by proxy. He believed that manufacturing could emerge despite the fact that there was not, and for a considerable period of time there would not be, a regional manufacturing class in the population. In his program, foreign business investment was the sine qua non of West Indian industrial development. Indeed, in Lewis's discussion of the initial sources of entrepreneurship essential for manufacturing he considered only private foreign investors and local governments. The local private sector was not taken into account. His view was that "the islands cannot be industrialized to anything like the extent that is necessary without a considerable inflow of foreign capital and capitalists and a period of wooing and fawning upon such people." There were two arguments behind this assertion. First was the fact that industrialization was expensive, "quite beyond the resources of the islands." The second was based on the fact that export promoting was too difficult for the region. It required breaking into foreign markets and building up new distribution outlets. These would most likely be accomplished if "the islands concentrate on inviting manufacturers who are already well established in foreign markets." Only after foreign businesses had been attracted to the Caribbean would, in Lewis's scheme, a role appear for the local private sector. With the rise in output produced by foreign investment, domestic income would increase. Then, "if local people are thrifty, they can build up savings which in due course enable them, having learnt the tricks of the trade, to set up in the business themselves." In the strategy, then, foreign businesses, in addition to promoting exports, had a tutorial role to fulfill. For, it is when "the local people have learnt the job and have built up their own savings that they can go right in." Thus it seems clear that the phrase coined by Lloyd Best, "industrialization by invitation," really does not do violence to the Lewis strategy.[15] Both the initial advance and even later development by the local private sector was dependent on the behavior of foreign businesses.

There has been a tendency to exaggerate Lewis's share of responsibility for the weaknesses of the program that ensued. But in fact two of the critical features of his industrialization scheme never were realized in practice. Lewis, in the first instance, insisted that manufacturing promotion in the region could function effectively only in the context of regional integration. His words on the subject were explicit: "it is idle to talk about a serious effort at industrialization until the whole area is brought within a single customs union." That such a union was not established until 1974 means that the program was undertaken without an institution that Lewis identified as critical. The second major departure from Lewis's plan concerned the question of exports. He had made it quite clear that the program would not accomplish its employment goals unless it successfully penetrated export markets. The whole purpose of the plan was job creation, but Lewis estimated that, of the 120,000 manufacturing jobs needed during the 1950s, production for the region's market would provide employment only for about 20,000 workers. Lewis thus concluded that manufacturing could not have the impact required "unless the islands start to export manufactures to outside destinations." This injunction to export, however, was in practice ignored. The region's manufacturing sector to date has not been able to achieve a significant export orientation. Indeed, early industrial promotion legislation was biased to import substituting rather than to exports. With such a bias the program could hardly attain the goals Lewis had set for it.[16] Thus, in one sense it is unfair to hold Lewis responsibile for the failure of programs carried out in his name. The region's industrial promotion program never contained elements that he considered to be fundamental.

Under the circumstances, it is not surprising that through its first two decades the industrial promotion effort largely failed to accomplish its employment targets. In the first place, the little foreign investment that did come to the region was largely confined to Jamaica and to Trinidad and Tobago. Not even Barbados was the recipient of much capital inflow for manufacturing during these years, not to mention the negligible amounts that went to Guyana and the smaller islands. But even in Jamaica and in Trinidad and Tobago, the effect of the investment that arrived from abroad did not approach the hopes that Lewis had held out. There were too few projects, the projects that were undertaken were too capital intensive, and, because the projects undertaken were branch-plant assembly activities, there were too few linkages established between them and the rest of the host economy. As a result of the latter shortcoming, the number of indirect employment opportunities created by the program was insufficient.

Overall, the employment creation dimension of the industrialization program was inadequate. Thus Edwin Carrington reported that in Trinidad and Tobago by June 1963, 99 factories employing a mere 4,666 workers had been put in place under that country's Pioneer Industries program. Adding to that number the 40 factories under construction, and anticipating an additional 2,255 jobs that would then be created, Carrington in 1967 wrote that "the estimate of 6,921 jobs from these 139 establishments and an investment of $257.8 million (TT) is to say the least, disappointing." It was all the more so in view of that fact that between 1950 and 1963 Trinidad and Tobago's labor force increased by nearly 100,000 whereas jobs in the country's dominant sugar and petroleum sectors had declined over the same years by about 3,800.[17] A similar account of failure in adequate employment creation is told for Jamaica by Owen Jefferson. There, while the labor force between 1956 and 1968 was growing by about 25,000 per year and the sugar industry was eliminating a total of 10,000 employment opportunities, the industrialization program created altogether about 13,000 jobs. Jefferson concluded for Jamaica in tones that echoed Carrington's summary for Trinidad and Tobago: "even though there has been a relatively rapid rate of increase of production, employment has not kept pace, with a resulting tendency towards an increase in the rate of unemployment."[18] The sad fact is that the roughly 20,000 jobs created in the 1950s and 1960s through the industrial development efforts in the region were just about the same number that Lewis cited as being inadequate for the 1950s alone. Industrialization by invitation, in short, did not come close to the employment goals that had been its raison d'être.

Despite the failure of industrial promotion to absorb the region's rapidly growing labor force, the pressures generated by that growth were somewhat offset by three developments. First, the region exported people, if not commodities, on a massive scale. Estimates prepared by Robert Harootyan and Aaron Segal suggest that emigration from the West Indies between 1950 and 1972 may have reached between 600,000 and 750,000.[19] The gigantic movement of people which these estimates represent can be appreciated when it is realized that the region's total population in 1970 was only about 4.6 million. Thus it seems likely that well over 10 percent of the Caribbean's population left the area in these years. Such a massive movement could not have helped but reduce the pressure of unemployment, as it substantially decreased the potential labor force growth. It thereby removed some of the cost of the failure of manufacturing. But Jack Harewood has been at pains to emphasize that such an emigration has associated with it costs as well as benefits. This was particularly true since the out-migration that occurred was increasingly composed of professionals and skilled workers. These are the kinds of workers, writes Harewood, "whom the developing Caribbean countries could ill afford to lose."[20] Thus while the out-migration may, in the short run, have relieved the pressure associated with the failure of manufacturing, it did so by making long-term development more difficult to achieve.

The second offsetting factor was the expansion of the raw materials extraction sectors of the largest of the region's territories and the effect this expansion had on the government's ability to employ labor. During the 1950s and 1960s bauxite in Jamaica and Guyana and petroleum in Trinidad and Tobago increased their output substantially. Foreign-owned, these sectors stood as enclaves in their respective surroundings. They engaged in little processing, established few linkages with other sectors of the economy, and employed relatively few workers. They did, however, contribute substantially to government revenues through taxation. With these revenues government itself became a substantial employer of labor in these years. To a very large extent in the three territories, government came to occupy the employer role which the manufacturing sector had failed to do and it did so largely on the revenues generated by the bauxite and petroleum enclaves. In Trinidad and Tobago, for example, the roughly 60,000 workers on the government's payroll in 1964 represented 30.4 percent of paid employees in the country and 20.2 percent of the total working labor force. The percentages for Jamaica in 1976, the earliest year for which such data are available, were nearly identical: government employees as a percentage of paid employees was 33.7 percent and as a percentage of all employed workers, 18.6 percent. No comparable data are available for Guyana, but it is almost certain that there too the government share in employment was quite high.

A third development was the emergence of tourism in the late 1950s and 1960s as a major economic activity in the region. The growth of this industry followed the model that had been established for manufacturing. Thus in Barbados the Hotel Aid Act of 1956 promised extensive fiscal concessions for the construction of tourist accommodations, and a Barbados Tourist Development Board was established in 1958. These efforts were designed to tap an increasingly affluent North American and European market, a market that had become accessible with the development of faster and less expensive means of travel. In fact, the number of tourist arrivals in Barbados in 1965 was almost twice that of 1960. A similar pattern was followed in Jamaica and somewhat later in the smaller islands. Only Guyana and Trinidad and Tobago failed to participate in the emergence of this industry. The former lacked the necessary environmental attractions while the latter seems to have eschewed the industry as a matter of policy.

Unfortunately for those who did pursue it, tourism—as a capital intensive and low-wage industry—was soon discovered to be a poor alternative to manufacturing. According to Delisle Worrell, tourism was the least labor-intensive sector in the entire Barbados economy. At the same time, wages in this sector were below those of all other sectors of the economy except public administration and agriculture. In 1975 Dawn Marshall estimated that only 3,628 jobs existed in the Barbados tourist industry, employing only about 3 percent of the labor force.[21] Thus this industry only to a very limited extent filled the gap left by the failure of manufacturing.

It can be seen, then, that a complex pattern of growth and change occurred in the Caribbean in the postwar years through about 1970. The conventional economic indices tended to record a favorable trend. With the emergence of new sectors of economic activity (tourism, manufacturing, and the extraction of bauxite and petroleum), the region's per capita income increased. The years between 1960 and 1976, Kempe Hope reports, experienced real growth rates per person of 5.1 percent for Barbados, 2.5 percent for Jamaica, 1.7 percent for Guyana, and 1.6 percent for Trinidad and Tobago. But none of these advances were sufficient to provide adequate employment for the region's growing labor force. Again, Hope's collection of data reveals unemployment rates in 1970 of 9.0 percent, 16.0 percent, 18.0 percent, and 12.5 percent respectively for Barbados, Guyana, Jamaica, and Trinidad and Tobago.[22] In every case these rates were higher than had been recorded a decade earlier and would continue to mount in the immediately subsequent years.

## State Intervention

The plantation-dominated economy of the Moyne Commission years had long since been radically transformed. Nonetheless, the high and rising unemployment rates were responsible for a continuing strong sense of dissatisfaction with the region's economy. Too many West Indian workers were unable to find employment at wages they considered adequate. The resulting open and disguised unemployment and, of course, massive emigration all made the successes suggested by the growth statistics seem irrelevant. Regardless of the favorable impression they provided, the economy had grossly failed in its employment-creating functions.

But the problem for the Caribbean was more profound than merely high unemployment rates. More fundamental was the fact that it had become apparent that the governments of the region were unable on their own to do anything about that major failing. Growth had occurred, but it was dependent growth; expansion was contingent on decisions made abroad. The region had been the passive beneficiary of those decisions, but it was that very passivity which now created the difficulty. For while those managerial decisions had not been adequate for the needs of the region, local leaders either in the private or public sector could do little to correct the situation. The strategy of dependent growth had not permitted the region to adjust the performance of the local economy, in this case to increase the demand for labor. Academically, the dissatisfaction with this outcome was most vividly expressed by Lloyd Best who scornfully referred to the post-World War II economy merely as a "plantation economy further modified." With this phrase, Best registered a nationalist's concern that the region's economy through these years had remained "as it has always been, passively responsive to metropolitan demand and metropolitan investment." None of the sectors of growth had been what Best calls "residentiary": locally owned, serving domestic markets, using an indigenously developed technology, and subject to local influence. Manufacturing, tourism, the extraction of bauxite and petroleum, and even the continued export of agricultural staples all involved "dependence on imported enterprise."[23] Such dependence meant that little could be done about unemployment. The output of those industries that had grown was very little affected by local policy. Output was primarily influenced by developments in the wider international economy. The demand for the region's tourist facilities most significantly was influenced by the rhythms of the business cycle in the metropolitan countries. The other three industries were, in their Caribbean operations, simply components of integrated production processes. Decisions concerning profitability were addressed primarily in an international, not a local context. Government's policy in the Caribbean therefore could have only a minimal impact with regard to decisions concerning levels of output carried out in the region.

Beyond this, the very strength of the foreign firms had aborted the development of indigenous enterprises. Local firms could potentially have been assisted by domestic policymakers. But the opening of the Caribbean economies to expatriate corporations had placed the financially and technologically weaker small businesses of the region in an untenable competitive situation. Local tailors and seamstresses in fledgling enterprises could not, for example, compete with international textile firms. They, therefore, were banished from the market. Furthermore, the kinds of branch plant activities that had been established had not proved to be suitable for teaching the "tricks of the trade." Even if management had been willing to undertake that teaching role, the fact is that issues of corporate strategy are not dealt with at the level of local assembly processes. And yet it was this kind of strategic thinking that was required for development. As a result nowhere in the West Indies was a locally, as contrasted to an expatriate, based productive capacity sustained and developed. The Caribbean, in short, experienced growth but not development. The result was that policymakers throughout the region were powerless to do anything to reverse the tendency for job creation to fall short of job need.

Under the circumstances it is not surprising that dissatisfaction with the economy increasingly took a political form. On one hand, the rise in unemployment and associated poverty put large numbers of the population under severe and direct economic pressure. Even with growth it seems likely that the number of households experiencing real deprivation increased. On the other hand, the new elites that had assumed power as the region moved to independence in the 1960s and 1970s found themselves in a vulnerable position. Dependent development had left them unable to influence the economy in a way necessary to diffuse mounting social tensions. Thus the unsatisfactory nature of dependent development was experienced at both the top and the bottom levels of West Indian society. Preeminently, pressure for change was generated by the poor and the unemployed. It was they who were the major participants in the 1970 Black Power revolt in Trinidad and they also who supplied the mass support for Michael Manley's shift to the Left in Jamaica in 1974. Yet it was the new elites, remaining in power, that moved to "cooperative socialism" in Guyana in 1973, to democratic socialism in Jamaica in 1974, and to a greatly enhanced role for the government in the economy of Trinidad and Tobago after 1968. Only in Grenada in 1979 was the Caribbean pattern of continuity in government personnel, but change in emphasis, violated. But even there, the change in strategy occurred in response to popular pressure. The new approach to the economy by the People's Revolutionary Government, however, did not involve a major shift away from elite rule in that country.

Thus during the late 1960s and the 1970s—either in the name of socialism or otherwise—there developed in the Caribbean a greatly enhanced role for the state in economic affairs. In some cases this took the form of direct nationalization, a process that occurred most extensively in Guyana. More typical is what Susan Craig describes as occurring in Trinidad and Tobago: "the power of patronage of the political elite and the Prime Minister has been enhanced, making even the local bourgeoisie dependent on the generous incentives, subsidies and fiscal policies of the state." Even in relatively conservative Barbados, government's share of the labor force grew proportionately more rapidly than any other sector of the economy.[24] These actions were defended as necessary to improve welfare conditions: in Guyana, they were described as making "the small man a real man." At the same time, however, they strengthened local ruling groups by providing them with leverage over significant aspects of the economy. Foreign investors still could not be controlled. But the discretionary provision of subsidies, licenses, and incentives not to mention the direct control of jobs gave the region's ruling groups influence over the economy in a way that the application of the Lewis model had not. In that sense the control of the state provided the means by which those groups helped solidify their rule.

But if it is true that out of self-defense West Indian ruling elites moved to increase the role of government in the region's economy, it is not at all obvious that such a change is of great significance in encouraging an indigenous technological capacity to emerge. The region's problems in this regard will not be resolved simply by changing the ownership structure of those industries already present in the region. The simple fact is that those industries, even when in an expansionary phase, are not the ones necessary to develop the Caribbean.

The major producing sectors in the region continue, in the 1980s, to be raw materials extraction, assembly manufacturing, tourism, and export agriculture. The latter represents the legacy of the plantation economy, whereas the other three have been underwritten by incentive legislation. They are thus all creatures of policy and the functioning of the region's institutions. The problem is that they are unsuitable for promoting an authentic process of indigenous development. Their presence does not encourage adequately the creation of local entrepreneurial, technologically sophisticated skills. As such, therefore, the existence of these industries is testimony to the continuing failure of West

Indian institutions and policy-making. As yet there has been no appreciation of the need to create an environment in which technology and science in production can flourish. Precisely the opposite occurred with "industrialization by invitation," which held that all that was needed in this regard could be imported. That strategy's fatal error, even more important than its failure to provide an adequate number of employment opportunities, was its overlooking the need to nurture indigenous technical and managerial capacities.

Thus raw materials extraction, even when it yields a windfall, requires few if any local initiatives. Trinidad and Tobago benefited from the oil price increases of 1973 and 1979 without even being part of OPEC. The benefits derived were strictly a rent. Though the income received by no means was insignificant, the experience did little to promote the competencies in business associated with technological advances.

The same is true with regard to assembly manufacturing. In recent years Barbados has been the most successful country in the region in attracting these kinds of businesses. But even in Barbados manufacturing's growth, though impressive, was less rapid than that of the island's economy as a whole. The sector was a virtual enclave with few linkages—forward or backward—with other sectors of activity. In all, manufacturing created only about 2,500 relatively low-wage jobs between 1970 and 1979. Of eleven sectors, wages in the manufacturing sector ranked ninth. Part of the reason for this was that, within this sector, female wage rates averaged only about half that of males. As exemplified in Barbados, the industry was not associated with local business competence, the stimulating of secondary sectors, or even the payment of high wage rates.

In recent years tourism has been a major sector of growth for the Caribbean. Particularly Antigua and Barbuda, Jamaica, Saint Lucia, and Barbados have been the beneficiaries of a major expansion in this sector. But tourism, like assembly manufacturing, contributes less to long-term development than the output statistics suggest. This sector also tends to be foreign-owned and characterized by few interindustry transactions within the local economy. And if Barbados's example is typical, it never was heavily labor-using and becomes progressively less so as it matures and accommodates less affluent consumers. Beyond this, an extensive and highly emotional argument is carried on in the region concerning the social costs associated with emphasizing this sector and becoming a "welcoming society."[25] Typically the nationalist Left objects to the social and racial implications of this industry, though, paradoxically, the People's Revolutionary Government in Grenada under Maurice Bishop was committed to its development as the country's leading sector. Nonetheless, tourism provides little of the kind of experience necessary to develop the business acumen and skills of economic modernity.

Finally, the case against the dual structure that still dominates the region's agriculture is the strongest of all. Export agriculture is inflexible in its crop choice and high cost, and is increasingly labor-displacing. But most important, the control of the region's best agricultural land in these large units denies to would-be commercial farmers the resources necessary for their growth. In the Caribbean there can be no higher opportunity cost. Entrepreneurial and business skills are learned; they could be developed in agriculture to an extent much greater than is the case now save for the unavailability of good land. It is because of this that even a centrist like Alister McIntyre calls for an extensive program of land reform, the goal of which would be to create "businessmen not peasants."[26] The aim would be not only to make these farmers market-responsive in producing more and better crops, but, in so doing, to create the incentive for other persons to go into related businesses as well. In such circumstances, there would be a heightened need for storage, distribution, processing, and marketing—all essential for an efficient agricultural sector. It is hypothesized that, if land reform succeeded in creating commercial farms, the opportunity to engage in profitable agribusinesses would attract other persons to these fields. A reorganization of farming along these lines might also increase the demand for tools and equipment appropriate to relatively small-scale operations, thus stimulating the development of comparable manufacturing activities. Finally, it is possible that the demand symbolized by such a sector would speed the pace of research and facilitate the diffusion of new productivity-raising crops, seed, and soil innovations. In short, it is possible to envision a land reform program as the means by which to create a leading sector in the general transformation of the region's economy.

## Prospects for the Future

Indigenous development requires that a honeycomb of business relationships be embedded deeply in society. Self-reliance need not require autarchy or even a substantial exit from international trade. What it does require is for local people to have the ability decisively to influence economic performance. For this to be done two essentials must be present. First, local firms must be involved in direct production and processing: a high proportion of the value added must occur locally. They must not engage simply in mercantile activities, as has been the tradition within the urban-based private sector in the Caribbean. And second, a substantial degree of interindustry linkage must be present in the economy. Expansion in one sector must stimulate production elsewhere in the region. In that way the Caribbean economy could be more self-generating. But such an increase in autonomy can occur only if there emerges a network of productive enterprises linked together through markets. One firm's output must become another firm's foundation for production. Such linkages, as we have seen, are necessary in agriculture, where a series of different business activities is necessary to connect the farmer to the food consumers. It is also necessary with regard to both manufacturing and services. A complex interlocking of productive activity is the stuff from which innovation and development emerges.

Nurturing the growth of local entrepreneurial activities is the key to establishing a developing West Indian economy with a reasonable degree of autonomy. But it is precisely the lack of serious effort in this direction that unites the otherwise contrasting economic strategies followed in Guyana, Jamaica, and Trinidad and Tobago in the 1970s and through the mid-1980s. In Guyana, the government of Forbes Burnham in late 1975 adopted an ideology of "cooperative socialism" and by 1977 virtually all of the economy's major economic sectors had come under state control. But other than government ownership, cooperative socialism never took on a recognizable institutional form. In particular the cooperative sector—a potential area of entrepreneurial development—was not permitted an autonomous existence and thus did not become an important component of the economy. But the managerial task that the government had imposed on itself was far beyond its competence. The resulting administrative difficulties that plagued the Guyanese economy were compounded by the fact that the Burnham regime, which always had only minority support, became increasingly estranged from the population and was required to expend increasing amounts of its energies in devising ways simply to survive. The result was an enormous decrease in the country's gross domestic product. In 1982 real per capita output in Guyana was only 65 percent of that of 1971 and only 42 percent of that of the sugar boom years of 1975. (See Table 11-3.)

At the other end of the Caribbean, Michael Manley's government in Jamaica adopted democratic socialism as its approach to development. In this case there was in practice only a minimal movement to nationalization, though verbally a radical language was adopted particularly with respect to foreign affairs. Apparently believing that practice would prove decisive, the Manley

**Table 11-3**

Real Gross Domestic Product in Caribbean Countries, 1970–1980

|      | Antigua & Barbuda 1975 Prices (thousands EC$) | Barbados 1974 Prices (millions B$) | Dominica 1977 Prices (thousands EC$) | Guyana 1970 Prices (millions G$) |
|------|-----------|-----------|-----------|-----------|
| 1970 | —         | —         | —         | —         |
| 1971 | —         | —         | —         | 490.3     |
| 1972 | —         | —         | —         | 499.3     |
| 1973 | 123,280   | —         | —         | 505.6     |
| 1974 | 127,646   | 640.0     | —         | 646.0     |
| 1975 | 120,556   | 627.0     | 77,474    | 758.8     |
| 1976 | 109,788   | 653.9     | 82,849    | 650.5     |
| 1977 | 117,795   | 678.0     | 85,021    | 593.3     |
| 1978 | 127,417   | 710.5     | —         | 577.9     |
| 1979 | 136,977   | 766.7     | —         | 509.5     |
| 1980 | 142,700   | 803.8     | —         | 430.3     |

Sources: Antigua and Barbuda, Barbados, Dominica, Jamaica, Montserrat, St. Vincent, and the Grenadines: United Nations, *Yearbook of National Accounts 1981*. Guyana: Bank of Guyana, *1982 Annual Report*. Trinidad and Tobago: estimated by splicing current

government seems to have been genuinely surprised by the magnitude of the flight of foreign capital that occurred after its declaration of democratic social-ism in 1974. As a result of this capital strike, the gross domestic product in Jamaica declined by 18.4 percent between 1973 and 1980 (see Table 11-3). The depressed economic conditions after 1974 foreclosed any possibility that, under Manley, local businesses in Jamaica could prosper. They were also directly responsible for the election of Edward Seaga and his Jamaican Labour party in 1980. The latter's return to the strategy of "industrialization through invitation" through its enthusiastic participation in the United States' Carib-bean Basin Initiative further compounded the country's problems. Inevitably, Jamaica received an insufficient inflow of capital; moreover, the capital that was invested created only a very limited number of job opportunities. The problem was joined with a decline in the country's bauxite market and, as a conse-quence, an International Monetary Fund-inspired austerity program was insti-tuted to attempt to correct its deteriorating balance of international payments.

| Jamaica 1974 Prices (millions J$) | Montserrat 1975 Prices (millions EC$) | St. Vincent & the Grenadines 1976 Prices (millions EC$) | Trinidad & Tobago 1960 Prices (millions TT$) |
|---|---|---|---|
| 1,982.2 | — | — | 1,259.9 |
| 2,042.2 | — | — | 1,340.2 |
| 2,231.3 | — | — | 1,427.6 |
| 2,263.4 | — | — | 1,494.5 |
| 2,169.6 | — | — | 1,847.8 |
| 2,156.7 | 21.9 | 66.73 | 2,024.2 |
| 2,026.1 | 21.2 | 70.95 | 2,145.9 |
| 1,987.3 | 20.7 | 73.47 | 2,389.4 |
| 1,982.0 | 21.7 | 84.34 | 2,359.4 |
| 1,953.4 | 24.9 | 83.76 | 2,732.2 |
| 1,848.0 | 26.8 | — | 3,317.1 |

dollar gross domestic product and retail price index as given in Trinidad and Tobago, Central Statistical Office, Annual Statistical Digest No. 23, 1974–75, and No. 29, 1982.

In all, unemployment increased dramatically as Jamaica's economic decline continued through the mid-1980s.

The republic of Trinidad and Tobago, on the other hand, was the beneficiary of the phenomenal increase in petroleum prices of the 1970s and enjoyed a period of genuine prosperity. But that very boom, by dramatically raising wages and the costs of other inputs, made it increasingly difficult for small-scale enterprises to survive. These businesses could not match the wages offered in the petroleum-related sector or by government. The resulting flow of resources away from the small business and agricultural sectors was compounded by government's decision to use its resources to establish large-scale "downstream" enterprises as its way to industrialize the country's economy. Some of these, like the iron and steel company, seem to have been misconceived from the start. Others suffered from a decision-making environment that encouraged a dysfunctional management style of extreme caution. The upshot was that when in the 1980s the price of oil softened, the economy had little resiliency. Output as a whole drifted downward in lockstep with petroleum.

The gross domestic product may have started to fall as early as 1981 and, as reported by the governor of the country's Central Bank, output by mid-1984 was 16 percent below that of 1983.

The Caribbean region thus still awaits the appearance of a government seriously embarked on a program to encourage indigenous development. In the cases of Guyana, Jamaica, and Trinidad and Tobago cited above, insufficient attention was paid to stimulating productive activity among the local population. Furthermore, not even the People's Revolutionary Government in Grenada between 1979 and 1983 was an exception in this regard. The latter's economic strategy heavily emphasized tourism, an industry that is incapable of raising technical proficiency. The fact of this common failure raises the possibility that the governments of the region may share more than is suggested by their obvious ideological differences. One hypothesis is that the professional middle class, which dominates the governments of the Caribbean, may be reluctant to encourage the rise of a production-oriented class, seeing in the latter a potential competitor for social dominance. A more benign hypothesis would be that the current ruling groups simply lack an appreciation of what is required to promote indigenous growth. Little scholarly work has been done on this problem and it is not possible, on the basis of available evidence, to choose among these or other interpretations. But the fact is that there is a need to explain the post-independence failure of the region to move beyond dependence and to nurture productive and technical skills.

It should be noted that when a government committed to self-reliant development does appear in the region, it need not eschew a commitment to egalitarian values. Alec Nove in arguing for "developmental socialism" does so in the name of opposition to the "extreme inequalities" of capitalist development. He advocates a mixed economy, one in which "a great many" small and cooperative firms coexist with a few nationalized ones and those international firms whose projects fit the local development strategy.[27] A model like his, when applied to the West Indies, engenders hope for the region. In it the foundations of the economy, like bauxite and petroleum, will be state-owned, while, through the careful selection of multinational firms, the region will have access to technology from abroad. Also present will be institutions and policies to promote and reward success on a smaller scale.

In the resulting mixed economy some inequality will exist, associated with market performance and the private ownership of firms. But in the search for equity as well as growth, agrarian reform and educational policies will have a compensating, positive effect. As noted above, land redistribution is a high priority in prompting the development of entrepreneurship. A substantial reallocation of productive land, by correcting the current maldistribution of this resource, will also profoundly influence the distribution of wealth and income and move both in a more egalitarian direction. The same is true with regard to education. A substantial increase in the educational and vocational levels of the West Indies' labor force will help encourage growth. In addition, a broad program of educational reform will tend to equalize incomes since the extension of educational opportunities provides a more equal distribution of human skills and capabilities. Thus the extensive endowment of the population either with tangible assets such as land or intangible human capital not only will tend to enhance the society's ability to produce, but also will help to promote equality. All of this, in conjunction with the use of the revenues generated by the nationalized sector to assist those in need, can go far to reconcile the competing claims of growth and equity.

Whereas development tends to demand the inequality associated with success and failure, equity requires substantial equality as a matter of right. It is possible to achieve a functional degree of each. But to do so requires the appearance of a government willing and able to carry out policies that will empower the region's people with regard to production, even as it refrains from looking abroad for a stimulus to its growth process. When that is done, finally the Caribbean will have escaped the dependency that has plagued it historically and will be in a position to shape its own future.

Finally, there can be no doubt that in adopting "development socialism" the region will risk the displeasure and hostility of the United States. The American response to all such efforts in the Caribbean has been hostile in the past and there is every reason to believe that it will continue to be so in the future. Obviously a satisfactory, and necessarily diplomatic means will have to be found to defuse, or at least neutralize, U.S. antagonism so the Caribbean can pursue its development policies unobstructed. If, in short, the region can avoid a confrontation by playing its foreign policy in a low key, it might be justified in doing so in order to get on with the job to which the highest priority should be attached, the promotion of a greatly enhanced regional productive capacity together with a substantial degree of equity.

## Notes

1. Kuznets, "Modern Economic Growth," pp. 171, 165–66.
2. Best, "The Choice of Technology Appropriate to Caribbean Countries," p. 6.

3. Eisner, *Jamaica, 1830–1930*, table 56.

4. Thompson, "The Plantation as a Social System"; Beckford, *Persistent Poverty*; Levitt and Best, "Character of Caribbean Economy"; Mandle, *Patterns of Caribbean Development*.

5. W. Arthur Lewis, "Introduction," in Eisner, *Jamaica, 1830–1930*, p. xxii.

6. Eisner, *Jamaica, 1830–1930*, table 67.

7. Mintz, *From Plantations to Peasantries*, p. 5.

8. Beckford, "Caribbean Rural Economy," p. 81.

9. *Report of the West India Royal Commission*, p. 18.

10. Ibid., p. 15.

11. *West India Royal Commission*, p. 27.

12. Ibid., pp. 247, 252, 254, 313, 317, 323.

13. W. Arthur Lewis, "Memorandum on Social Welfare," p. 6.

14. W. Arthur Lewis, "The Industrialization of the British West Indies," p. 1.

15. Ibid., pp. 38–39. In a 1976 lecture at McGill University, Best claimed authorship of the phrase. See Best, "The Choice of Technology Appropriate to Caribbean Countries," p. 2.

16. W. Arthur Lewis, "The Industrialization of the British West Indies," pp. 30, 11, 15, 16; Farrell, "Arthur Lewis," pp. 54–55, 59.

17. Carrington, "Industrialization in Trinidad."

18. Jefferson, "Is the Jamaican Economy Developing?" p. 7.

19. Harootyan and Segal, "Appendix," p. 219.

20. Harewood, "West Indian People," p. 123.

21. Worrell, "Economic Survey of Barbados," p. 37; Cox, "The Manufacturing Sector," p. 65; Phillips, "Development of the Tourist Industry," p. 124.

22. Hope, "Recent Performances and Trends in the Caribbean Economy," pp. 45, 4.

23. The most easily accessible example of Lloyd Best's work is an article he coauthored with Karl Levitt. See Levitt and Best, "Character of Caribbean Economy," pp. 37, 52.

24. Craig, "Background to the 1970 Confrontation in Trinidad and Tobago," 1:399.

25. Taylor, *Jamaica*.

26. McIntyre, "Adjustments of Caribbean Economies," p. 19.

27. Nove, *The Economics of Feasible Socialism*, pp. 195, 193.

## 12

Anthony P. Maingot

# Caribbean International Relations

f one were to choose a single word to encapsulate Caribbean history, that word would have to be "geopolitics," or the relationship between geography and international relations. The most important part of Caribbean geography has been the sea, which has historically served less as the clichéd "inner lake" and more as a series of maritime highways. In the fifteenth century the Caribbean became a center of activity as direct sea mobility and contact changed the nature of movement in the world from an essentially land-centered basis to one in which transoceanic mobility was the key to empire and riches. As testaments to that sea's importance were the competition that it invariably unleashed and the attempts to manage that competition through unilateral dictates. First came the Treaty of Tordesillas (1494) through which the pope wished to separate that which was "rightfully" Spanish from that which was Portuguese; other powers were to stay out. The Caribbean fell into the Spanish portion but, as would later be shown with another unilateral attempt at establishing a "demarcation line"—the Monroe Doctrine—it was easier to proclaim a geopolitical doctrine than to enforce it. Even the presence of the greatest concentration of fortifications in the world could not secure hegemony for any one power. Control of one small island off the coast of Haiti (Ile de la Tortue) was enough to provide an international band of pirates a base from which to harass all merchant shipping. In World War II German U-boats would do the same without a single base but many friendly allies among coastal plantation owners.

What the history of archipelagic areas teaches us is that even the mightiest of naval powers cannot totally dominate each and every square mile of sea or island in the area. The English, French, and Dutch breached Spanish domination, a domination which the United States brought to an end with the Spanish-American War of 1898. But, even before that, the relative decline of European threats to the area during the nineteenth century resulted from the paradoxical alliance of interests between the United States and Great Britain. The Monroe Doctrine was an American foreign policy principle enforced by the British fleet. The status quo of 1823 and later suited both nations well, and yet it did not stop France from attempting to colonize Mexico, Spain from re-colonizing Santo Domingo, or Britain from expanding its original claims in Guyana and Belize.

The Caribbean, thus, has long experienced dynamic tension between the enunciation of hegemonic principles, the incapacity to enforce them, and the reality of economic and political pluralism. What have continually changed—and will probably continue to change—are the particular configurations of that dynamic tension. As strategic actors constantly seeking to maximize the benefits of any situation, nations have varying and shifting interests in either stability or change. Those who seek stability do so through more than just military means: they also seek to preempt the agenda and rules of the game, control the mechanisms that enforce these rules, and influence the nature and direction of custom. Hegemony means controlling both law and culture. But mere physical possession does not guarantee hegemonic success, not in the age of Spanish conquest and colonization, and much less so in the twentieth century. In this century the United States has had an advantage in establishing the rules of the game; it has not, however, been able to monopolize them. Every change in the mechanisms governing international relations, every attempt at regional stability is evidence of existing or perceived instability; every military intervention, a confrontation with unwanted change. The history of Caribbean international relations especially in the first half of the twentieth century has been fundamentally that: international institution- and rule-building and interventions, military or otherwise. In the second half of that century the panorama has been more complex because the concept and ideology of decolonization have taken on new dimensions beyond the political: social, cultural, and, perhaps especially, economic. Both "outsiders" and local actors are players in different parts of the area at different times. As distinct from Latin America where the year 1810 signaled the move toward political independence, in the archipelago there has been no such watershed year. Yet, Caribbean international relations have seen some watershed phases or eras of somewhat unspecified chronology, and it is toward those eras and their major characteristics that this study turns.

## Establishing the Basic International Machinery, 1933–1953

More than anything else, the nations of the hemisphere had sought during the early part of the twentieth century to avoid unilateral interventions through provisions guaranteeing collective security.[1] In its broadest sense collective security means the assertion of collective rather than individual action to contain aggression. The decisions on how and when to proceed, since they must be collective decisions, are made within an international organization set up to that end. In spite of its failure in Europe, the principle of collective security was institutionalized by the nations of the Western Hemisphere, so strong was their fear of intervention by major powers, European and American. They sought to ensure the principle of sovereignty through an overarching provision against intervention. Since the Inter-American Conference at Montevideo in 1933 there had been a push in that direction. The question of nonintervention was again taken up at the conference in Buenos Aires in 1936 and in Mexico City in 1945. The Act of Chapultepec adopted at this meeting in Mexico provided the basis of the Pact of Rio de Janeiro, and must be regarded as the true cornerstone of the idea of collective security and nonintervention in the hemisphere—designed at that point to counteract Axis threats to the Americas. The pact declared that "every attack of a State against the integrity or the inviolability of the territory, or against the sovereignty or political independence of an American State, shall . . . be considered an act of aggression against the other States."[2]

The Inter-American Treaty of Reciprocal Assistance (known as the Pact or Act of Rio de Janeiro) was signed at the Inter-American Conference for the Maintenance of Continental Peace and Security in Brazil in 1947. According to Article 9 of the treaty, "aggression" was interpreted as "an armed attack by one State against the territory, the people, or the land, sea or air forces of another State." One year after the Pact of Rio de Janeiro institutionalized the concept of hemispheric collective security, the related concept of national sovereignty was given full recognition in the charter of the Organization of American States (OAS) signed in Bogota in 1948. Article 15 of the charter reads: "No State or group of States has the right to intervene, directly or indirectly, for any reasons whatever, in the internal or external affairs of any other State." Article 17 was even more specific: "The territory of a State is inviolable; it may not be the object, even temporarily, of military occupation or of other measures of force taken by another State, directly or indirectly, on any grounds whatever."

The categorical language of articles 15 and 17 states the principle of nonintervention. Article 6, however, established the machinery, and the very language of that article illustrates how geopolitics, by defining what or who belongs ("continental") and who does not ("extra-continental"), set important parameters for action. Article 6 is clearly a search for stability: "If the inviolability or the integrity of the territory or the sovereignty or political independence of any American State should be affected by an aggression which is not an armed attack, or by an extra-continental or intra-continental conflict, or by any other fact or situation that might endanger the peace of America, the Organ of Consultation shall meet immediately in order to agree on the measures which must be taken."

Under the provisions of the Rio treaty, the Organ of Consultation of the OAS would decide on the measures to be taken. How, why, and when it should do so is left fairly open-ended by the language "any other fact or situation" that might endanger "the peace of America." Law, and especially international law, is invariably a matter of interpretation. Its implementation is a matter of political will and physical capability. Between 1948 and 1953 the OAS Council met as the formal Organ of Consultation ten times; nine of these had to do with events in the Caribbean and circum-Caribbean. These nine cases concerned the general state of tension, intrigue, and enmity between the liberal-democratic forces in the Caribbean (led by José Figueres of Costa Rica, Juan José Arevalo of Guatemala, and Carlos Prío Socarrás of Cuba) and the dictatorial regimes in Nicaragua and Santo Domingo. The tenth dealt with the dispute between Peru and Colombia over the exile rights of Peruvian leader Raul Haya de la Torre.

The machinery for collective security seemed to work rather well when the disputes were not only intracontinental but, indeed, intra-Latin American/ Caribbean. In none of the ten cases adjudicated during these years were U.S. perceptions of its vital interests involved. It is fair to say, therefore, that the basic principles of collective security and nonintervention and the machinery so painstakingly assembled to enforce them had not really been put to the test by 1953. That test would come with the heating up of the Cold War, defined as an extracontinental force with local accomplices. It represented a major watershed and, again, the Caribbean would be the cockpit. In 1954, however, decolonization had not run its full course so that not every actor on the international scene was covered by the machinery of the OAS. Some of the critical early battles of the Cold War in the Caribbean were not covered by the rules and regulations of collective security. Unilateralism had free rein.

# Enter the Cold War, 1954–1961

The nature of the change in world and hemispheric politics was reflected in the agenda and conclusions of the Tenth International Conference of American States held in Caracas in March 1954. That conference ended with a "Declaration of Solidarity for the Preservation of the Political Integrity of the Americas against the Intervention of International Communism." Clearly the post-World War II U.S. confrontation with the Soviet Union was the mainspring of these new developments. The Great Powers had emerged from the war with an undeclared but quite evident acceptance of spheres of influence that had a nearly global reach. But there were also important local, Caribbean and Latin American, ideologies and events that contributed to the new anticommunism. Many of these ideologies and movements had roots in the period before 1954. It was in 1954, however, that the United States decided that there was a direct threat.

Perhaps the most important case to the post-1954 era began in Costa Rica in 1947 where the incumbent president, Teodoro Picado, attempted to annul the election results of that year. With strong support from the influential Communist party and in a strange alliance with the hierarchy of the Roman Catholic church and elements of the landowning aristocracy, Picado used the small army to put down an uprising led by José Figueres. The resulting civil war of 1948 took on Caribbean-wide importance when the close cooperation of democratically elected leaders helped put together a small fighting force called La Legión del Caribe. This alliance of Figueres with presidents Juan José Arevalo of Guatemala, Carlos Prío Socarrás of Cuba, and exiled leaders such as Juan Bosch of the Dominican Republic and Rómulo Betancourt of Venezuela would later be called the "Democratic Left" of Latin American politics.[3] Most would later join the resurgent European social democratic Socialist International. Their main targets were the traditional dictators, especially Rafael Leonidas Trujillo in the Dominican Republic and Anastácio Somoza in Nicaragua. Intervention was justified only when fighting dictatorships. This was their definition of the threat to hemispheric peace. The United States had a different definition and consequently the Democratic Left did not consider the United States an ally in this antidictatorial struggle. The United States, under the strong leadership of Secretary of State John Foster Dulles, regarded stopping communism as the fundamental task of U.S. foreign policy in the area and, if dictators such as Trujillo and Somoza helped in that endeavor, that was good enough for him. Yet, despite the differences in goals, the important point was that both groups were interested in stopping the Communist forces: the United States for global reasons and the Democratic Left for local reasons.

The Figueres victory in Costa Rica in 1948 and the formation of an alliance of social democrats throughout the Caribbean were the first major signs that even before 1954 there were important new actors in the international relations scene in the Caribbean. The second major event indicating that a Cold War theme would fall on receptive ears because anticommunism had already entered into local Caribbean politics took place in British Guiana (later Guyana). There a Marxist party, the People's Progressive party (PPP), won the 1953 elections but soon experienced a split between the Leninist wing led by Cheddi Jagan and a group led by the more pragmatic Forbes Burnham. While this split responded as much to ideology as it did to the Indian-black divisions of the local society, it was also part of a much wider, Pan-Caribbean battle which the Cold War would encourage and aggravate.

In the early 1950s, a major struggle was taking place between the Moscow-dominated World Federation of Trade Unions (WFTU) and the Western-dominated International Confederation of Trade Unions (ICTU). In the Western Hemisphere the anticommunist attack was led by the AFL-supported Inter-American Regional Workers Organization (IARWO). In 1952 and 1953 the ICTU and the IARWO scored major victories throughout the still colonial West Indies. In Jamaica, Norman Manley's party, the People's National party (PNP), expelled the major left-wing leaders of the Trade Union Congress. Manley's trade union, the National Workers' Union (NWU), joined its rival, the Bustamante Industrial Trade Union (BITU), in becoming members of the ICTU. In Barbados, Grantley Adams, first president of the WFTU-related Caribbean Labour Congress, called for disbandment of that congress, saying it was dominated by a Caribbean-wide clique of communists. In Trinidad, the few Marxist trade unionists had been isolated even further from the evolving political arena. In Guyana, Burnham's British Guiana Labour Union joined the ICTU in 1952, thus formally associating itself with such "moderate" West Indian politicians as Manley, Bustamante, and Adams—all subjects of virulent attacks as "bourgeois labor unionists" in Cheddi Jagan's paper *Thunder*.

The battle did not remain at the local level, however. Following major labor disturbances and conflicts between the PPP and the British governor in 1953, British troops landed, suspended the constitution, and threw the PPP out of office. This was the overt intervention; the covert intervention was being sponsored by the United States. Most Guyanese did not realize that what was unfolding was the first major anticommunist offensive by the United States in the Caribbean—an offensive in which the United States had substantial local support. A similar congruence of U.S. global and hemispheric interests and those of local groups occurred only a year later in Guatemala, the event which can be said to have ushered in a new era. The machinery for collective security proved to be of little use in this new era.

After the fall of the long-lived Ubico dictatorship (1931–44), Guatemala entered a period of truly progressive-minded government. The liberal regime of Juan José Arevalo began a trend that was continued by Colonel Jacobo Arbenz in even more dynamic fashion. It is a fact that the revolutionaries of 1944 were sincere but naive about the workings of international power politics. Robert Alexander explains that the 1944 revolutionaries came to power at a time when everything seemed to be "sweetness and light" between the democrats of the great Western powers and the communists inside and outside the Soviet Union. "The Guatemalan revolutionary leaders never got over this wartime honeymoon."[4] That the honeymoon between the two world powers had indeed ended, the Arbenz government soon discovered. Heavily infiltrated by members of Guatemala's resurgent communist movement, Arbenz's regime began to take a revolutionary reformist internal policy and an openly pro-Soviet international stance. On March 1954 the American and Latin American delegates at the Caracas conference adopted an anticommunist position aimed at the Guatemalan regime and events followed naturally from that act, to wit:

June 18: A well-armed force of Guatemalan exiles led by Colonel Castillo Armas invaded Guatemala from Honduras. Guatemala requested a meeting of the Organ of Consultation to consider this violation of the Rio treaty. None was called.

June 19: The United States blocked attempts by Guatemala to bring the case before the United Nations Security Council (at that time conveniently chaired by the American delegate, Henry Cabot Lodge).

June 26: Guatemala renewed its request for OAS action—in vain.

June 29: The Guatemalan army forced President Arbenz to resign.

July 2: The OAS called the Organ of Consultation into action but cancelled the meeting as a new government emerged in Guatemala.

In contrast to its prompt and effective action in the ten cases preceding 1954, the OAS suddenly developed leaden feet. Collective security no longer operated as a working principle. One key to the reason why might be found in the statement made in 1963 by Senator Thurston Morton, who recalled the following conversation he had with President Dwight D. Eisenhower and which illustrated the "tone" of the new era:

When the plans were laid to overthrow the communist government of Guatemala . . . the President said, "Are you sure this is going to succeed?"—he was reassured it would, and said: "I'm prepared to take any steps that are necessary to see that it succeeds. For if it succeeds it's the people of Guatemala throwing off the yoke of Communism. If it fails, the Flag of the United States has failed."[5]

The factor of "prestige" or "face" is evident in the U.S. attitude; it tends to be an important motivation of Great Power action in their spheres of influence but hardly one that would find support in the OAS charter. That support had to come from another source: the Monroe Doctrine.

One day after Arbenz had resigned, Secretary of State John Foster Dulles went on radio and television to inform the American public that "this intrusion of Soviet despotism in Guatemala was, of course, a direct challenge to our Monroe Doctrine, *the first and most fundamental of our foreign policies.* . . . For 131 years that policy has well served the peace and security of the hemisphere. It serves us well today."[6] But there was no hegemony possible in the Caribbean so that if the Monroe Doctrine was used successfully in Guatemala in 1954, it would fail miserably in Cuba only five years later.

To some extent the events unleashed in Costa Rica in 1948 played a role in what occurred in Cuba. Like Caribbean rebels had done for centuries before them, the Cuban rebels arrived by boat in 1956. The same hemispheric forces opposing dictatorships supported these opponents of Cuba's Fulgencio Batista who arrived in the "Granma." These social democratic forces could not, however, control the flow of Cuban events. Neither could the United States. Strains between the Eisenhower government and Castro were soon evident after Castro's successful revolution in 1959. Consciousness of the history of U.S. domination played an important role in that hostility. The Cuban government must have taken a cue from a State Department press release, dated July 1960, which stated that the principles of the Monroe Doctrine were "as valid today as they were in 1823. . . . Specifically the Organization of American States Charter and the Rio Treaty provide the means for common action to protect the hemisphere against the interventionist and aggressive designs of international communism."[7]

Again, the United States first tried to oppose the trends in Cuba by utilizing OAS machinery. In response to a U.S. request the OAS Council decided to convene a Seventh Meeting of Consultation in San José, Costa Rica, in August 1960. Despite strong pressure from Secretary of State Christian Herter to do so, the meeting failed to condemn Cuba directly. Failing to get multilateral approval for action against Cuba, the United States began to take unilateral action, the most important of which was the decision to arm, train, and supervise anti-Castro forces in Nicaragua, Guatemala, and Florida. This action was subsequent to its cancellation of all imports of Cuban sugar under the existing quota and otherwise tightening of the economic screws on Cuba.

The Bay of Pigs invasion occurred on April 19, 1961. Although actually presented with the invasion plans as a fait accompli by the preceding administration, President John F. Kennedy assumed personal responsibility for the affair. He then proceeded to provide an interpretation of U.S. obligations under the OAS charter which stretched the legal principles but, at least, was an honest and straightforward statement of basic American policy. Intervention, stated the president, was not involved since no U.S. troops were employed. "But let the record show," he noted, "that our restraint is not inexhaustible." He warned that should it ever appear that the inter-American doctrine of noninterference merely conceals or excuses a policy of inaction, that if the nations of this hemisphere should fail to meet their commitments against outside communist penetration, "then I want it clearly understood that this government will not hesitate in meeting its primary obligations, which are the security of our nation."[8] The events leading to the formulation and then reiteration of this position had all occurred in the Caribbean or circum-Caribbean. There was a continuity in U.S. responses from the entry into the Spanish-American War, the intervention in Panama in 1903, through the multiple interventions in Mexico, Nicaragua, Haiti, the Dominican Republic, and Cuba. What varied was the definition of the perceived threat. There has hardly been hemispheric agreement with that perception.

The missile crisis of October 1962 was an exception. It was played out on the Caribbean Sea as U.S. naval forces established a "quarantine" of Cuba. In this particular case, the collective security mechanisms of the OAS charter were called into play and the United States received complete hemispheric support for its actions. Ideology, legality, and political will were in harmony at the hemispheric level. It was a rare occurrence. Only three years later, in 1965, no such meeting of minds occurred when the United States invaded the Dominican Republic. The Marines were already on the beach when on April 29 the United States called for an emergency meeting of the OAS Organ of Consultation. The action was unilateral. Again, there were significant local and regional actors who applauded and supported it. Events in the Caribbean had given birth to the "Johnson Doctrine." To the extent that unilateral action was the core of that doctrine it was not new; neither was the fact that U.S. actions had strong local support. The only thing new was the concept of linkage, the perception that the threat transcended the boundaries of the Caribbean but was already present and alive in that region in Cuba. The legacies of this period included a shattered OAS treaty, a Marxist-Leninist Cuba committed to revolutions everywhere in the hemisphere, and a series of models of economic development designed to counteract the Cuban model—whose influence would go well beyond the Caribbean. Most important among these were Puerto Rico's "Operation Bootstrap" and the Alliance for Progress. The former had its inception well before the Cuban Revolution, but its success was heavily promoted as a model only after 1960. It was not something that could be easily imitated in the rest of the hemisphere, however. It involved the importation of U.S. capital to create manufacturing for export to the U.S. market. The special "commonwealth" political status of Puerto Rico made this possible. The leaders of the hemisphere could not expect, and often did not want, such close ties to American capital even though they welcomed the country's open markets. A new initiative was needed and the Alliance for Progress was born. The alliance was based on the theories of Argentine economist Raul Prebish and involved generating import-substitution industries based on local capital. Land reform and other structural changes were also visualized in the alliance, necessary counterparts to the Cuban reforms which were very influential.

Significant in both initiatives was the role of a group of Puerto Rican politicians who served as a bridge between the United States and the Latin Americans, especially with the hemisphere's Democratic Left. Men such as Governor Luis Muñoz Marín, Teodoro Moscoso, Jaime Benitez, and Arturo Morales Carrión were the first Hispanics to play a significant role in American foreign policy. They were not only the link with the Latin Americans, but also the critical bridge to the incipient nation-builders in the non-Hispanic Caribbean. This was made possible in part by the fact that during World War II the European colonial powers (Britain, France, Holland, and, later, the United States) had located their center of planning for what was to be the post-World War II decolonization process in Puerto Rico. The Caribbean Commission, as it was called, had as its deputy director of research a young historian and future prime minister of Trinidad, Eric Williams.

Clearly the new, post–World War II generation of Cuban, Puerto Rican, and other Caribbean leaders came on the scene in international relations at the height of the Cold War. How they individually and distinctly guided their nations through this turbulent period and toward relatively high levels of social and economic well-being is one of the extraordinary stories of Third-World development. It also demonstrated that aspirations or hopes of hegemony in this archipelagic region were unfulfilled. By the mid-1960s the Caribbean was a sea of variety: of political systems, of economic systems, of religions, and, critically, of varying degrees of diplomatic closeness to the United States. Adding to the mix and variety were a group of newly independent states whose only contact with the American military they had actively supported: a military presence that resulted from the Churchill-Roosevelt exchange of U.S. destroyers for U.S. bases in the area during World War II. Even though in some cases, such as that of Trinidad, the existence of an American base became a matter of some agitation during the early years of independence, nowhere was there the nationalist resentment of the American presence that had existed in, for instance, Cuba. As English speakers accustomed to the parliamentary system, civilian rule, and British common law, these new states had an identity of their own.

The challenge that these new nations faced in the 1960s was whether that identity could survive the presence in the new Caribbean cockpit which geography had assigned to them. It should already be evident that the machinery for collective security and nonintervention built in the region before their emergence as sovereign states was not in exceptional shape. Their survival would depend on their individual and collective (subregional) capacity to handle the pitfalls of international relations in the Caribbean.

## Enter the New Democracies, 1962–1980

When Castro came to power in 1959, only Cuba, the Dominican Republic, and Haiti were independent insular countries in the region. By 1980, however, that situation had changed dramatically; there were now thirteen independent island states and three mainland nations referred to here as West Indian. Other states such as the Netherlands Antilles, Puerto Rico, and the French West Indies exercised nearly total internal autonomy. None of these states, however, had the experience in foreign affairs that Fidel Castro and the Cuban Communist party had, certainly not in terms of the turbulent history of the Caribbean with its long-standing involvements across borders and seas. That involvement, more than anything else, dictated the responses to events in the Caribbean of the seven American presidents who had to deal with Fidel Castro between 1959 and 1982.

Over those years U.S. interests in the region had grown and diversified.

From a geostrategic viewpoint, some of the thirty-one "essential" U.S. foreign trade routes were in the Caribbean, and the busiest routes all bordered Cuba, following the Windward Passage (between Cuba and Haiti) and the Straits of Florida (between Florida and Cuba). Obviously, these routes were also crucial to the Latin American and Caribbean countries whose main market was the United States. By the early 1970s 55 percent of Caribbean exports and 43 percent of their imports were with the United States. In 1977, the assistant secretary of state for inter-American affairs calculated U.S. exports to the Caribbean at $2 billion and U.S. investments at $4.5 billion (excluding Puerto Rico). By 1982 those exports were $6.8 billion, investments stood at $5.65 billion, and U.S. imports from the area were $10 billion. In 1980, American tourists in the Caribbean spent $1.1 billion. The heaviest investments were in oil and bauxite. Two-thirds of the U.S. requirements for bauxite/aluminum came from the Caribbean; 25 percent of the petroleum imports as of 1980 were refined or transshipped in the Caribbean.

Even so, the development of a specifically Caribbean perspective as distinct from a hemispheric one had been problematic. The Eurocentric and Japan-oriented predisposition of top U.S. policymakers had always relegated Latin American policy to a secondary level; the Caribbean as such came in for even less attention. The reality was that despite the sizable West Indian presence in the United States and the cultural and political ties that such a presence brought, the United States never included the West Indies in its Latin American policy. Even during World War II, when the "bases-for-destroyers" deal provided the United States with important bases in the area, there was no distinctly Caribbean policy. Despite the presence of the Vichy-loyal fleet on the French islands and the heightened U.S. awareness after the sinking of over four hundred ships by German U-boats, the United States never challenged the European presence in the area or attempted to substitute a policy of its own. That presence always had coexisted nicely with the Monroe Doctrine, a doctrine which, on the other hand, had repeatedly been called on to justify actions in Central America and the Greater Antilles.

When the European withdrawal started in the 1960s, however, the search for a broader "Caribbean policy" began in earnest. The development of multiple, sovereign national systems and the traumatic experience of the Cuban Revolution (representing the first successful break with U.S. power in the area) speeded up the process. It is an important commentary on the evolving role of "border" states (such as Texas vis-à-vis Mexico) in U.S. foreign policy formulation, that it was Representative Dante B. Fascell of southern Florida, whose state and specific constituency had vital Caribbean-oriented interests, who led the search for a policy. As chairman of the House Subcommittee on Inter-American Affairs, Fascell had long attempted to emphasize the significance of the Caribbean for U.S. policy. To Fascell there was a need to go beyond the concerns with Cuba. During 1972 hearings on conditions in the Caribbean, Fascell noted that he had "a distinct feeling" that as far as the United States was concerned, "first, we don't care and, second, we are out."[9] In 1974, Fascell was happy to settle for the fact that the word "Caribbean" was now being used by the State Department—not as trivial a fact as it might at first appear. New language reflects new consciousness and this in turn is the essential first step in the formulation of discrete policy. It was Fascell who in April 1973 enunciated the most complete outline of a desirable U.S. Caribbean policy. Making a distinction between a U.S. "policy of self-preservation" and a "true" Caribbean policy, Fascell's proposals were premised on the beliefs that "while military considerations remain important to U.S. policy they are not likely to become of overriding concern," and that given the dangers inherent in a relationship involving such disparities of power, "the United States should play a support-ing and not a preponderant role in regional organizations."[10]

In fact, Fascell specifically recommended that the United States could and should stay out of the domestic affairs of the Caribbean. Intervention can only be legitimate, said Fascell, when there is a "clear and present danger to our survival." The stress was very much on the need for a concerted multilateral approach to the area and to the policy changes recommended. The Fascell approach, although new in its specific focus on the Caribbean, was actually part of a wider sentiment favoring change in inter-American relations generally in the early and mid-1970s. In very general terms there was considerable support for three crucial premises behind the call for multilateralism, all reflecting a post-Vietnam sense of disillusionment with excessive Cold War thinking: (1) the need to respect diversity in ideology and economic/social organization, (2) the independent role of Latin American/Caribbean nations in international affairs, and (3) the global significance of the principal issues of U.S.-Latin American/Caribbean relations.

These premises coincided with Latin American sentiment. The 1973 Gen-eral Assembly of the Organization of American States established a special committee on restructuring the inter-American system. The November 1973 meeting in Bogotá of Latin American secretaries of state was preparatory to the February 1974 meeting in Mexico with Henry Kissinger. The OAS General Assembly was then invited to meet in Atlanta, Georgia, in April 1974.

The official who opened this OAS General Assembly meeting in Atlanta was the then governor of Georgia, Jimmy Carter. The emphasis on multilateralism made its mark. Three years later, as president, Carter addressed the Permanent Council of the OAS, outlining a "new approach" to "Latin America and the Caribbean." That approach, said Carter, would be based on three elements: (1) a high regard for the "individuality and sovereignty" of each Latin American and Caribbean nation, (2) a respect for human rights ("You will find this country eager to stand beside those nations which respect human rights and promise democratic values"), and (3) a desire to press forward on the great issues that affect the relations between the developed and developing nations. "Your economic problems," said Carter, "are also global in character and cannot be dealt with solely in regional terms."[11]

The Carter initiative, then, emerged out of the debate of the preceding years. The approach would be multilateral: the International Monetary Fund (IMF), World Bank, General Agreement on Tariffs and Trade (GATT), the United Nations Commission on Trade and Development (UNCTAD), the Economic Commission for Latin America (ECLA), and Venezuela's chairmanship of the Paris conference on economic cooperation were all mentioned by Carter as elements of the new approach. Also available to the newly independent states in the area (and to those autonomous but not yet independent—see Table 12-1) were the provisions of the European Common Market's Lômé Convention which provided special arrangements for trade from former colonial areas. The array of agencies and organizations serving the African, Caribbean, and Pacific nations (the APC states) was great, as Table 12-2 indicates. The Third World was now a major battleground for the minds of people and the Caribbean was in the thick of this battle.

Aware of the stakes, the Carter administration launched a diplomatic campaign more intense than any since John F. Kennedy's Alliance for Progress; and now the Caribbean was included. There were traveling emissaries—including Jimmy Carter's wife, Rosalynn, his secretary of state, Henry Kissinger, his assistant secretaries of state for political affairs and inter-American affairs, and—very importantly—his ambassador to the United Nations, Andrew Young. In part reflecting the significance of race in Caribbean international relations but mostly reflecting Caribbean wishes for a more concerted effort by the United States, Young had extraordinary successes. There were also significant changes in the diplomatic appointments to Caribbean posts, and within the Department of State a Caribbean Task Force was set up to develop blueprints for possible policy.

Although the broad outlines indicated that the Kissinger notion of a multilateral approach to the area was embodied in the Carter proposals, there were important shifts in emphasis as to where vital U.S. interests lay. The concern

**Table 12-1**

Independent States and Dependent Territories of the Caribbean

| Country by Date of Independence | Independent States of the Caribbean | | | | |
|---|---|---|---|---|---|
| | Current Popu- lation | Area in sq. miles | Pop. Density per sq. mile | Gross Dom. Prod. U.S. $ millions | Per capita GDP U.S. $ |
| *French-speaking* | | | | | |
| Haiti (1804) | 6,000,000 | 10,714 | 549 | 1,500* | 289* |
| *Spanish-speaking* | | | | | |
| Dominican | | | | | |
| Republic (1844) | 6,200,000 | 18,700 | 308 | 6,800 | 1,341 |
| Cuba (1902) | 9,771,000 | 44,000 | 222 | 23,300 | 1,360 |
| *English-speaking* | | | | | |
| Jamaica (1962) | 2,100,000 | 4,411 | 504 | 3,400 | 1,360 |
| Trinidad and | | | | | |
| Tobago (1962) | 1,200,000 | 1,980 | 594 | 7,000 | 6,500 |
| Barbados (1966) | 252,000 | 166 | 1,518 | 819 | 3,271 |
| Guyana (1966) | 795,000 | 83,000 | 10 | 507* | 603* |
| Bahamas (1973) | 235,000 | 5,382 | 39 | 1* | 4,760* |
| Grenada (1974) | 107,000 | 133 | 821 | 50 | 459 |
| Dominica (1978) | 74,300 | 289 | 256 | 66 | 882 |
| St. Lucia (1979) | 119,000 | 238 | 513 | 133* | 1,079* |
| St. Vincent | | | | | |
| (1979) | 115,000 | 150 | 767 | 59* | 513* |
| Antigua (1981) | 78,200 | 108 | 715 | 83 | 1,039 |
| Belize (1981) | 148,000 | 8,864 | 16 | 185* | 1,200* |
| St. Kitts/Nevis | | | | | |
| (1983) | 44,404 | 104 | 427 | 48 | 1,072 |
| *Dutch-speaking* | | | | | |
| Suriname (1975) | 388,000 | 63,227 | 6 | 822* | 2,370* |

(continued on next page)

with military security (especially Soviet naval activities) was not abandoned, but clearly the focus was no longer primarily or exclusively military. The clearest indication of that was the Panama Canal Treaty, negotiated in 1977 and ratified by the United States Congress in 1978. Assistant Secretary of State Terence Todman explained that "we no longer see the Caribbean in quite the same stark military security context that we once viewed it" and noted that the security concerns were now regarded as more political. Rather than the threat

**Table 12-1**

(continued)

| Territory | Current Population | Area in sq. miles | Pop. Density per sq. mile | Gross Dom. Prod. U.S. $ millions | Per capita GDP U.S. $ |
|---|---|---|---|---|---|
| | | Dependent Territories | | | |
| *French Territories* | | | | | |
| Guadeloupe | 322,900 | 687 | 461 | 992 | 3,151 |
| Guiana | 73,022 | 35,135 | 2 | 120 | 1,935 |
| Martinique | 328,566 | 425 | 734 | 1,158 | 3,802 |
| *Dutch Territories* | | | | | |
| Netherlands Antilles | 250,000 | 383 | 634 | 1,000 | 4,320 |
| *British Territories* | | | | | |
| Anguilla | 6,500 | 35 | 185 | 3 | 420 |
| Bermuda | 72,000 | 21 | 3,496 | 787* | 12,000* |
| Cayman Islands | 18,285 | 100 | 167 | 72 | 4,800 |
| Montserrat | 12,034 | 40 | 304 | 20 | 1,736* |
| Turks/Caicos | 7,436 | 166 | 39 | 15* | 2,000* |
| British Virgin Is. | 12,244 | 59 | 210 | 29* | 2,456* |
| *U.S. Territories* | | | | | |
| Puerto Rico | 3,240,000 | 3,435 | 943 | 11,771 | 3,001 |
| U.S. Virgin Islands | 99,670 | 136 | 733 | 684* | 7,078* |

Source: Caribbean/Central American Action, *1984 Caribbean and Central American Databook.*
*Gross national product.

of foreign military bases at the U.S. doorstep, Todman spoke of "an even more troublesome prospect: proliferation of impoverished Third World states whose economic and political problems blend with our own."[12]

The emphasis, then, was on cooperation in definitions of problems and on multilateralism. Both necessarily meant that the United States was to adopt a supporting rather than a dominant role. Important in this context was the fact that although the United States had been holding bilateral discussions with many governments in the area, Venezuela, Costa Rica, and Trinidad and Tobago had been consulted the most and in turn had been supportive of this multi-

**Table 12-2**

Agencies and Organizations Serving the APC States

| Intergovernmental Organization[a] | Member States[b] |
| --- | --- |
| Customs Cooperation Council | Bhms, Guy, Hti, Jca, T.T. |
| Caribbean Community and Common Market (CARICOM) | A/B, Bhms, Bdos, Blze, Dom, Gda, Guy, Jca, St.C/N, St.L, St.V/G, T.T. |
| Caribbean Development Bank (CDB) | A/B, Bhms, Bdos, Blze, Dom, Gda, Guy, Jca, St.C/N, St.L, St.V/G, T.T. |
| European Economic Community, Lômé Convention (EEC-L) | A/B, Bhms, Bdos, Blze, Dom, Gda, Guy, Jca, St.C/N, St.L, St.V/G, Surme, T.T. |
| European Investment Bank (EIB) | A/B, Bhms, Bdos, Blze, Dom, Gda, Guy, Jca, St.L, St.V/G, Surme, T.T. |
| Group of Latin American and Carib Sugar Exporting Countries (GEPLACEA) | Bdos, Cuba, DomR, Guy, Hti, Jca, T.T. |
| Inter-American Development Bank (IADB) | Bhms, Bdos, Blze, DomR, Guy, Hti, Jca, Surme, T.T. |
| International Cocoa Organization (ICCO) | Dom, Gda, Hti, Jca, St.V/G, T.T. |
| International Bauxite Association (IBA) | DomR, Guy, Hti, Jca, Surme |
| International Sugar Organization (ISO) | Bdos, Blze, Cuba, DomR, Guy, Hti, Jca |
| International Coffee Organization (ICO) | DomR, Hti, Jca |
| International Telecommunications Satellite Organization (INTELSAT) | Bdos, DomR, Hti, Jca, T.T. |
| International Whaling Commission (IWC) | A/B, Blze, Dom, Jca, St.L, St.V/G |
| International Wheat Council (IWTC) | Bdos, Cuba, DomR, T.T. |
| Nonaligned Movement (NAM) | A/B, Bdos, Blze, Cuba, Gda, Guy, Jca, St.L, Surme, T.T. |
| Organization of American States (OAS) | A/B, Bhms, Bdos, Dom, DomR, Gda, Hti, Jca, St.C/N, St.L, St.V/G, Surme, T.T. |
| Organization of Eastern Caribbean States (OECS) | A/B, Dom, Gda, Montserrat, St.C/N, St.L, St.V/G |
| Agency for the Prohibition of Nuclear Weapons in Latin America (OPANAL) | Bhms, Bdos, DomR, Gda, Hti, Jca, Surme, T.T. |
| Latin American Economic System (SELA) | Bdos, Cuba, DomR, Gda, Guy, Hti, Jca, St.L, St.V/G, Surme, T.T. |

(continued on next page)

**Table 12-2**
(continued)

---

Key: A/B = Antigua and Barbuda; Bhms = Bahamas; Bdos = Barbados;
Blze = Belize; Dom = Dominica; DomR = Dominican Republic; Gda = Grenada;
Guy = Guyana; Hti = Haiti; Jca = Jamaica; St.C/N = St. Christopher and Nevis;
St.L = St. Lucia; St.V/G = St. Vincent and the Grenadines; Surme = Suriname;
T.T. = Trinidad and Tobago.

a. Does not include United Nations organizations.
b. Cuba is also a member of the Council for Mutual Economic Assistance (CEMEA),
International Bank for Economic Cooperation (IBEC), International Commission for
the Conservation of Atlantic Tunas, and International Investment Bank (IIB).

lateralism. Carter chose his closest allies from among the democrats in the
region.

The initiative was launched formally in Washington on December 15, 1977,
at a conference at the World Bank on economic development in the Caribbean.
The United States was to be just one member of the Group for Cooperation in
Economic Development that would begin to function in the spring of 1978. It
appeared to be a popular arrangement among Caribbean leaders who were
personally briefed by Ambassador Young.

It is virtually axiomatic in political analysis that the powerful will tend to
exercise a degree of influence consonant with the effects sought and with the
tenacity of opposition present or anticipated. The Carter administration sought
to influence Caribbean trends through an emphasis on human rights and on
political and social pluralism, and to do so in concert with other democracies
inside and outside the area. It practiced what it preached, substantially reducing the flow of U.S. military equipment to Latin America at a time when the
USSR was increasing its involvement.

With this decline in weapons transfer went further reductions in U.S. military visibility. The number of American military liaison officers serving in Latin
America went from 532 in 1970 to 115 in 1980; the number of Latin American
officers trained went from 3,700 to less than 1,700 during that same decade.
There can be no doubt that the early years of the Carter administration
represented a rare interlude in U.S. policy toward the area. The emphasis on
multilateralism and on human rights, the flexibility toward ideological pluralism all deviated from a traditional American emphasis on a Cold War-driven
geopolitics.

Yet, by 1979 this same administration began to harden its approach to Caribbean and Latin American affairs. Why? The answers lie in the complex and often paradoxical response of local actors to outside initiatives as well as the continued importance of both interests and ideology as motors of this local elite behavior. The response of the region's Marxist-Leninist leadership to the *apertura* (liberalization) provided by the Fascell-Carter policy was additional evidence that there still was no hegemonic power in the region. In 1980 the region was again a center of geopolitical and military concern.

## Back to Great Power "Realism"

By early 1980 it was clear that the Carter administration had reconsidered and reevaluated trends in the area and found that its multilateralism and virtual ban on military security assistance had not produced the results desired. It was precisely such a reevaluation that had long been advocated by those who considered themselves "realists" in international relations. They tended to argue that the North-South or rich-poor conflict Carter stressed had to be subordinated to this revival of the Cold War. What was important was to keep the area "in line" and to avoid blows to U.S. prestige. The view was of long standing in the United States and continued to be widely held, especially as it related to the Caribbean, an area which by 1980 included many more independent states than those of the Greater Antilles. The arena in which U.S. sensitivities about its national "honor" and "prestige" could be challenged was now expanded to include many more points of contact. It is evident that the greater the emphasis on subjective factors, the greater the possibility of misunderstanding, especially if the number of players increases and many of them are new to the game. This is exactly the situation that was faced by the Caribbean in 1980.

In 1967 Hanson W. Baldwin, military editor of the *New York Times*, admitted that "Cuba is not vital to us as a base," but concluded nevertheless that "its global importance is chiefly positional and political-psychological." Psychological factors usually are linked to the factor of prestige and all of these to the domino theory. "Revision of the treaty terms for Guantanamo," Baldwin asserted, "will inevitably lead to revisionism elsewhere—in Panama, in Trinidad, globally. . . . United States power and prestige are involved in Gitmo, whether we like it or not."[13]

In similar fashion, the panelists' findings of the 1971 Caribbean conference held at the Center for Strategic and International Studies of Georgetown University provide an interesting early insight into the thinking of an intellectual group that would become politically influential after 1980. It saw the Soviet challenge—exercised by itself and through Cuba—as the overriding threat to U.S. interests in the area, one endowed with special significance by the presence of the Panama Canal, U.S. territories, and military bases. Aside from this very real military importance, to the members of this group the area was "of great symbolic and psychological significance." Erosion of America's position in the Caribbean could adversely affect U.S. "prestige" worldwide.

Clearly, once the psychological and prestige dimensions of geopolitics are emphasized, then "objective" strategic and military factors become less significant.[14] Arguments about shifts in military technology and in the alignment of conventional forces carry little weight in the face of what are essentially subjective and reputational political variables. The panelists at the 1971 Georgetown conference made this clear in their conclusion that, in deciding how to respond to events in an area defined as vital (such as the Caribbean), what is of most importance is "not so much the reality of the situation" but whether the president and his advisers are convinced that the American public "believes" that vital U.S. interests are threatened. In other words, the perceptions to be considered are not only of those trained to evaluate such situations but indeed of the general public.

This, of course, was a correct evaluation of the complexities of foreign policy formulation in the American democracy. For the Caribbean it presented special problems: whether the United States had a specific Caribbean policy or not, American public opinion had invariably perceived the Caribbean as strategically important and the Panama Canal always had a special place in those perceptions. The concept of the "soft underbelly" was and is specifically a reference to the Caribbean border, never applied to the Canadian, Pacific, or Mexican borders. Now, with the multiplication of independent ministates in the American sphere of influence, there was fear that that "underbelly" had become even softer. The concept of "reverse manipulation" was being used to describe a situation where small states used their enormous disparity in size to manipulate the United States; when and where there was the additional suspicion that outside forces in turn manipulated the small states, then the question of prestige was added to a broader sense of military threat.

It was precisely this approach to Caribbean affairs (and, indeed, these same scholars) that emerged victorious in November 1980. Even before the inauguration of President Ronald Reagan their views were widely circulated and affected policies from Haiti and Guatemala to Argentina. Although retaining elements of the Kissinger-Carter multilateralism, Reagan now declared the Caribbean "vital." With this definition came a new and more aggressive approach to the Soviet threat in which "consultation" with friendly nations appeared to replace outright multilateralism; human rights no longer seemed a prominent feature even rhetorically. It was another "correcting shift" in U.S. policy toward the area. And, again, the United States found some strong support for such a shift among local actors. In 1980 this included many of the new ministates.

## The Ministate as Autonomous Actor

It is important to note that West Indian suspicion of Cuba increased during the period of U.S. emphasis on multilateralism and downplaying of hostile and belligerent rhetoric. It was the result of a series of intra-Caribbean events, incidents played out by Caribbean actors themselves. Most important by far was Cuba's surreptitious use of Barbados to airlift some 5,000 troops into Angola in 1975. It demonstrated Cuban audacity and Cuban logistical capabilities and at the same time showed how easily these small states could unknowingly be drawn into an East-West tangle. The airlift had a very negative effect on the relations among West Indian leaders; neither Michael Manley nor Forbes Burnham was overly concerned, but Eric Williams of Trinidad was particularly put out by the discovery of what old Cuba-hand, Herbert Matthews, called "this sensational development in hemispheric history."

It was in the context of this dramatic act by Cuba that West Indian apprehensions escalated when a coup d'état toppled the government of Eric Gairy in Grenada in March 1979. Cuba almost immediately had the only resident ambassador on the island, who soon presided over a growing Cuban presence. It seemed to replicate the situation in Guyana, where the Cuban mission took up nearly half a city block and where Cuba's multiple involvements had long been the talk of Georgetown. Some 15 Cuban doctors arrived; so did fishing trawlers and instructors for the growing new army. On November 18, 1979, Prime Minister Maurice Bishop told a rally that he expected 250 Cubans to start building a new international airport. Since he had just been in Canada seeking funds for a feasibility study for the same project, local and international surprise was understandable.

In 1980 an incident in the Bahamas "Out-islands" sent a chill through West Indian Cuba-watchers. A Cuban MIG aircraft sank one of the Bahamas's three gunboats and strafed the sailors while in the water. Cuban military helicopters later landed on Bahamian territory. Although the incident appeared to result from a genuine case of mistaken identity (the Bahamians were thought to be Cuban exiled "pirates") and apologies and reparations were eventually made, the harm was already done. A poll taken in the Bahamas showed that 85.9 percent believed that the attack had been deliberate and not a mistake and that 73.3 percent believed that Cuba still posed a threat to the islands. As a writer in Nassau put it, Cuba had attacked a "defenseless neighboring, friendly country." But even more important than this, he continued, it had attacked "a black developing nation at the same time that it purported to enjoy wide international prestige as a leader of the non-aligned movement."[15]

The 1980s were thus launched with a number of incidents that fed the growing perception of a Cuban threat in the area. All seemed to confirm the perception of a militarized and aggressive Cuba taking advantage of Carter's apertura toward multilateralism. Virtually anything emanating from Cuba or its ally, Grenada, elicited suspicion.

And yet, aside from the cases cited, how much of all this perceived Cuban involvement or subversion was real? Clearly in the 1970s there was at least a surface unity among the area's new and Cuba-leaning Marxist-Leninist groups. This could be seen, for instance, at the public launching of Jamaica's Communist party, Trevor Munroe's Workers Party of Jamaica (WPJ), formerly the Worker's Liberation League. In attendance were delegates from the Communist parties of the USSR, Britain, Canada, the United States, and Cuba; in attendance from the English-speaking Caribbean were representatives of Guyana's People's Progressive party and the Working Peoples Alliance, the Barbados Movement for National Liberation, Grenada's New Jewel Movement, Saint Vincent's Liberation Movement, and the Saint Lucia's Workers' Revolutionary Movement.

To see Cuban machinations behind this unity, however, is to ignore the long-standing ties between Caribbean radical groups—ties that predate the Cuban Revolution and that more often than not are the result of specific and independent decisions on each island. Furthermore, the coups in Grenada and Suriname involved the overthrow of unpopular regimes by small groups of men lightly armed. Like the rest of the Caribbean, these were "open" systems where the only protection was the degree of legitimacy of the regime, a legitimacy they appeared to have lost. Both cases show that Cuba's role tended to be most effective in situations where regime legitimacy was eroded and a process of antagonism had the makings of a broad-based social movement against the regime. The search seemed to be more for social redress and restoration of democracy and honesty than for sociopolitical revolution.

Yet by 1982 there was no evidence that Cuba actually posed a direct threat—military or otherwise—to any of the island states. To what degree there existed an indirect threat through subversion of local institutions and forces remains a matter of debate. What is undisputed is that by the early 1980s there was a widespread *perception* that this Cuban intervention was significant and threatening. There were additionally the overt diplomatic and military ties about which leaders in the unarmed ministates were apprehensive. By 1982 the Cubans had forged strong alliances with Grenada, Suriname, and Nicaragua; they had a massive banking and commercial operation in Panama; and they carried on a marriage of convenience with Guyana that gave them good access to the Movement of Nonaligned Nations. Their airlift capabilities extended far beyond the Caribbean, a fact demonstrated in 1975 and 1976 when they moved 11,000 troops into Angola and later into Ethiopia and elsewhere in Africa. The United States State Department assertion that Cuba had then a "substantial regional intervention capability" was not discarded by local leaders.

Be that as it may, and while it would be a mistake to underrate the significance attached by Caribbean observers to the political and ideological role defined by the Cubans and the capacity (indeed, audacity) of their intelligence and diplomatic corps, it is hard to tell to what extent the regional definition of the threat was a carryover of the U.S. national definition. Even, or perhaps especially, in spheres of influence, behavior tends to be strategically geared to deriving the maximum advantages from the dominant force in the sphere. The ministate was becoming an adept player of the geopolitical game, sensing Washington's not-too-subtle swings in foreign policy moods. The fact was that during the 1970s and early 1980s in island after island, radical, pro-Cuban parties were going down to overwhelming defeat in campaigns in which their Cuban and Grenadian connections had been made an issue. Since pro-Cuban governments such as Grenada, Suriname, and Guyana were also authoritarian ones, the Cuban issue became much more than a purely foreign policy matter: by the late 1970s it was central to the discussion of the type of society desired and the role that elections would play in making that decision. Popular sentiment was clearly on the side of retaining the parliamentary system, regardless of the type of economic system that was proposed within it. Elections were perceived as opportunities for change when such change was mandated by failure, especially economic failure. Nowhere in the Caribbean was this more evident than in Jamaica during Michael Manley's second of two terms (1976–80).

Faced with increasing economic problems due to a decline in the price of bauxite, the migration of significant numbers of native technicians, and a general sense of economic malaise, the Cuban connection became a handicap to the personally popular Manley. The Cuban mission in Kingston during the Manley years (1972–80) had become an impressive complex—complete with radio-transmitting antennas similar to those of their U.S. and British counterparts. The Cuban ambassador—not infrequently the center of political controversy—presided over an ever-increasing network of Cuban activities in health, education, construction, agriculture, tourism, sports, and—some maintained—politics. In international affairs the Manley government occasionally spoke of "party to party" relationships with Cuba, and their joint declarations had a strident and even revolutionary tone.

Even as Jamaica's elections of 1980 proved Cuba not to be as interventionist as thought and Manley a solid democrat, the perceptions of the Cuban menace contributed to the massive victory of Edward Seaga's anticommunist Jamaican Labour party (JLP). The change in Jamaican official attitudes toward Cuba in 1980 was even more dramatic than the changes had been in the United States: the Cuban presence was terminated overnight.

A preliminary conclusion would be that Cuba overplayed its hand in its zeal to support and assist ideologically like-minded groups in the area. The tenacious sense of independence and respect for nonintervention of the new nations of the region came into play in the face of Cuban diplomatic audacity. This same attitude was shown toward Venezuela, a country whose diplomacy—though much more circumspect than Cuba's—was still too presumptuous for some of these new leaders whose nationalism and defensiveness about their sovereignty had been brought close to the surface by events during the 1970s. But it was in Grenada that Cuba suffered its most serious defeat in the Caribbean. And, interestingly enough, it was also in Grenada that the ministates demonstrated their capacity for independent action in international relations.

## Grenada: The Limits of West Indian Solidarity

The leaders of the West Indian ministates bring several advantages to any international relations situation. Being democratically elected they know that they have the people's mandate; they also know, however, that a day of reckoning—elections—is never more than five years away. The international relations of small democratic states are no less linked to domestic politics than are those of large democratic states.

A second advantage that the leader of the small Caribbean state has is the formidable number of international organizations and institutions through which he or she can channel or screen decisions in the international arena. The West Indian state, for instance, is a member of the British Commonwealth which carries some symbolic weight and also allows a great deal of personal contact and thus, diplomacy, among the leaders. Because the Caribbean states are former British colonies, they participate in the provisions of the European Common Market's Lômé Convention which covers their traditional exports. As members of the United Nations they enjoy the benefits of its multiple agencies such as the Food and Agriculture Organization (FAO), the World Bank, and the International Monetary Fund. As members of the OAS they participate in that body's multiple agencies. The Caribbean Community and Common Market (CARICOM) which evolved out of the customs union (CARIFTA)—both following the failed attempt at a West Indian Federation (1958–62)—is perhaps the most successful regional arrangement for the promotion of economic integration outside of the European Economic Community (EEC) today.

Even though CARICOM has a permanent secretariat based in Georgetown, Guyana, the real decisions are made at the regularly held Heads of Government meetings which can also be called on an emergency basis. The smaller states of the Eastern Caribbean established their own collective organization in 1981, the Organization of Eastern Caribbean States (OECS). With its secretariat in Castries, Saint Lucia, it has seven full members (see Table 12-2); the British Virgin Islands are an associate member. Aside from its function of promoting general subregional integration, the OECS has two critical agencies which have already played key roles in their collective decision making: the Foreign Affairs Committee and the Defense and Security Committee. The OECS has created its own Eastern Caribbean Central Bank (ECCB) which administers the common currency, the EC dollar, and performs the other regulatory functions of a central bank.

An Eastern Caribbean state, thus, has access to both its own ECCB as well as the Caribbean Development Bank (CDB), established in 1966, of which all CARICOM states—plus Colombia, Venezuela, Mexico, Canada, the United Kingdom, and France—are members. The United States has been the CDB's principal nonmember donor. The larger West Indian states are members of the Inter-American Development Bank.

While all these memberships are positive contributions, they do put a strain on the resources in personnel available to the small state. This is a major weakness, a direct consequence of size. It is not, however, a fatal weakness; leaders of small states tend to compensate for this by actions of a collective type which reflect a solidarity going beyond the formal organizations to which they belong. In the British Caribbean this solidarity has been centered on the principle of regionalism.

In many ways the West Indian idea of regionalism was fed by a veritable club of men: Ebenezer Joshua in Saint Vincent, Vere Bird in Antigua, Robert Bradshaw in Saint Kitts, Herbert Blaize in Grenada. Like Grantley Adams and Errol Barrow in Barbados and Norman Manley and Alexander Bustamante in Jamaica, they had all emerged through trade union movements, all experienced the stigma of racism, and all shared a political culture which, in different degrees, was an amalgam of Christianity, Fabianism, and self-pride. They were politically and ideologically tolerant. After all, many of the "rebels" were either their children or mirror images of their own youthful radical days. Whatever the shortcomings of this rather Victorian generation, their commitment to the idea of a West Indian people as a whole, above and beyond state-to-state or rational legal treaties, was unquestioned. It gave West Indian elite responses to West Indian-related issues of a certain kind a degree of predictability.

It is an important conjunctural fact that the People's Revolutionary Government (PRG) of Grenada benefited from the predictability in West Indian international relations which this club of "giants" had legated. It would be impossible to understand either the acceptance of the PRG for the four and one-half years it existed or the decision to invade in October 1983 without understanding the nature of West Indian solidarity, both in terms of its depths and, of course, in terms of its inevitable limits.

In analyzing the West Indian responses to the PRG it is good to keep in mind that until its veritable self-destruction, the PRG gave every indication to friend and foe of being capable and willing to stay in power indefinitely. It is important to establish this fact to remove doubts that the basic assumptions about West Indian solidarity being analyzed were not, in fact, strategic, instrumental policy preferences based on a calculation that the PRG could not last and could therefore be cooperated with or ignored with impunity.

The first crucial response to the PRG was an act of cooperation: the West Indians established diplomatic relations with the regime. To be sure, this recognition responded to very specific historical, personal, and regional factors as well as being an act of solidarity. First, there was the fact that the deposed ruler, Eric Gairy, was universally disliked and ridiculed. He was regarded as an embarrassment to the kind of collective image West Indians were projecting to the world community. He was not a member of the club. Second, Maurice Bishop was regionally known and liked. The murder of his father engendered enormous sympathy for him, a fact which pointed to the distaste of West Indians for acts of state terror. Third, Bishop's personal friendship with Jamaica's Michael Manley, and the fact that Guyana's Forbes Burnham was a bitter enemy of Eric Gairy, helped the PRG leadership overcome the initial hostility of other West Indian leaders. A fourth factor was the "outside" one: the previous three years of a Carter-driven foreign policy which accepted "ideological pluralism" had also contributed to West Indian perceptions.

This last point illustrates the operation of a certain "cultural lag" between changes in U.S. perceptions and changes in the Caribbean similar to what occurred in Central America in the late 1940s. Nevertheless, it should be kept in mind that even though the United States recognized Grenada, U.S.-Grenada relations deteriorated almost immediately, and this occurred at a time when there were already some reevaluations in the Carter administration about Marxist initiatives in the area as discussed above. West Indian leaders were formulating their own responses to the PRG. This had not been the first time that they had shown their capacity to act in concert in less-than-rewarding circumstances.

Their policy toward South Africa was one of the earliest cases of a principled stance against racism while their recognition of Cuba in 1971 was equally autochthonous. But even these specific circumstances might not have been enough given the adherence of these leaders to electoral and parliamentary politics. After all, had one of the most influential of these leaders, Trinidad's Eric Williams, not punished those who in 1970 attempted a coup against him? The fact is that another fundamental assumption operated to make the recognition of a de facto government possible: the West Indian regional identity and sense of solidarity. Thus, there was no question that Grenada would continue in CARICOM and, indeed, be a signatory to the creation of the OECS in July 1981 even as it refused to agree to the principles of collective or coordinated actions in foreign policy and defense.[16] As events would later show (and captured documents corroborate), the PRG leadership had its own secret plans in those areas. Yet the collective spirit that led to any act of recognition of the PRG brought into play a very important characteristic of politics in archipelagic areas where a certain identity has already taken shape: despite the absence of specific reciprocal ties, processes of interaction (no matter at what level or type) tend to create norms and mutual obligations. This "diffuse reciprocity" is crucial to understanding the concessions made early on toward the unorthodoxy of the PRG, just as it had allowed Guyana's Forbes Burnham to be a member of the club despite the generalized sense that his regime was based on fraudulent elections.

The point is, of course, that initially the Grenadians also gave some "space," allowing West Indians to rationalize the acceptance of a de facto government.

To be sure, the PRG's decision to keep certain of the institutional structures of the ancien régime helped during this transitional period. Crucial among these was retention of the governor general (both the office and the actual occupant, Sir Paul Scoon); membership in collective associations, CARICOM, the Commonwealth, and the OAS; and the signing of the OECS charter. These, then, were acts that exposed Caribbean international relations as they operated "internally." Given the history of the U.S. interventions and general unilateral actions outlined at the beginning of this chapter, a critical question is: How did these ministates confront the growing American antagonism toward the PRG, an antagonism that escalated with the election of Ronald Reagan in 1980?

A few actions tend to show the strength of West Indian solidarity even in the face of American hostility. In April 1982 President Ronald Reagan, while vacationing in Barbados, invited five West Indian leaders to an informal miniconference. The leaders of Grenada and Saint Lucia (then governed by the radical wing of the Saint Lucia Labour party) were not included. The West Indian response was immediate and severely critical. Barbados's prime minister, Tom Adams—by then perhaps the PRG's most ascerbic regional critic and, in turn, its favorite target—led the response by telling the United States publicly that the West Indies did not wish to engage in ideological battles but to proceed with policies of economic development. Saint Kitts's Kennedy Simmonds put the essence of West Indian solidarity even more clearly by noting that they recognized Grenada as a member of CARICOM. They always had friendly relations with Grenada and wanted to continue working with it and other Caribbean countries. As the Reagan administration began to tighten the screws against the PRG—and, consequently, change the nature of the payoff matrix of Caribbean international relations—every vote took on meaning. Yet all attempts to exclude Grenada from Caribbean Development Bank funds and loans were strongly opposed by these leaders, again, including Tom Adams.

The clashes were numerous and increasing as the Cuban and Soviet presence increased and the general context of the Cold War began to envelop more and more actors in the area. And, yet, even the Edward Seaga regime in Jamaica voted with the other leaders gathered at the CARICOM Heads of Government meeting of February 1983 to accept "ideological pluralism" as a principle of their foreign policy. The underlying assumption was regional solidarity and the preferred policy was to accept variation, even ideological deviance if necessary.

For over four years, then, there were exchanges between West Indian leaders and the Grenadian leadership based on certain underlying values. These values also influenced commitments and shared obligations, that is, a diffuse reciprocity which operated in West Indian decision making. These underlying values, this diffuse reciprocity, operated for four and one-half years and in October 1983, when the West Indian leaders decided to act. An internal coup within the PRG had resulted in the murder of Maurice Bishop and dozens of others. The limits of West Indian solidarity had been reached. To negate the autonomy, the purposefulness of West Indian actions in 1983 would necessarily mean bringing into doubt the autonomy of their acts of cooperation during 1979–83.

Dominica's Prime Minister Eugenia Charles expressed well the nature of West Indian diffuse reciprocity when she spoke of "our kith and kin" being murdered on the streets of Saint Georges on October 19. The immense popularity of the Grenada intervention—even in those nations such as Trinidad which did not participate—spoke more clearly about the nature of inter-West Indian bonds and solidarity than all the official texts, treaties, and rhetoric. The same sentiments and values of reciprocal understanding that had led West Indians to cooperate with a "deviant" PRG led to the support for action against behavior generally regarded as totally outside anything West Indians had witnessed at least since the days of slavery. West Indians had responded to the fait accompli of Maurice Bishop in March 1979 partly for personal reasons. This was, in October 1983, also a part of their reactions to his murder.

## Conclusion

One way to approach the study of international relations in the Caribbean is to ask the question: Was the October 1983 invasion of Grenada legal?

If one accepts the argument that the relevant international treaties and agreements are those of the inter-American system—especially the charter of the OAS—then the answer is probably no. As such, the U.S. action can be interpreted as just another in a long string of naked, unilateral interventions. Intervention to rescue endangered citizens, such as the American medical students on the island, is allowed under international law. The problem was that no evidence was ever produced that showed these citizens to be in immediate danger nor was the invasion a rescue operation.

There is, however, another way of looking at the invasion: the arguments made by the governments of the Eastern Caribbean. None of the new states had had any participation in the construction of the inter-American system, and, though members of the OAS, they had weak historical and emotional links with it. Their attachment was to a different "community." To them, the charter of the OECS had precedence over that of the OAS. They were responding within the legal and sociological context of their subregional system to a legitimate call for assistance from Grenada. The governor general of Grenada, they argued, was empowered by the island's constitution to make such an appeal.

Clearly the legal arguments will continue for a long time. Meanwhile, sociological and political processes continue to give shape to a new Caribbean. As complex as this evolving Caribbean area is, some identifiable underlying characteristics can help in its study. First, rather than being purely secondary or derived versions of superpower rivalry, many of the conflicts and confrontations in the Caribbean are the result of independent Caribbean actors pursuing their perception of national interests as well as of their own survival in power in an area that has changed dramatically in the past twenty years. There are now some fifteen new actors with highly developed senses of national honor shaped by a very complex combination of traditional ideas of sovereignty as well as of racial and cultural solidarity on a global scale. Many more potential actors are waiting in the wings of the Caribbean stage. Final resolution of the political status of islands such as Puerto Rico, the Virgin Islands (American and British), the Netherlands Antilles, and the "Overseas Departments" of France (Martinique, Guadeloupe, and Guyanne) lies in the future.

Second, with few exceptions, these new nations are more interested in a North-South dialogue than in the East-West confrontation. This is because the traditional economic structure of the area is in crisis. From Cuba to Guyana, sugar is no longer profitable, nor are bananas; bauxite and even oil have questionable short-term futures. The hopes that U.S.-initiated programs such as the Caribbean Basin Initiative would attract substantial American capital to the area have not materialized. Migration to the United States especially continues to relieve the pressure from rapidly growing and youthful populations, but this cannot be a solution. The tourist industry is crucial as a source of employment and hard currency but tends to be fickle; it creates few "backward linkages" into other areas of the local economy.

The danger is that geography will again deal the islands a dirty hand: as stepping-stones or conduits of the astronomical amounts of illegal drugs flowing from South America to the United States. The return flow is of laundered dirty monies finding haven in the offshore banking systems of the Bahamas, the Caymans, the Netherlands Antilles, and Panama. The danger is that, as traditional economic sectors shrink or disappear, they will be replaced by a whole network of activities related to this perfidious trade.

Third, race and ethnicity will continue to be central to the Caribbean's

definition of itself. This emphasis will contribute to the retention of the archipelago's already strong, distinct identity. This identity will have broader implications for the area's international relations because this concern with race is
not purely psychological; it relates to a fundamental dimension of West Indian
ideology. Nearly all the leaders of the new nations of the Caribbean came to
power on platforms of social justice and condemnation of any form of racial
discrimination. Even as conservative a government as Edward Seaga's of Jamaica has had to reiterate periodically its traditional stand against South Africa.
Cuban behavior in certain critical areas of international politics thus is not far
removed from West Indian rhetoric. One such area is Cuban intervention in
Angola, which has been held to be a just response to South African involvement. Even as they feared Cuban audacity in foreign policy, West Indians
found it difficult to side with the American propensity to make linkages
between Cuban actions in Africa and in the Caribbean. As such, the Carter-
Fascell policy of multilateralism and pluralism appeared better suited to West
Indian perceptions and needs than did the post-1980 American hard line, even
as West Indians appeared to be shaping an anti-Marxist hard line of their own
in the 1980s.

Fourth, the "internationalization" of the region will provide a strong challenge to that regional sense of identity. The area is a battleground of ideas,
souls, and affiliations. Radio and TV programs blanket the area, as do traveling
representatives of every religious, political, and trade union organization conceivable. Students educated abroad return to govern and administer, and
membership in Intelsat (see Table 12-2) guarantees that they will stay in touch
with their colleagues around the globe.

Fifth, from the political-institutional point of view, and while stability is
never guaranteed, a general distinction can be made between those systems
that have essentially solved the problem of transition or succession of power
and those that have not. In the former category are the large number of
parliamentary systems with relatively stable electoral methods of succession; in
the latter, the essentially personalistic systems where unpredictable events will
probably follow the passing of the caudillo. In 1987 Cuba, Haiti, and Suriname
fell in that category. Shifts in international alignments may follow these local
transitions. Or then, again, they may not; for in international relations the
unintended and unexpected, the contingent and even the accidental, all play
their parts. And, yet, there is some order to these otherwise unpredictable
processes. In the final analysis it is good to begin the study of Caribbean
international relations with the assumption that any foreign policy initiative—
be it of a large or a small state—involved a trade-off between basic ideological

assumptions, preferred policy outcomes, realistic assessments of the environment, and national capabilities. Successful policies are those which, of course, eventually pay off, that is, maximize benefits and minimize costs to any part of the overall state agenda through wise trade-offs.

History shows that attempts at domination or hegemony have never fully succeeded in the Caribbean. Given the increasing number and variety of independent actors, this is becoming even less possible. Both history and contemporary analysis tell us that realistic trade-offs, national and collective, are the most productive routes to regional peace and progress.

## Notes

1. See the discussion in Henry Myron Blackmer II, *United States Policy and the Inter-American Peace System, 1889–1952* (Geneva: Institute of International Studies, Thesis no. 89, 1952).

2. For the text of the treaty see O. C. Stoetzer, *The Organization of American States* (New York: Frederick A. Praeger, 1965).

3. Cf. Charles D. Ameringer, *The Democratic Left in Exile* (Miami: University of Miami Press, 1974).

4. Alexander, *Communism in Latin America*, p. 354.

5. *Washington Post*, February 18, 1963, p. 1. CIA participation in the overthrow of Arbenz is plainly described by Allen W. Dulles, then head of the CIA, in *The Craft of Intelligence* (Illinois: Harper and Row, 1963).

6. U.S. Department of State Bulletin, 31 (July 12, 1954), pp. 43–44.

7. U.S. Department of State Bulletin, 43 (August 1, 1960), pp. 170–71.

8. U.S. Department of State Bulletin, 44 (May 8, 1961), pp. 658–61.

9. U.S. Congress, House Subcommittee on Inter-American Affairs, *Hearings on Soviet Activities in Cuba*, pt. 3, September 26, 1972, p. 28.

10. Speech by Dante B. Fascell, American Assembly-University of Miami Conference of the Caribbean, Miami, Florida, April 28, 1973.

11. *Weekly Compilation of Presidential Documents* 13, no. 6 (Washington, D.C.: Government Printing Office, 1977), pp. 523–28.

12. U.S. Congress, House Subcommittee on Inter-American Affairs, *Hearings on U.S. Policy Toward the Caribbean*, June 28, 1977, p. 30.

13. Baldwin, "A Military Perspective," p. 206.

14. Note the language of the important Kissinger Commission: "Beyond the issue of U.S. security interests in the Central American-Caribbean region, our credibility worldwide is engaged. The triumph of hostile forces in what the Soviets call the 'strategic rear' of the United States would be read as a sign of U.S. impotence." *The Report of the*

*President's Bipartisan Commission on Central America* (New York: MacMillan Publishing Co., 1984), p. 111.

15. Larry Smith, "The Flamingo Affair," *Image* (Summer 1980), pp. 48–53.

16. West Indian suspicions about Grenadian activities and intentions made West Indian leaders more defense and security conscious. This trend led eventually to the 1982 "Memorandum of Understanding" on security assistance between Barbados, Dominica, Saint Lucia, Antigua, and Saint Vincent. The Memorandum of Understanding became the nucleus of the later OECS decision to create a Regional Security System of eighty men on each island.

## 13

Roberto Márquez

# Nationalism, Nation, and Ideology

Trends in the Emergence of a Caribbean Literature

But today I recapture the
islands' bright beaches.—*Edward Brathwaite*

Reading Derek Walcott's (Saint Lucia, 1930– ) "Origins," a poetic meditation on the historic impact and legacy of the Enterprise of the Indies, one is struck by the holistic sweep of a single line: "Lost animist, I rechristened trees."[1] Pregnant with resonance and multiple reference, it points to and synthesizes a critical dimension in the historical and cultural evolution of the Caribbean: the continuous process of inventive, creatively adaptive creolization that, despite "those who conceive[d] of white cities in a raindrop / and the annihilation of races in the prism of the dew,"[2] ultimately gives the archipelago its essential and very distinct personality, its polychromatic ethnic and cultural particularity.

Walcott's line also underscores the dramatic tension between alienation and opportunity, irresolution and resolve, defeat and victory, at the heart of each successive "rechristening" of the colonized landscape. More subtly, it suggests the inextricable link of this dialectic to the problems—and possibilities—inherent in the postulation of a regional, "national," and literary identity that is an appropriate as well as authentic reflection of the vitality and complexity of Caribbean life. This is, finally, the poet's real subject. It is the recurring obsession that motivates and gives significance to everything he writes. As concept, esthetic creed, program, organizing metaphor, and historical commentary, moreover, Walcott's observation is virtually the signature of an entire generation. It echoes a sentiment that emerges—with varying emphasis, distinct focus, and nuance—in the work of writers as diverse in outlook, temperament, language, local origin, and circumstance as Jacques Stéphen Alexis (Haiti,

1922–61), Edward Brathwaite (Barbados, 1930– ), Alejo Carpentier (Cuba, 1902–80), Edouard Glissant (Martinique, 1928– ), Wilson Harris (Guyana, 1921– ), John Hearne (Jamaica, 1926– ), Pedro Mir (Dominican Republic, 1916– ), Luis Rafael Sánchez (Puerto Rico, 1936– ), and Simone Schwarz-Bart (Guadeloupe, 1938– ).

The list could be extended to include nearly every contemporary Caribbean writer worthy of note. Even V. S. Naipaul (Trinidad, 1932– ), his contemptuous disdain and haughty dismissal of the area as bereft of future possibility not-withstanding, cannot avoid its eminence in his fiction. Naipaul's best work, *A House for Mr. Biswas* (1961), for example, compellingly presents the unfolding, among the heirs of East Indian indentured immigrants, of the social, cultural, and historical drama of creolization that Walcott's line so forcefully conveys. When one completes that line with the one immediately preceding ("Between the Greek and African pantheon"), its applicability to Naipaul's—and the other writers'—work becomes all the more apparent. The pull of conflicting gravi-ties, the synthetic result of this taut polarity, is an inescapable part of their common inheritance as Antilleans. The rueful impassivity and sense of perpet-ual displacement typical of Naipaul's preoccupations, protagonists, and narra-tors; the edge of besieged panic and negrophobia that lace and finally under-mine the integrity of his later fiction especially, are so many signs of the peculiar effect the recognition of that inheritance and its immediate implica-tions have produced in this unusually gifted Trinidadian of East Indian ances-try. This panic is what lies behind his own feelings of alienation, his restless and peripatetic "search for a center."

These writers are joined in their differences no less than in their similarities by the consequences and vicissitudes of a shared history of colonialism, impe-rialist rivalry, interterritorial isolation, and ethno-class confrontation. They are all equally the product of the combined force of these not yet fully reconciled contradictions. They are simultaneously provoked, constrained, and chal-lenged by a vivid appreciation of the enduring significance of their "origins." Like Walcott, they are inevitably drawn to a critical reassessment of that same patrimony of conflict. They are all, directly or indirectly, compelled to come to terms with the structures—of economic, social, and political interaction, of feeling and perception—that have evolved from that legacy. Their writing, though not the strictly axiomatic correlative of those structures, is the expres-sion, in esthetic terms, of their ideological tensions and current experiential contours. Its thematic and formal characteristics are a testimony to that—evident or implicit—symbiosis. Whether in enthusiasm, uncertainty, indecision, or disapproval, these writers participate in, and their work reflects, the crises, reshufflements, and realignments that have been the substance of Caribbean reality during the last half century or more. Their reevaluation of and shared sense of urgency with regard to the past, the acknowledgment and postulation of a uniquely Caribbean genesis, is inextricable from their commitment to the perceived exigencies of the present and from their hopes for the future.

History, unreconciled and pressing, is their natural element; memory is their métier, the primum mobile of their reevaluative posture, the source of all prophecy. Edouard Glissant, in a passage as representative as Walcott's and which the latter would later use as an epigraph to his poetic autobiography, *Another Life* (1972), speaks explicitly to this point. "On the day when I finally fasten my hands upon its wrinkled stem and pull with irresistible power," he writes in *La Lézarde* (1958), "when my memories are quiet and strong, and I can finally translate them into words, then I shall perceive the unique and essential qualities of this place. The innumerable petty miseries, the manifold beauties eclipsed by the painful necessity of combat and birth."[3]

Caribbean literature has obviously reached this moment of maturity and conscious self-perception. These authors, among others, have been instrumental in the process of its articulation. The coincidence of thematic preoccupation (if not always of specific ideological response) found in their fiction and verse, without in the least diminishing the force of clearly manifest regional identities, also underscores the Pan-Caribbean scope of their defining experiences. Against the power of a tradition of derivative, "orbital," perceptions of the area, it argues the presence of a Caribbean ethos—and esthetic—whose elements cohere beyond the limiting colonial, specifically "national," or strictly linguistic premises of those perceptions. This increasingly distinguishing feature of their "rendezvous with history" has its antecedents: it represents only the most recent phase in a centuries-long process of cultural and literary evolution. What follows, then, is an effort, unavoidably synoptic and cursory, to place the achievement of contemporary Caribbean writing into the sharper relief and perspective an appreciation of its major stages can provide.

Occurring during the apogee of the system of slavery and in the most spectacularly profitable of the New World's colonies, the Haitian Revolution (1789–1804) marked a pioneering watershed. It represented, in the collective person of those who carried it out, the threatening coincidence of every primary social, economic, and political contradiction in which both the Caribbean planter class—which came to include *affrancis*, propertied mulattoes—and mercantile imperialism were enmeshed. Its impact was profound, long lasting, and palpably felt throughout the area.

The creation immediately after emancipation (1834–86) of an increasingly heterogeneous (though still caste conscious and pigmentocratically divided) working class of wage-earning ex-slaves, peasants, and indentured immigrants of largely East Indian and Asian origin was also a part of the attenuated fallout of the Haitian Revolution. As the ideological complement of its political independence, Haiti, finally, pioneered an entire cultural revolution. It opposed the notion of a *génie national* to a colonialist universalism that, at best, saw in the colonies so many inferior reproductions of European culture. It defined its historic originality in terms that focused on its ethnic and cultural uniqueness. It sought simultaneously to refute racist stereotypes of nonwhite inferiority; and, giving it specific weight and content, it accented its sense of a distinctively creole national sensibility. The features of the Haitian state's particular pigmentocratic emphasis in this regard would, of course, remain a matter of unceasing dispute among the black and mulatto elites that, once the dominant minority of whites had been expelled, continued their contention for hegemonic control.[4]

The *prise de conscience* manifest in their mutual affirmation of a Haitian identity and culture nonetheless once more implied a necessary rehistoricizing of the past that endowed it with a novel—even, to some extent, mythical—ontological significance.[5] This represented a crucial shift in the locus of cultural authenticity—a relative change of context, audience, and intention—that opened a modest, formally tentative, but still significant breach in the uncritical imitation of French metropolitan culture. In matters literary and otherwise, it gave incremental pride of place to the legitimacy of *creole* claims on the landscape, elucidation of the characteristic facets of the nation's singularity, and exploration of the emerging possibilities inherent in the facts of creolization—and conflict—in which it originates.

"We are quite like the American, transplanted and stripped of traditions, but there is in the fusion of the European and African cultures which constitutes our national character, something that makes us less French than the American is English," Emile Nau, one of the group of Haitian writers gathered around the newspapers *Le Républicain* and *L'Union*, declared in 1836. "This advantage," he went on to conclude, "is a real one."[6] Among the literary tasks it imposed, if it were not to remain an unrealized opportunity, was the need for "our poets" to "naturalize the French language in our culture." This, he averred, would "not be a question of taking the [French] language ready-made from [its] best exponents; it [would] be necessary [rather] to modify it and adapt it to our local needs."[7] The premises underlying Nau's observations were at once an echo and an anticipation of trends already manifest throughout the region and that, in the long wake of the Haitian Revolution, reached a certain crystallization.

Ushering in a period of unrelieved crisis and change, the harbinger of things to come, Haiti initiated a new stage of radical anticolonial self-assertion, uneasy accommodation, and conservative reaction. Part of the evolving process of regional class formation, caste and demographic differentiation, it heightened consciousness of a distinctively creole culture. Its salients included a sharpening of the white elite's racist fears of the "Africanization" of the Caribbean and stimulation of a climate in which the goal of maximum local autonomy, affirmation of a sense of specific "nationality," and the articulation of the constituent elements of an esthetic adequate to its expression became linked and allied aspirations. The contrasting purposes of some of these tendencies were not, necessarily, always mutually exclusive. They frequently complemented each other; more often than not, they came together in an odd blend of contradictory impulses that found in the evolving forms of romanticism—costumbrismo, realism, naturalism, and indigenous forms of symbolism—a vehicle for holding them in effectively dynamic stasis.

The Cuban abolitionist novel (from Petrona y Rosalia [1838], Cecilia Valdés [1838, 1882], and Francisco [1839] to Sab [1841] and El negro Francisco [1875]) managed thus to combine close observation of the physical environment, the social texture, sexual mores, and racial oppression of insular experience with confirmation of the patrician bias and still racially exclusive assumptions of the white Creoles who constituted the primary public, producers, and dramatis personae of scribal fiction, poetry, essays, and plays. A strict typology was established—master, señora, black mistress, illicit offspring, impossible loves—whose bathos, exoticism, and melodrama were so many stereotypical tributaries of the lyric "primitivism" of romantic convention.

Documentation of the indignities associated with chattel slavery did not prevent its creators from narratively closing off the possibility of slave rebellion as a legitimate option in the struggle to end them. In spite of the frequency of slave uprisings, slaves were invariably—wishfully—depicted as passively enduring their collective lot with stoic, if tragic, resignation. Historical veracity was less at issue than the requirements of internal security.

Narrative strategies, calculated to emphasize the morally debilitating influence of slavery on whites, made little attempt to examine the personality of the slave. When they did, they transformed him, culturally, politically, and psychologically, into a creole white in blackface. Sympathy for the mulatto was emblematic of the hybrid the ascendant creole ruling class felt itself to be—a people "neither European nor North American, but a mixture of African and the Americans who originated in Europe" as Bolívar, in another similar context, had succinctly put it.[8] It was the metaphorical transposition of the need to ground, in an image of etiolating conciliation between extremes, its pretension "to exercise an active domestic tyranny" of its own (the words, again, are Bolívar's) and, through purposeful ideological manipulation of that image, effectively—fictively—to impose it.[9]

Exploration of the many layers of Cuban society, revealing both a will to define its distinctiveness and the problematic centrality of the black—or mulatto—protagonist within it, did not preclude a posture that, except as they might be "bleached" or made gradually to "disappear," excluded the darker hues from any acceptable definition of Cuban nationality. "The task of all Cubans of hearts and of noble and sacred patriotism," Domingo del Monte, the liberal reformer who served as mentor, patron, and sponsor of much of this writing, argued, "ought to be, first, to end the slave trade, and then go on little by little to the suppression of slavery without convulsions and violence, and, in the end, to clean Cuba of the African race."[10] José Antonio Saco, del Monte's more conservative colleague and friend, was still more emphatic: "Cuban nationality," he declared, "is formed by the white race."[11]

The Ten Years' War (1868–78) created a radically new context. It was in this new context with the de facto abolition of slavery that Antonio Maceo's and José Martí's more sympathetic recognition of the strategic importance and social potential of the nonwhite masses engendered the latter's more radical and cohesively inclusive formula of the 1880s and 1890s: "Cuban is more than white, more than black, more than mulatto."[12] This formula was increasingly to become ideological common coin in more progressive liberal circles. Martí perceived something sui generis in the making and, foresightfully, pointed to the problem of its creative, firmly rooted, and lasting articulation. "[N]o nation on earth that turns from the way of life laid out by its origins, and follows a purpose other than that inevitable one presented by the elements composing it," he repeatedly emphasized, "can live long or prosperously."[13] There had moreover to be a fundamental congruence between the spiritual and material. "The problem of independence," Martí continually insisted, "did not lie in a change of forms but in a change of spirit."[14] He thus did not stop short of a frontal attack on the tradition of Europocentric mimicry and the tyranny of the model that remained an obstacle to the emergence of a genuinely original literary voice and sensibility. Informed by his resolute dedication to the revolutionary promise of a radically liberal vision of cultural efflorescence and social harmony, Martí saw each dialectically as an aspect of the other. A guiding premise of that outlook, concisely recorded in a journal entry of 1881 which points to a fully coherent *esthetica*, was the critical notion that

> To an irresolute nation, [an] irresolute literature! But as soon as the elements of a people approach some unity, the elements of its literature draw nearer together and condense into a great prophetic work. Let us now bemoan the fact that we lack this great work, not because we lack it but because it is a sign that we are not yet the great people of which it must be a reflection; for it must reflect, it must be the reflection.[15]

National independence, nation building, the ordering of the polity's social priorities, and the achievement of an autochthonous literary voice were all, in anticipation of the future, intimately related facets of a single imperative.

In Puerto Rico and the Dominican Republic, del Monte's identification of national purpose with the ascendancy of the white creole elite and paternalist liberal ideals produced, respectively, Manuel A. Alonso's *El Jíbaro* (1849, 1884) and Manuel de Jesús Galván's *Enriquillo* (1882). Like *Cecilia Valdés* and the novels mentioned above, each proved to be a work of foundational ideological and literary significance.

Alonso offers the reader a series of *escenas* or vignettes in prose and verse which seek to "give an idea of the customs of the island."[16] Because he was keenly conscious of the hovering threat of the official colonial censureship which made him initially reluctant to publish his observations, Alonso's intent is discreetly, sometimes obliquely, but as unambiguously as possible to demonstrate the "lack of harmony" between Spanish educational policy and the demands of local needs and experience.[17] Foremost among the latter was the creole elite's intensified commitment, its critical need, to promote the continued economic growth and expansion of an agricultural economy still at a distance of only a few decades from the two-centuries doldrums of officially sanctioned commercial isolation that the colony's function as a strategic *presidio*, or imperial military outpost, had traditionally imposed upon Puerto Rico. A trend away from the small independent peasant producer, incident to the privatization of land (1778) and its subsequent concentration within the ascendant class of sugar plantation owners and *patrones* of coffee haciendas between 1797 and the date of publication of *El Jíbaro*, forms the decisive backdrop of Alonso's preoccupation to responsively record those features of rural life that have already been or are in the process of being historically superceded by a creole-sponsored "progress." This is the context and subtext which gives force and meaning to the assumptions of value underlying Alonso's interwoven series of vignettes.

Alonso's choice of the romantic form of the vignette, he confesses, is itself directly related to both his consciousness of the censor and the didactic impulse of the prohacendado moralism of his evocative, reforming nationalist focus on, and critical evaluation of local customs. The form allows Alonso pithily to combine the ethnographic precision of his descriptions of "The Dances of Puerto Rico," "The Cockpit," "The San Juan Races," "The Saint Peter's Day Parade," and similar examples of a historically evolved, socially layered, distinctively Puerto Rican culture with an expressly declared concern that his scenes "give a not too disagreeable exterior to disillusionment [al desengaño]," "always with a view to improving local custom as [he] entertains" his reader.[18]

These several angles converge in the syncretically symbolic image of the titular Jíbaro or rural mestizo peasant. Emerging as a metaphor for "Puerto Ricanness," the figure pointed to the country's racially mixed origins while still managing to glide discreetly past any actual inclusion or direct engagement with the social, political, and cultural presence of the slave and his mingled legacy of descendants. Indeed, except for an incidental, wholly secondary appearance of the protagonist's mulatto manservant in the short story–like vignette, "The Bird of Ill Omen,"[19] and Alonso's affirmation earlier on that the dances "of the African blacks and the creoles from Curaçao do not merit inclusion" in his discussion of popular national dance forms,[20] the population of "coloured" Puerto Ricans does not enter significantly into the worldview of El Jíbaro.

Alonso's evocation of the jíbaro's way of life is not, however, motivated by any wish to nostalgically defend or symbolically idealize the rural peasant whose modes of speech and mores he strives faithfully, if humorously, to depict in pieces like "A Jíbaro Wedding" and "The Utuado Festival." Alonso's judgment about and even the depth of his identification with particular local customs are consistently informed by a perception of what he regards as their relative utility as a stimulus to the kind of economic growth on which the power and political future of the rising class of hacendados depends. Alonso affiliates with and is particularly sympathetic to that class's struggle to ensure that a formerly dispersed, perhaps still too "egotistically irresponsible" peasantry of subsistence farmers, agregados, and day laborers will be permanently transformed into the stable pool of reliable labor for hire with which contemporary (sugar and) coffee growers were then especially obsessed.

Thus, it is primarily "the deals, sales, and exchanges to which it gives rise," not any sentimental emotional attachment to it, that finally vindicates "a custom so usefully pleasing and so pleasingly useful" as the Saint Peter's Day Parade.[21] The same premise allows him to note the value of the cockfight "as a form of communication between some towns . . . encouraging the circulation of money" while simultaneously condemning it as "a mere holiday pastime" that, being "highly prejudicial" to progress, is destined to disappear.[22] By the same token, neither Alonso's meticulous attention to folkloric detail in depicting forms of peasant culture nor the obvious pride of his classically refined sonnet to "the Puerto Rican" Creole whose "love for the country none surpass" prevent him finally from concluding, it is

> the peasants [*labradores*], content with knowing how to govern their own homes as they please and limiting themselves to their town without caring what goes on in any other, [who] are promoting selfishness, which is the death of all progress; because confined within such narrow limits, they have given no thought to joining the merchants, manufacturers [*industriales*], and artisans in petitioning the government to create . . . [schools of agriculture] which are much more useful to the country than the dull routine which, with few exceptions, is still the rule in our country.[23]

Alonso's text thus combines the creole elite's defense of a distinctively Puerto Rican national personality with condemnation of the traditionalism of the jíbaro who, to a large extent, emerges as its historic repository and symbol. To the extent the image of the jíbaro actually corresponds to a historically specific and socially concrete class of people within the culture, it is that class's "selfish" refusal to gracefully and patriotically assent to the role reserved for it by its more favored fellow Puerto Ricans which ultimately proves to be the most formidable domestic obstacle in the way of the colony's future economic development. Ironically, to that extent, too, the jíbaro's recalcitrance is seen as impeding the island's cultural development. For, as Alonso argues in an escena devoted to "Puerto Rican Writers: D. Santiago Vidarte" (a commentary which incidently initiates a tradition of self-consciously national literary criticism), only "when our agriculture finally emerges from its ancient routine; in a word, when we can without disadvantage compare ourselves with the [more planto-crat-dominated] island of Cuba, will the terrain [of literary endeavor] be prepared."[24]

Alonso's image of El Jíbaro synthesizes, in sum, the colonial, racial, and interclass drama at the core of a historically evolved Puerto Rican culture and society during a period of radical transition in which "the old is passing away and is being replaced by the new";[25] in which the contributions of the slaves and their descendants are minimized or ignored; in which the traditional independence of the peasantry is at once being undermined and rejected as economically retrogressive; and in which the entrepreneurial spirit and emerging hegemony of the native creole ruling classes is at once the material and ideological measure of that culture and society's most advanced current state and of its best future prospects.

Less anti-Spanish in sentiment, Galván's *Enriquillo* invoked the cacique of an extinct population to the same effect. The Dominican Republic's proximity to Haiti, the complexion, annexationist inclinations, and general restiveness of the majority of its inhabitants, as well as a political atmosphere of unending internecine strife between different factions of the white creole elite, made the Dominican ruling class particularly nervous and sensitive to the disquieting portent of this volatile complex of forces. Its anxiety about the possibility of "Africanization" was, in consequence, all the more acute. That the country had for a time actually been annexed by Haiti and, after the achievement of independence from both Haiti (1844) and Spain (1865), had known the ravages of civil war merely intensified its fears about the hovering specter of both. Under the circumstances, the lyric evocation of—and symbolic identification of Dominican nationhood with—the loyalist opposition to Spanish abuse of Guarocuya, the novel's orphaned, Christianized, and Spanish-educated Enriquillo, offered several advantages. It not only permitted the author to circumvent, by in effect ignoring, the actual presence and wider significance of a national majority of blacks and mulattoes. As a conservative patrician alternative to the Haitian revolutionary solution, it had the additional merit of associating the origins of the republic with an aboriginal past. It provided its emergence with indigenous roots, a certain epic grandeur, enveloping in an aureole of historic authenticity the romantic excesses of Galván's *leyenda*. Interlacing the narrative with transcribed excerpts from the writings of Bartólome de Las Casas, who as the protagonist's mentor and protector serves as the ideological pivot of the piece, enhanced the effect of this documentary illusion. Galván thus invoked history itself to support an imaginative invention otherwise reminiscent of the exotic romances made popular by Chateaubriand's "Atala" and "René."

It proved a rather persuasive fusion. Dominicans, whatever their ethnic origins or color, could—would, and occasionally still do—identify themselves as descendants of Enriquillo and, hence, as in some sense "Indian." Blacks or darker-skinned mulattoes were, as a result of this double fiction, cast as "foreigners," "Haitians," or ceased effectively to exist. Enriquillo's eventual, grateful submission to the authority of Las Casas with which the novel concludes moreover redeems, in the person of one of its most sympathetic and enlightened representatives, the image of Spain's colonization of the New World. Like del Monte, Galván emphasizes the social dimensions and political virtues of a policy of assimilation and intermarriage that (as a reluctant concession to the facts of cultural and biological *mestizaje*) both perceive as a strategic necessity. As a cultural process, however, he regards it, at best, as an intermediary stage on the road toward a "more normal and civilized," proto-European "whiteness." No less significantly, Galván's denouement resolves, if only symbolically, the contradictions between the former metropole and its antagonist(s), between the creole elite and the masses over whom it rules, in a self-flattering image of domestic tranquility and harmonious accommodation that, ideally compelling as it appears, was as ideologically charged as it was wholly fictitious.[26] The burden of adaptation and conformity on which this vision of concord and collaboration depends is, logically, predicated on the "lower orders'" acceptance of the terms and jurisdiction of the ruling elite.

One need hardly note that, like the protagonists of the Cuban abolitionist novel, Enriquillo is esthetically and ideologically the metaphorical surrogate of a white creole consciousness. "[H]is dress, air of self-confidence and manners, as well as the regularity of the young cacique's features, gave him the appearance of one more among any number of sons of rich and powerful Spanish colonists on the island."[27] In the final analysis, Galván is essentially concerned with how continued confrontation and civil instability negatively affect the fortunes of this class. The vision of cultural synthesis and restoration of domestic harmony that allegorically emerges in *Enriquillo* is related to Galván's perception of that class's need to consolidate its economic, political, and social position. A climate of greater internal stability, under its aegis, would simultaneously represent the indispensable prerequisite and necessary proof of that consolidation. Its absence would, in any event, prove a discouragement to the foreign investment that was a crucial element of creole ruling class ideas of economic development. Successful incorporation of the Dominican elite into the world market system, which it properly regarded as the lynchpin and guarantor of its domestic ascendancy, lay at the center of its notions of progress. This is the subsoil of uneasy preoccupation that informs the novel's movement away from social and political crisis toward peaceful reconciliation and (apparently) mutual accommodation. It is a movement that, consistent with the characterization of its protagonist, faithfully represents the perspective and program of the "sons of rich and powerful Spanish colonists on the island." A further token of the creole elite's identification of its own interests with the authentic spirit of the "nation," whether figuratively embodied in the image of an assimilated "Indian," rural "peasant," creole black or mulatto, it registers, as fait accompli and continuing patriotic project, the circumscribed sociopolitical horizon and ethnic bias of that identification.

In the anglophone Antilles, where it was the almost exclusive province of transients, sojourners, or expatriates such as Michael Scott (*Tom Cringle's Log* [1836]) and James Rodway (*In Guiana Wilds* [1899]), the novel remained a casual, more rudimentary and circumstantial affair whose narrative point of view, even when most empathetic, remained primarily that of the outside observer. Not until the twentieth century would it reveal—structurally and aesthetically—the level of self-conscious "naturalization," affiliative sense of literary continuity, and formal sophistication already evident in the hispanophone islands. Memoirs, diaries, and poetry—with all the characteristics attributed to it by Edward Brathwaite—continued the predominate genres.[28]

The last half of the nineteenth century nonetheless witnessed the emergence of a core of Afro-West Indian intellectuals no less nationalist than their Hispanic creole counterparts. Its foundation lay, in significant part, in the impact of the ex-slave's post-emancipation flight from the plantation. That flight brought with it the burgeoning of new communities and townships with demands to make upon the resources of the state. Together with its effect on the economy and demography of existing towns, it accelerated the already developing process of formation of an articulated and politically cohesive middle class of mulatto and black proprietors, professionals, petty merchants, skilled artisans, and teachers. It provided this class with an expanded population base of potential political support—a "new" audience to be instructed, wooed, and cultivated—as well as, to a lesser extent, a replenishing source of potential new members. Primary and secondary school teachers, along with journalists, ministers, and lawyers, crucially important to the ideological cohesiveness and continued viability of this class, were particularly well represented among this new corps of Afro-West Indian intellectuals. In the pivot between a colonial administration of foreigners and expatriates, an oligarchic minority of white plantocrats, and the growing number of indentured Asian immigrants, they struggled to advance their own alternative to the assumptions of white supremacy, planter dominance, and metropolitan empire. More conscious of their (racial) victimization by and historic roots in pre-emancipation society, they were perhaps even more sensitive to the urgency of the need for social reform though not any less susceptible to the lures of liberal paternalism than their Hispanic creole contemporaries. They, too, saw themselves as the legitimate representatives of what they regarded as the only genuinely national majority. In contrast with them, however, they identified this majority with the indigenous population of creole descendants of the slave and, more specifically still, with the class of the more educated, prominent, and "competent" among them. Their reformist and anticolonial agitation lay the foundation for the populist alliances that set the stage for the achievement of formal independence in the next century.

The Trinidadian writer John Jacob Thomas (1840–89) was a notably acute, percipient example of this new breed of Afro-West Indian intellectual. His extraordinary career reflected the weight and larger implications of the above changes to which it was, more than partially, indebted. The son of humble parents of African descent, beneficiary of a newly inaugurated (1851) system of free secular primary schools and a partially subsidized normal school education, he himself eventually became a rural village schoolmaster. The perspective given him by that focal position between the illiterate masses of black agricultural workers and the rising group of educated blacks and coloreds to which he himself now belonged, stimulated Thomas—as pedagogue, autodidactic scholar, writer, and organizer of the island's first literary society—to contest the hegemonic assumptions still dominant in his society. Its unconsidered mimicry of inappropriate models and "pernicious idolatry" of racist categories were particularly favored targets of his censure.[29] Anticipating the substance of later debates on the issue, he insisted, in 1887, that the curriculum in West Indian schools did not go beyond "a servile imitation of the now almost entirely exploded English fashions of instruction. . . . [I]n many particulars hopelessly inapplicable to the training of the children of the tropics"—an observation that, beyond its pragmatism, pointed unequivocally to his awareness of a peculiarly non-English "national" reality.[30]

Like his Hispanic and francophone contemporaries, Thomas was keenly appreciative of the process of cultural amalgamation and differentiation that, in his region no less than in theirs, had produced a uniquely Caribbean species of person, with its own distinct national characteristics and style. As part of a larger argument in support of creole—in this case, Afro-creole—claims on the landscape and polity, he sought, like them, to substantiate materially and detail that self-assertive perception. His *The Theory and Practice of Creole Grammar* (1869), a pioneering description of the structure, internal logic, and cultural significance of the primarily oral speech of the folk, was in fact a sustained vindication of the linguistic integrity of the Creole's language. A work comparable in motivation and intent, if not in the racial identification of its specific constituency, to the novels discussed earlier, it proposed a reordering of the reigning linguistic paradigm by granting parity of cultural value to the local idiom. What others sweepingly dismissed as an inferior form of a presumptively "purer" European language, Thomas recognized as the manifestation of a dynamic process of confrontation, adaptation, and differentiation; it was prima facie evidence of a cultural distinctiveness and the palpable sign of an unmistakably decisive historical *achievement*. To the degree Thomas implicitly suggests the "literacy" of ordinary speech and its potential as an untapped reservoir of material and a vehicle for literary expression, one is reminded of the defenses of the creative vitality and insufficiently explored literary possibilities of the vernacular, as against Latin, written by, among others, Dante and Cervantes.

No less conscious than the Hispanic creole elite of the black population's increasingly strategic position, indeed more emphatically so, Thomas was certainly more sympathetic to the social, political, and cultural challenge it represented to the white creole ruling class. Like Martí's, his political vision combined an emphasis on the greatest degree of national sovereignty with a cultural definition of the "nation" that was more radically democratic and socioethnically inclusive. *Froudacity: West Indian Fables Explained* (1889), Thomas's rejoinder to the colonialist impertinence, national self-aggrandizement, and negrophobia of James Anthony Froude's *The English in the West Indies* (1888), brings both these dimensions into dramatic focus.

The product of touristically brief visits by one of England's most distinguished historians presented as an objective, comprehensive assessment of the character and condition of the Caribbean and its people under British rule, Froude's book was actually an apologia in defense of the traditional plantocracy, with which he closely identified, and an obliquely wistful excursus on the need to reinvigorate the metropole's imperialist resolve in the face of changing conditions. More pragmatically, it sought to win over British public opinion to the cause of the minority of white planters, a continuance of the narrow or nonexistent franchise, and the centralization characteristic of the Crown Colony system. "I believe the present generation of Englishmen to be capable of all that their fathers were and possibly more," Froude writes, "but we are just now in a moulting state, and are sick while the process is going on. Or to take another metaphor. The bow of Ulysses is unstrung. . . . They [the empire's colonial subjects] cannot string the bow. Only the true lord and master [England and its "English" Creoles] can string it."[31] Full of the social Darwinist clichés and conventions typical of the period, Froude's book is, finally, no more than a paean to the premise of the natural superiority of the English—and their overseas brethren—with which its author originally set sail.

Pointing to the sheer arrogance of trying to draw conclusions concerning the essential character of any people on the basis of a Cook's tour spent primarily among a minority of the privileged, Thomas immediately cuts to the heart of the matter, denouncing Froude's work as part of a "scheme to thwart political aspiration in the Antilles . . . by deterring the home authorities from granting an elective local legislature . . . to any of the colonies . . . [on the grounds that] it would avert definitively the political domination of the Blacks, which [Froude fears] must inevitably be the outcome of any concession of the modicum of right so earnestly desired."[32] He goes on to expose, systematically and in turn, each of Froude's "fables": his empirical failures of perception, the lack of sociological discrimination, analytical subtlety, or methodological reliability as well as the theoretical circularity and logical absurdities which are the consequence of his "singular contempt for accuracy" in support of the status quo.[33]

The result is far more than a critique of the casual effrontery and racial hauteur of an eminent metropolitan literary lion and man of affairs. *Froudacity* finally emerges as an adroit, passionately comprehensive nationalist reproof of the racist underpinnings of the colonial system itself. A vindication of the cultural singularity and self-directive capacities of each of the territories in question, Thomas's work is a cataloged enumeration of the inescapable centrality and historic basis of the Afro-creole population's legitimate claims to full citizenship and direct and equal participation in the conduct of its countries' affairs. An example of the ideological articulation of the vanguard of the newly emergent black elite of professionals, *Froudacity* placed particular emphasis on the obstacles colonialism put in the way of this class, despite its demonstrable achievements. The tone and intensity of Thomas's attack on race ideology, however, make clear his wider identification with the frustrations of the masses of blacks. "[D]oes Mr. Froude in the fatuity of his skinpride, believe," Thomas asks, "that educated men, worthy of the name, would be otherwise than resentful, if not disgusted, at being shunted out of bread in their own native land, which their parents' labour and taxes have made desirable, in order to afford room to blockheads, vulgarians, or worse, imported from beyond the seas?"[34]

Thomas rejected Froude's postulation of an inherent or necessary antagonism between the races. He stressed instead the conflict between the class of intransigent Anglo-West Indian ex-slaveholders and the remaining sectors of the population throughout the West Indies. This was, in his view, the primary contradiction. "There is no government by reason merely of skins," he insisted.

He envisioned a society open to talent of whatever color and, as a means to that end, argued in favor of a confederation of the different castes and classes that, drawing together the most "eligible and competent" from each, would look to the interests of all. "[W]e have hundreds of both races belonging to the class, competent and eligible," Thomas writes, "and hundreds of both races belonging to the class, incompetent and ineligible: to both of which classes all possible colours might belong. It is from the first mentioned," he concludes, "that are selected those who are to bear the rule, to which the latter class is, in the very nature of things, bound to be subject."[35] Thomas thus replaces Froude's pigmentocratic oligarchy with the gathering colored middle class's notion of a meritocracy, whose specific emphasis accentuates his conviction that blacks are "apt apprentices in every conceivable department of civilised culture."[36] His wording, in each case, is significant. It points to an essential paradox and epochally characteristic ambivalence. Like that of the great majority of his equally liberal Hispanic and francophone contemporaries, Thomas's incisive defense and contextualization of the "national" interests of an emerging domestic elite is only as democratic as rule by a patriciate of the "most competent and able" from among that elite will allow. He was, nonetheless, definite with regard to the ultimate meaning of what he recognized as a change of specific context in the Caribbean. In this regard, Thomas, whose tone of historical optimism contrasts sharply with Froude's edge of trepidatious historical foreboding, finally minces no words: "the ignoring of Negro opinion" by all those for whom Froude speaks, he warns, "though not only possible but easily practised fifty years ago, is a portentous blunder at the present time. Verbum sapienti."[37]

It was a prophetic warning. Its emphasis on the need for a rearticulation of "national" assumptions, guiding definitions, and priorities was unmistakable. Thomas's pointed notation of the crucial shift of axis implied by the growing consciousness, ever-looming presence, and portent of the anonymous majority of blacks was especially prescient. It framed the central thrust and challenge of dramas yet to come. Like Martí's essays and commentaries, Froudacity thus presaged—as it was itself symptomatic of—the crisis of hegemonic white creole dominion throughout the area. It prefigured the ideological exhaustion, eventual political deterioration, and eclipse of seignorial society whose consummation would occupy the first four decades of the twentieth century and serve as the backdrop and milieu of the new literary outlook of the writing produced then and immediately after. An eloquent exemplar of liberal nationalist Afro-creole opinion, Thomas's work, like Martí's, also constituted a penetrating adumbration of some of the salient features, as well the anticolonial tone and mood, of the world into which Walcott and his generation were born.

The expansion of the United States after 1898 and the progressive displacement of the effective power of European colonialism in the area by the force of its own neocolonial ambition was, undoubtedly, among the most distinguishing features of that world. By the 1940s, when the majority of that generation was on the threshold of entering its teens, the United States by a combination of political threat and maneuver (e.g., Roosevelt's "Big Stick" policy), increased economic penetration (e.g., Taft's "Dollar Diplomacy"), direct intervention (e.g., Cuba, Puerto Rico, the Dominican Republic, Haiti), negotiation (e.g., "Lend Lease" agreements), or purchase (e.g., the Virgin Islands) had clearly established itself as first among imperial equals in the Caribbean. Its burgeoning economic predominance and ultimate political cultivation of a moderately reformist middle class, only then coming into its own, further eroded the hegemony of the traditionally conservative agricultural oligarchies: tied to a system of seignorial, personalist, or superannuated production techniques, they found themselves increasingly unable to compete with the "modernizing" aggressiveness of American corporate capitalism.

In the prostrating wake of World War I, Europe also began to lose much of its luster as a model. With this accustomed paragon itself turning to new sources of spiritual revitalization and renewal, Caribbean intellectuals turned inward to a more sustained exploration of their own neglected reservoir of people and sources. They began not merely to highlight but increasingly to celebrate those characteristic features and populations that, though generally disdained, made their societies decidedly un-European. In response to the ebb of Europe and the disjunctures and dislocations that came with Yankee imperialism, a critical self-scrutiny and enucleating self-discovery became the order of the day. Where writers of the previous century typically regarded ethnocultural amalgamation (and its class associations) as something to be overcome or reluctantly tolerated, as an "exotic" liability or, more benignly, as an unavoidable, strategic necessity, the facts—and forms—of creolization would now be pointed to in the context of a more positive vision of synthesis, on the one hand, and a heightened appreciation of the contributions of the African ancestor, on the other. It was the cultural complement and reflection of a more broadly based call for a radical change in the traditional social order.

The developing self-consciousness, new political importance, and increasingly militant discontent of the rural and urban working classes, resulting in uprisings, strikes, riots, stoppages, and the formal crystallization of an organized labor movement during the twenties, thirties, and early forties, gave a particularly revolutionary edge to the force of that demand. It became more and more difficult, without risk of alienating this now crucial constituency, to entirely dissociate the long-standing aspiration to complete national sovereignty and a reinvigorated concern with ethnohistorical self-affirmation from the revolutionary and popularly felt urgency for the achievement of social justice. The push from below, as Martí foresaw, J. J. Thomas had warned, and the proletarianism of such as the Puerto Rican Ramón Romero Rosa and the radical black nationalism of the Jamaican Marcus Garvey now made palpably clear, could no longer be safely ignored.

A new "public" was beginning to flex its muscles and was to precipitate a decisive realignment of forces. It led the advancing mestizo, colored, and black middle classes to forge, as part of their own assault on the traditional distribution of power, that uneasy alliance with the working class which, on terms generally more favorable to themselves, effected the political demise of the old hacendado and planter elites. The nationalist populism to which these middle classes recurred to achieve it had, by the late fifties, effectively transformed them into the new arbiters of the domestic Caribbean scene: new middle-class regimes of either liberal populist (e.g., Puerto Rico, Jamaica, Trinidad) or despotic right-wing populist outlook (e.g., Haiti, the Dominican Republic, prerevolutionary Cuba, and Grenada) became increasingly characteristic. Though they demagogically clung to their earlier rhetoric, they were increasingly unable to deliver on promises to the working classes, save by encouraging their increasingly massive immigration abroad. Nor were they able to check—indeed their economic policies, growing political isolation, and defensiveness actually stimulated—neocolonial dependence on the United States and the systematic impoverishment of the unprivileged majority of their own people to which it contributed. The definitive collapse of those alliances, a characteristic feature of the decade of the sixties, made this reality all the more apparent. The general estrangement of the working classes and their supporters among the more liberal and radical wing of that middle class gave a renewed immediacy and vigor to the critique of the status quo and the defiant nationalism in which those alliances had, ironically, originated. It was to precisely those branches of the middle class that a community of writers struggling to establish its cultural and professional authority and demanding a functional and infrastructural recognition of the legitimacy and social value of their craft, in the main, structurally belonged.

Beyond a common nationalist denominator and the generally shared perception of the need to engage or somehow come to terms with the masses, the initial critique was neither monolithic nor univocal. Those being displaced naturally sought nostalgic refuge in the past with which they identified. To prevent any further erosion of their class's traditional prominence, they defended the stability, cultural superiority, and "national" integrity of its values. Denied by American intervention the "right" to a domestic hegemony it was poised to assume upon the collapse of Spanish colonialism, the Hispanic creole elite thus invoked, in the face of the cultural and economic threat of American imperialism, the alleged spiritual superiority of its traditional Spanish heritage. To the more conservative among them, the refusal of the peasantry and emerging proletariat to rally to its patrician cause became, in the event, evidence of what they regarded as either an endemic inertia and/or proof of a lack of patriotic, familial solidarity.

A radical Latinism, grounded in a platonic rejection of Yankee materialism and its putative lack of more transcendent virtues, became a symptomatic point of cohesion. It was a posture reminiscent of José Enrique Rodó's (Uruguay, 1871–1917) seminal essay, *Ariel* (1898). It shared an aristocratic repudiation of what was perceived as the era's tendency to an "inappropriately" democratic mediocritization to the lowest common denominator of society which Rodó's work shared with the Spanish philosopher José Ortega y Gasset's (1883–1955) equally influential *The Revolt of the Masses* (1937). José De Diego's (1866–1918) antiassimilationist protest against the imposition of North American culture and its pragmatism in Puerto Rico reflected its underlying premises. "We do not know in these historic reversals," he writes in one of his better known poems, "Aleluyas to the Gentlemen from the North,"

> The language and the meaning of English-speaking peoples.
> We have another language, another way of thinking . . .
> . . . . . . . . . . . . . . . . . . . . . . . . . . . . . . . . . . . . . . . . . . . . . .
>
> Unhappy scions of that sapless trunk,
> That flowered in the souls of Seneca and Hugo.
> We know the mysteries of pure Philosophy
> And of the art that reigns in Holy Poesy.
> But nothing do we know, in the land of the sun,
> Of the art of Government, as at Tammany Hall[38]

Conveniently disregarding the fact that Spain was the last of the colonial powers in the region to finally abolish it, and muting its more exploitative realities, a hyperbolic revision of the domestic history of slavery emerged that was calculated to demonstrate, as in the work of Tomás Blanco (1897–1975), an essential benevolence in comparison with the experience of the United States. It was another trope of the same ideologically charged claim to a certain moral superiority. The normative cultural paradigm for "the nation" remained, for all that, quintessentially white and Europocentrically Western. A reductive hispanophilia, exaggerated Catholicism, and idealist transformation of the local agrarian past into a benign national pastoral of cheerful jíbaros, enlightened landlords, and *hommes de lettres* were among its more distinguishing characteristics.

The (antiblack) racist determinism into which it could often degenerate, as in *Insularismo* (1934), Antonio S. Pedreira's (1899–1939) celebrated examination of the Puerto Rican personality, was another response to the crisis in which the Hispanic creole elite found itself as a class and the disquieting awareness, succinctly expressed by Pedreira, that "Given we're in the midst of a transition, we must take care to watch what belongs to us [*la propiedad*]."[39] The *francophonie* of the mulatto elite in the French Antilles and the Jamaicanism of a Herbert DeLisser (1878–1944) were rooted in a nationalism of a similarly conservative and genteel predisposition. This did not prevent DeLisser's novel, *Jane's Career* (1913), from being one of the first to focus on the displacement of the rural peasantry to the major cities and among the first by a native West Indian in which the central character is both black and a woman. It did, however, similarly texture his approach to the problem, and informed the patronizing attitude he took to the people and culture she represented.

*Negrismo*, in the Hispanic Caribbean, thus emerged as a more democratic liberal alternative to this dominant hispanophile discourse. Drawing inspiration from an untapped cornucopia of popular custom and experience, it acknowledged the ubiquitous cultural influence of the black. Its literary celebration of the oral traditions, verbal inventiveness, and generally suasive power of that disdained and neglected patrimony represented a substantive challenge to orthodox prejudice and dogma. It underscored the process of biological and cultural miscegenation that had taken place in the area. In only partial continuity with nineteenth-century liberal thought, from the perspective of its recognition of the demands of a distinctly new context, it pointed to the inevitably syncretic character of the national identity. "The Antillean," asserted Luis Palés Matós (Puerto Rico, 1898–1959), whose initial "afroantillean poems," "Pueblo negro" (1925) and "Danza negra" (1926), were among the first examples of the new modality, "is a Spaniard with the manner of a mulatto and the soul of a black."[40] The first of Alejo Carpentier's many novels, *!Ecué Yambá Ó!* (1927), was a quasi-anthropological attempt at a fictional exploration of the world of ñañigo ritual and belief premised on similar assumptions. The movement's faddish transience—by the late 1940s, interest in the "black theme" as such apparently exhausted, it faded from fashionability—was emblematic of the mediational and predominantly idealist posture that sustained it. The picturesque exoticism, uncritical susceptibility to an imagery of questionable racialist assumptions, and assumed formal distance from the world of their chosen protagonists manifest in the work of some of the movement's most representative figures—Ramón Guirao (Cuba, 1908–49), Emilio Ballagas (Cuba, 1908–54), José Z. Tallet (Cuba, 1893–1955), Manuel Del Cabral (Dominican Republic, 1907) and, indeed, Palés Matós himself—revealed that an emphasis on the syncretic facts, congregational, democratizing, and reconciliatory virtues of mestizaje was not always incompatible with confirmation of the traditional clichés of racist stereotyping. As in the redundancy of the term "Afro-Cuban" itself, it sometimes contained the latent suggestion that, for all its impact, the "Afro" contribution was an addendum affixed to an essentially inviolate national core that remained exclusively Hispanic.

Nicolás Guillén (Cuba, 1902– ), who shared the broadly consolidating emphasis on the historical and cultural importance of mestizaje, proved in this respect to be doubly exceptional. His affirmation of his country's *africanía* was neither temporary nor abstract. His identification with the concrete person of the black, moreover, evinced very little of that ambiloquy and distanced lack of internal consistency. "I deny the art that sees in the Negro only a colorful motif and not an intensely human theme," he demurred.[41] The notion of a constitutively Antillean *mulatez* is the guiding premise of an impressive corpus of poetry and prose covering more than fifty years of sustained intellectual activity from which a concern with the *specific material condition* of the black, as a barometer of a given society's overall health and condition, is never absent. "I am aware, of course," he notes with ironic audacity in the prologue to *Sóngoro cosongo* as early as 1931, "that these verses are repugnant to many people, because they deal with blacks and ordinary people. I don't care. Or more accurately: I'm pleased. That means that such fastidious spirits are not included in my lyrical agenda. They are, moreover, good people. They've risen with great difficulty into the aristocracy from the kitchen, and tremble as soon as they see a pot." "Someday," he reproaches his more priggish compatriots, "we will say: 'Cuban color'," adding "these poems wish to hasten its arrival."[42]

More than that of any other Hispanic contemporary, Guillén's work succeeded in dynamically grounding his negrismo in the socially concrete and in effectively transforming the black into the material embodiment and symbol of the nation's heterogeneous underclass as a whole. Regarding as that of the nation itself the collective aspirations of the latter, Guillén's affirmation of Cuba's ethnohistorical particularity and his radical anti-imperialism are, in both form and substance, inextricable from a critique of the narrowly culturalist discourse of his more conventionally liberal compatriots and from the wish to overthrow an ignominious social system that is not without its homegrown defenders. "[W]hat the black must aspire to . . . everywhere," he writes in 1950, "is not that there be ten or a hundred rich and cultured brethren . . . [domiciled in gilded ghettos] but that thousands of destitute blacks not rot in the misery, in the ignorance, in the pain . . . [of the nation's slums]."[43] He rejects the elitist preference for moral and "cultural" solutions as evasive, ineffectual indicators of a narrowly defined class self-interest:

> The bourgeoisie falsely affirms . . . that that terrible condition [of economic inequality] will disappear with [the acquisition of] "culture," and is willing to throw a bit of its money to entertain the blacks, domesticating them in the process . . . the liberation of the black lies very far . . . [from that] program of racist cultural intensification . . . as well as from that patriotic embrace that [Gustavo Urrutia] suggests between blacks and whites in the heart of imperialism. . . . No: the future holds a more profound, more drastic, more revulsive, more historically just solution, [one] derived from a powerful revolutionary upheaval.[44]

At one with him in affirming the mestizo essence, historical and cultural unity of the Antilles, Guillén's nationalism evinces neither the disconsolate pessimism nor the quasi-existentialist angst that informs Palés Matós's work. The elegiac undertone provoked in him by the nature of Cuban reality prior to 1959 is inseparable from the humorously satirical edge of his national self-scrutiny and the firm historical optimism which infuse his

> . . . simple song[s] of death and life
> with which to greet the future drenched in blood,
> red as the sheets, as the thighs,
>         as the bed
> of a woman who's just given birth.[45]

It is in the direction of this fusion between circumstantial discontent and historical optimism that, striving in its own way to be "universal y cubano," the expressionist historicism and documentary compactness of Carpentier's later proposition of a "magical realism" (in his preface to The Kingdom of This World [1949]) will evolve.[46]

Guillén's embrace of socialism was as logically continuous with his realism and the holistically subversive sweep of his version of "negrismo" as Palés Matós's more strictly metaphorical, "culturalist" evocation of a "Mulata Antilla," for example, was with the patrician populism to which his own sympathies inclined and as a result of which he was to become a representatively democratic and canonical figure.

In no case did Hispanic negrismo ever imply any denial or outright rejection of the nation's Spanish inheritance. Its coalescent emphasis on mestizaje as both a syncretic and unique cultural fact and as a creatively mediating historical force indeed came to be generally accepted as normative and, ideologically, became increasingly dominant. In the anglophone and francophone territories, the analogous nationalist reclamation and recuperation of the contemned African ancestor, though motivated by a similar set of anticolonialist perceptions, initially reflected a deeper sense of mutual estrangement and a much more immiscible temper. There, save for Haiti, the traditional colonial power was a continuing and very palpable presence (which, in the case of Guyana, Guadeloupe, and Martinique, remains still in formal control).

Unlike Spain, it constituted something still to be immediately contended with. The inescapable influence of American imperialism, for all its impact, had not changed that. Long-standing policies of cultural dependency and assimilation, adjunct to the economic and political integration of the colony within the metropolitan orbit, added both ire and urgency to anticolonial declarations of cultural and national independence. Idealization of the traditional metropoles, particularly as travel to them increased and widened its class base, became all the more difficult to sustain.[47] The image of a historically achieved resolution of the kind suggested by negrismo's convergent emphasis on mestizaje was, in this context, not always as immediately compelling. The mulatto as an image of mediating conciliation or a national symbol of a syncretic ethos proved, under the circumstances, to be rather more precariously uncertain and problematic. The truth of biological and cultural amalgamation, though recognized as salient, did not by itself offer any comforting sense of resolution. An anguished consciousness of irresolution and continuing contradiction, indeed, emerged as a leitmotiv.

Léon LaLeau's (Haiti, 1892–198?) much anthologized "Betrayal" ("This haunted heart that doesn't fit / . . . the words of France / This heart that came to me from Senegal"),[48] and Léon Damas's (Guyana, 1912–78) "Whitewash" ("they dare to / treat me white / though everything within me / wants only to be black"),[49] like Derek Walcott's later and still more tragically tormented "A Far

Cry from Africa" ("I who am poisoned with the blood of both [Africa and Europe] / Where shall I turn, divided to the vein?"),[50] are characteristic cases in point. Where (as in Martinique, Guadeloupe and, to a lesser extent, Jamaica and Trinidad) mulattoes and propertied coloreds had themselves become identified with—or emerged as a discrete element of—a pigmentocratically sensitive and privileged native aristocracy, the difficulty was naturally compounded. Haiti, where after the revolution and prior to the American occupation (1915–34) there were no whites at all in positions of proprietorship or power, provided the most pristine example of just such a ruling mulatto elite. Inured to snobbery, cultural mimicry, like some autarchic protocol, remained everywhere pervasive within its ranks. "Crammed full of white morality, white culture, white education and white prejudices . . . a faithful copy of the pale-skinned gentleman," Etienne Léro (Martinique, 1910–39) exploded in disgust, its members, he charged, took "a special pride in the fact that a white man can read [their] book[s] without ever guessing the color of [their] skin . . . [or ever coming upon] an original or meaningful accent . . . a trace of the black man's sensuous and colorful imagination or the echo of the hatreds and aspirations of an oppressed people."[51] His equally reform-minded anglophone colleagues, having little ground to quarrel with Léro, would have certainly sympathized with his assessment. Criticizing the reigning, submissively derivative tendency to a Victorian exoticism and contraversimilitude, one of them wrote: "We fail utterly to understand . . . why anyone should want to see Trinidad as a miniature *Paradiso*, where gravediggers speak like English M.P.'s. . . . The answer is obviously that the average . . . writer regards his fellow-countrymen as his inferiors, an uninteresting people who are not worth his while. He genuinely feels (and by this, of course, asserts his own feeling of inferiority) that with his people as characters his stories would be worth nothing."[52]

The combined force of these several factors gave point and substance to the more dramatically pronounced, specifically black radical emphasis and militantly defiant sense of the need for a radical divorce from the culture and traditions of Europe that, in contrast with Hispanic negrismo, is discernible in the texture, tone, and thematic foci of *négritude* and its equally anticolonial literary counterparts in the anglophone Antilles. Joined to the influence of more broadly international social and intellectual currents (Freudianism, Marxism, Nationalism, Pan-Africanism, Surrealism, Literary Realism), the catalytic impact of these factors also helps to explain the more intensely sustained concentration on the unique (double) alienation of the black in a racist environment. It accounts, too, for its focus on the rather complex psychological dimensions of racism, colonialism, and the process of decolonization which negrismo tended generally to slight or ignore altogether.

Reaching a kind of critical apogee in the penetrating, ideologically synthesizing commentaries of Frantz Fanon, this exploration of the internalized effects of colonialism on ego integrity proved to be particularly enduring and influential well beyond the French- or English-speaking Antilles. Their retrieval and defense of the African ancestor nonetheless often evinced a general tendency, later empathetically reproved for its mystifying idealism by Fanon, Walter Rodney, and René Dépestre among others,[53] to appeal to a virtually transhistorical Negro essence. Beyond any recognition of a denied heritage or the simple affirmation of internationalist solidarity with a common experience of racial oppression, this essence seemed to take precedence over, obscure, or otherwise absorb the black's specific contextual matrix. This oftentimes had the effect of diminishing the force of his or her national particularity, detaching it from its social and historical concreteness, even as it appeared to invoke it.

In a manner not unlike the more idealist versions of negrismo, it also minimized or avoided the problem of internal class conflict in favor of a larger ethnic-ethos identification. Though by a more dissociative contrast of cultures, anglophone and francophone varieties of negritude served the same nation-defining and broadly convergent purpose as the Hispanic emphasis on mestizaje. Rhetorically invoked and ideologically manipulated by a François Duvalier, an Eric Gairy, the later Eric Williams, or a Forbes Burnham, this indistinctiveness of contours—albeit with indisputable elements of accuracy—could easily degenerate into the self-promotional, populist demagoguery that helped to secure, as it concealed, the nationally hegemonic ambitions of the rising black middle class that each came finally to represent. Like negrismo, though, it was initially aimed at and, like it too, succeeded in opening a significant breach in an until then complacently dominant and all too decorous Europocentric discourse.

The opening salvos of this iconoclastic avant-garde sensibility were registered in the innovative, culturally rebellious little magazines and journals around which the vigorously nationalist temper of this new literary-political project crystallized. They served as a first launching pad which, in more than one case, would survive to provide a place of early apprenticeship for those, like many of the writers born in the thirties and after, destined to carry that project more critically forward: *Revue du monde noir* (1930), *Légitime Défense* (1932), *L'Etudiant Noir* (1934), and *Présence Africaine* (1947– ) in Paris; *Tropiques* (1941–45) in Martinique; *Trinidad* (1929) and *The Beacon* (1931–33,

1939) in Trinidad; the broadcast review, "Caribbean Voices" (1942–62), in London; *Bim* (1942– ) in Barbados; *Focus* (1943, 1948, 1956, 1960, 1983) in Jamaica; *Kykoveral* (1945–62) in Guyana; and *La Trouée* (1927), *La Revue Indigene* (1927–28), *Le Petit Impartial, Journal de la Masse* (1927–31), *Les Griots* (1938–40), and *La Ruche* (1946) in Haiti. The names themselves are a testimony to their specific cultural intent or allegiance.

The completed version of what to this day remains perhaps the single most celebrated, sustained, and representatively compendious lyrical monument to négritude, Aimé Césaire's (Martinique, 1913– ) *Cahier d'un retour au pays natal* (1939), in which the word itself made its most influential debut, was originally published in *Tropiques*. An apocalyptically visionary manifesto explicitly leveled at the hoary premises of the French concept and policy of *assimilation* ("Accommodate yourself to me / I won't accommodate myself to you"),[54] it describes the poet's journey back from physical and spiritual exile, his rejection of "the sterile attitude of the spectator," his rediscovery, embrace, and cultural repossession of his own country. The conceit of European technical progress, nature-overpowering pragmatism and rationality, in an inversion of the value-meaning of ancient stereotypes, is mockingly played against the deeper authenticity of "Those who give themselves up to the essence of all things / ignorant of surfaces but struck by the movement of all things / free of the desire to tame but familiar with the play of the world." Suggesting the universal identification of oppression, the *Cahier* expands outward beyond the landscape of Martinique eventually to encompass the whole of the black world. A journey in reverse across the Middle Passage made necessary by the consequences of the colonizer's *mission civilisatrice*, it is, as an antidote to the pained recognition of a historic fragmentation, marginality, and cultural inauthenticity, inextricable from a search for the source of cosmic harmonies. Infused with the imperative of this question of wholeness, the poem is, in effect, a lyrical catharsis. Evoking the word-magic of a surrealistic pantheism, Césaire "plunges into the red flesh of the soil [of Martinique and Africa]," breaking "the yoke-bag / that separates me from myself"; and, in an effort "to proscribe at last this unique race free," becomes "the furious WE." If the contours of an irreducible individuality—personal, sociohistorical, geographic, or national—fade into as they illuminate each other during the course of its powerful and multifaceted dialectic, Césaire's programmatic thrust is never in any doubt. Repudiating the inveterate paternalism and omnifarious pretension to superiority of the West he aspires, as his 1956 "Letter to Maurice Thórez," then secretary general of the French Communist party, put it, to "nothing short of a Copernican revolution, so deeply entrenched in Europe, in every party and in every sphere, from old guard right to red left, is this habit of making our arrangements, this habit of thinking in our behalf, in fine, this habit of contesting our right to initiative . . . which is ultimately the right to a personality of one's own."[55]

In Jacques Roumain (Haiti, 1907–44), Césaire's allegory of the return, of communal integration, and of affirmation of this "personality of one's own" took the form, in *La montagne ensorcelée* (1931) and the more accomplished and influential *Gouverneurs de la rosée* (1944), of a critical celebration of the organicity of Haitian peasant culture. Beyond its skillful handling of a contrastive imagery, figurative and structural use of voodoo ritual, and the *combite* as symbols of a dialectic between despair and possibility, Roumain's exploration of peasant life, in its language and narrative posture, argued its intrinsic esthetic potential as it insinuated his consciousness of the twin dangers of a slumming patronization and the diffusion, corollary to it, of intragroup and intraclass confrontation.

Early on, in his *Analyse schematique, 1932–1934*, Roumain took issue with the "attitude sentimentale" of those among the mulatto and black middle classes who, in defense of Haiti's African identity, appealed, as Duvalier and *Les Griots* were to do, to a psychobiological cluster "of abstractions which contain the entire world, precisely because they are no more than abstractions without any root in reality and which in the end commit themselves to nothing at all (racial consciousness, verbal and utopian nationalism, etc.)."[56] It was a criticism that, as the temporary alliance of the different classes began to collapse, would gain increasing currency. Like Roumain's fictional engagement with the remarkable complexity of the Haitian cultural landscape, it also intimated the need for a less hazily reductive, more imaginatively comprehensive yet scrupulously probing scrutiny of Caribbean culture and reality. His example would later inspire Jacques Stéphen Alexis's own notion of "Le Realisme Marveilleux Haitienne," and find echo in Glissant's complementary concept of *Antillanité*, as well as in Maryse Conde's (Guadeloupe, 1936– ) critical appraisal of the achievement and limitations of negritude. Negritude in the Antilles, she writes in *Présence Africaine* in 1972, "was a total, passionate, blind, refusal, born of the assumption of an acute awareness of the condition of being an exploited person, economically and culturally underdeveloped. The *Antillanité* we want to oppose to it, is no more than the second phase: that in which, after total refusal, the Antillean creates out of his complex inheritance and strives to express it in every one of its forms."[57]

It is to the challenge and esthetic exigencies of this program, with its more conceptually concentrated focus on regional specificity and its suggestion of a wider Pan-Caribbean resonance, that the writers of this generation have turned their attention with increasingly impressive verve and orginality—and in sometimes uneasy recognition of their debt to the predecessors whose achievements their own work extends.

Césaire's contemporaries in the English colonies, though perhaps without so immediately spectacular a success and, as a more intellectually eclectic and racially heterogeneous cohort lacking any single so fortuitously definitive a label as "négritude" proved to be, were motivated by an identical concatenation of forces and pursued similar goals. They, too, spurned the values of the smug, claustrophobic society colonialism and an unctuously pretentious native elite had produced. They condemned its "ubiquitous cruelty," its poverty, the pernicious indifference and torporific propriety that permeated its social and spiritual environment. They determined to lay siege, as Albert Gomes, founding editor of *The Beacon*, recalls in his memoirs, to their society's "ancient incrustation of psychic mildew and cobweb."[58] "Our right to be ourselves," they were also convinced (the words, again, are Gomes's), "was sacred."[59] Like that of their francophone colleagues, their esthetic program was informed by the commanding need to give material literary expression to these concerns. Ardent nonconformists, as Reinhard Sander points out, they demanded

> writing which utilized West Indian settings, speech, character, situations and conflicts. [They] warned against the imitation of foreign literature, especially against the imitation of foreign popular literature. Local colour, however, was not regarded as a virtue by itself. A mere occupation with the enchanted landscape of the tropics did not fulfill the group's emphasis on realism and verisimilitude. . . . Realism combined with and supported by the Trinidadian's social and political ideology resulted in fiction [and poetry] that focussed on West Indian characters belonging to the lower classes. [Though] The group around *Trinidad* and *The Beacon* consisted essentially of middle class people. . . . The barrack-yard was of particular interest to . . . [them].[60]

C. L. R. James's *Minty Alley* (1936), Alfred Mendes's *Pitch Lake* (1934) and *Black Fauns* (1935), and R. A. C. DeBoissiere's *Crown Jewel* (1952) and *Rum and Coca Cola* (1956)—whose authors collaborated in those journals—were the products of this outlook and mood. They mirrored their exploratory interest in the West Indian underclass, the peculiar formal tensions of a compassionate outside-narrator's view of it, and, especially in the case of DeBoissiere's novels, the intensity of the radically nationalist content of their proletarian sympathies.

James was to emerge as one of the modern Caribbean's most prolific, pioneeringly influential thinkers. Combining unorthodox Marxist with Pan-

African ideas, he went on to write his seminal examination of the unfolding, wider consequences and significance of the slave insurrection in Haiti, *The Black Jacobins: Toussaint L'ouverture and the San Domingo Revolution* (1938, 1963). The impact of his provocative analysis and commentaries on politics, society, and culture—from *The Case for West Indian Self-Government* (1933), *World Revolution* (1937), and *A History of the Negro Revolt* (1938) to *Party Politics in the West Indies* (1962) and *Beyond a Boundary* (1963)—was later gratefully acknowledged to have been one of their major sources of inspiration by the succeeding generation of activist West Indian intellectuals.

*The Beacon* group's linkage of its promotion of a more genuinely West Indian literary culture to the political project of decolonization and the establishment of an independent nation-state by which James himself was encouraged, and to which he significantly contributed, was characteristic of its sister journals in the region. In the two decades immediately before formal independence from Britain and the breakup of the West Indian Federation in 1962, they established the national ground and pioneered the esthetic dominion of a distinctly anglophone Antillean sensibility. Part of a progressive populist movement which, in the wake of universal suffrage and a political strategy of class convergence, eventually gave the middle class nominally representative control of the administrative apparatus of the state, this was one of their most lasting contributions to the process of formal independence. In the seventeen years of its existence its founder-editor, A. J. Seymour, tells us in *Growing Up in Guyana* (1976) that *Kykoveral*

caught and focussed in the first place the ideas and desires of a group of young Guyanese writers acting as an instrument to help forge a Guyanese people, making them conscious of their intellectual and spiritual possibilities, and then changed its form and pattern in response to the contemporary trends of writing in the region, to become a nursery for the expression of a West Indian literary cultural spirit, a new cultural sensibility which foreshadows a new nation, along with its contemporaries BIM in Barbados and the occasional FOCUS in Jamaica.[61]

These were the "nurseries" that, in addition to the work of those already mentioned, nourished, cultivated, or encouraged the prelusive fiction of Roger Mais (Jamaica, 1905–55), Edgar Mittelholzer (British Guiana, 1909–65), and V. S. Reid (Jamaica, 1913– ). Mais's pessimistic realism, his bitter denunciation, in *The Hills Were Joyful Together* (1953), of "what happens to people when their lives are constricted and dwarfed . . . girdled with poverty" and victimized by the callousness and ineptitude of the larger society,[62] added a dramatic vividness, an unsparing, naturalistic quality as well as a panoramic systemic scope and almost palpable sensual immediacy to Mendes's and James's comparatively more timid examination of life in the barrack yard. Its tough-minded exposé "of the real Jamaica and the dreadful conditions of the working classes"[63] included, in defiance of conventional middle-class prejudice, a precociously empathetic portrayal of the Rastafarian which he went on to develop more fully and symbolically in *Brother Man* (1954).

Mais effectively fused social realism with a symbolically resonant exploration of the tension-fraught dilemma of his own predicament as an artist in the allegorical portrait of a peasant blacksmith and sculptor he offered in *Black Lightning* (1955). An exceptionally gifted, self-absorbed visionary, his protagonist in that novel becomes the alienated victim of the exaggerated sense of self-sufficiency with which he protects himself against the uncomprehending community to which he is fully dedicated. It was Mais's metaphor for the anguishing feeling—shared by so many of his fellow West Indian writers at the time—of the sometimes unsustainable strain between their sense of loyalty and responsibility to a colonial, still underdeveloped society and an equally consuming dedication to their own development as artists that eventually compelled so many, including Mais himself, to temporarily emigrate to the metropole. Suggesting as it does the lack of organicity and unwholeness of anything short of a mutually sustaining interdependence between the artist and his community, the study of individual psychology *Black Lightning* presents, put in still starker relief, the overarching importance of the collective protagonist Mais had located at the center of his earlier works. The clearest forerunner of H. Orlando Patterson's (Jamaica, 1940– ) *The Children of Sisyphus* (1964), a no less grimly unrelenting but more deliberately existentialist depiction of the fragility and desperation of life in the Kingston slums, *The Hills Were Joyful Together* brought an unprecedented intensity to the emerging literature of the Yard. Taken as a whole, moreover, Mais's work intimated some of its still unexplored terrain. It widened the genre's repertoire of characteristic figures and, despite a sometimes too theatrical "staging" and occasional abuse of coincidence, extended the range of its formal, imaginative, and allegorical complexity.

In a similar way, V. S. Reid's fictional celebration of the *New Day* (1949), inaugurated by Jamaica's new constitution and the coming of universal suffrage in 1944, captured the early optimism inspired by the national movement and, in particular, Norman Washington Manley's People's National party. Its formal structure, choice of narrator, and privileging of the demotic gave literary prestige and validation to the social and cultural centrality of the country's rural black peasant core.

By contrast, Mittelholzer's Kaywana trilogy—*Children of Kaywana* (1952), *The Harrowing of Hubertus* (1954), and *Kaywana Blood* (1958)—made its author's obsession with the violent clash of racial and sexual potentialities, with the white-identified mulatto's tormented sense of "impurity" and the inimical power of his "dual nature" and irreconcilable "bloods," the prime mover of his fictional reconstruction of Guyanese history from its initial settlement by Europeans to the mid-twentieth century. Like Reid's, however, it was a work of foundational ambition. Despite their very different emphasis, both novels sought to give specific definition, historical coherence, and national integrity to local experience, "creating a tale that," in Reid's words, "will give as true an impression as fiction can of the way by which . . . [their respective countries and] people came to today."[64] Among the desiderata of the esthetic vocation of Seymour's "new cultural sensibility which foreshadows a new nation," this conceptual framework reflected, too, the spirit which animated his heroic little magazines.

As Seymour suggests, the magazines gave all these authors some impetus and a forum. They also provided the initial core of a sympathetic reading public, a mutually sustaining link, and the sense of an emergent community of common endeavor to the efflorescence of major writers in the fifties and sixties whose work would extend that of Mendes, James, DeBoissiere, Mais, Reid, and Mittelholzer to include a similarly motivated scrutiny of the populist fraudulence of a neocolonial independence. Colonialism had also to be examined, in the words of George Lamming, as "a continuing psychic experience that has to be dealt with long after the actual colonial situation formally ends."[65]

The common presumption in all this multivalently anticolonial, self-defining literary ferment throughout the archipelago was a growing conviction, succinctly enunciated by Jacques Stéphen Alexis in 1956, that "the forms in a national culture must, before anything else, correspond to the character and tendencies of the people in question," and serve to define it.[66] The essence of that character came more and more to be seen as inseparable from the style, speech, unsung experience, and primarily oral traditions of the popular masses. Even if only tacitly, unwittingly, or in the context of a continued opposition to the wider implications of their historic emergence, the anonymous masses increasingly assumed the role of clearly indicated or obliquely implied protagonist.

Beyond a certain democratization of the Caribbean literary landscape, forcefully affirmed in the pointed declaration and unadorned realism of the title of José Luis González's (Puerto Rico, 1926– ) collection of short stories, *El hombre en la calle* (1948), no less than in the work of Mais, Lamming, Guillén, Césaire, Roumain, and others, this shift of focal perspective was tantamount to proposing, by a rearticulation of the locus of its subject, a fundamental reassessment of the history—*another* rehistorization—of the Caribbean. The classic epic, turned on its head, thus gives way to the oftentimes deliberate articulation of a new epic: an epic of the wretched, the anonymous, the obscure and neglected—those hitherto absent from History. Underscoring their part in the historical formation of a uniquely Caribbean culture, the writer identifies the fate and national authenticity of his society as a whole—the authority and allegiance any government can legitimately claim—with the relative fortunes of its rural or urban, primarily black, underclass and the level of appreciation of its importance to the achievement of any sense of social health and spiritual integrity. The thematic forms and patterns of conception the artistic expression of this (re)appropriating, synthesizing epic assumes in the still evolving canon of the region's most recent writers reveal the persistent, recurring prominence of several interrelated tropes.

The first of these, as already suggested, involves a necessary engagement with History itself. "History," the novelist John Hearne writes, "is the angel with whom all we Caribbean Jacobs have to wrestle, sooner or later, if we hope for a blessing."[67] A critical encounter with the past as both the prehistory of the present—active, unreconciled, unpropitiated, contradictory, continuing or permanent presence—and the proper ground for establishing the entelechy, cultural and national, of a Caribbean ethos is indeed one of the premises and compositional principles of the current vogue of the historical novel in the region. "The constitution of History as it effects the Caribbean and the Guianas," Wilson Harris insists, requires its writers "to embrace the muse through an imaginative re-discovery of the past."[68] History must not only be confronted or, to the extent it has been neglected, ignored, denied, or remains enigmatic, revealed. It must, above all, be disenterred and (re)*constituted* as part of a larger effort to, in the words of Harris's preface to *The Whole Armour* (1962), "relate new content or new existences to a revised canvas of community. That new content ironically—on another level—is very old or eclipsed or buried material of consciousness which cries out for relief."[69] It is ultimately the haunting, only half-hidden specters that threaten a society borne of genocide, conquest, slavery, and colonization. For Harris, vision lies in the retrieval of "those 'monsters' back into ourselves as native to psyche, native to a quest for unity through contrasting elements, through the ceaseless tasks of the creative imagination to digest and liberate contrasting spaces rather than succumb to implacable polarisations."[70] Beyond pointing to a fundamental lack of achieved resolution and the tenuous stability of an already fragile enough polity, such polarizations threaten to imperil the actual or future possibility of an intrinsically viable society.

It is easy enough, Harris tells us in "The Unresolved Constitution" (1968), "to pronounce on [our] 'historylessness,' oppression, etc., . . . once one does not creatively descend into the disorder of it: an escape route which may well prove the best of two worlds and permit a skillful shortcircuiting of real crisis or confrontation in depth."[71]

One senses an edge of desperation creeping in on Harris's idealist optimism. In its essential motivation, however, this "act of memory" is very close to the concept of the "backward glance" which informs George Lamming's work. Particularly as exemplified in the formal construction and unfolding of *Season of Adventure* (1960), it is clear that Lamming, with Harris, regards it as at once revelatory and unavoidable, cathartic, redemptive, and epigenetic. An encounter with the past remains preliminary to any lasting resolution of the conflicts inherited by a colonial or, as in *Season's* prophetic focus on the public and private failures of the fictitious San Christobal's First Republic, the neocolonial West Indian society this fictitious island nation is meant to represent. Harris's poetic evocations of an exuberant, primal Guyanese hinterland, his experiments with time and Amerindian cosmology and legend, all of which are primary among his *spaces*, collapse the borders of Lamming's comparatively more "realistic" aesthetic to border on the far edges of the phantasmagoric and mythical. They also add a continental dimension to the more clearly insular concentration of the majority of his island-born colleagues. Thus the journey into the American interior of a racially representative crew of ill-fated conquistadores, in *Palace of the Peacock* (1960), is organized around "the odd fact" that his characters' "living names matched the names of a famous dead crew that had sunk . . . and been drowned to a man. . . . But this in no way interfered with their life-like appearance and spirit and energy. Such a dreaming coincidence [the participant narrator tells us] we were beginning to learn to take in our stride."[72] The past, far from being dead, is a quite vital *presence*.

These living-dead, in the prismatically resonant title of one of Lamming's other works, are Harris's *Natives of My Person* (1972). One is more immediately reminded of the contrastive simultaneity of historical epochs, the blend of documentable history and the only apparently marvelous—because *real*—

characteristic of Alejo Carpentier's fiction after *!Ecué Yambá Ó!*. The journey of Harris's crew is not unlike one of Carpentier's protagonist's attempts to (re) trace *The Lost Steps* (1959). Carpentier also is drawn, he tells us, by "the possibility of establishing certain possible synchronisms—American and recurrent—outside of time, which would relate one thing to another, past to present . . . [so as] to convey our truths . . . to understand and measure them in their proper dimensions."[73] His work also shares Harris's overarching ambition to demonstrate that an area to which Hegel himself would deny any independent historic particularity "is not without history but in fact is," in Harris's formulation, "pregnant with a native constitution—the 'lost' ages of men."[74]

The "Muse of History," as Derek Walcott calls it, is also at the heart of the combination of fiction, history, and popular (oral) tradition that Edouard Glissant seeks to synthesize in his work. It is a way of reclaiming—giving continuity, a distinct spiritual "itinerary," and form to—his *Antillanité*. "The child that I was and the man that I am," he writes in *La Lézarde*, "have this in common: they confuse legend and history."[75] In *Le quatrième siècle* (1964) that melding, evoked in the evolving relationship between Mathieu, the young "urban" intellectual, and Papa Longoue, the maroon-descendant *quimboiseur* who gives him a greater confidence in himself, is the source of a knowledge more true than the superficially logical "reporting in minute detail of dates and facts [that] masks the [subterraneously] continuous movement of our past."[76] Pointing to "a land of tremblings, of extinguished or forbidden truths," it is, most crucially, "profoundly rooted in the drama of West Indian soil . . . expresses *another* reality, *another* style of life."[77] As a principle of composition, Glissant's "confusion" represents a mode of historical reassessment, of national authentication, an act of faith in "the open, collective swelling and creative fertility of a culture which has been chosen,"[78] a registry of its contending divisions, and the projection forward of its distinct future possibilities.

The prologue to Andrew Salkey's epic poem, *Jamaica* (1973), significantly entitled "I into history, now," pithily condenses the different general aspects of this epochal obsession. Situated in the present, its anonymous speaker's speech denotes an ordinary, undistinguished member of the working class or rural peasantry. Invoking the authority of the mocking, cunningly inventive spider-man of West African and Caribbean folk tradition, he introduces his subject with the following self-affirming declaration:

I into history, now.
Is not'ing but song I singing
an' name I callin'

an' blood I boilin'
an' self I raisin'
in a correc' Anancy form,
a t'ing I borrow
an' makin' me own
wit'out pretty please
or pardon.

The ground from which it issues is an unpostponable question. "I sittin' down,"
he goes on,

scratchin' me 'ead
an' watchin' the scene,
an' I ol' as Anancy
but wit'out f'rim brain-box,
an' I say to me self,
"Is how the *mento* music go?"[79]

The question is analogous to Edward Brathwaite's "Where then is the nigger's /
home?"[80] Like Brathwaite's more broadly encompassing New World trilogy—
*Rights of Passage* (1967), *Masks* (1968), and *Islands* (1969)—the poem that
follows this prologue is an extended answer to the gravid, deceptively simple
query on which it concludes. Organized to highlight the historical evolution
and collectively representative moments that culminate in the present, it is
simultaneously a summation of the very process of articulation and primacy of
the question.

The assumption of a collective voice and condition—an expressed or implied "we" already seen in Césaire and inextricable from the work of nearly
every contemporary Caribbean writer—is generically corollary to the narrative
unfolding of this epos. The postulation of the claims of this "we" as against
those of the constrictively individualist "I" achieve a particularly transparent
formulation in Pedro Mir's *Viaje a la muchedumbre* (Journey to the multitude),
1972, especially in what are perhaps its two most celebrated poems: "Hay un
pais en el mundo" (There is in the world a country) and "Contracanto a Walt
Whitman (canto a nosotros mismos)" (Countersong to Walt Whitman [A Song
of Ourselves]). Drawing together the cultural and esthetic burden of both, Mir
writes in Canto 9 of the latter poem:

For
        what has a great unflagging poet ever been
        if not a limpid pool

in which a people discovers the precisions
of its face?

. . . . . . . . . . . .

And what
if not a string on an infinite guitar
on which the fingers of nations play
their simple, their own strong
and true and innumerable song?[81]

Mir's intertextual evocation of the *Leaves of Grass* effectively places the failed promise of Whitman's democratic vistas and the deterioration, in the contemporary United States, of nineteenth-century liberalism into the rigorously individualist egotism demanded by modern capitalism in critical counterpoint to the collective ethic and vision of a historically awakening Latin American. Thus, in Canto 15, he adds:

And now
the word is no longer
I
the word fulfilled
the touchstone word to start the world anew.
And now
now the word is
us.[82]

As all the above examples suggest, the engagement with history is intimately related to the search for an appropriately comprehensive metaphor in which to distill the essential element(s) of the Caribbean experience and condition. It is part of the quest for an archetypal symbol, a prototypical image, one that embodying the collective aspiration to a future whose promise remains unfulfilled might, by honest recognition and acceptance of the facts of continuing sociocultural conflict and contradiction, absorb and articulate as it strives to transcend the legacies of the past.

The figures most recently and frequently proposed—Ariel, Crusoe, Caliban—are, to some extent, a relative barometer of the ideological faith and wider programmatic outlook of those that invoke them. As the personification of the patrician middle-class, classically educated creole intellectual whose self-proclaimed mission is to properly educate the masses to an acceptance of its leadership as a civic-minded representative of an aristocracy of the spirit, Ariel has lost all the power of appeal it originally commanded. It has joined Prospero in being increasingly identified as the outdated emblem of a fundamentally conservative vision.

Those of more liberal, individualist predisposition, made uncomfortable by Marxist or black nationalist politics, by a too radically absolute insistence on the claims of any one class or racial group, regard the isolate Crusoe as a more persuasively compelling symbol. They see in his isolation, in his struggle to impose order and give meaning to his new insular environment, in his impulse to (re)create a society almost from scratch, the simile of their own predicament, the image of its anguish and the extent of its opportunity. In Walcott, for example, Crusoe is the embodiment of "a truly tough aesthetic of the New World [which] neither explains [n]or evaporates in pathos."[83] He emerges as the personification of a new Adam whose task, like the artist's, is that of "rechristening" the landscape and giving things their name. It is, at the same time, the oblique expression of Walcott's unresolved feeling of being "wrenched by two styles."[84] It has about it an element of the utopian. In John Hearne, whose novels disenchantedly record the deterioration and ultimate untenability of any alliance between the liberal middle class and the proletariat as a consequence of what he regards as the "irremediably anarchic" responses of the latter,[85] it is Crusoe's isolation and a sense of being out of sync with the time that emerges most forcefully.

In Naipaul, however, the image of the shipwreck achieves its most nihilistically conservative extreme. The token of his peculiar situation as "the late intruder, the picturesque Asiatic, linked to neither [ex-master nor ex-slave]," which he shares with the narrator of The Mimic Men (1967),[86] is also the expression of his vision of the inherent disorder and stasis of the West Indies, and of his antipathy for "this romanticism [which] begins by sympathizing with the oppressed and ends by exalting their values."[87] In Naipaul the image of the shipwreck, one of his favorite conceits, is an image almost wholly of abandonment and alienation, of a marginality the only answer to which is flight, recurrent and unending. It is the complement of his perception of islands and colonies as crushingly insular enclosures "incapable of supporting large events."[88]

As a symbol of the anonymous masses and quintessence of the full scope of the battle against a (neo)colonial condition, Caliban, the Antillean slave mocked but unceasingly struggling for his freedom in Shakespeare's Tempest, has by contrast emerged as the emblem of those most unambiguously identified with the black and mestizo underclass. In the cultural revindication and social challenge of that underclass they see the revolutionary potential for a truly egalitarian Caribbean society. Specifically invoked by Césaire, Brathwaite,

Lamming, Roberto Fernández Retamar (Cuba, 1930– ), and Anthony Phelps (Haiti, 1928– ), among others, this image of Caliban is also kindred to the spirit that informs the work of Jacques Stéphen Alexis, René Dépestre (Haiti, 1926– ), Edouard Glissant, Martin Carter (Guyana, 1927– ), and Luis Rafael Sánchez.

Whatever the emphasis in the choice of overarching metaphor (Andrew Salkey's almost protoplasmic "Caribbea" and José Luis González's description of Puerto Rico as an Afro-foundationed "four-story country" are another two),[89] its function is that of crystallizing, in a single synthetic image, the perceived tensions and traumas of a context and repertoire of preoccupations these writers all share in common.

As the primary instrument of the writer's craft and part of the problem of how best to give holistic expression to an authentically Caribbean *voice*, language itself is an unavoidable leitmotiv of contemporary Caribbean writing. It is at the crux of the struggle to forge a genuinely indigenous literary idiom. The essence of that idiom, beyond recording the region's linguistic personality, is a deliberate avoidance of even implicit apology, condescension, or narrative and linguistic distance from its subject. It must itself be a dramatic example of the dynamic process of creolization, of cultural confrontation and creation it attempts faithfully to examine and reflect.

The essence of this project is a continuing pursuit of internal consistency, of an intrinsically confirming cultural complementarity between *what* is said and *how*. This is of course the sign of an enhanced recognition of the linguistic complexity and rich diversity of Caribbean life and culture. But, beyond any semiotic appreciation of its multiple layers or any possible analytical reduction of them to a fetishlike exaltation of literary language for its own sake, this concern with language is reflective of its crucial role as a vehicle for directly engaging the problem of *who is* and speaks for the Caribbean. It is meant to convey the importance of a (re)consideration of who is speaking and being heard—and who *should* be. The choice of idiom(s) as a central element of this question of literary authenticity, then, is at once a choice of *person(s)* as well as *persona(s)*. It is, in addition, a way of signaling what in the lives and cultural experience of the people who are its subject is specifically unique and important. In that context, the concern with language is part of a challenge to the hegemonic, aristocratic pretension of a too narrow perception of Antillean culture, especially one premised on a rigorous, hierarchical divorce between the oral and scribal traditions—between a superficial "folkloric realism" of surfaces and one more deeply textured by the contagious "magic" of popular tradition and belief—to which even some of the most immediate predecessors of this literature made some obeisance. The establishment of what Glissant openly refers to as *Le discours antillais* (1981) requires, in consequence, the creative supersession of the limiting stasis and ahistorically purist negation these rigid dichotomies, sometimes unwittingly, ratify. "The era of Languages which are proud of their purity," Glissant writes, "must end for man: the adventure of speech (of the poetic theories of the diffracted but recomposed world) begins."[90] An exploration of the intersecting middle ground between social realism and an art that, in Alexis's words, "is indissolubly linked to the myth, the symbol, the stylized, the heraldic, even the hieratic"; that "achieves a new balance, more contrasted, a composition equally harmonious in its contradiction, a wholly internal grace, born of singularity and antithesis" is one of the facets of that adventure.[91] But it is especially the shared space between the oral and scribal traditions, originally hierarchically separated, that emerges as its most undisputably proper literary terrain. Beyond its national or regional appropriateness, as an aspect of the above balance, it is regarded as the space that holds the potential for a genuinely "universal" projection of the particular and the reconceptualization even of exhausted conventional notions of what is literature. "My language," Glissant says of his own work, "tries to place itself at the limits of writing and speaking, which seems to me something rather new in the literary enterprise. I am not talking about writing and speaking in the sense that one says a novelist imitates ordinary speech, that he has a style at writing degree zero, etc. I mean a synthesis, a synthesis of the syntax of the written and the syntax of the spoken, which I am interested in creating."[92]

Despite Derek Walcott's characteristic emphasis on his own "schizophrenia," the similarity of his comments on the issue is striking in its corroboration of a common mode, its intent, and aspiration. In "What the Twilight Says: An Overture," one of his most revealing statements about the sources and emergence of his art, Walcott recalls his early struggle to *find a voice* truly reflective of a colonial reality in which "both the patois of the street and the language of the classroom hid the elation of discovery." He concludes his recollection by noting the young writer's apprehension that

What would deliver him [the New World Negro] from servitude was the forging of a language that went beyond mimicry, a dialect which had the force of revelation as it invented names for things, one which finally settled on its own mode of inflection, and which began to create an oral culture of chants, jokes, folksongs and fables . . . a new melodic inflection meant a new mode, there was no better beginning. It did not matter how rhetorical, how dramatically heightened the language was if its tone were true, whether its subject was the rise and fall of a Haitian King or a small island fisherman, and the only way to recreate this language was to share in the torture of its articulation. This did not mean the jettisoning of "culture" but, by the writer's creative use of his schizophrenia, an eclectic fusion of the old and the new. So the people . . . [he adds] awaited a language.[93]

In the evocatively lyrical novels of Simone Schwarz-Bart (Guadeloupe, 1938– )—*Pluie et vent sur Telumée Miracle* (1972) and *Ti Jean L'horizon* (1979) —the lore of the folk, this culture of oral storytelling, of proverbs, "chants, jokes, folk-songs and fables" is thus no longer limited to and *contained* in dialogue sequences, the quasi-anthropological commentary of an aloof third-person narrator, or explicative footnotes. Infused into the very linguistic fabric, narrative posture, and tone of the text, it is at the compositional heart of the tale. Linguistically poised between the oral and scribal traditions, Schwarz-Bart's novels also blend and move smoothly between the "two worlds" of African cultural retentions and European empiricist convention, of a cyclical and lineal cosmology, of the apparently fabulous and the "real," of the peasants of Font-Zombi's here and now and their easy familiarity and sense of enduring connection with the "Bridge of Beyond." The fundamentally creole texture— and intent—of these novels is as manifest in the spaces they bring together in elegant synthesis as in the details of the Lougandor women's story of heroic endurance or Guadeloupe's unregarded "long history, full of wonders, bloodshed and frustrations, and of desires no less vast than those that filled the skies of Nineveh, Babylon or Jerusalem" to which they pay tribute.[94] As the sign of that history, Schwarz-Bart, too, regards that synthesis as the true emblem of her "unbroken and unbreakable" black peasants' Caribbean identity, the reflection of a "victory in the heart of darkness, and [the evidence of their] . . . inexhaustible patience longer than all future defeats."[95]

In Luis Rafael Sánchez's *La guaracha del Macho Camacho* (1976), it is the dramatically contrastive juxtaposition of class and cultural languages, rather than any achieved synthesis, that allows the author to heighten our awareness of their continuing confrontation and, simultaneously, to "liberate the language [from] academic finickiness or social anxieties" and "make space for a kind of language [that of the lower classes] that having been branded as crude had no real place in our literature."[96] The synthesis of self-consciously rhetorical speech or literary performance and the immediacy of the oral tradition, indeed, emerges through a kind of fused polyphony. The novel's contrapuntal structure underscores "the need to transform colonial reality in all spheres—political, moral, even in the realm of the physical" to which the sensuous, percussive rhythms of its overarching musical motif are directly related.[97] The speech of Sánchez's characters, including that of his narrator(s), its relative communicative efficacy and intrinsic authenticity, becomes the linguistic mirror of their moral or political outlook as well as the measure of the paucity—or untapped richness—of imagination and spiritual resources available in their universe of meaning. Language itself thus becomes the contested terrain of a national ethos exposed to both internal and external assault. What finally emerges is a book whose idiom requires it, in the words of one critic, "to be read in Puerto Rican."[98] Sánchez's declared concern, like that of his other Antillean contemporaries, is "to corrupt the traditional text, to redefine the form [of the novel, in this case] from the inside out."[99] The ubiquitous presence of the figure of the *guaracha*, moreover, is calculated to emphasize the national character and communicative power of the (oral, Afro-Hispanic) traditions from which the irrepressible popular dance tune draws its pervasively subversive authority.

The idea that "the forms in a national culture must, before anything else, correspond to the character and tendencies of the people in question," which informs the full range of all this creative ferment and experimentation, naturally received a considerable impetus from the socialist nationalism of the Cuban Revolution. It marked a crucial juncture in the Caribbean's perception of itself. Cuba's radical rejection of the neocolonial arrangements that had, in the decades immediately preceding, become the status quo revivified as it redefined the terms of the anticolonial movement throughout the archipelago. Its early successes in health, education, and welfare, in the face of all attempts to isolate Cuba's example or "destabilize" its social experiment, dramatized the failures of the "The Puerto Rican Model of Development" and the limits of the liberal populist vision that inspired it.

Like the Haitian Revolution before it, the revolution in Cuba also gave a new dimension and vitality to the cultural articulation of the area. It stimulated a growing confidence in the region's capacity to achieve a genuine independence as well as in the value and necessity of relying on one's own reservoir of native resources, courage, and imagination as the only sure guarantee of that independence. One of its real achievements was, precisely, the inauguration of what amounted to a cultural renaissance, an enthusiastic, multifaceted blossoming of cultural and intellectual activity. Extending the compass of their vision and the commitments of their publication programs to include the nonhispanophone areas of the region, institutions like Casa de las Américas also gave renewed vigor and currency to a Pan-Caribbean outlook that the collapse of the West Indian Federation and a long tradition of mutual isolation between and among imperial regions had prevented from emerging more forcefully. N. D. Williams (Guyana, 195?) is only one of the several young and not so young talents its annual prize revealed or introduced to the hispanophone islands and a wider international audience.

Guyana's inauguration, in 1972, of a periodic, Caribbean-wide Festival of the Arts of changing venue, Carifesta, is a tribute to the growing attraction of that outlook. It continues to contribute to a cross-fertilization in the creative—popular and scribal—arts. The Grenadian Revolution, up to the moment of the invasion of the United States in 1983, gave still further encouragement to these initiatives. Its promise became a magnet of attraction for the Caribbean, and in particular West Indian, intelligentsia. The two conferences of Intellectual Workers for Regional Sovereignty of the Caribbean Peoples (1981, 1983), which it sponsored, ratified the trajectory of already evident trends. Like the work of so many of the writers of the region, they called for "a more comprehensive definition of culture,"[100] a definition more in consonance with the character of the region.

This challenge, in all its infinite variety, continues to lie at the heart of the literature the Caribbean produces. It is reflected in the pain, and sense of outrage and resolve, of Nancy Morejón's (Cuba, 1945– ) Cuaderno de Granada (1984) and in Miguel Barnet's (Cuba, 1940– ) continuing commitment to the recuperatively "documentary novel." It appears in the provocative historicism of Edgardo Rodríguez Juliá's (Puerto Rico, 1946– ) recent fiction, La renuncia del héroe Baltasar (1974) and La noche oscura del Niño Avilés (1984), and in the keen interest in the contradictory vitality of popular thought and feeling that emerges in his essays, Las tribulaciones de Jonás (1981) and La muerte de Cortijo (1983). It is there in the piquant vibrancy of the salsa-peppered language of Ana Lidia Vega's (Puerto Rico, 1946– ) short stories, Encancaranublado y otros cuentos de naufragios (1982), no less than in her feminist Pan-Caribbeanism. It is evident in Michael Thelwell's (Jamaica, 1939– ) reimagining of Jimmy Cliff's character in The Harder They Come (1980) and in N. D. Williams's exploration of the familiar theme of the school in a colonial setting and in his character's pilgrimage among the Rastafari in Ikael Torass (1976). It is what compels Earl Lovelace's (Trinidad, 1935– ) defense of the world of the calypsonian against the encroaching corruption of its commercialization. Indeed, it is there in the most recent work of nearly all his equally well-established colleagues throughout the region.

One is everywhere struck by the continuing aptness of José Martí's shrewd observation, in Our America (1891). "Nations stand and greet one another," he wrote. "'What are we?' is the mutual question, and little by little they furnish answers." "The youth of America are rolling up their sleeves," he went on, "digging their hands in the dough, and making it rise with the sweat of their brow. They realize that there is too much imitation and that creation holds the key to salvation. 'Create' is the password of this generation."[101] It remains still a critical watchword.

The ongoing evolution of the region's diverse, multilingual literature also makes manifest just how compelling the salients of its historic trajectory remain. The common ground of its emerging foci and convergent lines of force, moreover, serve to illustrate the demonstrable truth, insofar as literary expression is concerned, of the French abolitionist Victor Schoelcher's (1804–93) even more striking comment of more than a century ago:

> Examining the position of the Antilles in the middle of the sea, looking at the map where they can be seen nearly touching each other, one is taken by the thought that they might well, one day, together constitute a social body apart in the modern world. . . . They would be united in a confederation by a common interest and have a navy, industry, arts, a literature that would be their own. That will perhaps not happen in one, in two, in three centuries, but it will happen because it is only natural.[102]

It was a prophetically incisive, visionary thought. It, in addition, eloquently synthesizes what is at once the de facto achievement and continuing promise of the literature of the Caribbean.

## Notes

1. Walcott, *Selected Poems*, p. 52.
2. Ibid., p. 55.
3. Glissant, *The Ripening*, p. 207.
4. For an excellent, detailed analysis of the various and complex dimensions of this continuing confrontation between the Haitian black and mulatto elites—its historical and class roots, social content, political impact, and ideological articulation as "Noirisme" and a competing "Mulatto Legend"—see Nicholls, *From Dessalines to Duvalier*, esp. chapters 2–4. The theme is taken up again, more synoptically, by the same author in his more recent *Haiti in Caribbean Context*, esp. pp. 21–60.
5. "Once more" because it displaced significantly the previous rehistorization of the Caribbean carried out by its "discoverers," conquistadores, settlers, and their various overseas governments and patrons. An epic assumption and narrative vision regarding the heroic scope of their collective mission in the New World filled the presumed tabula rasa of indigenous culture and the landscape it inhabited. The primary function of this

earlier reconstitution of history was to rationalize, legitimate, institutionalize, and give transcendent importance to "the enterprise of the Indies." As paradigmatic trope, this epic notion proved to be a powerfully cohesive, figuratively elastic, and especially adaptable image, which served equally well the very distinct and even contradictory interests of crown, conquistador, metropolitan investor, clergy, and settler.

6. *Le Républicain*, October 1, 1836. Quoted in Dash, *Literature and Ideology in Haiti*, p. 9. On the ideas of Nau and his colleagues, see Nicholls, *From Dessalines to Duvalier*, p. 74ff.

7. *L'Union*, November 16, 1837. Quoted in Dash, *Literature and Ideology*, p. 9.

8. *Selected Writings of Bolívar*, Vol. 1, *1810–1822*, Lewis Bertrand, trans., Harold A. Bierck, ed. (New York: Colonial Press, Inc., 1951), p. 181. See also pp. 110–11.

9. Ibid., p. 176.

10. Quoted in Bonilla, *Azúcar y abolición*, pp. 99–100, and Foner, *A History of Cuba, 1492–1845*, 1:198.

11. José Antonio Saco, *Contra la anexión* (Havana: Cultural, 1928), 1:224. Quoted in Foner, *A History of Cuba, 1492–1845*, 1:198. Saco was equally unambiguous as to the underlying concern of the class for whom he spoke: "In our present circumstances," he emphasized, "the political revolution is necessarily accompanied by a social revolution and the social revolution is the complete ruin of the Cuban [white] race" (p. 47).

12. Martí, *Letras fieras*, p. 101.

13. Martí, *On Art and Literature*, p. 307.

14. Martí, *Our America*, p. 90.

15. Martí, *On Art and Literature*, p. 306.

16. Alonso, *El Jíbaro*, p. 3.

17. Ibid.

18. Ibid.

19. Ibid., p. 115. It is only in the expanded edition of 1884, a decade after the decree of emancipation, that slavery emerges as a theme in the work—and then only to record, and applaud post factum, its legal abolition as a historic event, not to indicate or examine the substance of its larger social and historical significance, cultural legacy, or the continuing challenge of the ex-slave's presence to any reductive, noninclusive definition of the "national" identity.

20. Ibid., p. 40.

21. Ibid., p. 19.

22. Ibid., p. 53.

23. Ibid., p. 97.

24. Ibid., p. 62.

25. Ibid., p. 113. See also pp. 161–66 which include "1833–1883. Perdemos or ganamos," his generally favorable retrospective on the period added to the expanded edition of 1884.

26. For a perceptively sustained examination of the workings of this process in Galván's novel, particularly as it relates to his "patriarchal" assumptions about the

"Motherland," see Sommer, *One Master for Another*, p. 51ff. Sommer's critical examination of this "The Other Enriquillo," to which we are all indebted, is more analytically sound and comprehensive in its appreciation of Galván's ideological loyalties and programmatic outlook than any of his more conventional liberal and conservative commentators. It is also more sensitive to the concretely historical context out of which his novel emerges than is Selwyn R. Cudjoe's oftentimes anachronistically radical "materialist" critique. Ironically ignoring precisely the actual material circumstances to which Galván's novel is a response, Cudjoe misperceives it as "an almost literal retelling of the resistance of the Indians in precise historical details, in which Galván's sympathy seems to lie with the Indians," whose primary intent Cudjoe vaguely and much too rhetorically specifies as being "to remind the people of the constant need to resist foreign oppression." Neither "the people" nor the "foreigners," as Galván concretely understood these terms and their programmatic implications, are convincingly defined or delineated. See Cudjoe's *Resistance and Caribbean Literature* (Athens: Ohio University Press, 1980), pp. 83–89, 146.

27. Galván, *Enriquillo*, p. 267. My translation.

28. See his "Creative Writing of the West Indies during the Period of Slavery," p. 48. Those who wrote then, Brathwaite notes, "were Englishmen or English-oriented creoles" and "the work they produced was not 'West Indian' but 'tropical English.' Their models were the metropolitan masters. . . . Their limitations stems from the fact that few of them were able to record a truly convincing experience."

29. J. J. Thomas, *Froudacity*, p. 16. With pointed irony, he also spoke of the "ineffable privilege of whitemanship" (p. 117).

30. Ibid., p. 18.

31. Froude, *The English in the West Indies*, p. 14.

32. J. J. Thomas, *Froudacity*, p. 51.

33. Ibid., p. 75.

34. Ibid., p. 114.

35. Ibid., p. 155.

36. Ibid., p. 179.

37. Ibid., p. 120.

38. *Revista de Las Antillas* 5 (August 1913): 118–19. Quoted in José Luis Méndez, "Literature and National Liberation," p. 12. My translation.

39. Pedreira, *Insularismo*, p. 112.

40. Quoted in Quiñones, "La poesía negra de Luis Palés Matós," p. 23.

41. Angel Augier, *Nicolás Guillén: Notas para un estudio biográfico-crítico*, vol. 2 (Universidad de las Villas, 1964), p. 286.

42. Guillén, *Obra poetica*, 1:113–14.

43. Guillén, *Prosa de prisa*, 2:70.

44. Ibid.

45. Guillén, *Obra poetica*, 2:19.

46. Carpentier, *El reino de este mundo*, pp. 5–11.

47. As its class base dramatically widened to become increasingly defined as the almost inevitable journey of the economically marginal, displaced, and unemployed lower classes, the experience of emigration to the metropolitan centers, which had played so signal a part in the emergence of Pan-Africanism, négritude, and the work of the anglophone Antillean writers of the decade of the fifties, would by the late sixties and seventies produce a much more genuinely "settled" emigrant/migrant—as opposed to a transient student's, middle- or upper-class sojourner's—literature of Caribbeans in the metropolis to which Claude McKay's (1889–1948) work had already pointed. The writing of the Puerto Ricans Pedro Pietri, Edward Rivera, Nicholasa Mohr, and Caryl Phillips (Saint Kitts, 1958), novels (*The Final Passage* [1985], *A State of Independence* [1986]), and commentary (*The European Tribe* [1987]) are only some among the several most recent examples of a challengingly "new," although still theoretically "unlocated" and not yet fully examined, dimension of Caribbean writing.

48. Kennedy, *The Negritude Poets*, p. 15.

49. L. G. Damas, *Pigments* (Paris: Présence Africaine, 1962), p. 57. The translation by Ellen Conroy Kennedy is included in Kennedy, *The Negritude Poets*.

50. Walcott, *Selected Poems*, p. 4.

51. "Misère d'une poésie," *Légitime défense* (1932). Reproduced in Kesteloot, *Antologie négro-africaine*, p. 77. The English translation is by Shapiro, whose more extended excerpt appears in *Negritude*, p. 70.

52. Sander, *From Trinidad*, p. 5.

53. The pertinent texts in each case are Fanon, *Black Skin, White Masks*, *The Wretched of the Earth*, and, in *Toward the African Revolution*, the essays on "Racism and Culture" and "West Indians and Africans"; Rodney, *The Groundings with My Brothers*; Dépestre, *Bon jour et adieu a la négritude*; and "Jean Price-Mars y el mito del Orfeo negro," in *Por la revolución, por la poesía* (Montevideo: Biblioteca de Marcha, 1970), reprinted as "Jean Price-Mars et le mythe de L'Orphee Noir où les aventures de la négritude," in *Pour la revolution, pour la poesie* (Ottawa: Lemeac, 1974).

54. Césaire, *Return to My Native Land*. Unless otherwise indicated, all citations in this paragraph are from this volume.

55. *Letter to Maurice Thórez* (Paris: Editions Présence Africaine, 1957), p. 12.

56. Roumain, *Analyse schematique*, p. 28.

57. Maryse Conde, "Autour d'une littérature antillaise," *Présence Africaine* 81 (1972): 175. Quoted in Roget, "Edouard Glissant and Antillanite," p. 158.

58. Albert Gomes, *Through a Maze of Colour* (Trinidad: Key Caribbean Publications, Limited, 1974), p. 17.

59. Ibid., p. 77.

60. Sander, *From Trinidad*, p. 7.

61. A. J. Seymour, *Growing Up in Guyana*, p. 53.

62. Mais, *The Three Novels of Roger Mais*, p. 197. "[T]hey make animals without hope of the men who pass through here" (p. 211), which one of his main characters is

thinking in the prison, emerges as a metaphor for the larger society's treatment of its marginalized, poor, and destitute citizens.

63. *John O'London's Weekly*, May 1, 1953. Quoted in Ramchand, *The West Indian Novel*, p. 179, and Gilkes, *The West Indian Novel*, p. 35.

64. Reid, "Author's Note," in *New Day*, n.p.

65. George E. Kent, "A Conversation with George Lamming," *Black World* 22 (March 1973): 92. Quoted in Paquet, *The Novels of George Lamming*.

66. Alexis, "Of the Marvelous Realism of the Haitians," p. 265. This is a special issue devoted to the First International Conference of Negro Writers and Artists.

67. John Hearne, ed., *Carifesta Forum: An Anthology of 20 Caribbean Voices* (Kingston, Jamaica, 1976), p. vii.

68. Wilson Harris, "The Unresolved Constitution," *Caribbean Quarterly* 14 (March–June 1968): 44.

69. Harris, "Author's Note" to *The Whole Armour*, p. 9.

70. Ibid., p. 8.

71. Harris, "The Unresolved Constitution," p. 44.

72. Harris, *Palace of the Peacock*, pp. 23–24.

73. Stephanie Merrim, trans., "Tientos y diferencias," *Latin American Literature and Arts Review* 28 (January–April 1981): 28.

74. Harris, "The Unresolved Constitution," p. 46.

75. Glissant, *The Ripening*, p. 103.

76. Glissant, *L'Intention poétique*, p. 19.

77. Glissant, "Note sur une 'poésie nationale,'" p. 395.

78. Glissant, *L'Intention poétique*, p. 24.

79. Salkey, *Jamaica*, pp. 10–11.

80. Brathwaite, *The Arrivants*, p. 77.

81. Mir, *Viaje a la muchedumbre*, p. 50.

82. Ibid., p. 62.

83. Walcott, "The Muse of History," p. 2.

84. Walcott, *The Gulf*, p. 32.

85. John Hearne, *Land of the Living* (London: Faber and Faber, 1961), p. 84. For a more detailed discussion of this particular aspect of Hearne's work, see Roberto Márquez, "The Stoic and the Sisyphean: John Hearne and the Angel of History," *Anales del Caribe* (Havana) 3 (1983): 240–77.

86. Naipaul, *The Mimic Men*, p. 93.

87. Naipaul, "What's Wrong with Being a Snob," p. 37.

88. Naipaul, *The Middle Passage*, p. 29, and *The Mimic Men*, p. 160.

89. José Luis Gonzáles, *El país de cuatro pisos*.

90. Glissant, *L'Intention poétique*, p. 41.

91. Alexis, "Of the Marvelous Realism of the Haitians," p. 265.

92. Quoted in Roget, "Edouard Glissant," p. 166.

93. *Dream on Monkey Mountain and Other Plays* (New York: Straus and Giroux, 1970), p. 17.

94. Schwarz-Bart, *Between Two Worlds*, p. 4.

95. Ibid., p. 254.

96. Helen Calaf Aguera, "Luis Rafael Sánchez Speaks about *Macho Camacho's Beat*," *Latin American Literature and Arts Review* 28 (January–April 1981): 40.

97. Ibid.

98. Barradas, *Para leer en puertorriqueño*.

99. Ibid., p. 41.

100. From text of general letter of invitation to Second Conference of Intellectual Workers for Regional Sovereignty of the Caribbean Peoples, 1983.

101. Martí, *Our America*, p. 92.

102. Victor Schoelcher, *Les Colonies français* (1852). Quoted in Guérin, *The West Indies*, p. 174. Also cited in Roget, "Edouard Glissant," p. 155. My translation.

# Bibliography

## Newspapers

*Catholic Opinion* (Kingston, Jamaica)
*The Daily Gleaner* (Kingston, Jamaica)
*Guardian Weekly* (Port of Spain, Trinidad)
*Los Angeles Times*
*Moko* (Port of Spain, Trinidad)
*Public Opinion* (Kingston, Jamaica)
*Le Républicain* (Haiti)
*The Star* (Kingston, Jamaica)
*Sunday Guardian* (Port of Spain, Trinidad)
*Trinidad Guardian*
*L'Union* (Haiti)
*Washington Post*

## Published Materials

Adamson, Alan H. *Sugar without Slaves: The Political Economy of British Guiana, 1838–1904*. New Haven: Yale University Press, 1972.

Alexander, Robert. *Communism in Latin America*. New Brunswick, N.J.: Rutgers University Press, 1957.

Alexis, Jacques Stéphen. "Of the Marvelous Realism of the Haitians." *Présence Africaine* 8–10 (June–November 1956).

Alonso, Manuel A. *El Jíbaro*. Río Piedras, Puerto Rico: Editorial Cultural, 1968.

Anderson, Jervis. *This Was Harlem: A Cultural Portrait, 1900–1950*. New York: Farrar, Straus, Giroux, 1982.

Bailey, W., and Diffie, J. W. *Porto Rico: A Broken Pledge*. New York: The Vanguard Press, 1931.

Balboa, Troya y Quesada de Silvestre. *Espejo de paciencia*. Reprint. Miami: Ediciones Universal, 1968.

Baldwin, Hanson W. "A Military Perspective." In *Cuba and the United States*, edited by John Plank. Washington, D.C.: Brookings Institution, 1967.

Barradas, Efraín. *Para leer en puertorriqueño: Acercamiento a la obra de Luis Rafael Sánchez*. Río Piedras, Puerto Rico: Editorial Cultural, 1981.

Barrett, Leonard E. *The Sun and the Drum: African Roots in Jamaican Folk Tradition.* Kingston, Jamaica: Sangster's Book Stores, 1976.

Barry, Tom; Wood, Beth; and Preusch, Deb. *The Other Side of Paradise: Foreign Control in the Caribbean.* New York: Grove Press, 1984.

Bartlett, Christopher J. "British Reaction to the Cuban Insurrection of 1868–78." *Hispanic American Historical Review* 37 (August 1957): 296–312.

Basdeo, Sabadeo. "Walter Citrine and the British Caribbean Workers Movement during the Moyne Commission Hearing, 1938–1939." In *Politics, Society and Culture in the Caribbean,* edited by Blanca Silvestrini, pp. 239–55. San Juan: University of Puerto Rico, 1983.

Bastide, Roger; Morin, Françoise; and Raveau, François. *Les Haitiens en France.* Paris: Mouton, 1974.

Bauer, Arnold J. "Rural Workers in Spanish America: Problems of Peonage and Oppression." *Hispanic American Historical Review* 59 (February 1979): 34–63.

Beck, Horace. "The Bubble Trade." *Natural History* 85 (December 1976): 38–47.

Beckford, George L. "Caribbean Rural Economy." In *Caribbean Economy: Dependence and Backwardness,* edited by George L. Beckford, pp. 77–91. Mona, Jamaica: Institute of Social and Economic Research, University of the West Indies, 1975.

―――. *Persistent Poverty: Underdevelopment in Plantation Economies of the Third World.* New York: Oxford University Press, 1972.

Beckwith, Martha Warren. *Black Roadways.* Chapel Hill: University of North Carolina Press, 1929.

Bell, Ian. *The Dominican Republic.* Boulder, Colo.: Westview, 1981.

Bendix, Reinhard. *Nation-Building and Citizenship: Studies of Our Changing Social Order.* New York: John Wiley, 1964.

Benjamin, Jules. *The United States and Cuba: Hegemony and Dependent Development, 1880–1934.* Pittsburgh: University of Pittsburgh Press, 1977.

Benn, Stanley I. "Nationalism." In vol. 4 of *The Encyclopedia of Philosophy,* edited by Paul Edwards, pp. 442–45. New York: Macmillan and Free Press, 1967.

Benoist, Jean. *L'Archipel Inachevé: Culture et société aux Antilles française.* Montreal: Les Presses de l'Université de Montréal, 1972.

Bergad, Laird W. *Coffee and the Growth of Agrarian Capitalism in Nineteenth-Century Puerto Rico.* Princeton: Princeton University Press, 1983.

Bermann, Karl. *Under the Big Stick: Nicaragua and the United States since 1948.* Boston: South End Press, 1986.

Best, Lloyd. "The Choice of Technology Appropriate to Caribbean Countries." Working Paper, no. 15, July 1976. Centre for Developing Area Studies, McGill University, Montreal. Reprinted March 1979.

―――. "The February Revolution." *Tapia* (December 1970).

Bisnauth, D. "The East Indian Immigrant Society in British Guiana, 1891–1930." Ph.D. thesis, University of the West Indies, 1977.

Blanco, Tomás. *Prontuario histórico de Puerto Rico*. San Juan: Biblioteca de Autores Puertorriqueños, 1935.

Blanshard, Paul. *Democracy and Empire in the Caribbean*. New York: MacMillan, 1947.

Blasier, Cole, and Mesa-Lago, Carmelo, eds. *Cuba in the World*. Pittsburgh: University of Pittsburgh Press, 1979.

Bolland, O. Nigel. *The Formation of a Colonial Society: Belize from Conquest to Crown Colony*. Baltimore: Johns Hopkins University Press, 1977.

_____. "Systems of Domination after Slavery: The Control of Land and Labor in the British West Indies after 1838." *Comparative Studies in Society and History* 23 (1981): 591–619.

Bonilla, Raúl Cepero. *Azúcar y abolición: Apuntes para una historia crítica del aboliciónismo*. Havana: Editorial Cenit, 1948.

_____, and Campos, Ricardo. "A Wealth of Poor: Puerto Ricans in the New Economic Order." *Daedalus* 110 (Spring 1981): 133–76.

Bosch, Juan. *Composición social dominicana: Historia e interpretación*. Santo Domingo: Alfa y Omega, 1978.

_____. *De Cristóbal Colón a Fidel Castro: El Caribe, frontera imperial*. Santo Domingo: Alfa y Omega, 1979.

_____. *La guerra de la restauración y la revolución de abril*. Santo Domingo: Corripio, 1982.

Braithwaite, Lloyd. *Social Stratification in Trinidad: Preliminary Analysis*. Mona, Jamaica: Institute of Social and Economic Research, University of the West Indies, 1975.

Brana-Shute, Rosemary, comp. and ed. *A Bibliography of Caribbean Migration and Caribbean Immigrant Communities*. Gainesville: Center for Latin American Studies, University of Florida, 1983.

Brathwaite, Edward. *The Arrivants: A New World Trilogy*. New York and London: Oxford University Press, 1973.

_____. "Creative Writing of the West Indies during the Period of Slavery." *Savacou* 1 (June 1970).

_____. *Islands*. London: Oxford University Press, 1969.

_____. *Masks*. London: Oxford University Press, 1968.

_____. *Rights of Passage*. London: Oxford University Press, 1967.

Brereton, Bridget. *A History of Modern Trinidad, 1783–1962*. Kingston, Jamaica; Exeter, N.H.: Heinemann, 1981.

_____. *Race Relations in Colonial Trinidad, 1870–1900*. Cambridge: Cambridge University Press, 1979.

Bridges, Yseult. *Child of the Tropics, Victorian Memoirs*. London: Collins; Harvell Press, 1980.

Bryce-Laporte, Roy; Stinner, William F.; and de Albuquerque, Klaus, eds. *Return Migration and Remittances: Developing a Caribbean Perspective*. Washington, D.C.: Smithsonian Institution, 1982.

Cabranes, José A. *Citizenship and the American Empire: Notes on the Legislative History of the United States Citizenship of Puerto Ricans*. New Haven: Yale University Press, 1979.

Caine, William Ralph Hall. *The Cruise of the Port Kingston*. London: Collier, 1908.

*Caribbean Databook*. Washington, D.C.: Caribbean Central American Action, 1983.

Carnegie, Charles V. "If You Lose the Dog, Grab the Cat." *Natural History* (October 1983): 28, 30–34.

Carpentier, Alejo. *¡Écué Yambá Ó! Historia afro-cubano*. Madrid: Editorial España, 1933.

————. *El reino de este mundo*. [Caracas, Venezuela]: Organización Continental Festival del Libro, n.d.

Carr, Raymond. *Puerto Rico: A Colonial Experiment*. New York: Vintage Books, 1984.

Carrington, Edwin. "Industrialization in Trinidad and Tobago since 1950." *New World Quarterly* 4 (Crop Time, 1968): 37–43.

Cassá, Roberto. *Historia social y económica de la República Dominicana*. 2 vols. Santo Domingo: Alfa y Omega, 1979 and 1981.

Castellanos, Juan. *Elegía a la muerte de Juan Ponce de León: Donde se cuenta la conquista de Boriquen*. Reprint. San Juan: Instituto de Cultura Puertorriqueño, 1967.

Castles, Stephen. *Here for Good: Western Europe's New Ethnic Minorities*. London: Pluto Press, 1984.

Caulfield, Mina Davis. "Imperialism, the Family, and Cultures of Resistance." In *Capitalism and the Family*, edited by M. D. Caulfield et al. San Francisco: Agenda Publishing Co., 1976.

Césaire, Aimé. *Cahier d'un retour au pays natal*. Reprint. Paris, 1971.

————. *Return to My Native Land*. Translated by John Berger and Anna Bostock. Baltimore: Penguin Books, 1970.

Chernick, Sidney E. *The Commonwealth Caribbean: The Integration Experience: A World Bank Country Economic Report*. Baltimore: Johns Hopkins University Press, 1978.

Clark, Truman R. *Puerto Rico and the United States, 1917–1933*. Pittsburgh: University of Pittsburgh Press, 1975.

Clark, Victor S. *Porto Rico and Its Problems*. Washington, D.C.: The Brookings Institution, 1930.

Clarke, Colin G. *Kingston, Jamaica: Urban Development and Social Change, 1692–1962*. Berkeley: University of California Press, 1975.

Cliff, Jimmy. *The Harder They Come* (Sound track). Mango MLPS 9202, 1980.

Corbitt, Duvon C. "Cuban Revisionist Interpretations of Cuba's Struggle for Independence." *Hispanic American Historical Review* 43 (August 1963): 395–404.

Cortado, James W. "A Case of International Rivalry in Latin America: Spain's Occupation of Santo Domingo, 1853–1865." *Revista de Historia de América* 82 (July/December 1976): 53–82.

Cox, Winston. "The Manufacturing Sector in the Economy of Barbados." In *The Economy of Barbados, 1946–1980*, edited by Delisle Worrell, pp. 47–80. Bridgetown, Barbados: Central Bank of Barbados, 1982.

Crahan, Margaret E., and Knight, Franklin W., eds. *Africa and the Caribbean: The Legacies of a Link*. Baltimore: Johns Hopkins University Press, 1979.

Craig, Susan. "Background to the 1970 Confrontation in Trinidad and Tobago." In vol. 1 of *Contemporary Caribbean: A Sociological Reader*, edited by Susan Craig, pp. 385–423. 2 vols. Maracas, Trinidad and Tobago: The College Press, 1981.

Craton, Michael. *Testing the Chains: Resistance to Slavery in the British West Indies*. Ithaca: Cornell University Press, 1982.

Cripps, Louise L. *The Spanish Caribbean: From Columbus to Castro*. Cambridge, Mass.: Schenkman, 1981.

Cumper, George Edward. *The Social Structure of Jamaica*. Reprint. Millwood, N.Y.: Kraus, 1978.

Curtin, Philip D. *The Atlantic Slave Trade: A Census*. Madison: University of Wisconsin Press, 1969.

————. *Two Jamaicas: The Role of Ideas in a Tropical Colony, 1830–1865*. Reprint. New York: Atheneum, 1970.

Dash, J. Michael. *Literature and Ideology in Haiti, 1915–1961*. Totowa, N.J.: Barnes and Noble, 1981.

Davis, David Brion. *The Problem of Slavery in the Age of Revolution*. Ithaca: Cornell University Press, 1976.

————. *The Problem of Slavery in Western Culture*. Ithaca: Cornell University Press, 1966.

De A. Reid, Ira. *The Negro Immigrant: His Background, Characteristics and Social Adjustment, 1899–1937*. New York: Columbia University Press, 1939.

Debien, Gabriel. *Les esclaves aux Antilles Françaises XVII$^e$-XVIII$^e$ siècles*. Basse Terre: Société d'Histoire de la Guadeloupe, 1974.

DeBoissiere, Ralph. *Crown Jewel: A Novel*. Reprint. London: Allison and Busby, 1981.

————. *Rum and Coca Cola: A Novel*. Reprint. London: Allison and Busby, 1984.

de Kadt, Emanuel, ed. *Patterns of Foreign Influence in the Caribbean*. Oxford: Royal Institute of International Affairs, 1972.

DeLisser, Herbert George. *Jane's Career: A Story of Jamaica*. New York: Africana Publishing Corporation, 1971.

Delson, Roberta Marx, ed. *Readings in Caribbean History and Economics: An Introduction to the Region*. New York: Gordon and Breach, 1981.

Dépestre, René. *Bon jour et adieu a la négritude*. Paris: R. Laffont, 1980.

Deutsch, Karl W., and Foltz, William J., eds. *Nation-Building*. New York: Atherton, 1963.

Díaz Quiñones, Arcadio. "La poesía negra de Luis Palés Matós: Realidad y conciencia de su dimensión colectiva." *Sin Nombre* 1 (September 1970).

Dietz, James L. *Economic History of Puerto Rico: Institutional Change and Capitalist Development*. Princeton: Princeton University Press, 1986.

*Documents on the Constitutional History of Puerto Rico*. 2d ed. Washington, D.C.: Office of Puerto Rico, 1964.

Domínguez, Jaime de Jesús. *La anexión de la República Dominicana a España.* Vol. 1. Santo Domingo: Editora de la Universidad Autónoma de Santo Domingo, 1979.

Domínguez, Jorge I., ed. *Cuba: Internal and International Affairs.* Beverly Hills, Calif.: Sage Publications, 1982.

————. *Cuba: Order and Revolution.* Cambridge, Mass.: Harvard University Press, 1978.

Drescher, Seymour. *Econocide: British Slavery in the Era of Abolition.* Pittsburgh: University of Pittsburgh Press, 1977.

Dumoulin, John. *Azúcar y Lucha de Clases, 1917.* Havana: Editorial de Ciencias Sociales, 1980.

Duncan, Kenneth, and Rutledge, Ian, eds. *Land and Labour in Latin America: Essays on the Development of Agrarian Capitalism in the Nineteenth and Twentieth Centuries.* Cambridge and New York: Cambridge University Press, 1977.

Eaton, George E. *Alexander Bustamante and Modern Jamaica.* Kingston: Kingston Publishers, 1975.

Eisenstadt, S. N., and Rokkan, Stein, eds. *Building States and Nations: Models and Data Resources.* 2 vols. Beverly Hills, Calif.: Sage Publications, 1973.

Eisner, Gisela. *Jamaica, 1830–1930: A Study of Economic Growth.* Manchester: Manchester University Press, 1961.

Fagg, John E. *Cuba, Haiti, and the Dominican Republic.* Englewood Cliffs, N.J.: Prentice-Hall, 1965.

Fanon, Frantz. *Black Skin, White Masks.* New York: Grove Press Inc., 1967.

————. *Toward the African Revolution.* New York: Grove Press, 1967.

————. *The Wretched of the Earth.* New York: Grove Press, 1968.

Farrell, Terrence. "Arthur Lewis and the Case for Caribbean Industrialization." *Social and Economic Studies* 29 (December 1980): 54–59.

Fermor, Patrick Leigh. *The Traveller's Tree: A Journey through the Caribbean Islands.* London: J. Murray, 1950.

Fermoselle, Rafael. *Política y color en Cuba: La guerrita de 1812.* Montevideo: Géminis, 1974.

Fernández Méndez, Eugenio. *El significado histórico del Grito de Lares.* San Juan, Puerto Rico: El Cemí, 1973.

*Fidel y la religión, conversaciones con el Sacerdote Dominico Frei Betto.* Santo Domingo: Editora Alfa y Omega, 1985.

Foner, Philip S. *A History of Cuba and Its Relations with the United States.* 2 vols. New York: International Publishers, 1962–63.

————. *The Spanish-Cuban-American War and the Birth of American Imperialism, 1895–1902.* 2 vols. New York: Monthly Review, 1972.

Fraser, Peter. "The Fictive Peasantry: Caribbean Rural Groups in the Nineteenth Century." In *Contemporary Caribbean: A Sociological Reader,* edited by Susan Craig, 1:319–48. Maracas, Trinidad and Tobago: The College Press, 1981.

Friedlaender, Heinrich. *Historia económica de Cuba 1*. Havana: Editorial de Ciencias Sociales, 1978.

Froude, James Anthony. *The English in the West Indies or The Bow of Ulysses*. London: Longman, Green, 1888.

Frucht, Richard. "A Caribbean Social Type: Neither 'Peasant' nor 'Proletarian.'" In *Peoples and Cultures of the Caribbean: An Anthropological Reader*, edited by Michael M. Horowitz, pp. 190–97. Garden City, N.Y.: Natural History Press, 1971.

Galván, Manuel de Jesús. *Enriquillo: Leyenda histórica Dominicana*. New York: Las Americas Publishing Co., 1964.

García, Gervasio L., and Rivera, Quintero Angel G. *Desafío y Solidaridad: Breve Historia del Movimiento Obrero Puertorriqueño*. Río Piedras: Ediciones Huracán, 1982.

García Ochoa, María Asunción. *La política española en Puerto Rico durante el siglo XIX*. Río Piedras: Editorial de la Universidad de Puerto Rico, 1982.

Gates, Brian, ed. *Afri-Caribbean Religions*. London: Ward Lock, 1980.

Gayer, Arthur D.; Homan, Paul T.; and James, Earle K. *The Sugar Economy of Puerto Rico*. New York: Columbia University Press, 1938.

Geggus, David. "British Opinion and the Emergence of Haiti, 1791–1805." In *Slavery and British Society*, edited by James Walvin, pp. 123–49. London: Macmillan, 1982.

————. *Slavery, War, and Revolution: The British Occupation of Saint-Dominique, 1793–1798*. Oxford: Clarendon Press; New York: Oxford University Press, 1982.

Gellner, Ernest. *Nations and Nationalism*. Oxford: Basil Blackwell, 1983.

Genovese, Eugene. *From Rebellion to Revolution: Afro-American Slave Revolts in the Making of the Modern World*. Baton Rouge: Louisiana State University Press, 1979.

Gilkes, Michael. *The West Indian Novel*. Boston: Twayne Publishers, 1981.

Girvan, Norman. "After Rodney—The Politics of Student Protest in Jamaica." *New World Quarterly* 4 (High Season, 1968): 59–68.

————. *Aspects of the Political Economy of Race in the Caribbean*. Atlanta: IBW Press, 1975.

Glissant, Edouard. *Le discours antillais*. Paris: Editions du Seuil, 1981.

————. *L'Intention poétique*. Paris: Editions du Seuil, 1969.

————. *La Lézarde*. Paris: Editions du Seuil, 1958.

————. "Note sur une 'poésie nationale' chez les peuples noirs." *Les Lettres Nouvelles* 4 (1956): 391–97.

————. *Le quatrième siècle*. Paris: Editions du Seuil, 1964.

————. *The Ripening*. Translated by Frances Frenaye. New York: George Braziller, 1959.

González, José Luis. *El país de cuatro pisos*. Río Piedras, Puerto Rico: Ediciones Huracán, 1980.

González Vales, Luis. "Toward a Plantation Society (1860–1866)." In *Puerto Rico: A Political and Cultural History*, edited by Arturo Morales Carrión, pp. 79–107. New York: Norton, 1983.

Gordon, Shirley. *A Century of West Indian Education*. London: Longmans, 1963.

Gray, Obika. "State Power and Forms of Political Opposition in Post-Colonial Jamaica." Ph.D. dissertation, University of Michigan, 1983.

Guérin, Daniel. *The West Indies and Their Future*. London: Dennis Dobson, 1961.

Guerra, Ramiro. *Guerra de los 10 años*. Reprint. 2 vols. Havana: Editorial de Ciencias Sociales, 1972.

Guillén, Nicolás. *Obra poética, 1920–1958*. Vol. 1. Havana: Instituto Cubano del Libro, 1972.

———. *Obra poética*. Vol. 2. Havana: Instituto Cubano del Libro, 1973.

———. *Prosa de prisa, 1929–1972*. Vol. 2. Havana: Editorial Arte y Literatura, 1975.

———. *Sóngoro cosongo: Motivos de son*. Reprint. Buenos Aires: Ediciones Losada, 1975.

Hagelberg, G. B. *The Caribbean Sugar Industries: Constraints and Opportunities*. New Haven: Antilles Research Program, 1974.

Hagopian, Mark N. *The Phenomenon of Revolution*. New York: Dodd, Mead, and Company, 1974.

Hall, Douglas. "The Ex-Colonial Society in Jamaica." In *Patterns of Foreign Influence in the Caribbean*, edited by Emanuel de Kadt, pp. 23–48. London and New York: Published for the Royal Institute of International Affairs by Oxford University Press, 1972.

———. "The Flight from the Estates Reconsidered: The British West Indies, 1838–42." *Journal of Caribbean History* 10–11 (1978): 7–24.

———. *Free Jamaica, 1839–1865: An Economic History*. Reprint. New Haven: Yale University Press, 1959.

Haraksingh, Kusha. "Culture, Religion, and Resistance among Indians in the Caribbean." In *Indian Labour Immigration*, edited by U. Bissoondoyal and S. B. C. Servansing, pp. 223–37. Mauritius: Mahatma Gandhi Institute, 1986.

———. "Labor, Technology and the Sugar Estates in Trinidad, 1879–1914." In *Crisis and Change in the International Sugar Economy, 1860–1914*, edited by Bill Albert and Adrian Graves, pp. 133–46. Edinburgh: ISC Press, 1984.

Harewood, Jack. "West Indian People." In *Caribbean Economy: Dependence and Backwardness*, edited by George L. Beckford, pp. 1–33. Mona, Jamaica: Institute of Social and Economic Research, University of the West Indies, 1975.

Harootyan, Robert, and Segal, Aaron. "Appendix: Tables on Caribbean Emigration." In *Population Policies in the Caribbean*, edited by Aaron Lee Degal. Lexington, Mass.: Lexington Books, 1979.

Harris, Wilson. *The Palace of the Peacock*. London: Faber and Faber, 1960.

———. *The Whole Armour and the Secret Ladder*. London: Faber and Faber, 1973.

Haynes, Cleviston. "Sugar and the Barbadian Economy, 1946–1980." In *The Economy of Barbados, 1946–1980*, edited by Delisle Worrell, pp. 81–105. Bridgetown, Barbados: Central Bank of Barbados, 1982.

Healy, David. *The United States in Cuba, 1898–1902.* Madison: University of Wisconsin Press, 1963.

Hearn, Lafcadio. *Two Years in the French West Indies.* New York: Harper and Brothers, 1890.

Heinl, Robert Dels, and Heinl, Nancy Gordon. *Written in Blood: The Story of the Haitian People, 1492–1971.* Boston: Houghton Mifflin, 1978.

Henriques, Fernando. *Family and Colour in Jamaica.* London: Eyre and Spottiswoode, 1953.

Herskovits, Melville Jean, and Herskovits, Frances S. *Trinidad Village.* New York: Knopf, 1947.

Higman, Barry W. *Slave Population and Economy in Jamaica, 1807–1834.* Cambridge: Cambridge University Press, 1976.

_____. *Slave Populations of the British Caribbean.* Baltimore: Johns Hopkins University Press, 1984.

Hill, Errol. *The Trinidad Carnival: Mandate for a National Theatre.* Austin: University of Texas Press, 1972.

Hoetink, H. *The Dominican People, 1850–1900: Notes for a Historical Sociology.* Translated by Stephen K. Ault. Baltimore: Johns Hopkins University Press, 1982.

Hope, Kempe R. "Recent Performances and Trends in the Caribbean Economy: A Study of Selected Caribbean Countries." *ISER Occasional Papers Series,* no. 4. Saint Augustine, Trinidad: Institute of Social and Economic Studies, 1980.

Horowitz, Michael. *Morne Paysan: Peasant Village in Martinique.* New York: Columbia University Press, 1967.

Inter-American Development Bank. *Economic and Social Progress in Latin America: 1986 Report.* Washington, D.C., 1986.

Jagan, Cheddi. *Forbidden Freedom: The Story of the Suppression of the People's Constitutional Government of British Guiana.* New York: International Publishers, 1954.

Jamaica, Department of Statistics. *The Labour Force, 1976.* Jamaica, 1977.

*The Jamaica Hansard: Proceedings of the House of Representatives.* Kingston, 1953–54, 1963–64, 1968–69.

James, C. L. R. *Beyond a Boundary.* London: Hutchinson, 1963.

_____. *The Black Jacobins: Toussaint L'ouverture and the San Domingo Revolution.* Revised ed. London: Allison and Busby, 1980.

_____. *The Case for West Indian Self-Government.* London: Hogarth Press, 1933.

_____. *Minty Alley.* Revised. London: New Beacon Press, 1971.

_____. *State Capitalism and the World Revolution.* 3d ed. Detroit: Facing Reality Press, 1969.

Jayawardena, Chandra. *Conflict and Solidarity in a Guianese Plantation.* London: University of London, 1963.

Jefferson, Owen. "Is the Jamaican Economy Developing?" *New World Quarterly* 5 (Cropover 1972): 1–12.

Jesús Toro, Rafael de. *Historia económica de Puerto Rico*. Cincinnati, Ohio: South-Western Publishing Company, 1982.

Jiménez, Rodríguez, and Canelo, Rosajilda Vélez. *El precapitalismo dominicano de la primera mitad del siglo XIX, 1750–1850*. Santo Domingo: Universidad Autónoma de Santo Domingo, 1980.

Karch, Cecilia A. "The Role of the Barbados Mutual Life Assurance Society during the International Sugar Crisis of the Late 19th Century." In *A Selection of Papers Presented at the Twelfth Conference of the Association of Caribbean Historians (1980)*, edited by K. O. Laurence, pp. 95–133. Barbados: Government Printing Department, n.d.

Kennedy, Ellen Conroy, ed. *The Negritude Poets: An Anthology of Translations from the French*. New York: Viking Press, 1975.

Kerr, Madeline. *Personality and Conflict in Jamaica*. London: Collins, 1963.

Kesteloot, Lilyan. *Antologie négro-africaine: Panorama critique des prosateurs, poètes et dramaturges noirs du XXᵉ siècle*. Verviers, Belgium: Editions Gerard and Co., 1967.

King, Martin Luther, Jr. *Where Do We Go from Here: Chaos or Community?* Boston: Beacon Press, 1967.

Kingsley, Charles. *At Last: A Christmas in the West Indies*. London: Macmillan, 1871.

Kiple, Kenneth F. *Blacks in Colonial Cuba, 1774–1899*. Gainesville: University of Florida Press, 1976.

Kirkpatrick, Jeane J. *The Reagan Phenomenon and Other Speeches on Foreign Policy*. Washington, D.C.: American Enterprise Institute, 1983.

Klein, Herbert S., and Engerman, Stanley L. "The Transition from Slave to Free Labor: Notes on a Comparative Economic Model." In *Between Slavery and Free Labor: The Spanish-Speaking Caribbean in the Nineteenth Century*, edited by Manuel Moreno Fraginals, Frank Moya Pons, and Stanley L. Engerman, pp. 255–69. Baltimore: Johns Hopkins University Press, 1985.

Knight, Franklin W. *The African Dimension of Latin American Societies*. New York: MacMillan, 1974.

———. *The Caribbean: The Genesis of Fragmented Nationalism*. New York: Oxford University Press, 1978.

———. "Jamaican Migrants and the Cuban Sugar Industry, 1900–1934." In *Between Slavery and Free Labor: The Spanish-Speaking Caribbean in the Nineteenth Century*, edited by Manuel Moreno Fraginals, Frank Moya Pons, and Stanley Engerman, pp. 94–114. Baltimore: Johns Hopkins University Press, 1985.

———. *Slave Society in Cuba during the Nineteenth Century*. Madison: University of Wisconsin Press, 1970.

———. "The Social Structure of Cuban Slave Society in the Nineteenth Century." *Annals of the New York Academy of Sciences* 292 (1977): 259–66.

Knowles, William H. *Trade Union Development and Industrial Relations in the British West Indies*. Berkeley: University of California Press, 1959.

Kothari, Rajni, ed. *State and Nation Building: A Third World Perspective*. New Delhi: Allied, 1976.

Kuznets, Simon. "Modern Economic Growth: Findings and Reflections." In *Population, Capital and Growth*, edited by Simon Kuznets, pp. 165–84. New York: W. W. Norton and Company, 1973.

Labat, Jean Baptiste. *Nouveau Voyage aux îles de L'Amérique*. La Haye, 1722.

La Guerre, John Gaffar, ed. *Calcutta to Caroni: The East Indians of Trinidad*. London: Longmans, 1974.

Laguerre, Michel S. *American Odyssey: Haitians in New York City*. Ithaca: Cornell University Press, 1984.

Lalinde Abadía, Jesús. *La administración española en el siglo XIX puertorriqueño (Pervivencia de la variante indiana del decisionismo castellano en Puerto Rico)*. Seville, Spain: Escuela de Estudios Hispano-Americanos, Universidad de Sevilla, 1980.

Lamming, George. "I Do Not Sleep to Dream: Education, History and Society: A Caribbean Perspective." *Caliban* 3 (Fall–Winter 1980): 103–8.

Langley, Lester D. *Struggle for the American Mediterranean: United States-European Rivalry in the Gulf Caribbean, 1776–1904*. Athens: University of Georgia Press, 1976.

————. *The United States and the Caribbean, 1900–1970*. Athens: University of Georgia Press, 1980.

————. *The United States and the Caribbean in the Twentieth Century*. Revised. Athens: University of Georgia Press, 1982.

Laszlo, Ervin. *Individualism, Collectivism, and Political Power: A Relational Analysis of Ideological Conflict*. The Hague: Martinus Nijhoff, 1963.

Laurence, K. O. *Immigration into the West Indies in the Nineteenth Century*. Barbados: University of the West Indies, 1971.

Laviera, Tato. *Ame Rícan*. Houston: Arte Público Press, 1985.

Le Riverend, Julio. *Historia Económica de Cuba*. 4th ed. Havana: Editorial Pueblo y Educación, 1981.

Levine, Barry B. *Benjy López: A Picaresque Tale of Emigration and Return*. New York: Basic Books, 1980.

Levitt, Kari, and Best, Lloyd. "Character of Caribbean Economy." In *Caribbean Economy: Dependence and Backwardness*, edited by George L. Beckford, pp. 34–60. Mona, Jamaica: Institute of Social and Economic Research, University of the West Indies, 1975.

Lewis, David E. *Reform and Revolution in Grenada, 1950–1981*. Havana: Casa de las Américas, 1984.

Lewis, Gordon K. *The Growth of the Modern West Indies*. New York: Monthly Review Press, 1969.

————. *Puerto Rico: Freedom and Power in the Caribbean*. New York: Monthly Review of Books, 1963.

Lewis, W. Arthur. "The Industrialization of the British West Indies." *Caribbean Eco-*

*nomic Review* 2 (1950): 1–39.

———. *Labour in the West Indies: The Birth of a Workers' Movement*. Reprint. London: Beacon Books, 1977.

———. "Memorandum on Social Welfare in the British West Indies." Serial no. 45 in *West India Royal Commission Evidence*. London: HMSO, 1987.

Liden, Harold J. *History of the Puerto Rican Independence Movement*. Vol. 1 (Nineteenth Century). Hato Rey, Puerto Rico: Master Typesetting, 1981.

Lindsay, Louis. *The Myth of Independence: Middle Class Politics and Non-Mobilization in Jamaica*. Mona, Jamaica: Institute of Social and Economic Research, University of the West Indies, 1975.

Linz, Juan. "Early State-Building and Late Peripheral Nationalism against the State: The Case of Spain." In vol. 2 of *Building States and Nations: Analysis by Region*, edited by S. N. Eisenstadt and Stein Rokkan, pp. 32–116. Beverly Hills, Calif.: Sage, 1973.

Livingstone, William P. *Black Jamaica: A Study in Evolution*. London: S. Low Marston, 1899.

López, Adalberto. "The Birth of a Nation: Puerto Rico in the Nineteenth Century." In *The Puerto Ricans: Their History, Culture, and Society*, edited by Adalberto López, pp. 49–93. Cambridge, Mass.: Schenkman, 1980.

Lovejoy, Paul E. "The Volume of the Atlantic Slave Trade: A Synthesis." *Journal of African History* 22 (1982): 473–501.

Lowenthal, David. *West Indian Societies*. Oxford: Oxford University Press, 1972.

McIntyre, Alister. "Adjustments of Caribbean Economies to Changing International Economic Relations." In *Proceedings of the Sixteenth West Indies Agricultural Economics Conference*, edited by Lloyd B. Rankine, pp. 11–22. Trinidad and Tobago: Faculty of Agriculture, University of the West Indies, 1983.

MacMillan, W. M. *Warning from the West Indies*. Freeport, N.Y., 1971.

Mais, Roger. *Black Lightning*. Revised ed. Exeter, N.H.: Heinemann, 1983.

———. *Brother Man*. Revised ed. Exeter, N.H.: Heinemann, 1974.

———. *The Hills Were Joyful Together*. Revised ed. London: Longmans, 1978.

———. *The Three Novels of Roger Mais*. London and Kingston, Jamaica: Sangster's Book Stores and Jonathan Cape Ltd., 1970.

Maldonado, Rita M. *The Role of the Financial Sector in the Economic Development of Puerto Rico*. New York: Federal Deposit Insurance Corporation, 1970.

Maldonado-Denis, Manuel. *Puerto Rico: A Socio-Historic Interpretation*, translated by Elena Vialo. New York: Vintage Books, 1972.

Mandle, Jay R. *Big Revolution, Small Country: The Rise and Fall of the Grenada Revolution*. Lanham, Md.: North-South Publishing Co., 1985.

———. *Patterns of Caribbean Development: An Interpretive Essay on Economic Change*. New York: Gordon and Breach, 1982.

———. *The Plantation Economy: Population and Economic Growth in Guyana, 1838–1960*. Philadelphia: Temple University Press, 1973.

Marrero, Levi. *Cuba: La forja de un pueblo: Estudios y conferencias.* San Juan, Puerto Rico: Editorial San Juan, 1971.

Marshall, Dawn I. *"The Haitian Problem": Illegal Migration to the Bahamas.* Mona, Jamaica: Institute of Social and Economic Research, University of the West Indies, 1979.

Marshall, Woodville K. "Commentary." In "Roots and Branches: Current Directions in Slave Studies," edited by Michael Craton. *Historical Reflections* 6 (1979): 243–48.

————, with Trevor Marshall and Bartley Gihlis. "The Establishment of a Peasantry in Barbados, 1840–1920." In *Social Groups and Institutions in the History of the Caribbean*, edited by Thomas Matthews, pp. 84–104. Río Piedras, Puerto Rico: Association of Caribbean Historians, 1975.

Martí, José. *Letras fieras.* Havana: Editorial Letras Cubanas, 1981.

————. *On Art and Literature: Critical Writings.* Edited by Philip S. Foner. New York and London: Monthly Review Press, 1982.

————. *Our America: Writings on Latin America and the Struggle for Cuban Independence.* Edited by Philip S. Foner. New York and London: Monthly Review Press, 1977.

Martínez Vergne, Teresita. "An Experiment in Capitalism: Central San Vicente, 1873–1892." Ph.D. dissertation, University of Texas at Austin, 1985.

Mathews, T. *Puerto Rican Politics and the New Deal.* Gainesville: University of Florida Press, 1960.

Meeks, Brian. "The Development of the 1970 Revolution in Trinidad and Tobago." M.A. thesis, University of the West Indies at Mona, 1976.

Meinig, D. W. *Atlantic America, 1492–1800.* Vol. 1 of *The Shaping of America: A Geographical Perspective on 500 Years of History.* New Haven: Yale University Press, 1986.

Mejía-Ricart, Tirso, ed. *La sociedad dominicana durante la Primera República, 1844–1861.* Curso monográfico. Santo Domingo: Editora de la Universidad Autónoma de Santo Domingo, 1977.

Mendes, Alfred. *Black Fauns.* London: Duckworth, 1935.

————. *Pitch Lake: A Story from Trinidad.* London: Duckworth, 1934.

Méndez, José Luis. "Literature and National Liberation in the Caribbean." *Calibán* 1 (Fall–Winter 1975).

Mesa-Lago, Carmelo. *Cuba in the 1970s: Pragmatism and Institutionalization.* Albuquerque: University of New Mexico Press, 1978.

Millett, Allan R. *The Politics of Intervention: The Military Occupation of Cuba, 1906–1909.* Columbus: Ohio State University Press, 1968.

Mintz, Sidney W. "The Caribbean as a Socio-Cultural Area." In *Peoples and Cultures of the Caribbean: An Anthropological Reader*, edited by Michael M. Horowitz, pp. 17–46. Garden City, N.Y.: Natural History Press, 1971.

————. *Caribbean Transformations.* Baltimore: Johns Hopkins University Press, 1974.

————. *From Plantations to Peasantries in the Caribbean.* Washington, D.C.: Woodrow

354    Bibliography

Wilson International Center for Scholars, 1984.
————. *Sweetness and Power: The Place of Sugar in Modern History*. New York: Viking, 1985.
Mir, Pedro. *Viaje a la muchedumbre*. Mexico City: Siglo XXI editores, 1972.
Mittelholzer, Edgar. *A Swarthy Boy*. London: Putnam, 1963.
Monclova, Lidio Cruz. *Historia de Puerto Rico* (Siglo XIX). 3 vols. Río Piedras: Editorial Universitaria, 1962.
Moore, R. J. "East Indians and Negroes in British Guiana, 1838–1880." Ph.D. thesis, University of Sussex, 1970.
Morales Carrión, Arturo. *Puerto Rico: A Political and Cultural History*. New York: Norton, 1983.
Mordecai, John. *The West Indies: The Federal Negotiations*. London: Allen and Unwin, 1968.
Moreira, Neiva, and Bissio, Beatriz. "The Cubans in Africa." *Third World* 1 (May 1979): 6–35.
Moreno Fraginals, Manuel. *El Ingenio: Complejo Socioeconómico Cubano del Azúcar*. 3 vols. Vol. 1. Havana: Editorial de Ciencias Sociales, 1978.
————. *El Token Azucarero Cubano*. Havana: Museo Numismático de Cuba, n.d.
Mortimer, Delores, and Bryce-Laporte, Roy, eds. *Female Immigrants to the United States: Caribbean, Latin American and African Experiences*. Washington, D.C.: Smithsonian Institution, 1981.
Muñoz, Heraldo, and Tulchin, Joseph, eds. *Latin American Nations in World Politics*. Boulder, Colo.: Westview Press, 1984.
Muñoz Marín, Luis. *Memorias, 1898–1940*. San Juan: Universidad Interamericana de Puerto Rico, 1982.
Munro, Dana G. *Intervention and Dollar Diplomacy in the Caribbean, 1900–1921*. Princeton: Princeton University Press, 1964.
Munroe, Trevor. *The Politics of Constitutional Decolonization: Jamaica, 1944–62*. Mona, Jamaica: Institute of Social and Economic Studies, 1972.
Murch, Arvin. *Black Frenchmen: The Political Integration of the French Antilles*. Cambridge, Mass.: Schenkman, 1971.
Murray, David R. *Odious Commerce: Britain, Spain, and the Abolition of the Cuban Slave Trade*. Cambridge: Cambridge University Press, 1980.
Naipaul, V. S. *A House for Mr. Biswas*. New York: McGraw-Hill, 1961.
————. *The Middle Passage: Impressions of Five Societies: British, French, and Dutch in the West Indies and South America*. London: Andre Deutsch, 1962.
————. *The Mimic Men*. New York: Macmillan, 1967.
————. "What's Wrong with Being a Snob." In *Critical Perspectives on V. S. Naipaul*, edited by Robert D. Hamner, pp. 34–38. Washington, D.C.: Three Continents Press, 1977.
Nettleford, R. *Mirror, Mirror: Identity, Race and Protest in Jamaica*. Kingston, Jamaica: W. Collins and Sangster, 1970.

Newton, Velma. *The Silver Men: West Indian Labour Migration to Panama, 1850–1914*. Mona, Jamaica: Institute of Social and Economic Research, University of the West Indies, 1984.

Nicholls, David. "East Indians and Black Power in Trinidad." *Race* 12 (April 1971): 443–59.

———. *From Dessalines to Duvalier: Race, Colour, and National Independence in Haiti*. Cambridge: Cambridge University Press, 1979.

———. *Haiti in Caribbean Context: Ethnicity, Economy and Revolt*. New York: St. Martins Press, 1985.

Nichols, John Spicer. "The Mass Media: Their Functions in Social Conflict." In *Cuba: Internal and International Affairs*, edited by Jorge I. Domínguez, pp. 71–111. Beverly Hills, Calif.: Sage Publications, 1982.

Nietschmann, Bernard. "Ecological Change, Inflation, and Migration in the Far West Caribbean." *Geographical Review* 69 (1979): 1–24.

Nove, Alec. *The Economics of Feasible Socialism*. London: George Allen and Unwin, 1983.

Ortega y Gasset, José. *The Revolt of the Masses*. New York: Norton, 1932.

O'Shaughnessy, Hugh. *Grenada: Revolution, Invasion and Aftermath*. London: Sphere Books, 1984.

Ott, Thomas O. *The Haitian Revolution*. Knoxville: University of Tennessee Press, 1973.

Pagan, Bolívar. *Historia de los partidos Políticos Puertorriqueños, 1898–1956*. 2d ed. San Juan, 1959.

Paget, Henry, and Stone, Carl, eds. *The Newer Caribbean: Decolonization, Democracy, and Development*. Philadelphia: Institute for the Study of Human Issues, 1983.

Paget, Hugh. "The Free Village System in Jamaica." *Caribbean Quarterly* 1 (n.d.): 7–19.

Palmer, Colin A. *Human Cargoes: The British Slave Trade to Spanish America, 1700–1739*. Urbana: University of Illinois Press, 1981.

Paquet, Sandra Pouchet. *The Novels of George Lamming*. London; Kingston, Jamaica; and Port of Spain, Trinidad and Tobago: Heinemann, 1982.

Parry, J. H., and Sherlock, P. M. *A Short History of the West Indies*. 3d ed. New York: St. Martin's, 1971.

Pastor, Robert, ed. *Migration and Development in the Caribbean: The Unexplored Connection*. Boulder, Colo.: Westview Press, 1985.

———. "Sinking in the Caribbean Basin." *Foreign Affairs* 60 (Summer 1982).

Patterson, Orlando. *The Children of Sisyphus*. London: New Authors Limited, 1964.

———. "Migration in Caribbean Societies: Socioeconomic and Symbolic Resource." In *Human Migration: Patterns and Policies*, edited by William H. McNeill and Ruth S. Adams, pp. 106–45. Bloomington: Indiana University Press, 1978.

Payne, Anthony. *The International Crisis in the Caribbean*. Baltimore: Johns Hopkins University Press, 1984.

———. "The Rodney Riots in Jamaica: The Background and Significance of the Events of October 1968." *Journal of Commonwealth and Comparative Politics* 21 (July 1983): 158–74.

————, and Sutton, Paul, eds. *Dependency under Challenge: The Political Economy of the Commonwealth Caribbean*. Manchester: Manchester University Press, 1984.

Peach, Ceri. *West Indian Migration to Britain: A Social Geography*. New York: Oxford University Press, 1968.

Pedreira, Antonio S. *Insularismo: Ensayos de interpretación puertorriqueña*. San Juan: Biblioteca de Autores Puertorriqueños, 1934.

Pérez de la Riva, Juan. "Cuba: Población desarrollo." In *El barracón y otros ensayos*. Havana: Editorial de Ciencias Sociales, 1975.

Pérez Guzmán, Francisco, and Sarracino, Rodolfo. *La Guerra Chiquita: Una experiencia necesaria*. Havana: Editorial Letras Cubanas, 1982.

Pérez, Louis A. *Army Politics in Cuba, 1898–1958*. Pittsburgh: University of Pittsburgh Press, 1976.

————. *Cuba between Empires, 1878–1902*. Pittsburgh: University of Pittsburgh Press, 19[?]

————. *Cuba under the Platt Amendment, 1902–1934*. Pittsburgh: University of Pittsburgh Press, 1986.

Pérez, Víctor Manuel. *Las relaciones diplomáticas hispano-norteamericanos en torno al problema de Cuba, 1868–1898*. Colón, Panama: Hudson, 1973.

Perloff, Harvey S. *Puerto Rico's Economic Future*. Chicago: University of Chicago Press, 1950.

Phillips, Edsil. "The Development of the Tourist Industry in Barbados, 1946–1980." In *The Economy of Barbados, 1946–1980*, edited by Delisle Worrell, pp. 107–40. Bridgetown, Barbados: Central Bank of Barbados, 1982.

Picó, Fernando. *Historia General de Puerto Rico*. 3d ed. Río Piedras: Ediciones Huracán, 1986.

————. *Libertad y servidumbre en el Puerto Rico del siglo XIX*. Río Piedras: Ediciones Huracán, 1976.

Pluchon, Pierre. *Toussaint L'ouverture: De l'esclavage au Pouvoir*. Paris: L'Ecole, 1979.

*Pocketbook of Statistics: Jamaica, 1983*. Kingston: Department of Statistics, 1983.

Pons, Frank Moya. *La dominación haitiana, 1822–1844*. Santiago, Dominican Republic: Universidad Católica Madre y Maestra, 1978.

————. *Manual de Historia Dominicana*. 6th ed. Santiago, Dominican Republic: Universidad Católica Madre y Maestra, 1979.

Portell-Vila, Herminio. *Historia de la guerra do Cuba*. Havana: Historia Habanera, 1949.

Portes, Alejandro, and Bach, Robert. *Latin Journey: Cuban and Mexican Immigrants in the United States*. Berkeley: University of California Press, 1985.

Post, Ken. *Arise Ye Starvelings: The Jamaican Labour Rebellion of 1938 and its Aftermath*. The Hague: M. Nijhoff, 1978.

————. *Strike the Iron: A Colony at War, Jamaica, 1939–1945*. The Hague: Institute of Social Sciences, 1981.

Proudfoot, Malcolm J. *Population Movements in the Caribbean*. Port of Spain, Trinidad: Kent House, 1950.

Quintero Rivera, Angel. "Conflicto de clase en la política colonial." In *Relaciones inter-*

*nacionales y estructuras sociopolíticas en el Caribe*, pp. 22–57. Mexico City: Universidad Nacional Autónoma de México, 1980.

────. "Economía y política en Puerto Rico (1900–1934): Algunos elementos regional-structurales del crecimiento azucarero y el análisis de la política obrera." *Revista de Ciencias Sociales* 24 (1985): 393–454.

Ramchand, Kenneth. *The West Indian Novel and Its Background*. New York: Barnes and Noble Inc., 1970.

Ramos de Santiago, Carmen. *El desarrollo constitucional de Puerto Rico: Documentos y casos*. Río Piedras: Editorial Universitaria, 1973.

────. *El gobierno de Puerto Rico (desarrollo constitucional y política)*. Río Piedras: Editorial Universitaria, 1965.

Ramos-Mattei, Andres. *La hacienda azucarera: Su crecimiento y crisis en Puerto Rico (siglo XIX)*. San Juan: CEREP, 1981.

Ramsaran, Ramesh F. "Issues in Commonwealth Caribbean-United States Relations." In *Dependency under Challenge: The Political Economy of the Commonwealth Caribbean*, edited by Anthony Payne and Paul Sutton, pp. 179–203. Manchester: Manchester University Press, 1984.

Reid, Victor Stafford. *New Day*. Reprint. Kingston, Jamaica, and London: Sangster's Book Stores Ltd. with Heinemann Educational Books, 1970.

Renard, R. "A Social History of Guadeloupe and Martinique in the Post-Emancipation Nineteenth-Century." M.Phil. thesis, University of the West Indies, 1982.

*Report of the West India Royal Commission*. London: HMSO, 1897.

Reuben, Edwin P., and Reuben, Beatrice G. *Labour Displacement in a Labour Surplus Economy: The Sugar Industry of British Guiana*. Jamaica: Institute of Social and Economic Research, 1962.

Rice, C. Duncan. "Enlightenment, Evangelism, and Economics: An Interpretation of the Drive towards Emancipation in British West India." *Annals of the New York Academy of Sciences* 292 (1977): 123–31.

Richardson, Bonham. *Caribbean Migrants: Environment and Human Survival on St. Kitts and Nevis*. Knoxville: University of Tennessee Press, 1983.

────. *Panama Money in Barbados, 1900–1920*. Knoxville: University of Tennessee Press, 1985.

Richardson, Ronald Kent. *Moral Imperium: Afro-Caribbeans and the Transformation of British Rule, 1776–1838*. Westport, Conn.: Greenwood Press, 1987.

Riviere, William. "Black Power, NJAC and the 1970 Confrontation in the Caribbean: An Historical Understanding." University of the West Indies, Saint Augustine, 1972. Mimeographed.

────. "La Población Habanera." In *El barracón y otros ensayos*. Havana: Editorial de Ciencias Sociales, 1975.

Roberts, G. W., and Byrne, J. "Summary Statistics on Indentured and Associated Migration Affecting the West Indies, 1834–1918." *Population Studies* 20 (July 1966): 125–34.

Rodney, Walter. *The Groundings with My Brothers.* London: Bogle-L'Ouverture Publications Ltd., 1969. Reprinted 1971.

―――. *A History of the Guyanese Working People, 1881–1905.* Baltimore: Johns Hopkins University Press, 1981.

―――. "Plantation Society in Guyanas." *Review* 4 (Spring 1981): 643–66.

Rodó, Enrique. *Ariel.* Revised. Cambridge: Cambridge University Press, 1967.

Roget, Wilbert J. "Edouard Glissant and Antillanité." Ph.D. dissertation, University of Pittsburgh, 1975.

Roig de Leuchsering, Emilio. *1895 y 1898: Dos guerras cubanas: Ensayo de revaloración.* Havana: Cultural, 1945.

―――. *La guerra libertadora cubana de los treinta años 1868–1898: Razón de su victoria.* Havana: Oficina del Historiador de la Ciudad de la Habana, Colección Histórica Cubana y Americana, 1952.

―――. *Historia de Cuba en sus relaciones con los Estados Unidos y España.* 4 vols. Havana: Jesús Montero, 1938–41.

Rosenberg, Emily S. *Spreading the American Dream: American Economic and Cultural Expansion, 1890–1945.* New York: Hill and Wang, 1982.

Roumain, Jacques. *Analyse schematique, 1932–1934.* Editions: Idées Nouvelles, Idées Proletariennes, n.d.

―――. *Gouverneurs de la rosée.* Port-au-Prince, Haiti: Imprimerie de l'état, 1944.

Ryan, Selwyn D. *Race and Nationalism in Trinidad and Tobago: A Study of Decolonization in a Multiracial Society.* Toronto: University of Toronto Press, 1972.

Salkey, Andrew. *Jamaica.* London: Hutchinson, 1973.

Samaroo, Brinsley. "The Trinidad Labour Party and the Moyne Commission, 1938." In *Politics, Society and Culture in the Caribbean,* edited by Blanca Silvestrini, pp. 257–73. San Juan: University of Puerto Rico, 1983.

Sánchez, Luis Rafael. *La guaracha del Macho Camacho.* Buenos Aires: Ediciones de la Flor, 1976.

Sander, Reinhard W., ed. *From Trinidad: An Anthology of Early West Indian Writing.* New York: Africana Publishing Company, 1978.

Santos, Danilo de los, and Peguero, Valentina. *Visión general de la historia dominicana.* Santiago, Dominican Republic: Universidad Católica Madre y Maestra, 1981.

Saunders, G. "The Social History of the Bahamas, 1890–1953." Ph.D. thesis, University of Waterloo, 1985.

Scarano, Francisco A. *Sugar and Slavery in Puerto Rico: The Plantation Economy of Ponce, 1800–1850.* Madison: University of Wisconsin Press, 1984.

Schuler, Monica. *"Alas, Alas, Kongo": A Social History of Indentured African Immigration into Jamaica, 1841–1865.* Baltimore: Johns Hopkins University Press, 1980.

―――. "Myalism and the African Religious Tradition in Jamaica." In *Africa and the Caribbean: The Legacies of a Link,* edited by Franklin Knight and Margaret E. Crahan, pp. 65–79. Baltimore, 1979.

Schwarz-Bart, Simone. *Between Two Worlds.* New York: Harper and Row, 1981.

————. *Pluie et vent sur Telumée Miracle.* Paris: Editions du Seuil, 1972.

————. *Ti Jean L'horizon.* Paris: Editions du Seuil, 1979.

Scott, Michael. *Tom Cringle's Log.* Edinburgh: W. Blackwood, 1836.

Scott, Rebecca J. *Slave Emancipation in Cuba: The Transition to Free Labor, 1860–1899.* Princeton: Princeton University Press, 1985.

Scott, Robert E. "Nation-Building in Latin America." In *Nation-Building,* edited by Karl W. Deutsch and William J. Foltz, pp. 73–83. New York: Atherton, 1963.

"70-Years of Revolution." *Tapia* (December 1970): 9–13.

Sewell, William G. *Ordeal of Free Labor in the British West Indies.* New York: Harper and Brothers, 1862.

Seymour, A. J. *Growing Up in Guyana.* Georgetown, Jamaica: Labour Advocate Printers, 1976.

Shafer, Boyd C. *Nationalism: Its Nature and Interpreters.* Washington, D.C.: American Historical Association, 1976.

Shapiro, Norman. *Negritude: Black Poetry from Africa and the Caribbean.* New York: October House, Inc., 1970.

Silén, Juan Angel. *Historia de la nación puertorriqueña.* 2d ed. Río Piedras: Edil, 1980.

Silvestrini, B. G. "Women as Workers: The Experience of the Puerto Rican Woman in the 1930's," pp. 247–60. In *Women Cross-Culturally: Change and Challenge,* edited by R. Rohrlich-Leavitt. The Hague: Mouton, 1975.

Simey, Thomas Spensley. *Welfare and Planning in the West Indies.* Oxford: Clarendon Press, 1946.

Simpson, George Eaton. *Religious Cults of the Caribbean: Trinidad, Jamaica, and Haiti.* Río Piedras: Institute of Caribbean Studies, University of Puerto Rico, 1970.

Singham, Archie W. *The Hero and the Crowd in a Colonial Polity.* New Haven: Yale University Press, 1968.

Slater, Jerome. *A Reevaluation of Collective Security: The OAS in Action.* Columbus: Ohio State University Press, 1965.

Smith, Anthony D. *Theories of Nationalism.* London: Gerald Suckworth, 1971.

Smith, Michael Garfield. *Culture, Race and Class in the Commonwealth Caribbean.* Mona, Jamaica: Department of Extra Mural Studies, University of the West Indies, 1984.

————. *Dark Puritan.* Mona, Jamaica: Department of Extra Mural Studies, University of the West Indies, 1963.

————. *Kinship and Community in Carriacou.* New Haven: Yale University Press, 1962.

————. *Stratification in Grenada.* Berkeley: University of California Press, 1965.

Smith, Robert Freeman. "Twentieth-Century Cuban Historiography." *Hispanic American Historical Review* 44 (February 1964): 44–73.

Smith, Wayne S. *The Closest of Enemies: A Personal and Diplomatic Account of U.S.-Cuban Relations since 1957.* New York: Norton, 1987.

Snyder, Louis L. *Varieties of Nationalism: A Comparative Study*. Hinsdale, Ill.: Dryden, 1976.

Sommer, Doris. *One Master for Another: Populism as Patriarchal Rhetoric in Dominican Novels*. Boston: University Press of America, 1983.

Steward, Julian. *The People of Puerto Rico*. Urbana: University of Illinois Press, 1956.

Stone, Carl. *Class, Race and Political Behaviour in Urban Jamaica*. Mona, Jamaica: Institute of Social and Economic Research, University of the West Indies, 1973.

————. *Power in the Caribbean Basin: A Comparative Study of Political Economy*. Philadelphia: Institute for the Study of Human Issues, 1986.

Taylor, Frank. *Jamaica, the Welcoming Society: Myths and Reality*. Mona, Jamaica: Institute of Social and Economic Research, University of the West Indies, 1975.

Thomas, Clive Y. *Plantations, Peasants and State: A Study of the Mode of Sugar Production in Guyana*. Los Angeles: Center for Afro-American Studies, 1984.

Thomas, Hugh. *Cuba: The Pursuit of Freedom*. New York: Harper and Row, 1971.

Thomas, John Jacob. *Froudacity: West Indian Fables by James Anthony Froude Explained by . . .* London and Port of Spain, Trinidad and Tobago: New Beacon Books Ltd., 1969.

————. *The Theory and Practice of Creole Grammar*. Reprint. London: New Beacon, 1969.

Thompson, Edgar T. "The Plantation as a Social System." In *Plantation Systems of the New World*, pp. 26–36. Washington, D.C.: Pan American Union, 1959.

Tinker, Hugh. *A New System of Slavery: The Export of Indian Labour Overseas, 1830–1920*. London: Oxford University Press, 1974.

Tivey, Leonard, ed. *The Nation-State: The Formation of Modern Politics*. Oxford, U.K.: Martin Robertson, 1981.

Trinidad and Tobago Central Statistical Office. *Continuous Sample Survey of Population*. Publication no. 5. LF 1–4 (1966).

Troncoso Sánchez, Pedro. *Evolución de la idea nacional*. Santo Domingo: Museo del Hombre Dominicano, Serie Conferencias no. 2, 1974.

Trotman, David. *Crime in Trinidad*. Knoxville: University of Tennessee Press, 1986.

Walcott, Derek. *Another Life*. New York: Farrar, Straus, and Giroux, 1973.

————. *The Gulf*. New York: Straus and Giroux, 1970.

————. "The Muse of History." In *Is Massa Day Dead? Black Moods in the Caribbean*, edited by Orde Coombs. Garden City, N.Y.: Anchor Books, 1974.

————. *Selected Poems*. New York: Farrar, Straus, and Company, 1964.

Walters, R. M. "Cutting the High and Rising Food Import Bill, Reflections on a Caribbean Strategy That Worked: Trinidad and Tobago, 1939–1945." In *Proceedings of the Sixteenth West Indies Agricultural Economics Conference*, edited by Lloyd B. Rankine. Trinidad and Tobago: Faculty of Agriculture, University of the West Indies, 1983.

Watson, Karl. *The Civilised Island, Barbados: A Social History, 1750–1816*. Barbados: Graphic Printers, 1979.

Waugh, E. *A Handful of Dust*. New York: New Directions, 1945.

Weinstein, Brian. "The French West Indies: Dualism from 1848 to the Present." In *The African Diaspora*, edited by Martin L. Kilson and Robert I. Rotberg, pp. 237–79. Cambridge, Mass., and London, England: Harvard University Press, 1976.

Weinstein, Martin, ed. *Revolutionary Cuba in the World Arena*. Philadelphia: Institute for the Study of Human Issues, 1979.

Weisskoff, Richard. *Factories and Food Stamps: The Puerto Rico Model of Development*. Baltimore: Johns Hopkins University Press, 1985.

Welch, Richard E., Jr. *Response to Revolution: The United States and the Cuban Revolution, 1959–1961*. Chapel Hill: University of North Carolina Press, 1985.

*West India Royal Commission, 1938–39, Report*. Cmd., 6607. London: HMSO, 1945.

Wiarda, Howard J., and Kryzanek, Michael J. *The Dominican Republic: A Caribbean Crucible*. Boulder, Colo.: Westview, 1982.

Williams, Eric. *Capitalism and Slavery*. Chapel Hill: University of North Carolina Press, 1944.

―――. *From Columbus to Castro: The History of the Caribbean, 1492–1969*. New York: Harper and Row, 1979.

―――. *Inward Hunger: The Education of a Prime Minister*. Chicago: University of Chicago Press, 1971.

Williams, N. D. *Ikael Torass*. Havana: Casa de las Américas, 1976.

Wilson, Peter J. *Crab Antics: The Social Anthropology of English-Speaking Negro Societies of the Caribbean*. New Haven: Yale University Press, 1973.

Wood, Bryce. *The Making of the Good Neighbor Policy*. New York: Columbia University Press, 1967.

Wood, Donald. *Trinidad in Transition*. Oxford: Oxford University Press, 1968.

*The World Almanac and Book of Facts, 1987*. New York: Newspaper Enterprise Association, 1986.

Worrell, Delisle. "An Economic Survey of Barbados, 1946–1980." In *The Economy of Barbados, 1946–1980*, edited by Delisle Worrell, pp. 1–46. Bridgetown, Barbados: Central Bank of Barbados, 1982.

Zobel, Joseph. *Black Shack Alley*. Reprint. Washington, D.C.: Three Continents Press, 1980.

# Contributors

Herman L. Bennett is a Mellon Fellow in the Humanities and a graduate student in the Department of History at Duke University. He has received a Younger Scholars Grant from the National Endowment for the Humanities.

Bridget Brereton is Senior Lecturer in History at the Saint Augustine Campus, Trinidad, of the University of the West Indies. Between 1984 and 1987 she served as head of the Department of History. Her major publications include *Race Relations in Colonial Trinidad, 1870–1900* (1979) and *A History of Modern Trinidad, 1783–1962* (1981). Dr. Brereton is coeditor of volume 5 of the UNESCO General History of the Caribbean.

David Geggus is Associate Professor of History at the University of Florida at Gainesville. He has held fellowships from Oxford and Southampton universities as well as the Guggenheim Foundation, the British Academy, and the Woodrow Wilson Center. He is the author of *Slavery, War, and Revolution: The British Occupation of Saint-Dominique, 1793–1798* (1982).

Franklin W. Knight is Professor of Latin American and Caribbean History at the Johns Hopkins University, Baltimore. He has held fellowships from the Social Science Research Council, the National Endowment for the Humanities, the Center for Advanced Study in the Behavioral Sciences, the National Research Council, and the National Humanities Center. His publications include *Slave Society in Cuba during the Nineteenth Century* (1970), *The African Dimension of Latin American Societies* (1974), *The Caribbean: Genesis of a Fragmented Nationalism* (1978), *Africa and the Caribbean, Legacies of a Link* (1979), and *Atlantic Port Cities: Economy, Culture and Society in the Atlantic World, 1650–1850* (1988).

Anthony P. Maingot is Professor of Sociology at Florida International University, Miami, Florida. He was a Visiting Senior Social Scientist at the Rand Corporation between 1986 and 1988. His publications include "Cuba and the English-Speaking Caribbean: Playing the Cuban Card," in Barry Levine, ed., *The Changing Cuban Presence* (1983); "National Pursuits and Regional Definitions: The Caribbean as an Interest Area," in Basil A. Ince et al., eds., *Issues in Caribbean International Relations* (1983); and "Citizenship and Parliamentary Politics in the English-Speaking Caribbean," in Paul Sutton, ed., *The Contemporary Legacy to the Caribbean* (1986).

Jay R. Mandle is Professor of Economics at Temple University, Philadelphia. Previously he was a Fulbright lecturer in China. His publications include *The Roots of Black Poverty: The Southern Economy after the Civil War* (1978), *Patterns of Caribbean Development: An Interpretive Essay on Economic Change* (1982), and *Big Revolution, Small Country: The Rise and Fall of the Grenada Revolution* (1985).

Roberto Márquez is Clarence Robinson Professor of Hispanic American and Caribbean Cultures at the George Mason University, Fairfax, Virginia. He has held fellowships from the National Endowment for the Humanities and the Tinker Foundation and is the editor of *Caliban*. The official translator of the poetry of Nicolás Guillén, his publications include *Patria o Muerte: The Great Zoo and Other Poems by Nicolás Guillén* (1972), *Man-Making Words* (1972), *Latin American Revolutionary Poetry* (1974), *Racismo, cultura y revolución: Ideología y política en la prosa de Nicolás Guillén* (1979), and "The Stoic and the Sisyphean: John Hearne and the Angel of History," *Anales del Caribe* 3 (1983).

Teresita Martínez Vergne is Assistant Professor of History at the University of Puerto Rico, Río Piedras. Her publications include "The Attitudes of Influential Groups of Colonial Society toward the Working Rural Population in Puerto Rico, 1860–1873," in *Journal of Caribbean History* (1979); "History of Continental Puerto Ricans," in David Foster, ed., *Sourcebook of Hispanic Culture in the United States* (1982); and "New Patterns for Puerto Rico's Sugar Workers: Abolition and Centralization at San Vicente, 1873–1892," *Hispanic American Historical Review* 68 (February 1988).

Colin A. Palmer is Professor of History and Chairman of the Department of History at the University of North Carolina at Chapel Hill. He has held fellowships from the National Endowment for the Humanities, the American Philosophical Society, and the Rockefeller Foundation. His publications include *Slaves of the White God: Blacks in Mexico, 1570–1650* (1976), *Human Cargoes: The British Slave Trade to Spanish America, 1700–1739* (1981), and the forthcoming *Africa's Children: The Black Experience in the Americas*.

Bonham C. Richardson is Professor of Geography at Virginia Polytechnic Institute and State University. He is the author of *Caribbean Migrants: Environment and Human Survival on St. Kitts and Nevis* (1983) and *Panama Money in Barbados, 1900–1920* (1985).

Francisco A. Scarano is Associate Professor of History at the University of Connecticut at Storrs. He has held fellowships from the Ford Foundation, the Social Science Research Council, and the National Endowment for the Humanities. His publications include *Inmigración y clases sociales en el Puerto Rico del siglo XIX* (1981) and *Sugar and Slavery in Puerto Rico: The Plantation Economy of Ponce, 1800–1850* (1984), which won the Elsa Goveia Prize in Caribbean History in 1986.

Blanca G. Silvestrini is Professor of History at the University of Puerto Rico at Río Piedras. She served as president of the Association of Caribbean Historians between 1981 and 1984. She has held fellowships from the National Research Council, the Social Science Research Council, and the Center for Advanced Study in the Behavioral Sciences. Her publications include *El partido socialista y los obreros puertorriqueños, 1932–1940* (1979), *Violencia y criminalidad en Puerto Rico, 1898–1973* (1980), *Women as Workers: The Experience of the Puerto Rican Woman* (1976), and *Politics, Society and Culture in the Caribbean* (1983).